Also by IRVING KOLODIN

The Guide to Long Playing Records: Orchestral Music
The Musical Life
The Story of the Metropolitan Opera: 1883–1950
The Metropolitan Opera: 1883–1966

These are Borzoi Books published in New York by Alfred A. Knopf

The Continuity
of Music

IRVING KOLODIN

The Continuity of Music

A HISTORY OF INFLUENCE

ALFRED · A · KNOPF New York

1969

THIS IS A BORZOI BOOK
PUBLISHED BY ALFRED A. KNOPF, INC.

FIRST EDITION

Library of Congress Catalog Card Number: 68-23965

FOREWORD

T HIS IS THE RÉSUMÉ of one man's attitude toward the music being
made in his time, which, at 1968, is two-thirds of the twentieth
century. In this context "made" is not restricted to those who
speak of their performances in such a way. Rather it takes in creation
as well as re-creation. Necessarily, then, both past and present are
intimately involved. The reader, it may be hoped, will share the writer's
view that, music being the kind of continuously reborn, expanding,
altering experience that it is, what is chronologically past may be more
of the future than that which is chronologically present.

What follows is a statement of observations, correlations, and conclusions based on a listening experience available to few at any time,
and none prior to, say, 1935. This statement is put forth with no pride
or vanity, but to identify an opportunity as well as to state an obligation.

Having had the privilege, during more than thirty years of professional concern with the subject, of record-listening by day and
attendance at public events by night, I estimate my investment therein
to be something more than 40,000 hours.[1]

Total flight time does not of necessity make the best pilot, nor
does listening time alone assure responsible judgment. But insofar as
either is unique, so are the observations, deductions, and conclusions
thus made possible. They constitute a body of information beyond the

[1] A useful comparison may be derived from mention of statistics publicized in
1961, when Dick Merrill, first pilot to fly the Atlantic both ways in 1936, retired. He
had logged 37,000 hours of flight time (*Newsweek*, October 16, 1961, p. 71).

acquisition of anyone denied the opportunity, and merit public circulation, if not agreement and support.

The first evident fact about music in this century, and especially in the middle third of it, is that our time differs from times past, when what was played was, by definition, what was heard: at least two ranges of listening experience are being pursued in our time. To a degree, they overlap; but, as the concert-goer who considers "live" performance irreplaceable can turn his back on the reproduced kind, so the music lover who prefers to pursue his enthusiasm in private can order a world of sound in which he is arbiter of all he enjoys.

It is perhaps an accident that such latitude of choice coincides with a period in which larger quantities of music which communicates less to listeners are being created than ever before. It is not in the least accidental that in a period in which composers have tended more and more to write for each other, a large segment of the discriminating public has turned elsewhere for its satisfactions.

Some may condemn this as a withdrawal from the heat and the conflicts of our time, a statement of noninvolvement with the present and future of the art. But all such commitments must be reciprocal. If the composer cares not for me, the probability is that I—meaning the average well-versed music lover—will care not for him.

Free selection implies the equal, if opposite, alternative of free rejection. This places an additional, enormous burden of proof on the creator of today. He is competing not merely with mortal contemporaries, but with a whole historical totality of immortals whose masterworks are readily available in performances of incontestable authority.

Such being the case, it would seem ordinary common sense for the creator of today to be bent, beyond any predecessor, on clarity, conciseness, and intelligibility of statement. For the most part, the opposite tendency prevails, with considerably more that is complicated, diffuse, and obscure. The mode, the fashion, the vogue, that gives certain composers the honorary status they crave with their fellow practitioners has, largely speaking, separated them from the comprehension and the affection of the listening public. We are all familiar with the premise that the composer should lead, not follow. But at what distance, and for how long? Much so-called "representative" music written more than half a century ago has no wider appeal now—and far less impact—than it did when it was new.

There thus emerges this profound paradox in the musical life of our time: More people than ever before are being exposed to the music being created in their time and are getting little from it; more people are listening to the music of the past than at any previous time and are finding it a self-sufficient source of refreshment and sustenance.

Plainly, the supply-demand relationship is disturbed, the pipeline from creator to consumer clogged, the cogs not turning the wheels.

Such being the irrefutable circumstances, it strikes me as reasonable to inquire: Which element has failed to fulfill its function? Is the public at fault or is the music? Is it some of both, and not all of one or the other?

Is there some intrinsic, definable respect in which the music generically called "contemporary" differs from that which makes up the broad repertory of Western concert music and opera?

Would the isolation of it explain if not resolve the disaffection, among many who consider themselves possessed of an open ear as well as an open mind, toward music that gratifies neither the ear nor the mind?

It is in the interest of adducing answers to some of these questions—even, possibly, toward the resolution of a widespread perplexity—that this inquiry is addressed.

CONTENTS

Theme   3

I · Before Beethoven, and Beyond   8

II · The Line from Chopin   40

III · Wagner–Liszt and Liszt–Wagner   63

IV · "You, He, and I"   85

V · Berlioz at Home and Abroad (À Travers Champs)   116

VI · Wagner and Wagnerism   146

VII · Strains and Mutations   182

VIII · Shoots and Deviations   274

IX · Decision and Diffusion   322

X · Isolation or Synthesis?   356

Postscript   367

Index   *follows page* 367

MUSICAL EXAMPLES

	PAGE
Mozart: Piano Concerto No. 24, C minor (K. 491), finale	18
Beethoven: Violin Concerto (op. 61), finale	18–19
Mozart: Piano Concerto No. 24, C minor (K. 491), first movement	20
Beethoven: Piano Concerto No. 3, C minor (op. 37), first movement	21
Mozart: *Die Zauberflöte*, Act II, *"In diesen heil'gen Hallen"*	21
Beethoven: Symphony No. 3, E flat (op. 55), finale	22
Mozart: *Die Zauberflöte*, Act I (No. 5)	22
Beethoven: Choral Fantasy, C minor (op. 80)	23
Beethoven: *Fidelio*, Act I (Eulenberg miniature score, p. 380)	26
Wagner: *Lohengrin*, Act III	27
Beethoven: Symphony No. 3, E flat (op. 55), second movement	28
Brahms: Symphony No. 1, C minor (op. 68), first movement	29
Beethoven: Symphony No. 2, D (op. 36), second movement	30
Mendelssohn: *A Midsummer Night's Dream* (op. 61), Nocturne	31

PAGE

Brahms: Piano Concerto No. 2, B flat (op. 83), third movement — 35

Dvořák: Symphony No. 7, D minor (op. 70), first movement — 36

Chopin: Ballade No. 1, G minor (op. 23) — 48

Chopin: Prelude No. 23, F (op. 28) — 50

"Innsbruck, ich muss dich lassen" — 57

"Shenandoah" (arr. Cecil Dougherty) — 57

Chopin: Mazurka No. 5, B flat (op. 7, No. 1) — 59

Alfvén: *Midsommarvaka* (op. 19) — 60

Chopin: Mazurka No. 35, C minor (op. 56, No. 3) — 61

Chopin: Mazurka No. 41, C sharp minor (op. 63, No. 3) — 62

Wagner: *Eine Faust-Ouvertüre* (original version) — 80

Wagner: *Eine Faust-Ouvertüre* (1855 revision) — 81–2

Liszt: *Eine Faust-Symphonie*, Section I (Faust) — 83

Wagner: *Tristan und Isolde*, Act I — 84

Chopin: Mazurka No. 35, C minor (op. 56, No. 3) — 84

Gluck: *Alceste*, Act I (No. 15) — 93–4

Berlioz: *Les Francs-Juges Overture* (op. 3) — 95

Berlioz: *Roméo et Juliette, Jardin de Capulet* — 108

Wagner: *Tristan und Isolde*, Act III — 109

Berlioz: *Roméo et Juliette, Roméo seul* — 112

Wagner: *Tristan und Isolde*, Act III — 113

Berlioz: *Absence* (*Nuits d'été*, No. 4) — 114

Wagner: *Tristan und Isolde*, prelude to Act III — 115

Berlioz: *La Damnation de Faust*, Scene 6 — 118

Gounod: *Faust*, Act II — 119

Berlioz: *Harold en Italie*, second movement — 120

Gounod: *Faust*, Act I — 121

Berlioz: Requiem (*Dies irae*) — 126–7

Verdi: Requiem (*Dies irae*) — 128

Glinka: *Russlan and Ludmilla* (Chernomor's March) — 131

Glinka: *Kamarinskaya* — 135

Wagner: *Lohengrin*, Act I — 142

Tchaikovsky: *Lac des cygnes* (op. 20), introduction — 142

PAGE

Bruch: Violin Concerto No. 1, G minor (op. 26) 149

Wagner: *Der fliegende Holländer*, Act I 149

Wagner: *Tristan und Isolde*, prelude 151

Thomas: *Mignon*, overture 152

Wagner: *Die Meistersinger*, overture 164–5

Brahms: *Academic Festival Overture* 166–7

Brahms: Piano Sonata No. 3, F minor (op. 5) 168

Wagner: *Die Meistersinger*, Act III 168

Bruckner: Symphony No. 3, D minor, first movement 172

Beethoven: Symphony No. 9, D minor, second movement 173

Bruckner: Symphony No. 7, E, adagio 175

Beethoven: Symphony No. 9, D minor, scherzo 175

Bruckner: Symphony No. 9, D minor, adagio 178

Brahms: Piano Concerto No. 1, D minor, maestoso 187

Strauss: *Burleske* 188

Brahms: String Quartet, A minor (op. 51, No. 2), *andante moderato* 194

Strauss: *Don Juan* (op. 20) 194

Strauss: *Tod und Verklärung* (op. 24) 196

Wagner: *Tristan und Isolde, Act III* 197

Beethoven: Symphony No. 3, E flat, finale 202

Strauss: *Ein Heldenleben* (op. 40) 203

Lehár: *The Merry Widow*, Act I 218

Mahler: *Lieder eines fahrenden Gesellen*, No. 2 219

Bartók: Concerto for Orchestra, Intermezzo 220

Mahler: Symphony No. 1, D, third movement 221

Grieg: *Peer Gynt* Suite No. 1 (op. 46), No. 3 222

Wagner: *Die Walküre*, prelude to Act I 225

Mahler: Symphony No. 2, C minor, first movement 225

Schubert: Symphony No. 9, C, first movement 227

Mahler: Symphony No. 2, C minor, "Auferstehen" 228–9

Beethoven: String Quartet No. 16, F (op. 135), *lento assai* 231

Mahler: Symphony No. 3, G, langsam 231

Wagner: *Siegfried Idyll* 232

Mahler: Symphony No. 3, G, langsam 233

PAGE

Mahler: *Das Lied von der Erde* 245–6

Brahms: *Alto Rhapsody* (op. 53) 247

Mahler: Symphony No. 10, adagio 251

Bruckner: Symphony No. 9, D minor, langsam 252

Wagner: *Eine Faust-Ouvertüre* 253

Fauré: *Après un rêve* (op. 7, No. 1) 277

Debussy: *Beau soir* 277

D'Indy: *Symphony on a French Mountain Air* (op. 25) 279

Debussy: *La Damoiselle élue* 280

Chabrier: cadence formulation 282

Falla: *El Sombrero de Tres Picos* 297

Stravinsky: *Pulcinella* 298

Wagner: *Parsifal*, Act II 304

Stravinsky: *The Firebird* 305

Debussy: *Nuages* (Nocturnes, No. 1) 313–14

Stravinsky: *Le Sacre du printemps* 315

Stravinsky: *Le Sacre du printemps* 320

Puccini: *Turandot*, Act III 321

Wagner: *Tristan und Isolde*, Act III 327

Berg: *Traumgekrönt* 327

Berg: String Quartet (op. 3) 328

Strauss: *Tod und Verklärung* (op. 24) 329

Wagner: *Tristan und Isolde*, Act III 347–9

Brahms: String Quartet, A minor (op. 51, No. 2), andante 365

CONTINUITY: *"Identity with respect to a series of changes."*

Webster's New International Dictionary
(second edition)

AN INQUIRY INTO HISTORY

THIS INQUIRY is put forth with no belief that it assembles all the relevant fact or deals with all the pertinent data relating to the continuity of music written in the period betwen 1685 and 1950.

It is, rather, offered as a stimulation to thought, with the purpose of provoking addenda and invoking assistance toward the (probably) illusive objective of assembling all the relevant data.

It is, in short, a probe along a line clearly defined by innumerable examples, though with no presumption that these are all, or even most, of the incalculable total. It presumes refutation, as well as inviting support.

Above all, it seeks to make a beginning toward the better understanding of a phenomenon so familiar that it has never been analyzed previously.

The Continuity
of Music

Theme

ROM A VAST STOREHOUSE of music written in Europe, or anywhere
else in the world where the European tradition prevailed, between
1685—the year in which Johann Sebastian Bach, Domenico Scarlatti, and George Frideric Handel were born—and 1964—the year in
which both Paul Hindemith and Francis Poulenc died—there emerges
a strong sense of interaction and cross-influence among the works of
the greatest composers. I am not referring to the facile, superficial re-
semblances that might be described as model and imitation, or even
to those specific instances in which a later composer has openly confessed admiration for the works of a predecessor (Debussy's *Hommage
à Rameau*, Ravel's *Tombeau de Couperin*, Tchaikovsky's *Mozartiana*,
etc.).

I refer to something deeper, more fundamental: the ways in which
turns of thought or flashes of ideas thrown out by one composer of
eminence (Gluck, Mozart, Haydn, Beethoven, Weber, Schubert,
Chopin, Liszt, Mussorgsky, Debussy) became the impulse from which,
in large measure, the style of another (Berlioz, Schumann, Brahms,
Bruckner, Mahler, Strauss, or Schoenberg) evolved. A mating of two
sources seemingly remote from each other may grow the flower and
bear the fruit in which the seed of a wholly new strain is contained: a
blend of Schubert and Wagner producing Wolf, or Chopin and Liszt
becoming Scriabin, or Mussorgsky-Tchaikovsky-Debussy emerging as
Stravinsky.

If many of the names in the preceding citation are Central European or even, more precisely, Germanic, the reasons are twofold:

a) for much of this time, the music of greatest vitality and communicative power was Germanic;

b) it is the music on which I was reared and know best.

I put this statement clearly on the record to save effort for whoever may choose to assemble such evidence as proof of "bias." Evolving from this central position outward as this study has progressed, the skein of relationships has become infinitely more far-reaching. There is, in fact, a likeness to a network of waterways traversing a vast topography, save that in this fanciful pattern some streams may disappear before reaching a terminal point, others branch off and return to the main flow, forced by a current from another direction to form a surprisingly powerful new confluence.

Certainly the same kind of continuity can be traced or adduced in the torrential flow of Italian writing for the stage from Paisiello to Puccini, with Gluck, Rossini, Bellini, Donizetti, Verdi, Ponchielli, and Giordano as other participants. Italian instrumental music took another trend with Paganini, becoming Northernized (Tommasini-Martucci-Busoni) through Schumann and Liszt. When brought back by Respighi after studies with Rimsky-Korsakov, it was no longer true to its heritage, from which it has been led even further afield by Nono-Berio-Dallapiccola. The Russian sequence is shorter, more compact, as is the Spanish.

I hold no brief for a national heritage per se, save as it tends to produce a strongly defined species of its own, such as Italian opera, German *Lieder*, or French piano music. My premise, rather, is that there is a common heritage from which local types have developed, that these in turn exerted an influence—like the return flow of air around a storm center—on the sources from which they emanated. In some instances, influence and consequence are as strongly established as Bach's conversion to his own purposes of models by Vivaldi. In others, it may be wholly unconscious and nonvolitional, as in Mozart's contacts with works of Cimarosa and Paisiello in Vienna, or Rossini's in turn with Mozart's, or Dvořák's with Wagner's. Instances are abundant of such impulses leaping national boundaries, whether mere lines on a map or the natural barriers of mountains and rivers.

It was out of this interchange over centuries that there developed the kind of musical language Western minds flatter themselves by calling "universal." Our present concept of a universe extending to spaces beyond the most distant stars, and the Western portion of our own globe being a correspondingly smaller portion of the whole, we may merely describe it as a musical language well and widely understood.

Edvard Grieg gave verbal consent to this concept of interchange, hence of continuity, when in writing about Robert Schumann's song-technic, he stated:[1] "Schumann was . . . the first . . . who utilized the relationship between song and accompaniment which Wagner has later developed to a degree that fully proves what importance he attached to it. I refer to the carrying of the melody by the piano, or the orchestra, while the voice is engaged in the recitative."

Then, anticipating cries of outrage from Wagnerians, Grieg added what is, in this context, the key statement: "But, for all that, it is a fact that most contemporaries influence each other, whether they want to or not. This is one of nature's eternal laws to which we are all subject . . ." Grieg gave assent to his own formulation of what might be called Grieg's Law in more than a verbal way in the A-minor Concerto, favorite of three generations of pianists. Not only did he choose the key of the Schumann concerto; he also paralleled many structural details of the earlier work, such as the sequence of themes in winds and strings, the plan of the development, and the design of the coda. This is, to be sure, an overt example of what more frequently happens less consciously, but it demonstrates the degree to which cross-fertilization may produce a new growth.

Across this span of more than two and one half centuries there have been innovations and experiments, reforms and emancipations, manifestos and exordia to clarify aesthetic practices, fancied returns to Grecian ideals, bold proclamations of "The Art Work of the Future" (a terminology now as passé as the evils it sought to correct). There has been in all these times a section of opinion resistant to change. There have also been powerful voices urging the merits of one composer or another. In neither case has a permanent outcome been achieved by special pleading for, or the efforts of a minority faction against. Schumann for Niels Gade, the Maharajah of Mysore for Nicholas Medtner, this piano virtuoso for Anton Rubinstein or that one for Charles Alkan have not succeeded in creating a worth not inherent in the music itself. An implacable, if unorganized, generally-agreed-upon conception of value will prevail.

It is, moreover, rare for a master's value to elude recognition for very long, assuming reasonable opportunity for complete judgment. The "neglect" of Bach is the classic case to the contrary; it was much related to the vastness of his output and the inaccessibility in usable, printed form of some of his greatest glories until Mendelssohn revived them in the 1830's. But it is well to remember that long before (1805), Beethoven phrased his praises of the Bach *he knew* (see p. 14) in the

[1] From an article in *Century Magazine*, January 1894.

highest possible terms. Even the recent surge of interest in Vivaldi has not added a hitherto unhonored name to the list of music's masters. It is the abundance of the works recently restored to circulation which enforces his greatness rather than a newfound quality that establishes it.

In the case of some composers who now enjoy an esteem denied to them in their lifetime—Mahler, Nielsen, Janáček, to mention three—the general condition that prompts the writing of this survey may very well be basic. That is, the failure of the best composers of today to match the quality of communication achieved by the second-, third-, or fourth-best of yesterday has caused a revision of judgment, a reconsideration of merit in some composers previously overlooked. When no new works equal to Puccini's fourth-best are being written, even *La Fanciulla del West* may be welcome.

In any case, the revaluation of Mahler, Nielsen, and Janáček has come within the fifty-year span which has, in most past circumstances, been accepted as a reasonable time in which to determine the worth or resolve the issue of idiom affecting works considered "controversial" when first performed. Indeed, the same period of time has now elapsed for Schoenberg's *Pierrot lunaire* of 1912 and Stravinsky's *Le Sacre du printemps* of 1913, though with rather different results.

Each imparted a profound shock to the body of music as it existed. Accepted practices were questioned, ties to the past were strained, as even the value of a heredity itself was decried by one influential coterie of trend setters.[2] One manner—Stravinsky's—has found a wide, responsive audience. The other—Schoenberg's—has not.

During this century, composers have been liberated from virtually all the restraints known to the previous generations of composers: every man has been as emancipated as any man would want to be.

What has been the result? Largely speaking, rather than profiting from such freedom to broaden the range of music's expressive power, and therefore of its appeal to a wide public, the composers who have grown up with all these resources at their disposal—if not always at their command—interest a constantly shrinking portion of the public. This contracting circle excludes not only the casual visitor to the concert hall or opera house who might easily be discouraged, but also a large part of the indoctrinated, devoted, indeed dependent public which is willing to exert an effort to add breadth to its musical experience. This is the portion of the public to which music is not merely something with which to pass time, but is as necessary to bodily well-being as water or air.

2 André Hodeir: *Since Debussy* (New York: Grove Press; 1961), p. 11.

If, as I propose to show, an enduring continuity pervaded the whole time before, is its steady decline and sometimes total absence in the music being created today a clue to that music's lack of appeal?

Let us pose an even more essential question:

What has been offered in replacement for what has been taken away? When the shock effect of the latest successor to Ornstein's tone clusters, or Cowell's arm thumps, or Cage's idiosyncrasies has run its course, what remains?

What puzzles me beyond all other perplexities encountered in the length of this inquiry is the willingness, nay the eagerness, of composers without number to give up the resources, advantages, and values evolved through years of trial and error by their most talented predecessors.

It was, perhaps, for Schoenberg, a crucial personal dilemma. But it could hardly be such a dilemma for one born long after the shadow cast by Wagner had ceased to lengthen.

It might, of course, have to do with the realization by composers that Schoenberg's talented predecessors are also their talented predecessors. Thus, his evasion of responsibility—by contrast, say, with Bruckner's persistent search for self-fulfillment and his eventual attainment of it in the musical terms with which he had begun—is also their evasion of responsibility. If that is so, it would make them as inferior in confidence, superior only in cowardice, to all who have answered the call to music over the past sixteen decades.

These are harsh words, but so are the sounds that call them forth.

If the interruption of continuity has coincided with the disruption of spiritual community between creator and listener, would it not be well to recognize the fact? A reasoned review of the nature of music and of its manner of regenerating itself across decades would add to order, contribute to clarity, and perhaps clear the ground of entanglements and intellectual underbrush.

It might even suggest that the new order changeth, giving place to the old.

I

Before Beethoven, and Beyond

I

TWO ABSORBING ASPECTS of the continuity of the music as it exists for me are these:

    a) it is much more a matter for the ear than for the eye;

   b) it is constantly revealing itself in new and unsuspected relationships as listening experience broadens and deepens.

The first fact is of exceptional importance. It goes beyond restatement of the obvious reality that the ear is the true organ of musical perception. It bears, rather, on the subtle capacity of the ear to make associations that would be masked or invisible to the eye. Conversely, it may reject totally values and relationships that gratify the eye. It is said of a great sculptor that he regarded his art, essentially, as taking away from the block of marble what was extraneous to the image in his mind. It might also be said of the great composer that he put nothing in his score that was not meant to be intelligible to the ear.

The continuity of music as I conceive it is a network of values perceived by the ear, subject to verification by the eye. Without the action of the mind's ear in making such associations by reference to the card file of music it contains, many instances of considerable significance might not emerge from a scrutiny of the printed page. It is a root, garden variety of fact about music that things may sound quite differently than they look, especially in combination or when a change of medium is involved.

The second factor is hardly less important. The more music we have heard and can retain, the more we can sense and appreciate what has been happening to the musical language in the Handel-Bach-Scarlatti-Strauss-Hindemith-Poulenc parenthesis. I do not, let it be noted, talk about progress or improvement, but of change.

2

FOR HANDEL'S PURPOSE, as for Bach's, the musical language of the time was a functional extension of himself, in which he found immense, not to say inexhaustible, latitude for what he strove to express. Indeed, where imagery and portraiture were concerned, a single flute, by the measure of sound in an ensemble where woodwinds were scanty, might have an effect equal to the whole interrelated scheme of Ravel's woodwinds in *Daphnis et Chloé*, or a pair of trumpets in *Solomon* be as brazen to the ear as the brass band interpolated by Dimitri Shostakovich into his instrumentation of Mussorgsky's *Boris Godunov*.

What that same language became in the usage of a younger contemporary or direct successor to Bach or Handel depended, in more than slight degree, on how much of it was actually transmitted to him, how much he had to rediscover for himself. Indeed, there is doubt that Bach himself knew much of the literature of Handel, his exact contemporary. Whether apocryphal or not, his celebrated journey of fifty miles on foot to hear Buxtehude symbolizes the difficulty with which impressions were acquired or influences transmitted at that time.

Such was the insulation of one court from another, one city-state (now part of a general community) from its neighbor, that a piece written for an occasion, whether gay or solemn, might not travel a hundred miles in a decade. When the occasion had passed, so, more often than not, did the music created for it. There was scant, if any, thought of posterity, even less of a "literature." C. P. E. Bach probably meant no disrespect when he referred to his illustrious father as "the old peruke." It was the reduction to a phrase of a prevailing attitude that what was past had had its day, and that something else had to be provided in its place. If there was a "body of music" to which one referred back, or which endured beyond the life of its creator, it was music for the Church or that which had become traditional in rituals of a particular court.

It was not until well into the nineteenth century that the concept began to emerge of a body of music possessed of a past as well as a present, or roots and a trunk as well as branches. It even began to be recognized that not all the best blossoms grew at the top. Or to phrase it otherwise, that there was a vast trove of musical treasure which made up a repertory: in the true sense of that word, it had values in which interest could be "found again." From it began to emerge a literature in which the best of the new was supplementary to the old, not a replacement for it.

That there were certain physical facts at work is hardly in question. There had, in the first place, to be a means by which music written to be played in one place could become known in another. There had to be ways by which persons identified with the musical life of one locality extended their influence to another.

For his time, Handel was a relatively traveled man. Bach was all but untraveled. As for the other of the extraordinary trio born in the same year, Domenico Scarlatti's relocation in 1728 to Madrid, where he spent the last twenty-seven years of his life, unquestionably exercised a long and profound influence on Spanish music as well as on keyboard music generally. Thus, three varying patterns of existence flowed from these three exact contemporaries, with a profound effect on the kind of continuity that emerged from their long life spans (a total of 211 years, or an average of slightly more than seventy years per individual).

Much is made of the "imposition" of Leopold Mozart in touring his famous son as a virtuoso, with possibly damaging effects on his physical well-being, even to the shortening of his life span. But it is altogether probable that Mozart would have been quite another kind of musician without the first journey to France, England, and Italy, as a child, and the later visits to Munich, Mannheim, Stuttgart, Paris, Milan, and Vienna. When, finally, he came to live permanently in Vienna, and ply his trade there (which was, more or less, how his activities were regarded by the native and foreign notables attached to the Austrian court), he was, without question, the most worldly musician known up to that time, the one most widely versed in the practices and prejudices of musical Europe from the Danube to the Thames. That the freedom of choice thus granted to Mozart (in selecting the elements that pleased his taste and rejecting those that did not) profoundly affected the kind of artistic expression he evolved can hardly be doubted.

With Haydn, travel came almost too late: had he not gone to England at Salomon's invitation in 1790, he would have been denied the experience of the Handel Festival at Westminster Abbey in the spring of 1791 with the voices of thousands performing such works as *Zadok the Priest, Israel in Egypt,* and *Messiah.*[1] After hearing "The nations tremble," from *Joshua,* Haydn said that he "had long been acquainted with music, but never knew half its power before he heard it."[2] It was by no means accidental that it was in the aftermath of these experiences that Haydn wrote his greatest choral works, *The Creation* in 1798 and *The Seasons* in 1801. At another extreme, it was after hearing "God Save the King"[3] (known in the United States as "America") that Haydn created *Gott erhalte Franz den Kaiser* in 1797, later utilizing it for the superb variations in the "Emperor" (Kaiser) Quartet of opus 76.

Such products of happenstance were curiously associated with Haydn. It was Mozart's chance hearing of Haydn's opus 33 quartets (written in 1781) that aroused the impulse to emulation which he embodied in the celebrated six quartets dedicated to Haydn. It was the kind of symphonic writing that Haydn produced in response to Salomon's invitations to London that, a decade later, turned Beethoven's impulses to the direction evident in his early symphonies.

Or, perhaps, the seemingly "curious" instances of accident were not so curious. Haydn had served a long, arduous apprenticeship to the art in the services of the Esterházy family before coming on the world stage of music. His fame among younger musicians was such that any opportunity to benefit from association with him was a cherished privilege. Nevertheless, it is clear from the citation of such specific, limited happenings that, in these conditions, continuity was capricious and intermittent. It occurred or did not occur according to who was where at a given time, what rare, engraved score or set of parts came to whose hand, what chance invitation (such as Salomon's to Haydn) affected an otherwise routine way of life. The chain of influence flourished or languished, added a link or none at all as years passed, and great men hardly knew of each other's existence—or, even if they did, had no means of profiting from it.

As has been suggested earlier (p. 10) "something happened" in the early years of the nineteenth century to alter this situation almost beyond recognition, indeed to bring about a wholly new one. It did not happen all at once, of course: intellectual revolutions are slower to mature than political or industrial ones. But all the evidence points to

[1] H. C. Robbins Landon: *Symphonies of Haydn* (London: Universal Edition; 1955), p. 458.
[2] Ibid., p. 458.
[3] *Grove's Dictionary of Music and Musicians,* 5th edn., IV, 159 (article on Haydn).

a particular set of circumstances, and a particular man who was exposed to them as the known factors which, in combination, might produce the "unknown" for which we are searching.

3

ONE MIGHT START with the venture of Bernhardt Christoph Breitkopf into the printing business in Leipzig in 1719. Prosperity flowed from the start (with a Hebrew bible). His son, Johann Gottlob Immanuel, had wider aspirations when he became head of the firm in 1745. It was his introduction of movable musical type in 1750 (the year of Bach's death) that produced, in the words of the Viennese critic and historian C. Ferdinand Pohl, "a revolution in the music trade."[4] By 1756 he had produced an opera in score. In the next two decades, he improved his methods and broadened his scope to include works of C. P. E. Bach and Leopold Mozart.

One of Johann Gottlob Immanuel's two sons (Bernhard Theodor) became a resident of St. Petersburg, where his taste inclined to national affairs as well as to publishing. The other (Christoph Gottlob) fulfilled, in almost every detail, the classic figure of the third-generation family businessman. He enjoyed the profits from his ancestors' hard work, but turned over the continuation of both to a friend. Soon (1798) the firm name ceased to be Breitkopf und Sohn, taking the world famous name of Breitkopf und Härtel a few years after the advent of the friend, Gottfried Christoph Härtel. It has ever since, as B. and H., asserted a pre-eminent place among music publishers though there has never been another Breitkopf in the business. Through such massive publication projects as the works of Mozart in seventeen volumes, a complete Haydn in twelve, Clementi in thirteen, etc., Härtel utilized the development of lithography by Alois Senefelder to enrich enormously the amount of music in print by 1820.

It will not escape the attention of the reader that the period 1790–1820 straddles the crucial years of development and productivity for one of music's most influential composers. Nor is it too much to assume that the outpouring from the presses (first those of B. and H., soon enough those of numerous others) fed his curiosity like rain on receptive soil.

Even before the young Ludwig van Beethoven went to Vienna to live in 1792, the new emerging technology exerted an influence on him denied to his predecessors. Thanks to the biographies of Thayer

[4] *Grove's*, I, 923 (article on Breitkopf).

and others, which document Beethoven's day-to-day existence more closely than that of any preceding composer's, we know that he played viola in the orchestra of the Electoral Theater in Bonn from the age of nineteen to twenty-one (1789–91). Among the works he performed and re-performed, and thus came to know intimately, were: Mozart's *Entführung aus dem Serail, Don Giovanni,* and *Nozze di Figaro*; Paisiello's *La Frascatina* and *Barbiere di Siviglia*; Gluck's *Die Pilger von Mekka*; Grétry's *L'amant jaloux* and *La fausse magie*; Cimarosa's *Il Convivo*; and Dittersdorf's *Der Doktor und Apotheker*, plus as many more by composers of lesser consequence.[5]

From the time of his arrival in Vienna in 1792, Beethoven fed on all the nourishment that the thriving musical life of that city afforded. Haydn accepted him on a teacher-pupil basis, though Beethoven stubbornly insisted that he learned little from the older man. This, perhaps, may have been true of their formal lessons, but he could not conceal, even if he had been so disposed, what he learned from his informal exposure to the new symphonies Haydn was writing for London at this time. They were, indeed, as much a part of Beethoven's conditioning in his crucial twenties as the music of Mozart, which began to have wider public prominence after his death in 1791.

As much as Beethoven profited, financially, from the offers of publication that came for his own new creations, so he profited as much, artistically, from the works of others that were turned out by the same presses. The earliest Ricordi came from Italy to learn the printer's art in Leipzig in the early years of the century, and by 1808 what was produced in the theaters of Italy was reproduced by the presses of Milan. For those who did not travel across the Alps (which, of course, included Beethoven) the flow of printed music from the peninsular sources was a new, provocative source of stimulation. By the time of Beethoven's death, virtually the entire alphabet of famous German firms was in being, from Artaria to Schlesinger. Their counterparts elsewhere followed swiftly.

Within Beethoven's productive lifetime—which is to say, from the time of his exposure to the works of others as a child until his death—there was a steadily increasing opportunity for him to experience the continuity of music in multiple, nonaccidental ways denied to his predecessors. It was coincidence that Beethoven's own first performance of the piano part of his B-flat Concerto[6] occurred on a program of De-

[5] Alexander W. Thayer: *Life of Ludwig van Beethoven,* ed. and rev. Henry E. Krehbiel (New York: Beethoven Association; 1921), I, 107.

[6] The first to be composed, though published as No. 2.

cember 18, 1795, in which Haydn, just returned from his second visit to London, conducted three of his new Salomon symphonies in the Redoutensaal. But it was part of a larger, emerging design that, when he was asked (in 1801) to endorse a project to increase greatly the amount of Bach in print, he knew enough about his great predecessor to describe him as "this ancestral father of harmony."[7] Handel's art he always esteemed though it was not until late in his life (1824) that Arnold's forty-volume edition revealed its full magnitude to him.[8]

It is hardly necessary to add, in the light of Beethoven's epochal achievements, that this proceeded from no static acceptance of established values or docile veneration of celebrated names. It was part of a life-long quest among alternatives for the means to feed the dynamics of his own growth and development. If he rejected Haydn's preachment, he was nevertheless responsive to his practice. If he disclaimed description as "Haydn's pupil" (a form of endorsement the older man craved), that was not without relevance to his total character. Proud, independent, not to say iconoclastic, Beethoven preferred to go his own unfettered way. That this was not unknown to Haydn may be read into his inquiry to a mutual friend, when he had not heard from Beethoven for some time: "How goes it," he asked, "with our great Mogul?"[9]

Among contemporaries, Beethoven attached great worth to the gravity of Cherubini, the volatility of Clementi, and the ingenuity of C. P. E. Bach, who died in 1788. Writing to Härtel in 1809, Beethoven observed: "Of Emanuel Bach's clavier works I have only a few, yet they must be not only a real delight to every true artist, but also serve him for study purposes; and it is for me a great pleasure to play, for real art lovers, works I have never seen, or seldom see."[1] Enclosed was an order for all the scores the firm could provide by Haydn, Mozart, and the two Bachs.

Out of this intense curiosity, quick susceptibility, and incredibly acute intuition (Spohr he mostly rejected and Rossini he esteemed very selectively), Beethoven formulated an idiom ever more distinctively his own. The times provided everything he needed to nourish his genius, as the society in which he enjoyed high esteem fed his ego. He was encouraged from youth by discriminating patrons, enabled to devote

---

[7] Thayer: *Beethoven*, I, 281.
[8] Ibid., III, 277–8.   [9] Ibid., I, 248.
[1] Friedrich Kerst: *Beethoven, the Man and the Artist, as Revealed in His Own Words*, ed. and tr. Henry E. Krehbiel (New York: B. W. Huebsch; 1905), p. 55.

himself to his major concern—composition—without too severe a burden of other activities. He was appreciated abroad as well as at home by persons whose praise was meaningful. After a while, he was able to choose among publishers, or entertain competitive offers. Very little for which he is celebrated today was not in print or on press during his lifetime, from the trios of opus 1 (Artaria brought them out in 1795) to the final quartet, opus 135 (which Schlesinger produced in Berlin in 1827).

Combined with these favorable outward circumstances were such productive inward ones as a passion for concentration, a compulsion to hard thought and final solutions, an indifference to temporal enticements, and an intransigence about enduring values. Together they enabled him to make the most of his sizeable gifts. The grinding process of refinement that typified his compositional method was, in effect, a pulverizer that packed everything he learned, all he felt, and much that he merely divined into a hard core of meaning unlike any previously known.

So much romantic lore is attached to the outward occurrences of Beethoven's life, his battle against physical handicaps and bodily disabilities, that the much greater drama of his struggle for supremacy over musical means is underplayed. This is two ways regrettable, for it was on a more epochal scale and continued throughout his life. Only those who appreciate the difference between the state of music as he found it and the conditions of future growth which he bequeathed to it can understand how much has not been fully absorbed or wholly explored a century and a half later.

Most particularly, in the short compass of a single lifetime, Beethoven, fed by the new conditions that came into existence as he did, grew to personify the nature and shape of the continuity to come, the typical pattern of its procedures. First there was a gathering together of retrospective elements, from which the lessons of the past were learned; then, a period of revaluation and consolidation, in which the lessons were applied in a new spirit by a gifted individual; finally, a summation of old and new, bringing with it implications and intimations of things to come. If the individual was not merely gifted, but possessed of a compulsion to seize the Promethean fire, the summation could be, as Beethoven's was, a molten force flowing into all known molds—instrumental, vocal, orchestral, choral, even operatic—exerting an irresistible pressure that changed the shape of many and the content of all.

4

THESE, OF COURSE, are the two ways in which continuity is manifest: shape and content. Or to put it in more specific terms, by the procedural, which is readily intelligible to the eye, and by the substantive, which is primarily perceived by the ear. In the higher forms of achievement, the two may be so closely interrelated that the form and what it contains are scarcely separable. In the highest, the fusion is so complete that the listener is oblivious to procedure in absorption with substance, as in Beethoven's C-sharp-minor Quartet, opus 131. Who thinks of a given subject in terms of an ABA procedure, rondo, or aria da capo? In such a totality, the composer has achieved the highest degree of identity with the listener by so absorbing him with meaning as to leave him unconcerned with procedure, form, technique, or any other mechanical detail.

In the nine symphonies, sixteen quartets, and thirty-two piano sonatas (not to mention the many duo sonatas, trios, songs, etc.), there are hundreds of examples of the ways in which Beethoven's relentless pursuit of musical possibilities, his far-ranging comprehension of tonal combinations produced sonorities, relationships, and procedures previously unexplored, in some instances still unexploited. His was, without question, the most inclusive musical brain history has known, and its product dominated the musical functioning, for decades to come, of masters as well as of neophytes.

For supporting testimony, one may refer to Sir Donald Tovey's discussion of the First Symphony.[2] Within the space of a few lines, he refers—without, of course, stating it in such terms—to an essential dualism in the subject of continuity. This is the adaptation from the past to the present of an unfulfilled resource, which thus becomes a part of the future. It could be likened to a series of reflecting mirrors in which back, side, and front views show likenesses to grandfather, father, and child. Thus Tovey: "Beethoven got the idea of using C and G drums in this F major movement from Mozart's wonderful Linz symphony [No. 23 in C, K. 425]." Farther along on the same page, in presenting some views on the trio of the minuet, Tovey observes: "The trio, with throbbing wind band chords and mysterious violin runs, is, like so many of Beethoven's early minuets and trios, prophetic of Schumann's most intimate epigrammatic sentiments."

[2] D. F. Tovey: *Essays in Musical Analysis* (London: Oxford University Press; 1935), I, 24.

Thus, in an early work of Beethoven which does not enjoy a reputation as strongly individual, Tovey identifies a line of continuity stretching from Mozart's "Linz" Symphony of 1785 to Schumann's D-minor of 1841–5 without even considering the existence of such a concept.

Staying, for the moment, with Tovey, one finds in the space of three pages (25, 26, 27) references, in a discourse on Beethoven's Symphony No. 2, to "The Heavens are telling" from Haydn's *Creation*, Schubert's Grand Duo for four hands, Schumann's Symphony No. 4, and the opus 11 Serenade of Brahms. Remarks Tovey, in fair wonderment at the card file of music in his mind: "The echoes are by no means confined to imitative or classicist efforts: they are to be found in things like Schubert's Grand Duo and Schumann's Fourth Symphony, works written at high noontide of their composer's powers and quite unrestrained in the urgency of important new developments." For those who have had the opportunity (denied Tovey) of hearing and rehearing at will most of the important and some of the unimportant music written between 1700 and 1950, to juxtapose the sound of Bach with the sound of Brahms, or the idiom of Haydn with that of Hindemith, such links, attachments, and affinities are the rule rather than the exception to it. Much will depend, of course, on the "card file of music" in the individual listener's mind and his ability to recognize a link, attachment, or affinity when it presents itself.

Of Beethoven's response to the work of his predecessors, there are many generic or inferential references, but few so specific as one bearing on his knowledge of the C-minor Piano Concerto (No. 24, K. 491) of Mozart. It was in 1799 that Beethoven visited the Augarten (a part of Vienna, situated on an island in the Danube where outdoor concerts were given at the time) in company with a fellow musician, the pianist-composer-publisher Johann Baptist Cramer. As they strode back and forth listening to the playing of the concerto, Beethoven paused and said: "Cramer! Cramer! We shall never be able to do anything like that."

In his massive biography Thayer elaborates:[3] "Directing his companion's attention to the exceedingly simple but equally beautiful motive which is first introduced toward the end of the piece [measures 168–204] . . . Beethoven, swaying his body to and fro, marked the time and in every possible manner manifested a delight rising to enthusiasm."

Admiration was recast as emulation in the following year when he came to produce his own C-minor Piano Concerto (No. 3, opus 37).

[3] Thayer: *Beethoven*, I, 219.

Mozart: Piano Concerto No. 24, C minor (K. 491), finale

His version of the "Mozart effect" may be heard in the unexpected appearance, at a comparable point in the finale, of a major-key theme (E flat) at a place where a reversion to something in keeping with the minor mode of the rondo would be expected. This instance has the special interest of being linked to a specific, citable incident. Moreover, it is one in which the means of perception was through the ear, the essential instrument of continuity.

One might relate the same Mozartian precept to an eloquent stroke of contrast in the finale of Beethoven's Violin Concerto. As the motival thread is spun out, Beethoven provides the contrast of G minor to the movement's basic D major, and then drifts off into C major before returning to the rondo theme itself. Thus he has added a variant of his own to a variant of the "Mozart effect," as well as recalling his source in a background figure for the bassoon, an instrument more prominent in the finale of the C-minor than in almost any other piano concerto by Mozart.

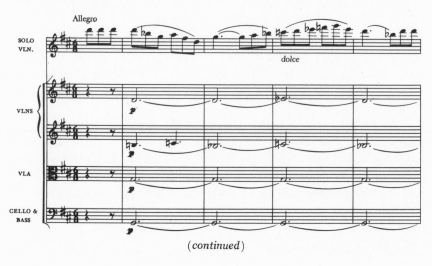

(*continued*)

Beethoven: Violin Concerto (op. 61), finale

Still another outcome of Beethoven's acquaintance with K. 491, possibly a product of the same Augarten experience, had a much longer projection into continuity. In it, for nearly the first time in his total (to then) of more than twenty piano concertos, it occurred to Mozart to bring back the opening theme of the whole work in a solo statement by the piano *after* the cadenza. It is in Beethoven's C-minor Concerto (the Third, to which reference has already been made) that this procedure appears for the first time in one of his major works for solo instrument and orchestra (see examples, pp. 20–21).

So singularly right and functional a part does this procedure play in the rounding out of the musical structure, as a reminiscence, in a quiet, contemplative mood, of the preceding conflicts and tensions, that music lovers have been conditioned for decades to wait for those exalted moments "after the cadenza" which Beethoven wrote into all the solo concertos that followed (Nos. 4 and 5 for piano, and the D-major for violin).

For later composers, especially Brahms, whose reprise (just before the end of the D-major Concerto's first movement) of the opening theme of the violin in its highest register is a winged flight he rarely exceeded, the procedure was no longer an experiment or innovation. It was *de rigueur*, the final "strike home" of the symphonic ballad.

Thus from a single work of Mozart, of which we know that Beethoven had certain knowledge, he evolved two basic concepts that passed through him into the stream of continuity. One might mention, as other examples, the E-major scale played by the violins behind Sarastro's words in *Die Zauberflöte*, "*Dann wandelt er an Freundes Hand, vergnügt und froh ins bess're Land*" ("And guided forth by friendship's hand,

Mozart: Piano Concerto No. 24, C minor (K. 491), first movement

They journey to a better land" is one translation), which became the
E-flat scale at the climax of the variations-finale of the "Eroica" (Symphony No. 3). It was later recalled by that insuperable Mozart-Bee-
thoven idolator Richard Strauss at a peak moment of his "Eroica" (*Ein*

Beethoven: *Piano Concerto No. 3, C minor (op. 37), first movement*

Mozart: Die Zauberflöte, *Act II, "In diesen heil'gen Hallen"*

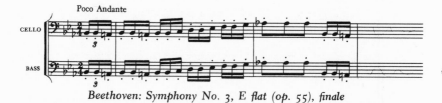

Beethoven: Symphony No. 3, E flat (op. 55), finale

Heldenleben). And in the vocal finale of his Choral Fantasy, opus 80 (example, p. 23), Beethoven turned to a formulation very much like the Dritte Damen in *Die Zauberflöte* (example, below). It was not until he had discharged this obligation to the continuity of Mozart that Beethoven found the way, some years later, to incorporate the thought into the choral finale of the Ninth. Certainly the French horn duo behind Fiordiligi's "*Per pietà*" in *Così fan tutte* is brought to mind by the French horn trio behind Leonore's "*Komm, Hoffnung*" in *Fidelio*.

For his response to the example of Haydn, one need only consult Beethoven's first piano trio, the first symphony, the first quartets, indeed almost every one of his fledgling flights. From these examples and the transformation of them through his own personal impulse, Beethoven evolved such monumental additions to precedent (in the procedural) as the magnificent coda to the first movement of the "*Eroica*." Here, one by one, the choirs join in a universal chorus rising to a shout of praise for the Hero, personified by the opening theme.

Mozart: Die Zauberflöte, Act I (No. 5)

Beethoven: Choral Fantasy, C minor (op. 80)

A simple concept in itself, it was unknown previously on such a scale: but it became the model for an infinity of alternative versions, not excluding Ravel's *Boléro*. Also a revolution in procedure was the link-by-bridge-passage from the scherzo of the C-minor Symphony to the finale. In like manner, the finales of Beethoven's later concertos (Nos. 4 and 5 for piano, and the D-major Violin Concerto) were joined to their slow movements. This was quickly acted upon by Mendelssohn to produce the ideal of an integrated work in his E-minor Violin

Concerto. There are no interruptions between movements; all the cadenzas are written out by the composer; nothing is left to interpretative whim or improvisatory chance. One could see as a further extension the compact all-in-one-movement concerto pioneered by Liszt in his E-flat, and, in the farther future, the single-movement symphony of Sibelius (No. 7) and the *Kammersymphonie* of Schoenberg.

In his familiar, familial role as Father of the Symphony, Haydn bequeathed the minuet-turned-scherzo of the symphonic sequence. What Beethoven effected in the character of the adopted "son" was not merely a leavening of Haydn's earthy humors to produce a more sophisticated kind of levity, but also a broadening and strengthening of its whole body by the addition of second trios, replacement of the literal repetition by a varied, written-out second statement. Here was malleable material for Schubert, Schumann, Brahms, Dvořák, and Bruckner to hammer into new shapes. In the hands of Chopin, the scherzo became a separate work in a special category of its own.

From both Haydn and Mozart, Beethoven received a ground plan of the symphony which provided for a slow introduction (optional with the composer). Most often it was utilized to define the key center, either by stress upon it or by digression from it (as in the introduction to Beethoven's First Symphony). Now and then, as in Mozart's E-flat (No. 39) Symphony or in Haydn's D-major (No. 104), it was utilized for a play of sonority which mapped the tonal cosmos to come as well as the specific areas within it. Well after the first function of the slow introduction for a symphony had passed from Beethoven's scheme, he found reason for and purpose in utilizing the second. Indeed, it provides the means for setting in motion the five-octave chord at the opening of the Seventh Symphony, in which the modern orchestra raises its voice for the first time. A responsive spirit, such as the young Hector Berlioz's, would not require much more than such a demonstration to deduce that the orchestra was his predestined instrument. He soon saw in it a voice that could speak in many more tongues and subtly varied dialects than those few Beethoven had discovered for himself.

5

IT IS OF THE ESSENCE in contemplating the current of continuity to reckon with two factors: a) the degree of flow at a given time; b) the accessibility to that flow of a specific individual. It was of little effect on the music of Bach for him to be a contemporary of Handel if the latter's accomplishments were unknown to him or if they were known to him but unavailable for study. With Beethoven, there were not only sources but also opportunities for exposure to them which, together with his capacity for self-development, produced the forces now so well known.

In the presentation of the case to this point, evidence has been restricted to the variety usually called direct: that is to say, each contention is related to a specific, identifiable source. This may permit the liberty of one reference to the circumstantial. I know, for example, of no printed reference pointing to Beethoven's familiarity with the C-minor (K. 475) Fantasia of Mozart, or of the sonata in the same key with which it is affiliated. But such knowledge strikes me as implicit in the strong suggestion it contains of certain substantive elements in Beethoven's idiom. To my ear, these are as much a part of the assimilation and stimulation that make up the continuity of music as the "anticipations" of Schumann's idiom noted by Tovey in the First and Second symphonies of Beethoven.

It is the kind of Beethoven familiar in so early a work as the C-minor Piano (*"Pathétique"*) Sonata, opus 13. In its introduction, one finds a strain of earnest, brooding (not to say impassioned) statement from which later emerged some of his most characteristic achievements. As they surge upward, fall back, and surge again in a chromatic tension, they reach toward an outline decidedly Wagnerian, not to say Tristanish.

This is one of those occurrences of "anticipation" often remarked, of the sort that make up, in the words previously used, "a phenomenon so familiar that it has never been analyzed previously." What spurs interest and prompts analysis is the recent availability, in recorded form, of the piano music Wagner was writing in his late teens (between 1829 and 1831, when Beethoven's life had barely ended). One can hear, especially in the B-flat Sonata and the F-sharp-minor Fantasy (both dated 1831), a disposition on the part of the young Wagner toward a comparable idiom, a drive toward the domination of it. Already (1830) Wagner's enthusiasm for the composer whom, for the half century of his life still to come, he revered above all others had prompted him to make his own piano reduction of the Ninth Symphony because none was available in print.

Some might say, with a full weight of contemporary skepticism, that if Wagner had been exposed to the *"Pathétique"* and the introduction had made such an impact on him, it was a long time—twenty-five years—in manifesting itself. Considering the originality of *Tristan* and the far-reaching effect of its vocabulary, a gestation period of twenty-five years was hardly excessive. Beethoven, for example, first thought of setting Schiller's *Freude*[4] in 1790, but did not translate the impulse into action until 1822, though the musical mate for it had begun to emerge, as we have seen, in the Choral Fantasy of 1808. There was with Wagner, too, a way-point of striving without complete success: the first version of the *Faust Overture* of 1840 shows a composer striving to make this idiom his own and not quite succeeding.

A more specific example of Wagner-in-Beethoven is to be found in the "*Komm, Hoffnung*" section of Leonore's first-act "*Abscheulicher*" in *Fidelio*. I have in mind a passage built on the C-major chord which begins "*So leuchtet mir ein Farbenbogen.*"[5] Its Wagnerian counterpart

Beethoven: Fidelio, Act I *(Eulenberg miniature score, p. 380)*

is heard in the third-act "Grail Narrative" in *Lohengrin*, in which the son of Parsifal sings the words "*liegt eine Burg die Montsalvat genannt*" (example, p. 27). It is one of the fascinations of this endlessly ramified subject that the same aria already cited for the evidence it shows (in its horn passages) of Mozart-in-Beethoven may also be cited for the projection forward of Beethoven-in-Wagner.

Suggestions of the substantive Schumann (as distinguished from the procedural one cited by Tovey) may be found at several points in the piano music of Beethoven, but nowhere as strongly as in the first measures of the E-minor (opus 90) Sonata. A charming work of 1814 (being neither early, middle, or late, it is usually passed up by pianists who think of Beethoven in such terms), it poses a vigorously rhythmic, melodically assertive opening statement whose thrust is parried by a languorously syncopated counter-statement. Together they depict, to the life, Schumann's Florestan and Eusebius moods. Rather than pursu-

[4] Ibid., 132.
[5] Eulenburg miniature orchestral score of *Fidelio*, p. 380.

Wagner: Lohengrin, *Act III*

ing them into the decade after next, Beethoven goes back to being Beethoven, leaving to Schumann the privilege of discovering himself.

If there is Schumann in Beethoven, one might ask (in paraphrase
of Shelley) can Brahms be far behind? One need look no farther than
the swirl of musical motion that Beethoven brought into play at a
climactic moment of the Funeral March in the *"Eroica"* Symphony for
the answer. It begins at measure 44 and ends a mere five measures
later (example, p. 28); but in that span the tread and power of Brahms
at his most "Olympian" rise before us almost visibly. The details may be
itemized thus: the first violins launch a repeated figure in triplets, the
second violins sing the main melody against violas doubling the cellos a
sixth below. In the woodwinds, the oboes and clarinets move in contrary
motion, the bassoons cling to clashing suspensions doubling the flute
two octaves higher. All is sustained by a bass pedal D.

Brahms, who knew a good musical thing when he heard it or
absorbed it unconsciously, used the general idea more than once, but
most conspicuously in his First Symphony (measure 495). Here the
triplet movement is in the timpani, the contrary motion in the violins
and cellos (going up), the flutes, oboes, clarinets, and oboes (going
down). Supporting all is a pedal point (C) in the doublebass, contra-

Beethoven: Symphony No. 3, E flat (op. 55), second movement

bassoon, and horns. It is the identical textural concept, augmented by additional instruments (example, p. 29).

Rather than being merely an incidental element of the first movement, it plays a generative part in its character, affecting shape as well as content. It brings to a pounding climax the whole action of the opening movement after a build-up of nearly 500 measures, in a *poco*

Brahms: Symphony No. 1, C minor (op. 68), first movement

sostenuto that echoes its use at the very beginning. Like many a deep-seated artistic impulse, it assumed a life of its own which outgrew its creator's original estimation of it. Albert Dietrich, for whom Brahms played a preliminary form of the movement in 1862, noted that the introductory passage was absent at that time. During the fourteen years that elapsed before Brahms deemed the whole work ready for a *première* at Karlsruhe in 1876, it asserted its predestined place as the impelling force of the movement, hence of the whole symphony.

The range of Beethoven's expression is reflected in the variety of minds and temperaments that found stimulation in one kind of work but not in another, or even in one movement of a specific work but not in any other part of the same work or in any different work. Thus, the suggestion of Schumann is strong in the B-flat (Fourth) Symphony but not in any other. Both Tchaikovsky and Falla (in *El Sombrero de Tres Picos*) recalled their affection for the C-minor (Fifth). With Berlioz it was the "Pastorale's" atmosphere and the orchestral range of the Seventh that were immediately influential. Mendelssohn, it might be said, was responsive to the color of the allegretto of the Seventh Symphony, and perpetuated it in his A-major ("Italian") Symphony's slow movement, to the exclusion of most other aspects of Beethoven. One learns not to be dogmatic about such matters when the realization dawns, as it did on me only recently, that the essence of the evocative nocturne in his *Midsummer Night's Dream* music (example, p. 31) is the larghetto of Beethoven's Second Symphony.

Beethoven: *Symphony No. 2, D (op. 36), second movement*

It is an instructive comment on the difference between "classical" and "romantic" to observe the kind of embellishment utilized by Mendelssohn, in addition to the "poetic" coloration of the French horn, to produce the results for which this section is famous.

Mendelssohn: A Midsummer Night's Dream (op. 61), Nocturne

It also makes one wary of "definitive" pronouncements to realize that one has known both creations and admired them, independently, for decades without perceiving the family likeness they share. One might, when least expected, find some projection into the continuity of music of Beethoven's Symphony No. 8. The Eighth, a reversion to Beethoven's earlier, lighter style, has no descendant presently known to me.

But its tremendous successor is without question the most influential of all. Whether or not one attributes to its formidable example the proliferation of later orchestral works with choral appendages is, even, beside the present point. Nor do I have in mind such a celebrated parallel to its chorale theme as the broadly flowing finale of Brahms's First Symphony (when its paternity was suggested to the composer, he commented: "Any fool can see that"), or such an uncelebrated one as occurs in the finale of Schubert's C-major Symphony[6] written half a dozen years after the *première* of the Ninth in 1822.

I have in mind, rather, the extent to which its formulation of tonal shapes, its expansion of design, its juxtaposition of ideas with less and less of the preparation previously considered indispensable, all come to selective, highly dispersed productivity in the work of his greatest progeny—using the term in the sense that all those who share in this continuity are offshoots of their elders.

For Berlioz and Wagner (see p. 67, re the *Faust Overture*), the Ninth had profound philosophic and spiritual implications which will be dwelled upon in a later chapter. With Bruckner first and Mahler afterwards, the organization, sequence, and compositional conception

---

[6] It appears first at the beginning of the development section (measure 386) and is a recurrent factor in the movement thereafter.

of the Ninth were very much at the heart of many of their procedures now only beginning to be understood. This common antecedent may, indeed, be a stronger reason for putting them in a bracket—however unaccommodating otherwise—than other reasons previously adduced.

6

HAVING PROJECTED A LINE of thought extending over a period of at least two centuries—binding Bach to Beethoven and Beethoven to Mahler —it is perhaps appropriate to state some general principles. In none of the instances thus far cited, whether affiliating Beethoven with Mozart, or Mendelssohn, Berlioz, Schubert, Schumann, Wagner, Brahms, Bruckner, Mahler, and Richard Strauss with Beethoven, is there the slightest suggestion of imitation: least of all, the faintest implication of plagiarism.

Rather, as has been suggested in the reference to Grieg's Law, it is a relationship inherent in the nature of music, what Grieg termed an "eternal" factor in its process of generation and regeneration.

One may therefore state as Axiom I of this subject:

When a composer produces an atypical effect or mode of expression, one may say that he anticipates. Thus the point reached by Beethoven at measure 44 of the Funeral March of the *"Eroica"* is atypical, something he never did again in so conspicuous a way.

This leads directly to Axiom II:

In extending such an atypical trend of Beethoven's thought, in giving new meaning and an added dimension *to it through the addition of his own resources, Brahms is participating in a century-spanning sequence of continuity.* He is, like so many others in their different ways, the instrument of history through which the prophetic vision of Beethoven is fulfilled and acquires an identity of its own.

Conversely, Axiom III:

When a composer DUPLICATES *a typical vein of a predecessor without adding anything substantial to it from his own resources, he is indulging only in imitation. If it is volitional, it then, of course, becomes plagiarism.*

More likely than not, the recipient of an influence may pass through one or more preliminary phases on the way to becoming capable of anticipating, on his own, a later man's predestined manner. In the case of Brahms, for example, it may be noted relative to the early (opus 1) Sonata in C, written when he was not yet twenty, that he had selected the manner of the *"Hammerklavier"* Sonata for himself, that he was trying on—and not finding very accommodating—the wings on which Beethoven soared to such heights at nearly fifty. This being a typical idiom of Beethoven which its originator exploited to its utmost—or, at least, one to which Brahms at this time of life could add very little—its use can only be termed imitation. If one thinks well of the Brahms who eventually evolved procedures of his own which entered deeply into the being of such an innovator as Schoenberg,[7] the impact may be softened somewhat by describing the results as "derivative."

The fundamental distinction between typical and atypical may be formulated as follows: the propagation of the atypical is an act of continuity, advancing a dormant tendency toward latent fulfillment; the duplication of the typical is, essentially, an act of imitation, adding nothing to a mode of expression fully realized by a predecessor.

Curiously, a composer who imitates convincingly enough and with some discrimination may, during his lifetime, have more success than one who seems to be "old-fashioned" or, as current terminology has it, "conservative." The former is consonant with current trends (whether his music is dissonant or not) and thus possessed of official validity, however short-lived these trends may be. It is only when an objective view of the whole period has become possible and the persons who have used its fashionable idiom only fashionably are separated from those who have added something to it from their own capacities, or have resolutely pursued a direction of their own, that a measure of relative durability may be achieved. One might cite, on the international scale, the current interest in the works of Carl Nielsen or Leoš Janáček, who were eclipsed, in their lifetimes, by many more fashionable composers.

Is it possible that without imitation there can be no propagation? It is not merely possible, but also demonstrable. It depends, of course, to what degree the imitation flourishes, and for how long. To invoke Mozart in this context may be only to make child's play of what should be a man's work, but it serves to affiliate the argument with one who was both imitator and propagator. At the ages of five, six, and seven, he was writing—with the aid of his father, no doubt—competent imitations of Johann Christian Bach, in his earliest (so-called) symphonies. By the time he was ten and eleven, these began to assume the shape of individual utterances of his own, especially in the slow move-

[7] Arnold Schoenberg: *Style and Idea* (New York: Philosophical Library; 1950), p. 185.

ments. At fifteen, sixteen, and seventeen, the question was no longer whose music Mozart's was like, but who had ever written music like this before.

If this is an extreme of precocity, there can also be an extreme of latent development, of a musical manifestation as original as Borodin's and as late-blooming (he was thirty-six when he began his most famous work, *Prince Igor*). There is, indeed, no manner of measurement or dependable guide to the age at which musical individuality may assert itself or provide a sufficient refinement of data to account for all the innumerable variants. They range from the early bloom that withers on the vine (Korngold) to the hardy perennial (Verdi), from the sporadic producer (Wolf) to the vine-like creeper that rises ever higher (Wagner). These are but a few of the mutations that come to maturity in such an unpredictable idiosyncratic way that nothing like a type can be evolved.

All that can be evolved is a law of probability reading: the composer who has a "style of his own" from student days is more likely an impostor than a genius. The reflection of Beethoven in the mirror Brahms held up to himself in the opus 1 Sonata has its equivalents in the development of many, perhaps of nearly all, others. A convenient and interesting example is provided by Dvořák. In works of small scope, but which are by no means of slight artistic value, he was intensely himself almost from the start (allowing for Smetana's prior discovery of the Czech musical soul and his direct participation in Dvořák's realization of its existence within himself, too). Certainly this is evident in the *Slavonic Rhapsodies* and *Slavonic Dances* of 1878, also in the lesser-known Suite (opus 39) of the same year, when Dvořák was in his mid-thirties.

In works of larger scope, however, in which problems of form and internal architectural relationships were more demanding, Dvořák leaned heavily on others for the shape of a second theme here, the beginning of a development there, the treatment of a transitional passage or coda elsewhere. The recent publication (and recording) of Dvořák's first four symphonies (in the sequence of nine ending with the "New World")[8] bears additional witness to his response to one line of prior thought after another as his musical culture expanded. Wagner remains a constant, for Dvořák played in an orchestra conducted by him in a Prague concert of 1863, and he tended to revert to that early enthusiasm even after he had steeped himself in the examples of Beethoven, Schubert, Schumann, and Brahms.

[8] In deference to its chronological occurrence, it is now commonly described as No. 9 rather than No. 5.

Brahms: Piano Concerto No. 2, B flat (op. 83), third movement

In the D-minor Symphony of 1885 (now No. 7), the second subject of the first movement (example, p. 36) is such close kin to the slow movement of Brahms's B-flat Concerto (No. 2) for piano and orchestra (example, p. 35) that one wonders how so honest a man and conscientious a musician as Dvořák failed to perceive the likeness. It is rather another thing that the first movement of the same D-minor Symphony ends with much the same kind of dying fall as the first movement of Brahms's Symphony No. 3, for Dvořák's admiration for that work was freely confessed, as was the spirit of emulation it aroused in him.[9]

Perhaps because *Tannhäuser* was one of the works[1] he played

[9] Ottokar Sourek: Quoted in liner of Artia ALP 177.
[1] On February 8, 1863, together with the *Faust Overture*, the preludes to *Die Meistersinger* and *Tristan*, plus Siegmund's "*Winterstürme*" from *Die Walküre*, Pogner's address and the entrance of the Guildsmen from *Die Meistersinger*. Ernest Newman: *The Life of Richard Wagner* (New York: Alfred A. Knopf; 1937), III, 202.

Dvořák: Symphony No. 7, D minor (op. 70), first movement

under Wagner's direction, pieces of it creep into the earliest symphonies (No. 3 especially). But it is surprising to discover in the *Carnival Overture* of Dvořák's mature years a bridge passage reproduced whole from Wagner's blueprinting of it in the same *Tannhäuser* overture. The work begins in a rush of jollification and boisterous energy, in a manner decidedly Dvořák's own. However, when the need for a change of scene arises, it is a violent change indeed—straight into the Venusberg by way of arpeggios, scampering strings, the glinting punctuation of the cymbal, the whole unmistakably distinctive coloration. Again I express wonder that what is patent fact to me was not patent fact to Dvořák.

Had Dvořák written no other symphonies, not found the true voice we hear in the E-minor Symphony, he would have left as equivocal an impression in this aspect of his writing as, say, Lalo. But, in this absorbing instance of **continuity** and the development incidental to it, we hear a composer of unmistakable gifts, if not the highest degree of intellectual disposition toward the biggest musical structures, in the full endeavor of finding a way of his own. Meanwhile he stands on the shoulders of his elders until he is able to plant a next stride firmly on ground of his own. Once attained, it has remained ground where no one has set foot since.

All this is by way of interesting contrast with Tchaikovsky, who had much the same kind of difficulty with bridge passages, junctures, and joints as Dvořák. But, perhaps, because he was too self-critical, or merely too proud, to borrow, he suffered to "let his seams show" (as he phrased it in a letter to Nadejda von Meck in 1878) most of his life. Indeed, he promulgated his own version of Grieg's Law, which found expression in a letter of the same year to Taneyev.[2] Provocatively enough, the subject was a comparison of *Eugen Onegin* with *Aida* (whose "effects" Taneyev apparently deemed a contribution to that work's success). Wrote Tchaikovsky: "I spit upon 'effects'—my music which, *entirely against my will*[3]—is impregnated with Schumannism, Wagnerism, Chopinism, Glinkaism, Berliozism, and all the other 'isms' of our time would be as out of keeping with the characters of *Aida* as the elegant speeches of Racine's heroes—couched in the second person plural—are unsuited to the real Orestes or the real Andromache. Such music would be a falsehood and all falsehoods are abhorrent to me."

Thus, if Tchaikovsky may be stigmatized for abrupt breaks in his symphonic structures and the "solecism" of an opening theme in the B-flat-minor Piano Concerto which is never heard again, he cannot be condemned for plagiarism or even patronized for the kind of unconscious imitation of another bird's call to be noted with Dvořák. Such outside assistance might have brought him to a solution of his problem sooner. But it is part of the consistent pattern that made him abhor "falsehood" that when he did come to full mastery of his symphonic problem it was under such compulsion as the emotional truth of the *"Pathétique."* The results are intuitively right, full-fashioned, the shoulders joined to the arm (with heart on sleeve), and no seams showing. To accept Tchaikovsky's analogy, it could be said that the seams no longer showed because the form in which the music was molded was his own.

Clearly if Dvořák, in accordance with Grieg's Law, acted in the continuity of his predecessors and contemporaries half knowingly, half unknowingly and Tchaikovsky did so without being able to help himself, the existence of the fact if not of the name was recognized by two

[2] *Life and Letters of Peter Ilich Tchaikovsky*, ed. Rosa Newmarch (London: John Lane The Bodley Head; 1906), pp. 255-6.
[3] Italics added.—I.K.

enormously gifted men and vouched for by a third. The singularity of it all is not that the same work may say different things to different minds, but that it may say nothing at all to a blood brother and musical kinsman.

Continuity might be compared to the distribution of radio waves, which also travel through the air. In such a system, there can be no meaningful communication unless there is a receiver as well as a sender. Turning the image in the other direction, it could be said that there are, still, suggestions and implications in the later works of Beethoven—quartets and variations, as well as sonatas and symphonies —which he would have strengthened, developed, perfected, had he lived on for another productive decade. But to "receive" them and profit from the musical meaning they contain would require a man of equally subtle mind, of which music has seen very few.

Brahms studied Beethoven's chamber music closely, and profited to the extent, at least, of the texture he evolved for the opus 51 quartets. Wagner's devotion to the C-sharp-minor Quartet (opus 131) is as famous (see p. 70) as Berlioz's (see p. 96) is not. But neither pursued the issue to a final outcome. Bartók clearly modeled his own early (and admirable) quartets on Beethoven's, but it was not until the Music for Strings, Percussion, and Celesta of his mid-fifties (1936) that he began to rethink late Beethoven in his own way, a rethinking that also shows itself in the final quartet that followed. As for the last outpost of Beethoven's unapproachability—the *Grosse Fuge,* opus 133 —Schoenberg paid it the musical compliment of recollection at a moment of some consequence in his Piano Concerto of 1942, as well as a verbal compliment in unmistakable terms (see p. 260).

By projecting his mind into areas of music that would not be totally explored for decades to come, Beethoven foresaw not only solutions (the lines of his projection followed by Schumann, Brahms, Wagner, etc.), but also many problems. Like the later works of several of his eminent predecessors—including Bach, Haydn, and Mozart— Beethoven's final sonatas and quartets tend more and more to a chromatic rather than a diatonic texture. This is to say, simply, that the older he grew, the more inclined he was to prefer the closer relation, note to note, of chromatic writing to the more open spaces of diatonic procedures. What this chromatic texture came to be in later works of Wagner and Strauss, and then in Schoenberg, will be discussed in due course.

Certainly Beethoven was conscious of the tyranny of the cadence, and strove mightily, especially in his later years, to make it melt, dissolve, or otherwise lose its identity in order that music might flow on and on. Richard Strauss came closer to a solution of the problem in his *Metamorphosen* of the 1940's than anyone else, but its lessons are still to be learned. Beethoven was acutely aware that melody is the out-growth of harmony rather than its seed, that fresh ways of combining notes into chords, and chords into sequences, will do more to regenerate melody than anything else (as Poulenc, Prokofiev, Shostakovitch, and others who have recently fashioned durable melodies from harmonies of new pungency and flavor give proof). He was one of the first to write across rather than within bar lines, in prophecy of an impulse that would become a compulsion with Stravinsky and others. He not only projected the idea of the scherzo as an independent piece, but also set a pattern for a whole category of variations for orchestra with the finale of the *"Eroica."*

A fitting summation to the pre-eminence of the man and the enormous influence he exerted is the comment of the late Paul Hindemith, whose name has not had prominent place in this discussion previously. Asked by an interviewer[4] "Whom do you consider to be your closest musical antecedents?" Hindemith replied: "I suppose Bach, Mozart, and Haydn. Beethoven also, in a sense: but then, he is everybody's predecessor."

Hindemith might have added that Beethoven was "everybody's" preceptor in two ways still unmatched: the amplitude of his intent, the magnitude of his achievement.

[4] Jay Harrison, in the New York *Herald Tribune*, February 15, 1959.

II

The Line from Chopin

I

HINDEMITH'S GENERALIZATION is a welcome endorsement of the point of view thus far expounded, the more gratifying for the eminence of its source. But it is, clearly, no more applicable to all the ramifications and involutions of so large a subject than any other generalization. If one conceives of Schubert, Schumann, Berlioz, Brahms, Bruckner, Mahler, Elgar, Sibelius—to select more or less at random among Hindemith's artistic forebears—as "everybody," such an all-embracing line of continuity might be acceptable. But it is quite plain that such a sequence does not lead to a whole host of "nobodies," such as Liszt, Fauré, Saint-Saëns, Debussy, Ravel, Granados, and Poulenc, least of all to Stravinsky and his part in continuity; and, no more than partially, to so all-important a phenomenon as Wagner.

This, however, is not to say that such a line does not exist—one must, rather, look for it elsewhere. And if it is of sufficient stature to coexist as an influence comparable to Beethoven's, it should not be too hard to find. Indeed, it is the validity of the premise that dictates the direction of the search. If one sector of an organism—in this case, the body of music—can be seen to follow a recognizable pattern of development and regeneration, it is reasonable to suppose that another part will function similarly.

2

FOR THOSE WHO HAVE HEARD a sufficient sampling of the music written from the maturing of Beethoven to the death of Debussy, the indications lead unmistakably to one individual. Like Beethoven, he came from a provincial center to live in a great musical capital. Rather than Bonn, the place of origin was Warsaw. And, rather than settling in Vienna, he was almost magnetically attracted to Paris.

Beethoven was forty, with a sizeable share of his enduring accomplishment in being, when Frédéric Chopin was born about 1810. This of itself gave Chopin an advantage of immense importance. By the time he would come to an age of artistic awareness in his later teens, all of Beethoven's music would have been written, as would Weber's and substantially all of Schubert's. The publication of instrumental works by J. S. Bach would have vastly expanded, and the singular perceptions of Mendelssohn would also have been added to the resources of music. If Chopin rejected the thinking embodied in all or any of these, they were at least there to be experienced and evaluated, accepted or rejected. He could set aside all the substance of Beethoven that did not appeal to him, and still find, in Beethoven's enlargement of the scherzo, a design that could be propagated as a form in itself.

By the time Chopin was ten, Beethoven had already written the Sonata in B flat (opus 106) known as the *"Hammerklavier,"* expounding the resources of the improved piano as it then existed. Symptomatic of the developments in the range and carrying power of the keyboard instruments built between 1770 and 1820 was the emergence of a new phenomenon—the traveling virtuoso personified by Johann Nepomuk Hummel, John Field, and Friedrich Wilhelm Kalkbrenner. Warsaw was a place where they could be heard before Chopin left it in 1830.

As early as 1840, writing of the Nocturnes, opus 37, and the F-major Ballade (No. 2), Robert Schumann—who, as well as being a composer of inimitable style, shared with Berlioz the distinction of being one of the first critics to think in terms of a repertory—observed: "Chopin may now publish anything without putting his name to it: his works will always be recognized." In the relatively short span of ten years, Chopin had achieved not merely a reputation, but an identification with a historically distinctive idiom of his own. In it were embodied not only the creative personality of the composer, but also the characteristic sound and the barely exploited potentialities of the instrument on which he performed.

As the instrument was to become the one most commonly available to the composers and music lovers of the next ten decades, it might be worthwhile to consider the components of that idiom. Fortunately, one need not start from scratch or rely wholly on self-instituted search. Gerald Abraham has given convincing exposition of its fundamental elements in the provocative study entitled *Chopin's Musical Style* (London: Oxford University Press; 1939). Abraham's quest for the connective threads from the past and their place in the texture of Chopin leads to a series of conclusions in which are embodied several of the recognizable factors of continuity as herein expounded: the procedural and the substantive, typical and atypical, plus several others previously unremarked.

Well before Schumann made his familiar comment on the wholeness of Chopin's identity, François-Joseph Fétis, one of the first notable music critics and founder (in 1827) of the long-lived *Revue musicale*, perceived the singularity of the Pole's musical personality. Writing of Chopin's debut in Paris on February 26, 1832[1]—the date tells the Chopin-indoctrinated that he had just turned twenty-two—Fétis wrote: "Here is a young man who, giving way to his natural leanings and taking no models, has . . . an abundance of original ideas of which the type is nowhere to be discovered. . . . Beethoven has composed music for the piano, but here I am speaking of music for pianists, and in this realm, I find, in the inspirations of M. Chopin, indications of a change of form that may in the future exercise considerable influence on this branch of art . . ."

Here is a sample of criticism (omitted, naturally, from such a monument to critical confusion as Nicolas Slonimsky's *Lexicon of Musical Invective*, in which Fétis is recalled only for his doubts of Berlioz) as perceptive as it is prophetic. It is no less than audacious in linking the young man newly arrived from Warsaw with the towering memory of Beethoven, then only five years dead and in the flood tide of rising esteem in Paris. Against this background it is all the more remarkable that Fétis not merely sensed Chopin's gifts, but also saw the implications of his innovations *vis-à-vis* Beethoven. This is heartening evidence of two things: the possibility that a critic can, despite all the citations to the contrary, correctly evaluate the importance of an art change as it is happening, and foresee its probable effect on the future of that art. (It also suggests that every critic should be judged in specific rather than general terms: the same Fétis who heard Chopin truly questioned the objectives of Berlioz and misunderstood the purposes of Wagner.[2])

If an issue must be taken with Fétis's statement, it would—with

---

[1] The program included the F-minor Piano Concerto (opus 21) and the Variations on "*Là ci darem la mano*" from Mozart's *Don Giovanni*. Herbert Weinstock: *Chopin, the Man and His Music* (New York: Alfred A. Knopf; 1949), p. 74.

[2] Ernest Newman: *The Life of Richard Wagner* (New York: Alfred A. Knopf; 1937), II, 219.

no derogation of any kind—concern his description of the composer as "a young man who, giving way to his natural leanings and taking no models" produced results of which "the type is nowhere to be discovered." Here Fétis is assigning to Chopin a degree of autogenesis which, in the light of such studies as Abraham's, we know *neither he nor any other great composer* possessed. Obviously, many links in the chain of circumstances were unknown to Fétis.

He could hardly know, for example, that among the virtuosos who included Warsaw on their tours was Hummel, whom Chopin heard in 1828. As Abraham's exposition makes clear, the F-minor Concerto of Chopin's Paris debut program is related to a now forgotten work of Kalkbrenner. Chopin's indebtedness to Field is rather better known. It went, however, beyond Field's invention of the nocturne, which Chopin raised to a higher plane of individuality, to include his style of performance. This contributed no less substantially to Field's place in the continuity of Chopin than his style of composition did.

The interaction of Hummel and Chopin brings to prominence an element of continuity which merits formulation as Axiom IV:
The obvious source is not always the true source.

From our present knowledge of the greatest music being written between 1815 and 1835, it would seem certain that Chopin was thoroughly acquainted with some, at least, of Schubert's music. Not only in the embellishment of melodies and the formulation of harmonies, but also in the typically "Schubertian" kind of arpeggios and broken chords, there are many suggestions of procedures typically Chopinesque. But, as is well known, Schubert's music did not circulate widely outside of Vienna in that period. Furthermore, one of Chopin's earliest and most responsible biographers, Frederick Niecks, is authority for the statement: "Chopin knew too little of his [Schubert's] music to be appreciably influenced by him."[3]

Nevertheless, the impression persists in such typical works of Schubert as the Impromptus (1827) and the Quintet for Piano and Strings based on *"Die Forelle."* Looking into the origins of the latter, one discovers that it was written during a holiday trip to Steyr, at the suggestion of an amateur cellist named Paumgartner. It was Paumgartner's thought—perhaps because he was none too sure of himself—that the cello line should be supported by the doublebass. This was hardly a spontaneous improvisation by Paumgartner: it was, rather, based on a practice of Hummel which can be heard in recordings of

[3] Frederick Niecks: *Frederic Chopin As a Man and Musician* (London and New York: Novello, Ewer and Co.; 1890), I, 213.

his celebrated Septet, opus 74, written in 1815.[4] And, as Hummel's work included a movement of variations, so does Schubert's, perhaps better to please his "patron." The choice of *"Die Forelle"* also related to Paumgartner, it being his favorite among Schubert songs.[5]

That Schubert substantially exceeded the worth of the work he chose for a model[6] was hardly part of Paumgartner's purpose. But the pinpointing, through Paumgartner, of the source of the work's special features leaves little doubt that the "Schubert-in-Chopin" was Hummel in both instances. Hummel's taste in harmony (in his essay on the composer in Cobbett's *Cyclopedic Survey of Chamber Music* [I, 578], Rudolf Felber cites modulations from "F to F sharp," a deviation "to C major through B major and E minor" in the first movement of the Septet, and equally unconventional effects elsewhere) and his fondness for cascades of piano sound rippling down the keyboard plainly appealed to the young Schubert as they did to the even younger Chopin a decade later. Indeed, Schubert's esteem for Hummel was manifest in its highest form in the same year (1828) that Chopin heard him play in Warsaw. It took the form of the dedication to Hummel of his three last piano sonatas (in C minor, A major, and B flat).

Thus Axiom IV (*The obvious source is not always the true source*) has a counterpart, Axiom V:

Two well-known manifestations of a similar impulse may be related not to each other, but to a common source.

It is especially important to be wary of a false conclusion when the source—in this case, the music of Hummel—is all but forgotten, whereas those who derived strength from it are widely admired and frequently performed. Sometimes it may derive from a *portion* of a common source which has had its day and disappeared from prominence even though other works of the same creator may be universally known and performed.

I am mindful here of a strong likeness in Chopin's use of ornaments—grace notes, mordents, trills, etc.—to certain stylistic traits of Bellini familiar to many from *"Casta diva"* in *Norma*. It is well known

---

[4] The annotation of its performance on the Lyrichord label vouches for this date.

[5] Otto Erich Deutsch: *Memoirs of Schubert* (New York: Macmillan; 1958), p. 148 (letter of Albert Stadler, dated 1858).

[6] W. W. Cobbett: *Cyclopedic Survey of Chamber Music* (London: Oxford University Press, Humphrey Milford; 1930). The citation here does not answer convincingly the question of whether Schubert, of his own volition, omitted the wind instruments for which Hummel wrote, or whether he was acquainted with the work in its alternate form as a quintet. Stadler's reference to the "recently published Hummel Quintet (originally a Septet)" is at the least ambiguous (II, 356).

that Chopin and Bellini shared a mutual admiration in Paris which ended with the latter's death in 1835 at the tragically early age of thirty-four.

A contrary view is expressed by the Chopin scholar Arthur Hedley in his essay on the subject in *Grove's*:[7] "One must exclude Bellini from the list of those who have had a particular influence on Chopin: anything 'Italian' in Chopin had been acquired before the Pole made the acquaintance of Bellini's music." In another part of the same essay (p. 253) he states: "Italian opera of the Rossini school was the staple fare of Warsaw when Chopin was growing up there." Concludes Hedley: "That he should have been fond of Bellini's work was natural: it appealed to a taste already formed."

But was it not perhaps the other way around: that the refinements of *Il Pirata* and *La Sonnambula*, operas of Bellini that were current in Paris when Chopin arrived in 1831,[8] corrected that taste and gave it something to feed on which it had not known before? Certainly Amina's "*Ah! vorrei trovar parola*" (Act I of *La Sonnambula*) is a "Chopinesque" formulation before there was any such in print from which it could have been derived.

Whether the Bellini-in-Chopin (like the Hummel-in-Schubert) was really Rossini (and Abraham and Weinstock present *different* evidence for their conclusions that Bellini as well as Chopin was affected by their mutual interchange) is not of profound moment. It is not essential to this inquiry that the continuity in every instance be traced from a specific source which must be given "credit." It is essential for my purpose only that the *existence* of such a connective tissue be confirmed, and that it operate through the width and breadth of the musical organism.

What is perhaps most illuminating in Hedley's reference to "a taste already formed" is the background and influence of that taste on Chopin's work as a whole. All through Chopin's early letters (during his travels in the late 1820's before he broke away from Warsaw) there are repeated references to the operas he attended (in Vienna, Berlin, and elsewhere) as well as to the concerts he attended or in which he participated. In his first letters from Paris, he dwells as much on the singers to be heard—Lablache, Rubini, Malibran, Pasta, Nourrit—as on the instrumentalists. From this predilection, formulated taste or externally induced enthusiasm, there emerged

---

[7] *Grove's Dictionary of Music and Musicians,* 5th edn., II, 261.
[8] *Chopin's Letters,* coll. Henryk Opiénski, ed. and tr. E. L. Voynich (New York: Alfred A. Knopf; 1931), p. 157.

an interest in vocal as well as instrumental practices. It was their synthesis that brought into being a new kind of musical formulation—Chopin's own.

In this respect Chopin stood closest to Mozart, whose sonatas for piano bear many evidences of the same musical thinking as is contained in certain of his operatic expressions (especially in the slow movements of a *romanza* character), and whose ensembles, especially the act-finales, frequently remind one of the interwoven chatter of the piano concertos. In a more than figurative sense, Chopin found in the Italian operatic writing of the time a new voice for the piano, which entered into the alteration of emphasis detected by Fétis when he said that Beethoven wrote music for the piano, Chopin for pianists.

It is almost laughable to encounter, from time to time, a disparagement of Chopin phrased in such words as "he wrote 'only' for the piano." It is, rather, the opposite that is more to the point. He had the single-mindedness of purpose to concentrate almost wholly on the medium he knew best because its stimulation was so strong that he required no other. Within its world of sonorities were enticingly unexplored continents, hidden canyons, and subterranean caverns, climates and atmospheres for whose mapping, charting, and close investigation one lifetime of a mere thirty-nine years was simply not enough.

3

THE EXISTENCE OF A CHOPIN LINE as well as a Beethoven line of continuity implies a difference as well as a distinction, a fundamental divergence of musical impulse among those magnetized to one or the other. With a full awareness of the peril inherent in generalizations, one may be attempted: Beethoven, and those who profited most from his example, worked primarily in terms of themes and their development; Chopin, and the composers who comprise his line, fulfilled themselves through melody and its elaboration.

Out of these distinctions arose differences of immense importance, even in their effect on harmonic character. Thematic development and its contribution to the structure of the sonata form (as Tovey so often demonstrates) utilize modulation, the juxtaposition of keys and the by-products thereof as mortar for its architecture. Melodic elaboration can wander much more freely into chromatic colorations and subtle plays of transitory shadings, along the horizontal dimension of music rather than the vertical.

Basically, the challenge in thematic development is to distill a thought to its essence and to liberate from that essence a dynamic, forceful expression. In melodic elaboration, the art is embodied in the elaboration of the possibilities contained in a melodic entity. The objective in each case is the same: to engage, retain, and satisfy the attention of the listener. The means to that end may be as different as embroidery is from sculpture.

We are talking here in terms of disposition rather than of limitation. As fully formed masters of musical resources, each had access to the strengths of the other: Beethoven knew how to ornament or elaborate when it suited his purpose, as Chopin knew how to develop when need be. But the overriding, characteristic difference between them reposes in the compulsion toward what each did most and did best. Beethoven wrote no less than thirty-two piano sonatas out of endless absorption with the formal possibilities thus presented. Chopin wrote three, and found his interest in those possibilities satisfied.

With Beethoven and those who responded to his example, the totality of an expression is of far greater concern than the individual details that enter into it. With Chopin and those who inherited his disciplines, the infinity of detail in every measure, taken together, makes up the totality of value. Varying Fétis, one might say that Beethoven expressed music through the piano, whereas Chopin expressed the piano through music. This was the nature of the challenge to which each responded, and it remained a challenge as long as life itself.

Well over a century after his death, Chopin's music remains the most pianistic of all. What I have in mind goes well beyond the usual connotations of those words (music which lies well for the hands, does not require them to oppose their natural functional design, fulfills the totality that the Germans call *klaviermässig*). Rather it is, in ways much more far-reaching than occurred to any composer before him, directly derived from contact with the keyboard.

As an example: if one places the thumb of the right hand on middle C, the fifth (little) finger falls comfortably a seventh above, on B flat. Random placement of the fingers in between gives them ready access to D, F sharp, A. Pivoting around G for the middle finger, Chopin artlessly—or artfully, depending on the degree of premeditation one assigns to the outcome—arranges them to form the germ-cell of a melody from which sprouts the strong central trunk of such a unique growth as the G-minor Ballade. It is inconceivable, for example, that this pattern could have occurred to one whose basic orientation to music was through the human voice.

Such procedure is frequent in Chopin and has, of course, been identified and analyzed by many (Abraham cites it relative to the *Études*). But implications and extensions of the first fact can lead to many more remote ones. Among them is the conclusion that the hand could discover what the mind could not imagine. From this could emerge a quite different world of sound than might be "reality" for another—as was the case of Berlioz, soon to be considered. What it led to, as the resources of the piano expanded and one keen mind after another applied itself to the exploitation of them, provided a stimulus by which kindred spirits of the continuity-to-come were encouraged to fulfill themselves.

In this same G-minor Ballade, Chopin precedes his main discourse with an introductory statement setting the stage for the narrative drama to follow. Like a minstrel preluding on his harp, he moves the pattern in a wide upward and downward arc across the keyboard. When a point of rest is attained, it is in terms of a chordal formation that presents D-G-E flat in the left hand, B flat in the right:

Chopin: Ballade No. 1, G minor (op. 23)

To some writers of the nineteenth century and even the early years of this one, the E flat was a vexing intrusion, perhaps even a misprint. In his *Chopin, the Man and His Music*,[9] Huneker devotes several paragraphs to this subject, which, says the author, "has caused some controversy." Of the E flat, he notes that Guttman and Mikuli, among other Chopin pupils, "use it," but, he adds, "Xavier Scharwenka has seen fit to edit Klindworth and gives a D natural in the Augener edition." And he also cites Charles Willeby (an English

[9] James G. Huneker: *Chopin, the Man and His Music* (New York: Charles Scribner's Sons; 1900), p. 278.

biographer of Chopin) as "one who personally prefers the D natural." On the other hand, the authoritative Frederick Niecks heard the E flat as the critical coloration of the composer's thought "the emotional keynote of the whole poem."

In his treatment of the subject (post-Huneker) the author of A *Handbook to Chopin's Works*, C. Ashton Johnson, describes the chord as one "which forms the subject of such dispute among commentators. A comparison of a similar device in the 34th bar, however, leaves no doubt that the effect was intended by the composer."[1]

For the most illuminating comment on this vexing issue—if that is what it is—it is well to seek out the most authoritative voice. Such a one was that belonging to Camille Saint-Saëns, who was fourteen when Chopin died in 1849, but who outlived Debussy. From the intimates of the Polish composer whom he met in his long span of years, he derived the following view of the matter:[2]

> At the beginning of the famous Ballade in G minor, in the last bar of the Introduction, we find in the original edition that a D manifestly had been written down, though it was corrected into an E (flat). This supposed E (flat) gives an expression of pain, quite in harmony with the character of the *morceau*. Was this a printer's error? Was it the original intention of the composer? The note produces a dissonance, with unexpected effect. Now, dissonances were at that time dreaded, though nowadays as welcome as truffles. From Liszt, whom I questioned on the matter, I could obtain nothing except that he preferred the E flat. So do I, but that is not the point. The conclusion at which I have arrived is that Chopin, when playing the Ballade, sounded the D, but I am still convinced that the E flat was his first thought, and that the D was adopted on the advice of timid and maladroit friends.

For the reader whose ear is attuned not only to Chopin's thinking but also to its extension through the many who responded to what he set in motion, the significance of this bygone "controversy" may seem wholly academic. It stands, however, at a crossroad of thought which is sufficiently well traveled since then to merit at least this much consideration.

Clearly there is nothing in the least arbitrary about Chopin's procedure, whether or not he yielded to the sensitivities of his well-meaning "friends" when he played the ballade in their presence.

[1] C. Ashton Johnson: A *Handbook to Chopin's Works* (New York: Charles Scribner's Sons; 1910), p. 146.
[2] Camille Saint-Saëns: *Outspoken Essays on Music* (London: Kegan Paul, Trench, Trubner and Co.; 1922), p. 155.

It is, clearly and unmistakably, a way of blending into a single piquant sonority the tonic chords of the two keys that come and go in the work: G minor and E flat. Ever fastidious of good musical manners, even in such an "adventurous" moment, Chopin does not let the E flat hang in the ear, unresolved, before launching into the ballade. He salves the ear irritated by this "stinging dissonance" by sounding the desired D—two octaves away in the bass to be sure, but there nevertheless.

It is not too far-fetched to hear in this modest example of polytonality a foreshadowing of the clustered chords, the vaguely indeterminate harmonic colorations of Debussy and others who received, and then advanced, the line of Chopin's continuity. It is typical of the kind of effect that would occur to one who was keyboard-oriented. It came to have the kind of meaning ascribed to it here only when submitted to the rigorous discipline of Chopin's discriminating ear, found good, and made part of an artistic whole.

Discussing the antecedents of Debussy's way of writing, Nadia Boulanger has said:

The origins of Debussy's harmonic style are to be sought . . . in Liszt, Chabrier and Fauré, rather than in Moussorgsky . . . In 1915 Debussy published his two volumes of 'Études' for the piano and dedicated them 'to the memory of Frederic Chopin.' The inscription is significant, for it represents a conscious homage to the composer whose influence was a chief and guiding force in the formation of Debussy's piano style . . . We shall have to re-discover Chopin, re-appreciate his amazingly original harmonies, the individuality of his piano style, with its wide, delicately sonorous spacing of chords and realize anew the astonishing prophetic qualities of measures like these:

"In these final measures of the F-major 'Prelude,' " Boulanger con-

Chopin: Prelude No. 23, F (op. 28)

tinues, "Chopin has dared to add the seventh harmonic to the triad and to treat it as a consonance, as a point of final repose. In that single E flat [curiously persistent, that vibrant tone!] is implicit all the delicate and sensuous delight in sonorities so characteristic of modern music."[3]

4

As THE VARIETY OF OPINIONS hitherto cited, from Niecks to Johnson, Klindworth to Saint-Saëns, and now Boulanger, may suggest, there is continuity not only in consonance but also in dissonance. Indeed, it is an unquestionably profound factor in the continuity we are considering that the line between the two is by no means impassable, that, in a generation, the ear can be taught to tolerate what was intolerable previously. Much would relate, of course, to the purpose of what rates as a "dissonance" before it becomes accepted as something else, what transformations in the tonal language must occur before, in the expressive image of Saint-Saëns in 1922, it becomes "as welcome as truffles" (and, in the same sense, an acquired taste).

Such a clash of sound, for Mozart, was restricted to a purpose of momentary musical mystification (as in the introduction to the C-major Quartet, K. 465, which caused it to be known as the "Dissonant" Quartet), or reserved for the expression of some grave emotional disturbance (as in the G-minor Viola Quintet, K. 516), or invoked as the acid of humor to produce the slightly soured cream of the jesting parody known as *Ein musikalischer Spass* (K. 522). It was, in short, an asset borrowed from outside the normal range of his vocabulary to make a particular point in a special way, rather than its common coin.

With Beethoven the usage of dissonance in a prominent way is sufficiently rare to be individually known and chronicled: the false entry of the French horn in the first movement of the *"Eroica,"* where it clouds the onset of the recapitulation with the suggestion of a wrong entrance; the persistently out-of-key bassoon in the village band of the *"Pastorale,"* for a humorous allusion; the wild clamor in the introduction to the finale of the Ninth, where a "brutal" clash of chords is invoked to attract maximum attention to what follows. As with Mozart, the norm is presumed inviolable, the frame in which the deviation is exploited.

With Chopin, however, the intermingling of E flat and G minor is not only, as Niecks viewed it, "the emotional keynote of the whole

[3] In the published form of her *Lectures on Modern Music,* p. 167.

poem," but also a play of sonority for the sake of sonority itself. A concept then quite new in music and one rarely sponsored before in quite the same way (Bach, who did almost everything in his enormously productive life, did something comparable in the choral prelude *Schafe können sicher weiden*), it may well rank among Chopin's most provocative keyboard innovations. Largely speaking, however, it remained for him—as Boulanger's remark suggests—an atypical procedure, for others (such as Liszt, Fauré, and Chabrier) to appreciate, exploit, and make part of their functioning before being converted into a wholly new idiom by Debussy and Ravel.

In pursuing the destiny, outlined by Fétis, of writing music not for the piano but for pianists, Chopin wove ever more engaging patterns from the threads of material that formed under his hand. Some of his brightest blends of color emerge from the traceries of inner voices that modify (in the grammatical sense) and inflect so much of Chopin's harmonic thinking. What was a somewhat static device for Beethoven (as in the allegretto of the Seventh Symphony) became a wholly dynamic one with Chopin. This was a pattern of shifting harmony under a stationary tone which imparted to that top line a melodic character that it would otherwise have lacked. In the F-minor Ballade, it becomes a motivating factor in the development of the tonal texture. Here the inner fingers—sometimes all ten fingers—at extremes of the keyboard are engaged in seeking (and finding!) shades of color, tints of sound otherwise unimaginable. It might be likened to the discovery of inner rhythms, or a new pattern of *onomatopoeia* which adds a resource to the language (as Poe did).

It is conceivable that some of Chopin's predecessors, such masters of improvisation as Beethoven, Wölffl, and Hummel,[4] made contact with comparable discoveries. But reducing them to the permanence of a written record was something else. This was a respect in which the particular nature of Chopin's gifts came into its sharpest focus. If he lacked the inclination of a Beethoven to concentrate, to file, to hammer and shape an idea until it became a diamond-hard core, he had in superabundance the patience required to set down precisely and in the most elaborate detail every quaver and minim, every accent, nuance, and agogic indication required to transmute his imagery from its audible form as a shower of sound in a prelude or the rainbow arc of an arpeggio in a waltz into a permanent, written equivalent. In this he far exceeded even his adored Mozart, who, in more than one famous work, left in-

---

[4] Alexander W. Thayer: *Life of Ludwig van Beethoven*, ed. and rev. Henry E. Krehbiel (New York: Beethoven Association; 1921), I, 216–17.

complete passages requiring embellishment. Scholars have exhausted themselves—and us—in assembling the data to repair such omissions and make contemporary performers more informed representatives of Mozart's meaning than many others before them. But, in a manner that paralleled his own fastidious taste in tailors and clothes, Chopin's manuscripts are models of neatness. They may vary in detail from one version to a later one, but each will be as explicit as the other of his purpose as he conceived it.

How such care affected his place in music's continuity may be readily understood from an observation by Berlioz,[5] who was frequently in Chopin's company when they were fellow-rebels in the 1830's. Writing in the *Rénovateur* of December 15, 1833, of the sensation newly arrived from Poland, Berlioz commented:

> Chopin as an executant and composer is an artist apart: he has no point of resemblance with any other musician of my acquaintance. His melodies, impregnated with Polish forms, have something naïvely wild which charms and captivates even by its strangeness; in his Études one finds harmonic combinations of astounding profundity; he has imagined a sort of chromatic embroidery, reproduced in several of his compositions, whose effect is indescribable: it is so piquant and bizarre. Unfortunately, it is almost only Chopin himself who can play his music and give it this original turn, this unexpectedness which is one of its principal charms; his playing is marbled [*marbrée*] with a thousand nuances of which he alone has the secret and which could not be indicated.

As of 1833, when relatively little of Chopin's characteristic work was in print, and that little not widely circulated, Berlioz's observation was valid enough. But it is a commentary on the diligence and care with which Chopin addressed himself to the problem that it was substantially solved before it became the impossible hazard Berlioz evoked. Perhaps no one but this "Trilby of the Piano" (as Berlioz called him) ever played Chopin as Chopin did; but he not only passed on, through his pupils, his practice, but also, through his written scripts, his preachment.

Had the order of impulse been otherwise, there might have been as much disagreement, even mystery, about his true intentions as there is about the vocal writing of such contemporaries as Rossini, Donizetti, and Bellini. Fortunately for Chopin—and for us—the creator and the re-creator were embodied in the same person. Because he was the personification of the *fioriture* that he invented, Chopin could imagine all

---

[5] W. J. Turner: *Berlioz, The Man and His Work* (London: J. M. Dent and Sons; 1934), p. 183.

the variants he chose to have associated with them and convert them into permanent symbols. The only thing he could not write out and formalize was that eternal intangible, *rubato*. It stands as the final mystery, the one imponderable, whose successful solution separates from all others the elect, the elite, of Chopin players.

This passion for precision, this devotion to the creation of a completely documented, wholly explicit text perpetuated Chopin's influence long beyond his own life span, or the life spans of such others as Liszt, who lived for decades longer. His example became their credo, to be learned, lived by, and if possible, improved upon. Sometimes it led to the dead end of virtuosity, which is to say that absorption with procedure took precedence over concern for substance. But there remained, finally, the written thing itself, to be judged, evaluated, accepted, or rejected, the typical processes by which continuity is maintained or perishes. With Liszt's *Les Jeux d'eaux à la Villa d'Este* of 1877 as a link, Ravel's *Jeux d'eau* of 1901 could be said to be part of the musical stream propelled by Chopin.

5

BECAUSE THERE IS SOME TENDENCY to mark Chopin down for not being able to manage certain things well—the disciplines of sonata form, the resources of instruments other than the piano, or the combination of them in the orchestra—it might be well to enumerate the range, extent, and variety of the things he did superbly. With the exception of the nocturne, whose impulse he derived from Field and immeasurably expanded, they were not merely in categories not previously considered consequential, but in many instances self-invented: ballades, preludes, waltzes, mazurkas, polonaises, scherzos, impromptus, études, tarantellas, and so on to the berceuse, barcarolle, and bolero. Within each category, the examples range from one to more than fifty. Characteristically, even where the discipline is the least flexible and the number of examples the greatest, in the mazurkas, it is mere statement of fact to say that no two are exactly alike.

The sum of it is that such loose formulations suited Chopin's inclinations ideally. That was not because each was less a formulation, with problems of proportion and balance, than a rondo or a sonata allegro, but because, being "loose," each could be shaped, draped, or manipulated to accord with the necessities of the musical ideas that moved him. Freedom with discipline is basic in any musical expression worth the name, and all composers of consequence have had to find their own solutions to the problems of integration thus posed. More than a few (beginning with Schumann and Liszt) found the examples of Chopin not merely stimulating but also instructive; some (such as Scriabin) were almost completely possessed by them. The list is long, the names are all familiar and not in the smallest need of repetition here, save perhaps as a measuring rod of the deep well of music Chopin contained within himself and which others drew upon. In a sentence, the summation could be that the continuity from Chopin is, with a few notable exceptions, the continuity of piano music up to and including Poulenc (not excluding Gershwin or Prokofiev).

Generically, Chopin was a short-story writer among composers, a description that may, like its literary parallel, accommodate everything from the short-short (prelude) to the novelette (*Fantaisie-Impromptu*). Always and ultimately, however, the emphasis was on *story* covering an expanse, long or less long, as circumstances decreed. Undoubtedly Mendelssohn contributed to the formulation of the *morceau* or character piece (acting on Schubert's lead in the *Impromptus* and *Moments musicaux*) in his Songs Without Words, as Schumann did to the family portraiture to come of Bizet (*Jeux d'enfants*), Mussorgsky (*Nursery Cycle*), and Debussy (*Children's Corner*) in his intimate *Kinderscenen, Fantasiestücke, Album für die Jugend*, and *Kinderball*.

But Chopin remains the generator *sui generis* of the narrative for the keyboard, of incidents without name, case histories in tone which are designated, like the contents of a filing cabinet, opus 10, No. 3, or opus 28, No. 7. Debussy added name value to similar impulses with such titles as *Jardins sous la pluie* ("Raindrop" Prelude) or *Le Vent dans la plaine* ("Winter Wind" Étude).

Schumann paid his own tribute to the continuity of music (without, of course, using the phrase) when he wrote: "In the course of time the distance between sources diminishes. Beethoven, for instance, did not need to study all that Mozart had studied—Mozart, not all that Handel, Handel, not all that Palestrina—because these had already absorbed the knowledge of their predecessors . . ."[6] In a similar way, Chopin's distillation of Hummel and Field drew their essence into the stream of music, even though neither embodied a single, distinctive flavor strong enough to survive unaided.

In a retrospect of what music had been before and what it became after him, the evidence seems clear to me that Chopin possessed the singular distinction of surviving as a *totality*, though so many of his

[6] Robert Schumann: *On Music and Musicians*, ed. Konrad Wolff (New York: Pantheon; 1946), p. 93.

individual attributes were absorbed by others. One reason for this, without question, was his capacity for lavishing as much artistry and effort on a prelude as on a polonaise. Each creation was a cosmos in itself, to be realized with all the resources at his command. As with such a poet as Keats or Shelley, his determination to "load every rift with ore" transformed the enrapturing into the enthralling, drawing us back again and again to the most familiar of his works with an ever new sense of discovery and delight.

It is in this respect beyond all others that Chopin made a formidable appeal to the French temperament and its musical predilection. The French were, almost without exception, predisposed to the "loose design," exponents of meticulous workmanship, devotees of the enamoring detail, jewelers and lapidarians rather than hewers, hammerwielders, or stonecutters. In seeing themselves in the mirror held up by Chopin, such composers as Saint-Saëns, Fauré, Chabrier, and Chausson not only prepared a way for Debussy and Ravel, as well as Satie, but also rediscovered a line of succession from the then (1850) all-but-forgotten Rameau and Couperin.

Paraphrasing Hedley's observation that acquaintance with Bellini's music appealed to "a taste already formed," it might be said that in aiding the French to recover a part of their own heritage, Chopin was appealing to a predispositon of his own. For it should not be forgotten that Chopin was French-descended on his father's side, that his adaptability to Parisian ways, Parisian modes of thought, Parisian values of art and life was not without blooded affinity.

6

TAKEN TOGETHER, these things would certainly be sufficient to certify Chopin for high rank among those who have been—in the earlier image —both receivers and transmitters in the wire-less world of musical continuity. But potent as they are, they do not fully measure the strength of the signal he broadcast. His work embodied another characteristic of the most embracing sort, by which the artists who had the wisdom as well as the opportunity to profit by his examples were immeasurably enriched.

Guy de Pourtalès gave one phraseology to it in a paraphrase of Paderewski in which he refers to Chopin as "the ingenious smuggler who would allow the prohibited Polonism to escape across the frontier in his portfolios of music."[7] But, in addition to the political aspect of national "Polonism," there was another, ethnic kind, which Berlioz

[7] Guy de Pourtalès: *Polonaise* (New York: Henry Holt; 1927), p. 67.

(in a continuation of the remark quoted previously, page 53) described as early as 1833 as "his melodies, impregnated with Polish forms, have something . . . wild which charms and captivates even by its strangeness."

Clearly Chopin bore with him into exile treasure of a special sort. This was not merely the folk spirit of Poland in the abstract, but its airs and melodies, rhythms and dances, the whole sonorous stock from the wistful to the heroic which makes up the audible heritage of that incomparably endowed, perpetually partitioned land.

There had, of course, been folk influences on the cultivated music of Central Europe from the time that the *Wanderlied* entitled *"Innsbruck, ich muss dich lassen"* was converted into the hymn *"O Welt, ich muss dich lassen"* in the sixteenth century.[8] Haydn's Croatian ancestry

"Shenandoah" (arr. Cecil Dougherty)

has been identified with certain trends of thought in his symphonies and quartets, and there is abundant evidence that Mozart and Schubert were drawing on deeply subterranean folk springs in some of their finest works (*Die Zauberflöte*—in the first instance, certainly—many songs,[9] piano pieces, and chamber music movements). By the time of

[8] *Grove's*, IV, 546. Americans who are acquainted with the shanty "Shenandoah" (example above) will find a surprising carry-over in it of these ancestors.

[9] *"Der Lindenbaum"* has been promoted to "folk" status in some collections I have seen, in that category of *Volkslieder* made up of works universally popular, whether by a known composer or not. It is the kind of borrowing best exemplified by the universal acceptance of *"Die Lorelei"* as a folk song, though it is unquestionably the creation of Friedrich Silcher to words of Heinrich Heine.

Schumann, the *volkstümliches Lied,* or song made up in the manner of a folk song, was a recognized genre of writing.

The distinction between their response to folk sources and Chopin's would be this: The earlier composers used folk tunes either for a special kind of color (as Haydn did in his G-major "Gypsy" Trio) or for atmospheric purposes (as Beethoven did in his opus 59 quartets, to honor his Russian patron, Count Rasumovsky, who had commissioned them); Chopin evolved a whole style—melodic, harmonic, and rhythmic—from the folk idioms he had grown up with in youth. It might be likened to the difference between a scroll or other exterior decoration that is added to a basic design and an inlay that becomes an inherent part of a design.

Whether Chopin would have followed the same pattern had he remained in Poland is a diverting speculation, worth a moment's consideration. Perhaps it would have all seemed too provincial, a fetter from which he would have been forced to free himself. But in the plan of life which found him an émigré, if not an exile, it provided a nostalgic link to what he had left behind, as well as sounding an exotic note (even for such a sophisticate as Berlioz) in his new milieu.

In association with the taste, the meticulous workmanship, and the fastidious elaboration of which mention has been made, this affection for the folk idiom of his native land infused the art music of the time with a wholly new impulse. Competent authorities rate the occurrence of actual folk tunes in Chopin as relative rarities,[1] but the component elements are rarely absent.

Of several categories that present themselves for investigation and observation—including the waltzes, polonaises, ballades, études—the mazurkas provide the most profitable study of Chopin's transformation of the raw materials of a folk expression into an art form. They are not only the kind of work Chopin wrote more often than any other—fifty-eight times in all—but are also the simplest in formulation, the least encrusted with decoration or embellishment. For the most part, a melodic line in a lean succession of single notes and a rhythmically regular bass (with, perhaps, alto and tenor in the "thumb" position of the two hands) are the elements of these musical etchings whose very spareness makes subtleties all the more audible.

These subtleties derive, above all, from the manipulation of two components: the oddly inflected scale with the sharpened fourth (in the key of D minor it would be G sharp rather than G natural) and

---

[1] In a discussion of Chopin in *Saturday Review* of February 27, 1960, Arthur Rubinstein alluded to the trio of the B-minor Scherzo, based on the Polish Christmas song *"Lulajze Jezuniu,"* as the "only" actual folk song known to him in the piano works.

the empty-fifth, drone bass, derived from the characteristic wheezing sound of the *koza* or *koziol,* a kind of pipes often used in Poland to accompany the mazurka. This is music of the soil brought into the salon, with the rude vigor of the farmhouse and the tavern adapted, but not adulterated, to serve the more cultivated tastes of the gentlemen and ladies of the ballroom.

Czeslaw R. Halski observes in his comment on the mazurkas:[2] "He used the national material as a basis, eliminating all vulgarities and extending its original forms, and developing them into fuller beauty, containing almost unidentifiable folk tunes, by the force and striking individuality of his genius." Thus transformed, they present in microcosm the compelling blend of the naïve and the sophisticated in Chopin, the earthy and the elegant, the rural as well as the urban, which cast a spell not merely romantic but also necromantic.

As early as opus 6, No. 3 (the third in the published sequence of mazurkas), Chopin has transformed the drone from a mere bass support to a middle-voice coloration. In opus 7, No. 1, it becomes a delicately drawn "trio," magically reached as if by shifting a lever on the keyboard. (Hugo Alfvén remembered its measures 4, 5, and 6 when he came to write his popular *"Midsommarvaka"*—"Midsummer Vigil"—years later [example, p. 60]. Opus 7, No. 3, has Griegish overtones—to

Chopin: Mazurka No. 5, B flat (op. 7, No. 1)

backdate the character of a composer who was six when Chopin died— in its sliding harmonies, and undertones, too, in its slyly inflected bass figures.

In the next series, opus 17, we encounter the mazurka-as-nocturne, with Wagnerian embellishments (in opus 17, No. 4, measures 15 and 18, and again measures 31 and 34) of the *"Liebestod"* to come. By opus 24, No. 1, Chopin is convinced that the listener's ear can do without the intermediate chord in a modulatory series. He performs what came to be classified, eventually, as an elision (more properly, a transition by evasion) when Liszt, Wagner, and Strauss made it a staple of their musical manner. Opus 24, No. 4, for many their most favorite mazurka,

[2] *Grove's,* V, 643.

Alfvén: Midsommarvaka (*op. 19*)

is a particular example of the kind of "handy" pattern noted in the discussion of the G-minor Ballade. It begins with the octave stretch F to F in the right hand, closing the interval half a step at a time down to a fourth before the dance tune begins. When it does, it has the shape of a mazurka-as-rondo.

Opus 30, No. 2, charms the ear with eight repetitions of a two-measure figure, always different (actually four changes, done twice). The device pleased Chopin so much that he wrote another entire mazurka in the same manner (Fokine made this opus 67, No. 4, into one of the most appealing moments of *Les Sylphides*). Opus 30, No. 4, suggests the kind of "chain" dance pattern pioneered by Weber in his *Invitation to the Dance*. Indeed, whereas its predecessor (opus 30, No. 3) is a mere forty-odd measures in length, the mingling here of stroke and counterstroke approaches two hundred and fifty. And so it goes to opus 56, No. 3, in which, pursuing the implications of the harmonic thought to the uttermost, Chopin arrives (measures 135–7) as close to the shores of Tristan's Cornwall as any composer prior to Wagner.

Chopin: Mazurka No. 35, C minor (op. 56, No. 3)

In some structural elements—basic rhythm, meter, pace—this is phylo-genetically a mazurka, but it has clearly evolved into the higher musical type of free-flowing fantasy, unbounded by spatial perimeter or prior practice, restrictive key relationship or preconceived concept of design.

Whether it was "nationalism" per se that found its outlet in Chopin's music, or the kind of music he succeeded in evolving which freed his own and others' nationalistic impulses, it is clear that his precepts of the 1830's became the practice of others in the 1840's, 1850's, and later decades (in a rippling pattern from the original point of impact, like the afteraction of a stone dropped into a pond). What Chopin demonstrated could be done with the materials of the mazurka and the polonaise, others were impelled to accomplish with the czardas, the polka, the furiante, the tarantella, the jota, the myriad variants of dance rhythms in other lands. Liszt made one contribution to con-tinuity with his rhapsodies, as Glinka did with material he found in Spain. The path soon became a highroad traveled by Smetana, Dvořák, Grieg, Granados, and others.[3]

For that matter, in later times the inheritors of Chopin not only followed his philosophic path, but also, in forsaking their native land, as he had done, followed his physical example to become Francophiles themselves. Albéniz, Granados, Falla, Villa-Lobos, Enesco, to some ex-tent Stravinsky, all were formed, in part, by time spent in Paris when they were growing up. Whether in the Conservatoire or in the École Boulanger (whose influence in shaping the first generation of composers to be properly described as American can be traced to the initial ex-perience of Aaron Copland), they continued a sense of being, experi-enced an atmosphere, and shared a mode of life which, however changed

[3] In writing of Granados after his death by drowning when the *Sussex*, in which he was returning to Europe from America, was torpedoed, Ernest Newman noted: "The most original mind must, of course, have a progenitor. Granados de-rives ultimately from Chopin—that source as fecund for certain forms of life in modern music as the classical stream itself." Ernest Newman: *Testament of Music* (New York: Alfred A. Knopf; 1963), p. 193.

in a century, are still closer to the influences that shaped Chopin than those to be found anywhere else.

As for the continuity that extended elsewhere, one explicit statement emanating from another end of musical Europe than Boulanger's merits consideration. Directing attention to still another mazurka (opus 63, No. 3) as influential in the formation of certain ideas embodied in

Chopin: Mazurka No. 41, C sharp minor (op. 63, No. 3)

his *Snegurochka* and *Mlada*, Rimsky-Korsakov told his admirer and Boswellian disciple (August, 1894) V. V. Yastrebtsev: "In Chopin you will find many of the real roots of contemporary music."[4]

As one whose pupils included Igor Stravinsky, Rimsky is worth heeding, whether or not he could have foreseen that the E flat-G minor ambiguity of the first ballade would lead to the bitonality of *Petrouchka*.

[4] Gerald Abraham: *Chopin's Musical Style* (London: Oxford University Press; 1960), p. 99.

III

Wagner-Liszt and Liszt-Wagner

I

NOBODY KNEW THE MUSIC of Chopin better than Franz Liszt, and nobody knew Franz Liszt and his music better than Richard Wagner. Thus if Rimsky's remark—a typically musical kind of "anticipation" before Boulanger's verification of the fact—was meant to embrace within the then (1894) meaning of "contemporary" the works of Wagner, who had died eleven years before, it could be said that the step from Chopin to Wagner was as direct as Liszt alone could make it.

Whether Wagner derived it directly or by way of its effect on Liszt, he was certainly not insensitive to the stimulus in Chopin. He was as responsive to it as he was to his feeling for Mozart, Beethoven, Weber, Schubert, Schumann, Mendelssohn, Marschner, Meyerbeer, Berlioz, Spontini, Nicolai, Bellini, and sundry others who became part of his continuity. That is the equivalent of saying that they became, through him, an even more integral part of the larger continuity than they might have been otherwise.

Those who have, for one reason or another, deemed it a deprecation of Wagner to cite this or that instance of such linkage have failed only to reckon with one thing: Wagner was the great synthesizer of his time, one who absorbed into his being all that he heard and experienced from youth to old age. Or, as Newman phrases it: "Nothing

—that had once found its way into Wagner's mind was ever lost."[1]

Those who today play the game of disparagement usually stop short of *Tristan* or *Parsifal,* for the simple reason that they would find little in them rewarding to their purpose. Many things went into the formation of the idiom from which they were evolved, but once it was formed, what Wagner achieved was unlike anything anybody had ever achieved before. As for *Die Meistersinger,* even avowed anti-Wagnerites find themselves helpless to resist its spell. It is as though it had been written by some other composer who happened to have the same name.

Wagner's particular kind of development had other, complementary reasons. To a larger extent than perhaps any other composer of comparable stature (the "perhaps" is by way of recognizing Berlioz and Schumann as the exceptions), Wagner was a musical enthusiast and music lover before he was anything else. Unlike almost all of his great predecessors who were destined, by prodigious talent demonstrated at an early age, to become persons of musical consequence, Wagner was not, in any common understanding of the term, a prodigy. At an age when Mozart had written many representative works (all the violin concertos, for example), when Beethoven's rich gifts impelled his patrons in Bonn to finance his studies with Haydn, when Schubert had composed *"Der Erlkönig"* and Mendelssohn had immortalized his name with the *Midsummer Night's Dream* overture, when Chopin was on the verge of his Parisian debut and Liszt was the first pianist of Europe, Wagner was still trying to express something of the admiration he felt for those whose music he loved best. At nineteen and twenty he was writing piano works which, when they were not Beethoven-like, were Weberish. Their fascination lies not in how much they suggest the later Wagner, but how little.[2]

One might go a step further and say that what distinguishes these works—a pair of sonatas, fantasies, etc.—is not the evidence of talent they display, but the degree of perseverance they embody despite their evident lack of outstanding talent. Lacking such perseverance, another youth of the time might have concluded that composing was not for him, and found another outlet for his enthusiasm. Possessing it, as well as being possessed by it, Wagner strove on to achieve results utterly incompatible with his beginnings as we know them.

[1] Ernest Newman: *The Life of Richard Wagner* (New York: Alfred A. Knopf; 1937), II, 124.
[2] They may be heard in admirable performances by Bruce Hungerford on a pair of disks devoted to Wagner's piano music which are available on order from the Festspielhaus, Bayreuth.

A particular reason for this disparity is that these "beginnings as we know them" are only distantly related to the end product of the whole intellectual-emotional ferment. In the same way that Chopin's mind was dominated by everything to do with the keyboard and Beethoven's impulses were challenged by thematic development in all its diversity, so Wagner's true creative drive related to what he could see on a stage or imagine being performed by singers and an orchestra. Paul Bekker states the analogy directly: "In Wagner's development as a composer the stage and its phenomena hold the place occupied by the clavier and the laws of musical form in that of Mendelssohn or Chopin . . ."[3] In the end, of course, it is the music that redeems many of his stage situations for us. There is little doubt, however, that it was an atmosphere, a conflict, that could only be depicted theatrically which became the leaven of his ferment.

Recollections of this predisposition flowed back to Wagner's mind in maturity when he came to dictate *Mein Leben* (*My Life*) in his 1869–75 period of residence at Triebschen. "Everything connected with a theatrical performance had for me the charm of mystery, it both bewitched and fascinated me."[4] This comment was related to the endeavor of the then barely teen-aged Wagner to organize a performance of Weber's *Der Freischütz,* a work for which his affection was deep and enduring. As well as playing at theater, he was already working at it by writing four- and five-act tragedies. In one, several characters had to be brought back as ghosts because most of the *dramatis personae* had been killed off.[5]

This literary product had been meant for musical setting, although Wagner's compositional skills were then even more rudimentary than his dramatic. Already evident, at fifteen, was a tree-and-vine relationship that bore the fruit of his greatest works. Eventually it was the tree— music—which supported the vine—text. This was altogether fortunate. Had Wagner been a better poet, he might have been a lesser musician. What he created verbally was strong enough to provide a structure for musical elaboration without the intrusion of a collaborator whose ego might have opposed his own. Sometimes the musician was overindulgent of the poet—listening to Wagner reading the text of *Tristan,* say, without hearing the music must have been one of the most pulverizing ex-

---

[3] Paul Bekker: *Richard Wagner, His Life in His Works* (New York: W. W. Norton and Co., Inc.; 1931), p. 4.
[4] Richard Wagner: *My Life* (New York: Tudor Publishing Company; 1936), p. 14.
[5] Ibid., p. 29.

periences to which a friend could be subjected—but, when he chose to allow his musical fancy to flow, in Siegfried's Rhine Journey or the Good Friday Spell in *Parsifal,* he had no one to argue with save himself. Clearly, Wagner relished his *poetizing,* and all the evidence suggests that the ultimate musical values were gestating in his mind even while it was activating words.

Providentially, then, the economic need that impelled Wagner to an apprenticeship in the musical theater was clearly as meaningful a part of his development as Beethoven's attraction to Vienna or Chopin's gravitation to Paris. It permitted him to soak up the literature of the German musical theater of the time while learning the craft of conductor, which was of enormous use to him later. In such works as *Der fliegende Holländer, Tannhäuser,* and *Lohengrin,* the accepted *Jugendwerke* of fiery strength and idealistic love, Wagner is pursuing a continuity of impulses and inclinations, trends and practices from Beethoven (*Fidelio*) and Weber (*Der Freischütz* and *Euryanthe*), to cite sources relatively well known today. Mingled with them were such other, forgotten matter of the time as Heinrich Marschner's *Der Templar und die Jüdin,* with its ballade similar to Senta's and its prayer akin to Elisabeth's. It was also as an apprentice conductor that he was exposed to Bellini's *Norma* and *I Capuleti ed i Montecchi.* As collector of impressions rather than conductor, he went, heard, and remembered as much of Spontini and Meyerbeer as suited his purposes.

The first strong influence of another sort came during his first visit to Paris between 1839 and 1841. It was a time of prominence for Berlioz, during which performances of his *Symphonie fantastique, Roméo et Juliette, Harold en Italie,* and *Grande Symphonie funèbre et triomphale* were being given under his own direction. Wagner heard them all and reacted with the interest to be expected of a young man from the provinces. From the later pinnacle of Meistership in the 1870's—when Berlioz's life had come to its unhappy end—Wagner could be both honest and generous: "It is a fact that at that time I felt like a little schoolboy by the side of Berlioz."[6]

The importance to Wagner of his discovery of the Berlioz orchestra, even more of Berlioz the orchestrator, can hardly be overstated. What was crude if powerful in the half-formed *Rienzi* (1838–40) overture became, in the bristling curtain-raiser for *The Flying Dutchman,* the expository introduction to *Tannhäuser,* and the atmospheric prelude to *Lohengrin,* stirring summations of the drama in their subjects. Unintentionally, but far from unimportantly, they served to stimulate interest

[6] Ibid., p. 235.

in Wagner's output when the operas themselves could not be prepared or were not being performed.

Something of equal influence befell Wagner in Paris: the first sound of the Beethoven Ninth Symphony in a properly prepared performance (directed by Habeneck). Years later he recalled: "I owed the recovery of my old vigor and spirits to the deep impression the rendering of the Ninth Symphony had made on me when performed in a way I had never dreamed of . . . In this mood I sketched an overture to *Faust* which, according to my original scheme, was only to form the first part of a whole *Faust* symphony . . . This is the same composition that I rewrote in several parts fifteen years later: I had forgotten all about it, and I owed its reconstruction to the advice of Liszt . . ."[7]

If one regards the tremendously compelling if incompletely realized *Faust Overture* as a true portent of things to come eventually, the ones that came immediately, if better realized, were not so compelling. They took Wagner through the working-out of the problems of self-recognition which confront every consequential artist, but, in a manner of speaking, showed only one side of his profile. The recurrence to his attention of the *Faust Overture* came through the intercession of Liszt. It provides a direct, indispensable link to the circumstances in which Wagner ceased to be primarily a product of the past, living on the assets of his predecessors, and began to fulfill his destiny as a conceptual force in the music that would be written for decades to come.

2

IN THE CONSTANTLY ABSORBING PANORAMA of Wagner's mature life, relatively little attention is paid to the years between 1849 and 1858, which he spent in Zürich. His participation in the Dresden phase of the revolutionary uprising of 1849 had made him a fugitive from Saxony. Because of reciprocal arrangements among the German states, he was unable to live or work in any of them. He took refuge in Zürich, where he could correspond with friends in Germany and have freedom of travel to France, Italy, and England. Venice, which was still under Austrian domination, presented a special case, for which permission was required.

The Zürich period terminated in the dramatic entanglement with the Wesendoncks, a readily recognizable symbol of his absorption by then (1858) with *Tristan*. But for half of the preceding time (1849–53) Wagner wrote no music at all in Zürich, a self-sufficient reason for

[7] Ibid., p. 215.

most persons concerned with outcomes rather than causes to pass it by as fallow and nonproductive, hence of slight interest.

Fallow, perhaps—but by no means unproductive and, on close view, teeming with interest. In the passing weeks and months it might have seemed a time of inaction, of diffusion of effort, of marking time and awaiting developments, with days spent on prose-writing unaffiliated with texts for music, let alone music itself. It was, in fact, a time of ingestion and digestion, of nourishment to the mind and spirit by exposure to elements of the past and the present which were to influence, profoundly, what Wagner was soon pleased to call "the art work of the future."

It was less a time awaiting developments than a time of creating the conditions in which developments would be brought about. There was tedium in it and a good deal of frustration, but gain far outweighed loss. Dominating the whole period was the gradual strengthening and tightening of the ties to Liszt. The gap between them had been wide when they had met in Paris a decade before, during Wagner's miserable years of starvation and neglect. Since then Liszt had become even more a dominant figure in Europe's musical life from Weimar, where he had settled as animator of its artistic activities. But the surge of Wagner's creative effort gradually narrowed the gap between them, first through Liszt's production of *Tannhäuser*, in 1849, and then with the initial performance anywhere of *Lohengrin*, under his direction, on August 1, 1850.

Important as its success was to the future of Wagner, in sustaining belief in his estimate of its qualities, the impact of this "sublime work"[8] on Liszt was even more important. It stimulated him to a resumption of interest in composition, which had become dormant, to pursue plans he had projected during several previous years, and to generate other, even more ambitious ones. In all of these Wagner had a part as adviser, consultant, or participant. Out of their absorption in common tasks and shared interests there arose, during the next decade, an artistic interchange between Liszt and Wagner which could be likened to that of Goethe and Schiller, or of Rimsky-Korsakov and Mussorgsky when they were living together.

In some basic respects it could be said that the two men were living one musical life simultaneously. In these years, when Wagner "wrote no music," the "Liszt part" was racing ahead to the accomplishment of such major works as *Tasso, Orpheus, Mazeppa,* and *Les Pré-*

---

[8] Liszt-Wagner Correspondence, I, 78 (dated September 2, 1850).

ludes, the B-minor Sonata for piano, and the *Faust Symphony*. It was, in short, the time in which the talent of Liszt as composer of something more than rhapsodies and travelogues began to take form.

Concurrently, Wagner devoted more than a casual amount of his time (while pursuing lines of thought that would eventually bring the scenario of the *Ring* into being) to the musical life of Zürich. Its resources were limited to a now-and-then operatic enterprise and an orchestra of smallish size and uneven quality. After a year or so, his initial enthusiasm for the opera (based on hope that imported talent could supplement the local supply) diminished, but not before he had conducted Bellini's *Norma*, Mozart's *Die Zauberflöte*, Beethoven's *Fidelio*, Weber's *Der Freischütz* (twice), and Boieldieu's *La Dame blanche* and Mozart's *Don Giovanni* (each three times).

He found conducting the orchestra more rewarding, and his activity with it extended over a five-year span, during which he participated in more than twenty concerts. Customarily the evening began with an assistant conducting the portion that included a vocal or instrumental soloist; following this Wagner would conduct two or so works with the orchestra. His usual preference was for an overture (Weber's *Freischütz* or *Euryanthe*, Spontini's *La Vestale*, Gluck's *Iphigénie en Aulide*)[9] followed by a Beethoven symphony. Sometimes he indulged his enthusiasm for Beethoven by devoting his part of the program exclusively to him, as on the occasion when the Symphony No. 8 was paired with all the incidental music to *Egmont*. Mozart's "Jupiter" occurs once, as does a D-minor of Haydn (more likely the early No. 26 rather than the later No. 80, especially as it was performed at Christmastime and the former bears the subtitle "*Weihnachts*" Symphony as well as "*Lamentatione*").[1]

In the course of three seasons, Wagner refreshed his acquaintance with all the Beethoven symphonies save Nos. 1 and 2. No. 9 was scheduled for performance in 1854, but put off for lack of suitable personnel. He also conducted the *Coriolan Overture*, the Concerto No. 5 (on behalf of a youthful disciple who played the piano part), and the E-flat Septet (opus 20). On a rare occasion he undertook a work of his own, such as the *Tannhäuser* overture.

Also of musical consequence in this "nonproductive" period was a visit to Paris during October 1853. In his autobiography, Wagner recalled it later in these words: "One of the artistic pleasures I enjoyed

---

[9] It was for a Zürich performance that Wagner wrote his well-known concert ending for this overture.

[1] *Grove's Dictionary of Music and Musicians*, 5th edn., IV, 172.

most was a concert given by the Morin-Chevillard Quartet Society at which they played Beethoven's Quartets in E flat and C sharp minor. The excellent rendering of this last work impressed me in very much the same way as the performance of the Ninth Symphony by the Conservatoire Orchestra had once done. This was the first time I really became intimately acquainted with the C sharp minor quartette, because I had never before grasped its melody.[2] If, therefore, I had nothing else to remind me of my stay in Paris, this would have been an unfading memory."[3]

The profound impression of this experience had a further, better-known result. In the course of the next winter's music-making in Zürich, Wagner persuaded the principal string players of the orchestra to form a quartet. With them he spent many hours rehearsing opus 131 "with infinite patience."[4] It was for the public performance in Zürich that Wagner wrote his celebrated commentary on this great work. (It later became a part of his lengthy essay on Beethoven published in 1870, the centennial year of the composer's birth.) It begins, in evocation of the music's mood: "The long introductory Adagio, than which probably nothing more melancholy has been expressed in tones, I would designate as the awakening on the morn of a day that throughout its tardy course shall fulfill not a singe desire, not one."

Edward Dannreuther, editor of *Beethoven* by Richard Wagner (London: William Reeves) directs attention (p. 82) to the extent to which these words echo a passage in the first act of *Faust*: "*Den Tag zu sehen, der mir in seinem Lauf, Nicht einen Wunsch erfüllen wird, nicht einen.*" But it touches a deeper autobiographical note in reproducing a complaint voiced by Wagner to Liszt in a letter dating from many months before: "My nights are mostly sleepless; weary and miserable, I rise from bed to see a day before me which will bring me not *one* joy."[5] (Italics in original.)

This expression preceded the Parisian visit of October 1853 by seven months. It preceded by about a year his verbal exposition of Beethoven's C-sharp-minor Quartet and what it meant to him. He was ready and ripe, then, to hear its "inner melody" for the first time when he encountered it in the Paris performance of the Morin-Chevillard

---

[2] In his *The Life of Richard Wagner*, II, 394, Newman renders the same passage as: "The inner melody of Beethoven's C sharp minor quartette was revealed to him for the first time."

[3] Wagner: *My Life*, p. 608.

[4] Newman: *Wagner*, II, 447.

[5] Liszt-Wagner Correspondence, I, 270.

Quartet. The impression it made was so close to his emotional state of the time that he was impelled to organize rehearsals and see them through to a public performance, complete with verbal analysis, when he returned to Zürich. Before very long its singular kind of chromaticism became a germinating element in the idiom predestined for a work in which "melancholy" is as keenly felt as it is in *Tristan und Isolde*.

In the span of his Zürich years, Wagner engaged in one other public musical activity of major scope and important consequence: a series of concerts in London at the invitation of the Philharmonic Society. During a four-month stay, beginning on March 12, 1855, he conducted eight concerts at intervals of two weeks. He found much pleasure in the orchestra, especially the principal players and the instruments they used. The public was less responsive than he thought was his due, and he soon concluded that the visit was artistically futile. But he had a chance to perform all the Beethoven symphonies including the Ninth, Mendelssohn's "Scotch," Mozart's E-flat, and Spohr's C-minor (No. 3). Other works included the *Anacreon* and *Wasserträger* overtures of Cherubini, and such concertos as the A-flat of Hummel, Beethoven's B-flat, and the Chopin E-minor.[6]

Of even greater long-range consequence was the renewal of acquaintance with Berlioz, who happened to be in London for concerts of his own. Among the works Berlioz presented at a concert on June 9 were sections of *Roméo et Juliette*, and among those present was Wagner. This was his third exposure to the score (the first, in Paris in 1839–41, was followed by a partial performance under Berlioz in Dresden in 1843), and it left him an admirer. A few weeks later the two men met at the home of a mutual friend. Both reported on their meeting to Liszt with decided enthusiasm and some reservations.

Whatever the latter—and they were no more than might divide any two men of such strong individuality—Wagner was prompted to pursue Berlioz's musical initiatives farther. On his return to Zürich he asked Liszt to send him whatever scores of Berlioz he had available, and petitioned the composer similarly. Berlioz could offer only *L'Enfance du Christ*, *Lélio*, and the *Te Deum*, for the publishers no longer provided him with earlier scores. From Liszt, Wagner received nothing, his Berlioz scores being on loan (there are no references to the subject in later published letters).

So much for the ingestion publicly. There was much more privately, of which the most considerable part, in scope and influence, was the

[6] Myles Birkett Foster, ed.: *History of the Philharmonic Society of London, 1813–1912* (London: John Lane, The Bodley Head; 1912), pp. 241–4.

new works that Liszt was creating in this period. He brought them along to Zürich in July 1853, at which time the two men met for the first time in four years. In *Mein Leben* (p. 599), Wagner gave this account of the reunion: "Now for the first time I enjoyed the delight of getting to know my friend as a fellow composer. In addition to many of his celebrated piano pieces which he had only recently written [the *Consolations, Harmonies Poétiques et réligieuses,* and Ballade No. 2 might qualify] we went through several symphonies with great ardour, and especially his Faust symphony . . . My delight over everything I heard by Liszt was as deep as it was sincere, and above all, extraordinarily stimulating . . ." The most important consequence was left to the last. Wagner adds: "I even thought of beginning to compose again." Newman notes what he considers a contradiction in Wagner's statement and information from other sources, saying "Liszt did not begin work on the *Faust* symphony until August 1854."[7] He suggests that Wagner might be confusing his memory of this visit with another of a later date. However, the Liszt-Wagner Correspondence contains a letter dated February 7, 1854, in which there is the pointed inquiry: "How about the *Faust* symphony?" (In the original: *"Wie steht es mit der Faust-Symphonie?"*)[8] There is the possibility that Liszt might have been mulling some of it mentally and played it for Wagner at their meeting of the previous summer, even as Wagner had parts of future projects sketched or in mind well before the time of formal composition.

With or without the *Faust Symphony,* however, the evidence is clear that the ultimate effect of this warming contact with Liszt's works was to dissolve internal obstacles that had blocked Wagner's compositional flow for a full six years. It was just weeks later (September 5, 1853) that he began to write again, after a lapse since the completion of the last, summarizing part of *Lohengrin* (the orchestral prelude) on August 28, 1847. The task to which he now turned was another orchestral prelude: the introduction to the gigantic panorama of the *Ring* that rises from the depths of the Rhine in *Das Rheingold.* During the next three years, Wagner sketched *Das Rheingold, Die Walküre,* and the first two acts of *Siegfried,* before the ever-lessening possibility of having the *Ring* performed caused him to set aside the whole project and begin *Tristan.* It was while *Die Walküre* was in progress that Wagner made the previously mentioned visit to London. There, in addition to conducting his own concerts and renewing his acquaintance with Berlioz, he heard Karl Klindworth perform the new B-minor Sonata of Liszt.

[7] Newman: *Wagner,* II, 386.
[8] Ibid., I, 12.

Wagner's expressions of admiration in a letter to Liszt of April 5, 1855, run to such terms as "great," "noble," "sublime," "beautiful beyond anything."

Thus, whether the *Faust Symphony* became a part of Wagner's experience at the earliest date I have suggested (July 1853) or at a later one (a letter of January-February 1855 which accompanies Wagner's transmission of the revised *Faust Overture* to Liszt states that it "will appear very insignificant by the side of your Faust Symphony"[9]), both it and the B-minor Sonata were unmistakable parts of the events that preceded *Tristan.* The first scraps of ideas directly associated with *Tristan* were noted by Wagner in December 1856,[1] a fragmentary form of a touching thought familiar from Act III. Indirectly, the aura of *Tristan* begins to glow for the first time in the revised version of the *Faust Overture*, which Wagner created many months earlier (January 1855). As previously noted (p. 67), Liszt had performed the original version in Weimar in 1852, thereafter passing on to Wagner his observations. Among them was the following: "The work is quite worthy of you: but if you will allow me to make a remark, I must confess I should like either a second middle part or else a quieter and more agreeably colored treatment of the present middle part . . . and— forgive my opinion—the motive in F is not satisfactory; it wants grace in a certain sense, and is a kind of hybrid thing . . . If instead of this you introduced a soft, tender, melodious part modulated *à la* Gretchen, I think I can assure you that your work would gain very much . . ." Wagner's response was surprisingly acquiescent: "You beautifully spotted the lie when I tried to make myself believe that I had composed an overture to Faust . . . You have felt quite justly what is wanting: the woman is wanting."[2]

When the time came for Wagner to take the work up again, he reported the results to Liszt (January 19, 1855) as follows: "I have been taken with a desire to remodel my old *Faust* overture. I have made an entirely new score, have rewritten the instrumentation throughout, have made many changes and have given more expansion and importance to the middle portion . . ."[3]

The "glow" to which I have referred occurs in measure 120 of the revised score. It is a sighing chromatic phrase directly prophetic of the

[9] Liszt-Wagner Correspondence, II, 63.
[1] Ernest Newman: *The Wagner Operas* (New York: Alfred A. Knopf; 1949), p. 195.
[2] Lawrence Gilman: *Orchestral Music* (New York: Oxford University Press; 1951), p. 459.
[3] Ibid., p. 459.

intervals to which Isolde speaks the word *"Tristan!"* after the drinking of the potion in Act I (in the Wagner canon it is officially known as the "glance" motive; it may be found in the Schirmer piano score on p. 92). But, no less remarkable, the same idea, indeed the same intervals, even the same sequence of notes—B flat, C, D flat down to E—say "Faust" for Liszt when they appear in the first movement of his *Faust Symphony* (he writes it in the flute, around "high" C, Wagner in the same register for first oboe, doubled in the lower octave by the second oboe).[4] Here is more than an instance of contributory thought flowing from one to the other: it is, substantially speaking, a duplication of idea, in circumstances under which some precise guidance as to priority would be helpful.

For many months, in consideration of this coincidence, I was guided by a statement in the Eulenburg score of the *Faust Overture* to the belief that it was insoluble. In the words of Dr. Ernst Praetorius, a comparison of the earlier and the later version was impossible because *"die Urfassung nicht . . . im Liszt-Museum in Weimar ruht, sondern wohl nicht mehr existiert."* ("The original version does not repose in the Liszt Museum in Weimar . . . but probably no longer exists.")

However, a series of inquiries, including one to the composer's granddaughter Friedelind, turned up a substantial discussion of the subject by Olin Downes, in *The New York Times* (June 1950). Downes had based his observations on a monograph by Dr. Joseph Braunstein, a member of the faculty of the Mannes College of Music in New York celebrated for authoritative writings on many aspects of music.

Through the kind co-operation of Dr. Braunstein, I was able not only to see the whole of his monograph, in which many interesting aspects of Wagner's style before and after the first version of the *Faust Overture* are considered in detail, but also a photostat of the score itself, clearly bearing the date Paris, January 12, 1840. It was obtained by Dr. Braunstein from the archives in Bayreuth in the postwar period when jurisdiction over Bavaria was held by the American Military Government.

For its meticulous treatment of the two *Faust* overtures and their differences, it is urgently desirable that the whole of Dr. Braunstein's excellent study be published, and with it the musical text of the

---

[4] Ibid., p. 459. In the annotation from which these and the preceding quotations have been taken, Lawrence Gilman observed: "Neither Gretchen nor the Devil, it has been noted, appears in the score. But Tristan is there and so is Isolde; yet they were not born, musically, until almost three years later . . ." The parallel to Liszt's work did not occur to him.

original overture. As for its bearing on the present subject, the original is as absorbing for what it does *not* contain as for what it does contain.

Positive. The restless, ascending idea is Wagner's, for it appears in the original at much the same place. It is also worked up in a way strikingly similar to the procedures of Beethoven in the *Coriolan Overture*. Thus it would have been familiar to Liszt from the performance of the original version he gave in Weimar in 1852.

Negative. It is only in the revised version of 1855 that Wagner pursued the idea to its present crux of interest and the warmth of expression which produced the *Tristan* "glow." Whereas in the first version Wagner had been restricted to the mordent (or turn, to which he resorted in the *Rienzi* overture, the Entrance of the Guests in *Tannhäuser*, and other early works) for expressive emphasis, he now found other, more sophisticated ways of attaining the same objective. He also recognized the impurity of style conveyed by the mordents by removing them in almost every instance.

On balance, the judgment would have to be that Wagner's original mind gave birth to the thought, but that Liszt's greater musical resources enabled him to expand it in ways impossible for Wagner to achieve as of 1840. When the thought came back to him as amended by Liszt, the path was open for Wagner to push on with it to expressive destinations quite beyond those of his great contemporary.

When the body of *Tristan und Isolde* began to form musically two and a half years later (October 1857), there went into it, in my view, a good deal of all the musical experience to which Wagner had been exposed during his Zürich years. That would include, among many others, not only the harmonic explorations that Liszt had been pursuing in the wake of Chopin, the suggestions contained in the C-sharp-minor Quartet of Beethoven, and some aspects of the re-acquaintance with Berlioz's *Roméo et Juliette*, but even a half-buried recollection of Haydn's *Creation*,[5] whose introduction has some provocative procedures.

Thus it is inescapable that in his "nonproductive" Zürich period, Wagner merely channeled into his own being the two main tributaries of continuity thus far mapped (Beethoven's and Chopin's) and a third that will be considered shortly (Berlioz's). From the mixture and the addition to it of his own strong individuality, Wagner proved himself capable of creating a new confluence with branches and directions evolving out of it which gave the whole stream of music a new impetus.

---

[5] A work that Wagner described as "a great joy to me" when he directed it in Dresden during the 1840's. Wagner: *My Life*, p. 397.

3

To SAY THAT, however, is still only to phrase the matter in the most general terms, to omit the illuminating detail of what was evolved and how it came about. First there was the stimulation of Liszt from what he learned of Wagner's ideas when he became absorbed in *Lohengrin*. Then there were the corollary effects on Wagner: first, the boost to his self-esteem which resulted from this endorsement by an artist he admired and respected; second, the new, adventurous compositions that Liszt created in the aftermath of his absorption with *Lohengrin*, and which, in turn, stimulated Wagner to a renewal of his creativity. For the next six years Wagner and Liszt were in each other's minds almost constantly, each experiencing the other's discoveries almost as they were made, and reacting to them with an enthusiasm that creators usually reserve for their own work. To speak of Wagner "borrowing" from Liszt or "appropriating" his ideas is to view in the most superficial way the seething mass of music that was almost communally generated.

To see it in proper perspective one need only take note of Liszt's inscription in the score of his *Dante Symphony*, which he sent to Wagner in 1859:

> As Virgil guided Dante, so you have guided me through the mysterious regions of life-tone imbued worlds. From the bottom of his heart there calls to you: "Tu se' lo mio maestro, e'l mio autore!" and dedicates this work to you with invariably faithful love
>
> Your
> Weimar Easter 59   F. Liszt.

While relishing the compliment, Wagner felt that it would not be wise for it to appear in print just then. He replied:

> Let me tell you, however, that we had better keep the dedication written in my copy to ourself. I at least shall not mention it to a soul. Your words have positively made me blush, you may believe me. I cannot tell you too often how miserably weak I feel as a musician. I know, in the depths of my heart, that I am an absolute blunderer.[6]

Continuity here is as close as the words written on paper. For, Wagner goes on, he could hardly deserve such praise from Liszt: "You, whose pores are running over as with streams, fountains, cataracts . . ."

[6] Liszt-Wagner Correspondence, II, 297.

to which the latter replied, as quickly as the words could be transmitted: "The noblest reward of my work would be if I were to bring home to you the truth that you are and remain an *immense musician*."[7] Here the impact of one nature on the other is not limited to musical suggestion or artistic stimulation. It takes almost the form of physical interchange, of assured strength nourishing less assured strength with the kind of adrenalin it craved.

Such assurance was as important to Wagner as it is to most creative artists. Curiously, the need tended to grow greater as his accomplishments did. Writing to Liszt while absorbed with the *Ring* (May 2, 1854), he said: "While I am composing and scoring I think only of *you*, how this and the other will please you: I *am always* dealing with you." In time Mathilde Wesendonck would serve as the immediate object of his thoughts (even before *Tristan*, for the manuscript of the first act of *Die Walküre* is full of coded allusions likening himself to Siegmund and her to Sieglinde). And then it would be Cosima. But Liszt remained the one whose praise he cherished most.

In the aftermath of Liszt's Zürich visit of 1856, when he played piano versions of the *Faust* and *Dante* symphonies to Wagner, the latter wrote:

"All that I lack, especially as a musician, owing to my nature and insufficient education, my intercourse with you and no one else alone can give me. Without this stimulus my limited musical capacity loses its fertility; I become discontented, laborious, heavy, and producing becomes torture to me. I never had this feeling more vividly than since our last meeting."[8]

For Liszt the association was no less, if differently, rewarding: "Several of my intimate friends," he answered, "for example, Joachim and formerly Schumann and others, have showed themselves strange, doubtful, and unfavorable toward my musical creations. I owe them no grudge on that account and cannot retaliate, because I continue to take a sincere and comprehensive interest in their works. Imagine then, dear Richard, the unspeakable joy which the hours at Zürich and St. Gallen[9] gave me when your beaming glance penetrated my soul and lovingly encompassed it, bringing life and peace."[1]

[7] Ibid., II, 301. The italics are in the original letter, dated May 14, 1859.
[8] Ibid., II, 173 (December 16, 1856).
[9] A reference to a concert they gave together in November 1856 in the town a few hours from Zürich. The public purpose was to encourage interest in the work being done there by the town's music director Sczadrowsky; the private profit was the opportunity for Liszt to direct *Orpheus* and *Les Préludes* in the presence of Wagner, whose part of the program was Beethoven's "*Eroica*" Symphony.
[1] Ibid., II, 187 (April 19, 1857).

Who is to say, then, whose "borrowings" or "appropriations" were literal, whose spiritual? To take note of the suggestion of Lisztian arpeggios in the prelude to *Das Rheingold*, of an allusion to *Les Préludes* in Act II of *Die Walküre*, of a sparkle of color in the Fire Music, or other indebtedness of Wagner[2] is merely to see the outward, immediately recognizable symbols of the inner, much more subtle transformation. The probability is that without interaction with the other neither Liszt nor Wagner would have become exactly what he became.

For the most part, Wagner left the typical Liszt for his friend to develop, and found his stimulation in the atypical. That is to say, in such harmonic formulations as Liszt projected in the *Faust Symphony*, but did not follow through as rigorously as he might have. It remained for Wagner, in obedience to Axiom I of this subject, to make from Liszt's atypical his typical.

Previously, Wagner had found nourishment and example in Schumann and Schubert as well as in Beethoven (the first act of *Die Walküre* begins, of course, with a figure very much like the bass "storm" of "*Der Erlkönig*," and the first confidences of Siegmund and Sieglinde are carried on in much the terminology of "*Widmung*"); in Mendelssohn (figures very much like those of his "Hebrides" Overture come and go in the "Ride of the Valkyries"); and in Weber (horns for woodland atmosphere, etc.).

By the time of *Tristan*, Wagner was not only speaking a new harmonic language, but was also speaking it with another national accent. Compared with the density and power of the *Ring*, with its essential Germanness, the orchestral texture of *Tristan* is more of a network, less of a weave; it was derived in part from Liszt, but in larger part from their common source, Berlioz. No longer does it depend on the general power inherent in an orchestra which Wagner had experienced in his first Parisian days. Rather it exploits such acoustical considerations as the interplay of instrument against instrument, in which ordinary concepts of dissonance are canceled out by the distance between the clashing tones. This would, in time, become what Schoenberg and his followers would call *Klangfarbenmelodie* ("melody of timbres"). Some part of this skill was coming to Wagner as he refined his palette to produce the pictorial content of *Siegfried*. It was the impact of the next, wholly new subject that led him farther and wider along the highroad pioneered by Liszt.

[2] Arthur W. Margret: *Liszt and Parsifal* traces the phrase associated with "*Durch Mitleid wissen der reine Thor*" to Liszt's *Excelsior*. *Music and Letters* (London), May 1953.

Whether there was such a highroad or not, and whose impulse came first need not be left to speculation, conjecture, or guesswork. Confirmation was clearly entered on the record by Wagner in an epilogue to and summation of the entire period. Addressed to Bülow, his letter of October 7, 1859, deals primarily with an article by Richard Pohl (a musical journalist acquainted with Berlioz as well as with Wagner and Liszt) in the *Neue Zeitschrift für Musik,* of which he was the editor. It discussed exactly the subject of this inquiry: the harmonic innovations of Liszt and their impact on Wagner. It was prompted by Bülow's fears that *Tristan,* upon which Wagner rested so much hope, might not turn out to be a success. Observed Wagner: "I have read your letter concerning *Tristan.* It doesn't increase my admiration for you. The generous and beautiful things you say I will disregard—they are your personal opinions. But I resent your remark that the opera might not be popular and deem it an impractical consideration. Things like that are never said among ourselves: they are usually uttered by strangers . . . What do you, I, and our few friends care about popularity? Why even touch on the question? There is indeed much that we will admit to among ourselves. For instance, since becoming acquainted with Liszt's compositions, I have become a completely different person harmonically.[3] But when friend Pohl applauds this secret *à la tête* in a short discussion of the *Tristan* Prelude—and for all the world to hear—then an indiscretion is committed."

The instance previously alluded to, in the revised *Faust Overture,* is as explicit as any imaginable, for it shows Wagner altering, reshaping, and improving an earlier idea in the light of Liszt. In the earlier version, Wagner's first, youthful impulse exhausts itself at the barrier of a cadence that he can only delay or try to intensify through the use of a mordent. In the revision of fifteen years later, two significant things happen: The figure overlaps itself through the introduction of antiphonal voices in other instruments; it climbs past the previous melodic crux by means of passing tones and contrary movement in the lower voices, and then partially evades the cadence before settling into the A major needed to attach it to the next phrase. In the area of the work in which Wagner told Liszt he had given "more expansion and importance to the middle portion" (second motive) there is even more of the same sideslipping and evasion.

---

[3] The original reads: "*Dass ich seit meiner Bekanntschaft mit Liszt's Compositionen ein ganz andrer Kerl als Harmoniker geworden bin, als ich vordem war . . .*" *Richard Wagner to Hans von Bülow,* pp. 125–6.

Wagner: Eine Faust-Ouvertüre *(original version)*

What had been happening in the harmonic formulations of Liszt and Wagner and where it was heading has been well described as follows by Gerald Abraham:

"Though very different from true polyphony, this passage is thoroughly typical of the breaking up of vertical harmony into horizontal thematic lines characteristic of Wagner's mature style. Just as in the seventeenth century the old fluid contrapuntal techniques already began to solidify into the chordal homophony that was the rule in the last half of the eighteenth century and the first half (if not more) of the nineteenth, so in Wagner this temporarily all-predominant monophony began again gradually to dissolve into linear elements—a tendency that

The musical example should be deleted; the relevant example is complete on page 82.

(*continued*)

Wagner: Eine Faust-Ouvertüre (*1855 revision*)

Liszt: Eine Faust-Symphonie, *Section I* (Faust)

led eventually through Strauss and early Schönberg to the linear counterpoint of Hindemith . . ."

What Abraham is describing here was neither a work of Liszt nor one of Wagner, but a series of measures in a Chopin mazurka (opus 56, No. 3, measures 37–5 from the end). Without this transmission of

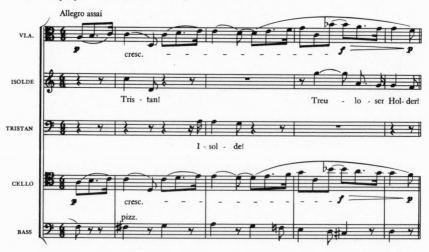

Wagner: Tristan und Isolde, *Act I*

influence from Chopin to Wagner through Liszt, the "mature style" of Wagner might very well have never come into being.[4]

Chopin: Mazurka No. 35, C minor (op. 56, No. 3)

[4] Gerald Abraham: *Chopin's Musical Style* (London: Oxford University Press; 1960), p. 100.

IV

"*You, He, and I*"

I

FROM THE HUNDRED-ODD YEARS that have elapsed since the *Tristan* music was first performed at Wagner's Parisian concert of early 1860, few opinions of a musical kind are as thought-provoking to me as the one then expressed by Berlioz as critic for the *Journal des débats*. After rating on several planes of interest the other matter of the occasion—the overtures to *The Flying Dutchman* and *Tannhäuser,* and the prelude to *Lohengrin,* of which he found the last-named "admirable in every respect"—Berlioz turned his attention to the new music of the evening. This is what he had to say of the prelude to *Tristan*:

"We have a slow movement, begun *pianissimo*, increasing gradually to *fortissimo* and returning to the nuance of its starting point without any other theme than a sort of chromatic sigh; but full of dissonant chords, the harshness of which is still further increased by extensive modifications of the real notes of the harmony. I have read[1] this again and again besides listening to it with profound attention and an earnest wish to discover what it means, but am constrained to admit that I have still not the least idea of what the composer wanted to do."[2]

The literature of composer-opinion, whether in formal criticism or in informal comment (letters, conversation, etc.), is full of no less sweeping judgments, some profound, some superficial. It is rare, how-

[1] Wagner had sent Berlioz, a short time before the concert, one of the first published scores of *Tristan*, inscribed: "To the dear and great composer of *Roméo et Juliette,* the grateful composer of *Tristan und Isolde.*" The score is now in the Bibliothèque Nationale (see p. 86).

[2] Hector Berlioz: *À travers chants* (Paris: Calmann Lévy, Éditeur; 1880), pp. 310–11.

ever, to find so general a confession of bafflement by one bold and venturesome spirit by the work of another, equally enterprising one. I am, out of respect for Berlioz's probity as a critic, accepting his statement as a forthright reading of his own mind, without respect to the pique or irritation that some have attributed to him vis-à-vis Wagner. What he is saying, in effect, is: I Berlioz, composer of the *Symphonie fantastique, Harold en Italie, Roméo et Juliette,* the Requiem, *Les Troyens,* and other works too numerous to catalogue, do not comprehend what you, Wagner, are about in the *Tristan* prelude.

To the generalities made public in his article, the student of today can add private specifications of Berlioz's dissatisfaction which were entered in the score sent to him by Wagner. Despite the well-intentioned efforts of some unknown custodian of the copy in the Bibliothèque Nationale to remove the "blemishes,"[3] Berlioz's marginalia can still be made out: seventeen notations in Act I, twenty-seven in Act II, a scanty eight in Act III (when, perhaps, he had tired of his pastime). At the words "*O zahme Kunst der Zauberin*" in Act I, Weinstock makes note: "Berlioz underlined the place at which the short, rising notes B, C, C sharp, and D are heard against a longer-held A flat and F while Isolde repeats and holds an F." In several of the subsequent passages singled out by Berlioz for disagreement, similar harmonic clashes are at issue—as, for example, just before the curtain rises on Act II. Here, to continue the quotations from Weinstock's article, "An outburst leaves resounding through the garden of King Marke's castle the untroubled harmonies of G minor and B flat major. It consists (bass clef) of the F below the staff, B flat, E flat, F sharp and (above the staff) A." In his quest for an explanation, Weinstock adds, "Why did this unquestionable dissonance 'infuriate' Berlioz? More than a century later, of course, any effect of shock which it once had has vanished." Weinstock suggests that its justification on the grounds of "dramatic relevance" might have eluded Berlioz, who had not seen *Tristan* performed and could not read German.

That there might be some deeper, more fundamental factors at work provides not only a reason for closer consideration of Berlioz's attitude *vis-à-vis Tristan,* but also a challenge to discover their identity. For here, certainly, is a confluence in the streams of continuity which, like any similar juncture of forces, puts us in the middle of eddies and

[3] The condition of the volume, as of a few years ago, was amusingly recounted by Herbert Weinstock in his article "Wagner Corrected by Berlioz" published in the *Metropolitan Opera Program* during November 1966.

whirlpools. Unlike some Germans,[4] Berlioz did not reject *Tristan* because of revulsion from its subject matter; unlike some Frenchmen, he had no anti-Teutonism in his makeup (some of his greatest successes had occurred in German cities). Nor do I find persuasive the suggestion that Berlioz was influenced by dislike of Wagner as a person, or by his wife's dislike of Wagner, or jealousy of his success in achieving a concert of his works in Paris. One or the other might have caused a lesser critic than Berlioz to write the unfavorable review that appeared in *Journal des débats,* but neither can explain the specific objections to Wagner's practice entered into the score of *Tristan.*

2

IT IS IN THE NATURE OF its involvement with Hector Berlioz's part in the continuity of music that a search for a clue to his point of view starts late in his life and goes backward, rather than beginning early and going forward. Continuity is a force that ebbs as well as flows, and when blocked it may, like some rivers, make a U-turn and seek a new channel. A clear line of distinction must be made between Berlioz and the influence exerted by others considered thus far in this survey:

Deepened familiarity with Beethoven, and with Wagner, gives endless intimation of things to come.

Increasing familiarity with the works of Berlioz brings a sharpened awareness of what has already happened.

The musical "character" of Berlioz familiar to us through such often-played works as the *Symphonie fantastique,* the *Carnaval romain* and other overtures must, in the light of what we have learned lately from such less frequently performed works as the Requiem, *Damnation de Faust,* and *Roméo,* be sharply or subtly amended. It may be otherwise for the next generation, which will, through the availability of recordings of his complete *œuvre,* be able to discover his innovations as they occur rather than to rediscover them *after* their appearance in Verdi's *Requiem,* Gounod's *Faust,* and Wagner's *Tristan.* Even so, it will be years before all his major works will be available in printed form, and thus provide the student of Berlioz with access equal to that enjoyed by the student of his contemporaries. In order to render unto

---

[4] Clara Schumann's diary of September 8, 1875, reads: "We went to *Tristan und Isolde* this evening. It is the most repulsive thing that I ever saw or heard in my life." Clara Schumann: *An Artist's Life* (Leipzig: Breitkopf und Härtel; 1913), II, 312.

Berlioz what is Hector's, we must rethink this phase of continuity and conceive it as it came into being and exerted its influence, not as we belatedly have come to understand it.

Among those so influenced was, of course, Wagner himself, as he generously acknowledged in *Mein Leben*. But with his own blend of awareness and brashness, he expressed himself somewhat differently when the experience was fresh. Writing to his friend Ferdinand Heine from Paris in 1841, he said:

> Permit me to say a few words about the personal impression which my acquaintance with Berlioz has made on me. The first of his works I heard was his *Roméo et Juliette*, in which the tasteless-ness of his extreme economy has repelled me violently from his genius as a musician. I see the matter as follows: Berlioz stands among the Frenchmen so entirely *alone* that, lacking any congenial foundation, he is forced to feel his way about in a fantastic maze, thus very much hampering the beautiful development of his enormous powers, perhaps making it even impossible. He has been and remains an isolated phenomenon, but he is French in the full sense of the word. We Germans are fortunate, for we have our Mozart and Beethoven in our blood, and we know how to let our pulse beat. But Berlioz has no predecessor and is doomed to a perpetual fever . . .[5]

This, like the statement of Fétis apropos Chopin is acute up to a point. Wagner, aged twenty-eight and with little beyond *Rienzi* and the first version of the *Faust Overture* to his credit, endorses the concept of continuity by putting himself firmly in the line of those with "Mozart and Beethoven in their blood." But as Fétis spoke of Chopin's "taking no models," so Wagner, decrying Berlioz's lack of "foundation," misread the complex of elements which had produced the *Symphonie fantastique*, *Harold en Italie*, and *Roméo et Juliette*. It was, merely, another kind of foundation than his own, indeed one different from that on which any composer of comparable stature had ever taken his stand. Is it not possible that, as many aspects of Berlioz's originality seemed to Wagner evidences of "tastelessness" because they emanated from a continuity of which he was not a part, so eventually Wagner's innovations were rejected by Berlioz because they, in turn, were not derived from the continuity in which *he* was formed?

Stated as Axiom VI, this antithesis would read:

The range of music can accommodate values exactly opposite but no less valid.

[5] *Letters of Richard Wagner*, The Burrell Collection, ed. John N. Burk (New York: The Macmillan Company; 1950), p. 465.

It could be accompanied by a codicil—Axiom VII—stating: *The range of music is greater than any single individual's comprehension of its component parts.*

Before proceeding to a consideration of the elements that formed the foundation that Wagner considered "nonexistent"—and Berlioz would doubtless have argued that he was at least as devoted to Mozart and Beethoven as Wagner was—one further comment may be introduced. It comes from another composer with a strong feeling for the written word—Robert Schumann. An outspoken partisan of Berlioz since 1835, when he had come upon the Liszt reduction for piano of the *Symphonie fantastique*, Schumann was nevertheless troubled by many things in other works, such as the *Waverley Overture*, which he termed "foreign and repellent to the German ear."[6] Thus two of Berlioz's most perceptive contemporaries were agreed that the music of Berlioz disquieted as well as delighted them, that there were some things in it that were repellent, that these things were, at the least, non-German and probably were French.

3

WHETHER WITH A FULL AWARENESS of its implications or not, Wagner had chosen with exquisite justice in characterizing Berlioz as "French in the full sense of the word." For it is of the essence to the distinctions of Berlioz that he brought something to music, both in his lifetime and enduringly, that was broadly French rather than narrowly Parisian. One sometimes has the feeling that this distinction has escaped some of his own countrymen, such as Léon Vallas and Charles Munch. In his lengthy article on Berlioz in the latest (fifth) edition of *Grove's Dictionary*,[7] Vallas states that the composer's harmony is marked by "poverty," "astonishing insufficiency," "mistakes, banalities and platitudes," "ignorance and bungling." In *I Am a Conductor*, Munch finds it in his heart to forgive Berlioz "his clumsiness and his bad basses" because "he succeeds in making the tempestuously romantic impression" for which he strove.[8]

Characteristic as these are of the conventional complaints against Berlioz, they are uncharacteristic in being made by men who would, nevertheless, assert their devotion to him. What it means, merely, is

[6] Robert Schumann: *Music and Musicians* (London: William Reeves; 1891), First Series, p. 226.

[7] *Grove's Dictionary of Music and Musicians*, 5th edn., I, 665.

[8] Charles Munch: *I Am a Conductor* (New York: Oxford University Press; 1955), p. 54.

that, having suffered through life from the derogation of his enemies, Berlioz seems fated to endure through eternity the forgiveness of his friends. Certainly the man who wrote the perfectly balanced cadence at the end of "The Royal Hunt and Storm" in *Les Troyens*, having held it cunningly in reserve during a dozen earlier involutions of the melody, could have written any number of similar cadences had it been his will or desire (as he did in one affecting moment of *Harold en Italie*). His basses are what they are not for lack of skill to make them otherwise, but because they serve precisely the purpose for which Berlioz intended them. These insights are two among the preconditions to understanding without which Berlioz seems more than necessarily an enigma.

As well as being broadly French rather than narrowly Parisian, Berlioz brought into his music modal, melodic, agogic, and rhythmic traits more than slightly related to his area of origin, near Grenoble.[9] He became a musician through the election, decision, or intercession of no one but himself. Most baffled of all, perhaps, was his father (a doctor), who could see little correlation between a son with a talent for playing the flute (and guitar) and a man with a passion to be a composer. Berlioz was a prodigy of nothing but the imagination, whose like has appeared but a few times in the history of music.

His affinities were expressed with no less strong emotion than his antipathies. As a mature master he wrote to a young friend for whose pianistic talent he had a high regard: "Remember the 12th of January 1858. It is the day when, for the first time in your life, you approach the marvels of dramatic music and make the acquaintance of the sublimities of Gluck. As for me, I shall never forget that your artistic instinct unhesitatingly recognized and rapturously worshipped a genius new to you."[1]

With these words, Berlioz might almost be reliving his own "artistic instinct" of thirty-five years before, when he first went to Paris in 1821, aged eighteen. Not yet an avowed music student, he was, to placate his father, engaged in what would today be called pre-medical studies. But he was already hopelessly affianced to music, mentally and spiritually married to the genius of Gluck, whose *Orfeo* he had played at home on the flute. Now, in Paris, he found in its stage performance a glorious fulfillment of this enticing prospect. In turn came *Armide*,

[9] Jacques Barzun: *Berlioz and the Romantic Century* (Boston: Little, Brown and Company; 1950), I, 38.
[1] *Letters of Berlioz* (London: Remington and Co.; 1882), I, 255–6.

Alceste, and the two *Iphigénies,* which led to related works of Méhul and Spontini. He became a member in good standing of the enthusiasts in the pit, where he heard his favorite works again and again.

While still unable to persuade his father that his future lay in music, Berlioz became a pupil of Jean-François Lesueur, a respected composer and eminent pedagogue. Berlioz's burning impulse to communicate musically found expression in a choral work concerned with the Israelites' crossing of the Red Sea, but arrangements for its performance had to be suspended for lack of rehearsal funds. He did manage to have a *Messe solennelle* performed at the Church of Saint-Roch in 1825. However, his meaningful debut as a composer may be dated May 26, 1828, when his overtures entitled *Waverley* and *Les Francs-Juges* were performed at the Conservatoire, where he had been a student for two years.

Neither then nor later did Berlioz indulge in trial runs with piano-oriented sonatas, rondos, nocturnes, etc. The reason for this was simple. He lacked even the rudimentary keyboard skill that Wilhelm Richard Wagner was simultaneously acquiring as a youth of fifteen in Leipzig. Doubtless this was a handicap of sorts. But it also conferred some benefits of no small consequence. Unlike earlier composers, he was never limited, orchestrally, to the reproduction of what he first conceived at the piano. He was at liberty to let his fancy roam, restricted only by what he could hear inwardly. He was the living embodiment, perhaps the progenitor, of the creative process defined by Rimsky-Korsakov when he corrected those who referred to his *Capriccio espagnol* as "magnificently orchestrated." Rather, he said, it was a "brilliant composition for orchestra."[2] Even Weber, whose orchestral palette aroused Berlioz's admiration and emulation, was a composer whose first affinity was to the piano.

A literary-minded musician of my acquaintance, Robert A. Lawrence, said, when asked to summarize his views on Berlioz's innovations: "He ventilated the orchestra." That is, he let air into its mid-range thickened by figurations derived by Beethoven from his piano-conditioning, light into the dark corners of the treble and the bass. This may have been related to his own experience as a wind-instrument player, or it may have been evolved from observation. But the inclination was present even in the two youthful works heard at the Conservatoire concert of 1828.

[2] N. A. Rimsky-Korsakov: *My Musical Life* (New York: Alfred A. Knopf; 1923), p. 246.

It is particularly evident in the earlier of the two,[3] the strongly assertive, much-too-seldom-heard overture *Les Francs-Juges* ("Judges of the Secret Court"), opus 3. If, according to Wagner's formulation, Berlioz was "without congenial foundation," everything about *Les Francs-Juges* should have been his own. But a penetrating commentary on it by the late Julien Tiersot indicates otherwise. Says Tiersot: "In it, among motives in whose interweaving one may recognize the influence of a former period, he introduced a broad and sustained melody twice repeated by the powerful voices of all the trombones combined."[4] As the author of works not only about Berlioz, but also about Gluck, Jean-Jacques Rousseau, and Couperin, Tiersot has a superior point of vantage from which to discern the elements of continuity in Berlioz's earliest orchestral work. Conspicuous among them is Méhul, a composer whose "new and ingenious combinations," according to Gustav Chouquet, "sometimes anticipate those of Berlioz."[5]

Even those denied more than casual familiarity with works of Méhul can hear in *Les Francs-Juges* another strong impulse from music of "a former period." This is the brief instrumental preparation for the imperious tune in A flat with which the free-striding spirit of Berlioz makes its debut on the world stage of music. Not only in its bass pulsations and cross-bowed syncopations in the violins, but also in its total color and musical feeling, the preparation arouses aural expectations of *"Divinités du Styx"* from Gluck's *Alceste*. The greatest compliment one can pay to this allusion is to say that Berlioz's flashing melody, when it enters, is not an anticlimax (see examples, pp. 93, 94, 95).

Returning to Tiersot, it is pertinent to note his emphasis on the originality of Berlioz's use of the trombone when *Les Francs-Juges* was written in 1826. That was the year (March was the month) of Weber's visit to Paris en route to London to produce *Oberon* (he died in June). Writing years later of the awe with which he regarded the composer of his beloved *Der Freischütz*, Berlioz said that it was from his studies of "the three modern masters, Beethoven, Weber, and Spontini" that he "perceived the subtle connection which subsists between musical art and the special art of instrumentation." He adds that it was his own discovery: "No one ever pointed this out to me."[6]

Perhaps the subtlest comment on the difference between Weber's

---

[3] For those who might challenge this statement of priority because *Waverley* bears the designation opus 2, the composer's own words can be invoked. Writing to Robert Schumann in 1837 (*Letters of Berlioz*, I, 134), he described *Les Francs-Juges* as "the first piece of instrumental music I ever wrote."

[4] *The Musical Quarterly* (New York), July 1917.

[5] *Grove's*, V, 654.

[6] Hector Berlioz: *Memoirs* (New York: Alfred A. Knopf; 1932), p. 46.

use of the orchestra and Berlioz's is the instrumentation by the latter of the former's *Invitation to the Dance*. With all the dash and flair and vibrant life that Berlioz imparted, orchestrally, to Weber's invention, it remains an orchestrated piano piece, lacking the special flexibility and color inherent in such another waltz as *"Un Bal"* in the *Symphonie fantastique*. As between those who "orchestrated" and those who "wrote orchestrally," the historic line of separation clearly puts Weber on one side, Berlioz on the other.

Begin on pg. 94, continue here

(*continued*)

Begin here
continue
on pg. 93

Gluck: Alceste, Act I (No. 15)

4

IT IS THUS CLEAR that Berlioz, at twenty-five, was on his way to the command of a robustly unconventional instrument. The open question, of course, was: How would he utilize it? Would it be to go on writing overtures based on literary sources, or would he be propelled in the

Berlioz: Les Francs-Juges Overture *(op. 3)*

direction of something more ambitious musically and more indicative of a personal point of view artistically?

What Berlioz had derived from his enthusiasm for opera and his selection of affinities from his days among the enthusiasts in the pit is evident enough. The new influence came from another direction and coincided with his exposure to the orchestral works of Beethoven when they began to be played systematically in Paris for the first time in the spring of 1828. François-Antoine Habeneck (later to be extolled by Richard Wagner) founded the Société des Concerts du Conservatoire in 1828 and persevered in his propagandizing of Beethoven for twenty years thereafter.

If Habeneck's enterprise did not originate Berlioz's interest in Beethoven (he had already studied two of the symphonies in score), it vastly accelerated it. Between March 1828, when the *"Eroica"* was chosen to open the new series, and 1830, when Berlioz went to Italy as winner of a Prix de Rome, Habeneck played the Fifth Symphony seven times, the Seventh four times, the Sixth and the *"Eroica"* three times each, the Fourth twice, the First and Second once each.[7] The Ninth was not played until 1832, but the inflamed mind of the young Berlioz could not accommodate itself to such a leisurely pace. He threw himself into a study of the score and, indeed, found work proofreading its French edition.

His enthusiasm for the Ninth was also responsible for one of his earliest, typically bold critical pronouncements. In a tribute to the recently deceased Beethoven for *Le Correspondant* in 1829, he proclaimed the view that the Ninth was the greatest of the symphonies, that it was not the product of a master suffering decline of his faculties,

[7] Barzun: *Berlioz*, I, 89 *n.*

as some detractors contended, but a work that opened doors on the future of music.[8]

Equally provocative was the high opinion Berlioz expressed in the same year of the C-sharp-minor Quartet, opus 131. One might have anticipated the high opinion from the nature of his musical mind, but one would hardly have expected, from a beginning critic of twenty-six, the provocative conclusion he derived from the experience of hearing its first performance in Paris by the Baillot Quartet. This was the scene as depicted in Berlioz's article of October 8, 1829:

> About two hundred persons were in the hall listening religiously. After a few minutes, the audience grew restless; people began to talk, each telling his neighbor of his increasing discomfort and boredom. Finally, unable to stand such weariness of spirit, nine tenths of the audience got up and left, complaining aloud that the music was unbearable, incomprehensible, ridiculous—the work of a madman defying common sense.
>
> Silence was at last restored on the demand of a few, and the quartet was concluded. Thereupon the voice of condemnation broke out again. M. Baillot was accused of making fools of the public by presenting extravagant nonsense. A few Beethoven devotees apologized, pleading the composer's mental derangement. "What a pity that such a great man should have produced deformities after all his masterpieces."
>
> Yet in one corner of the room there was a small group—and, I must confess, whatever one may say, that I was among them—whose thoughts and feelings were altogether different. This tiny fraction of the audience, suspecting what was going to happen, had huddled together so as not to be bothered in their contemplation. After a few bars in the first movement, I did indeed fear that I might be bored, though I kept listening. Shortly the chaos began to unwind, and just when the public's patience gave out, mine revived, and I fell under the spell of the composer's genius. Here is music, then, which repels almost all those who hear it and which, among a few, produces sensations wholly out of the ordinary. Whence this enormous discrepancy?[9]

Berlioz's answer to his own query, as synopsized by Barzun, runs as follows: "Each generation . . . fears change: and the envious oppose what is new, knowing their own incapacity to create."

Taken together, these are expressions of influence, testimonials to understanding, which leave in the limbo of mere speculation Wagner's estimate of Berlioz's "foundation." Indeed, it was Berlioz's character, at twenty-six, to be moved not only to admiration, but also to emulation. Chamber music was hardly in his line, but music for instruments and voices could be. It was part of his impulsive nature not to wade in cautiously, but rather to strike out boldly toward the flood tide of Beethoven's accomplishment, the Ninth Symphony. The outcome was the *Eight Scenes from Faust* (1829).

In announcing to his friend Humbert Ferrand his intention to write that work, Berlioz referred to it as *Symphonie descriptive de Faust*: "Listen to what I say, Ferrand; if ever I succeed, I feel beyond a doubt that I shall become a colossus in music; for some time past I have had a descriptive symphony of *Faust* in my brain; when I set it at liberty, I want to astound the whole world with it."[1]

Within a year, the work was "liberated"; but it did not succeed either in astonishing the world or in making Berlioz a colossus. Indeed, he decided that the *Eight Scenes from Faust*, as they were then titled, did not fulfill his intentions, and he recalled the copies in circulation and suspended further publication. Not until a decade later (1845), when he reworked much of the old and added a good deal that was new, did it take the form now known as *La Damnation de Faust*.

Berlioz's next new step was not so long, but it landed him with both feet on tenable ground. Rather than attempting to combine orchestra and voices where Beethoven had left off, he undertook to rethink some of Beethoven's procedures in the orchestra alone. To speak of the *Symphonie fantastique* in terms of Beethoven's orchestra may strike some as rash, considering its inclusion of four harps (the first time that instrument occurs in the symphony orchestra), heavy percussion, and low brass, chimes, and piano. It *begins*, however, with almost exactly the orchestra of the Ninth Symphony, adding to it as Berlioz travels farther along the path projected by his idol.

Such an orchestra might, in time, have evolved from the combination put together by Berlioz in *Les Francs-Juges* and *Waverley*. But it is improbable—lacking his newly stimulated interest in Beethoven—that it would have happened so soon, or, even more to the point, that the mind which had previously relied upon the free association of ideas possible in an overture would have found the sense of order to organize five sharply differentiated movements around so superbly serviceable a concept as the *idée fixe*, or central theme, which recurs throughout.

5

TO BE SURE, nowhere in Beethoven does one find a symphony with a verbal program, a scene in the country, a march to the gallows, and

[1] *Letters of Berlioz*, II, 42 (February 2, 1829).

an *idée fixe*. But one does find—supposing one is possessed of the selective genius of Berlioz—suggestions of each in *different* works. When brought together and fired by the heat of an extraordinary imagination, the suggestions provide a new example of continuity parallel to that propounded as Axiom I of the subject (p. 32). Rather than being concerned with substantive matter, however, it is the atypical *procedure* of Beethoven which became a typical procedure of Berlioz, in the *Symphonie fantastique, Harold en Italie,* and *Roméo.*

For the verbal program, one might instance the *"Pastorale."* It also contains a scene in the country which is interrupted by a storm, as Berlioz's is threatened by one. The *"Eroica"* contains a march on a grand scale, also a finale utilizing a theme and variations. The finale of the Ninth builds much of its effect from the variations imposed by Beethoven on its chorale theme.

Taken together, these provide the structural elements from which Berlioz evolved the framework for the *Fantastique.* But even more consequential for the continuity of music to come was the *idée fixe.* Its transformations and deformations are the essence in the portrayal of the hero's domination by his beloved. From it came the thematic metamorphosis practiced by Liszt in his greater tone poems and E-flat Piano Concerto. From the seeds sown by Berlioz came the fruit reaped by Wagner in his altered, elaborated, and transformed motives, with their later effect on Verdi, Bizet, Massenet, Puccini, and, of course, Debussy and Strauss. In either case, the power of music to arouse a retrospective association was utilized for psychological purposes previously unknown.

To mention "the power of music to arouse a retrospective association" is to remind the reader reasonably acquainted with the Ninth Symphony of what he can hardly forget: the moment of sublime originality just after the harsh chord dismissing the reverie of the adagio has introduced the finale. A rude command to reality after the otherworldly serenity of the slow movement, its eight-measure clamor is answered, with almost verbal explicitness, by the doublebasses and cellos. Again the outburst, and once more the rejoinder.

Thus begins what is known to some as the "Rejection" section of the Ninth Symphony, as the main themes of the preceding movement are put forward in the sequence of their original occurrence. To what end? Tovey has explained it well:[2]

[2] D. F. Tovey: *Essays in Musical Analysis* (London: Oxford University Press; 1935), II, 36.

Beethoven's first idea was that a baritone should explain this procedure [he has alluded to it in the previous sentence as "rejection"] in words . . . The orchestra was to start with a confused din expressing terror and violence: the singer was to rebuke it; whereupon the orchestra was to give out the opening of the first three movements, after each of which the singer was to point out why it was not to the purpose . . .

Evaluating Beethoven's difficulty in finding just the right words, Tovey continues:

Away, then, with these paragraphs of amateur prose attempting to describe emotion which only music can express. Let the basses of the orchestra seem on the point of articulate speech with their passionate recitative. Everything is there without words: nor could any words do justice to the pathos with which the recitative, after furiously rejecting the tragic solemnity of the first movement, seems to hope wistfully for something better . . .

After reviewing the claim to consideration of each movement's main theme, Tovey says: "For a moment the passion breaks out again in despair: and now comes the new theme [a foreshadowing of the Chorale melody]. At once the situation is changed; the recitative of the orchestral basses greets the new theme with exultation."

In the manner of the great military strategist planning a campaign, Beethoven has two objectives, one limited, the other unlimited. But, as perhaps only genius (military or musical) can, he achieves them both. The limited one is to recall the material of the preceding movements, to assess the suitability or unsuitability of each part of it for the purpose at hand. The other, unlimited and unprecedented, is to recall the mood, atmosphere, and emotional impact of each movement by this device of a memory-jogging quotation. Thus, though using music to recapture emotions "which only music can express," Beethoven is also employing the equivalent of a verbal "aside" to test, establish, and exploit the associative power of music.

For all its novelty on such a scale, it must be noted that the procedure itself was neither invented nor pioneered by Beethoven. Mozart introduced an early version of the "power of music to arouse a retrospective association" in Act II of *Le Nozze di Figaro.* It occurs[3] when Figaro enters the boudoir of the Countess caroling a phrase of *"Se vuol ballare."* This is a musical way of indicating that Figaro's mind is still on the situation that existed when he voiced his defiance of

[3] P. 95, Boosey and Hawkes piano score. The aria "quoted" is on p. 29.

the Count with this tune in Act I, that he has not yet been brought up to date on the plot as it is known to the Countess and Susanna. It makes a charming point charmingly; but it is a long way from the use of reminiscence as it had developed by the time Wagner wrote Act I of *Tristan*. When Tristan exclaims *"Wo sind wir?"* Isolde's reply *"Hart am Ziel"* ("Near the goal") suggests only the approaching end of the voyage at Cornwall, unless one knows that the music to which her words are sung is the death motive.[4]

Thus, like much else in the continuity of music, this associative power was latent in its resources for decades before it was exposed and expounded. It was to Berlioz's credit not only that he recognized the capacity of music to make such allusions, stimulate such recollections, underscore dramatic contrasts through tonal means alone—quotation, alteration, distortion, transformation, intensification, augmentation, inversion—but also that he was able to wield that power in a purposeful, artistic way. Even more to his credit, he was able, in future works, to employ the power to advantage without duplicating the form it had taken in the *Symphonie fantastique*.

In *Harold en Italie*, which combines the Beethoven kind of symphonic concerto with the Berlioz kind of dramatic symphony, the "fixed idea" is drastically altered to suit quite another purpose. Nevertheless, the "power of music to arouse a retrospective association" is as much a functional part of the work's atmosphere as is the timbre of the solo viola itself. Here it is broached in a melodic statement—mournful, brooding, yet passionate—first heard from the viola on its entrance. Its transformations (of a sort later echoed by Tchaikovsky and Glazunov in their violin concertos) are basic in the lively first section depicting "Harold in the Mountains." It underlies the "March of the Pilgrims" that follows, a flowing stream of melody on which the chanting of the pilgrims,[5] first heard from a distance, seems to float by. Not at all surprisingly, the melody they intone is a perfect counterpart of the preceding one, which in this case means that in due course it becomes a perfect counterpoint as well.

What could be described as a paraphrase of the Harold theme introduces movement three ("Serenade of a Mountaineer of the Abruzzi to his Beloved") on the English horn, an instrument with little history of prominence in earlier symphonic writing. There is no doubt who is standing by when the viola enters with Harold's doleful

[4] G. Schirmer piano score, p. 81.
[5] An advance guard, no doubt, of those who later went to Italy in Wagner's *Tannhäuser*.

song at double length (augmented). As for the final "Orgy of the Brigands," it deals so much in the "retrospective" as herein defined that it has been described by Barzun as "clearly a borrowing from Beethoven's Choral Symphony."[6]

As embodied in Berlioz's own terminology, it may be spelled out thus: a brief introduction (eleven measures, *allegro frenetico*) is followed by a reminiscence of movement one bearing the designation *Souvenir de l'introduction*; this is put aside brusquely (by, among other things, an outburst in the doublebasses) for a *Souvenir de la marche des pèlerins* which does not please any more than does the following *Souvenir de la sérénade*. Then the viola tentatively ventures the Harold theme, not very successfully to the taste of the orchestra. Various other "souvenirs" are tendered and rejected. Eventually the "Brigands" win out, in a riotous Tchaikovsky-Liszt coda that somehow occurred to Berlioz decades before it occurred to either of them.

As well as perpetuating the important adjunct to musical thought defined by Beethoven in the "Rejection" section of the Ninth, *Harold en Italie* clearly shows the way for the use of the "motto theme" as it became known in the works of Franck and Vincent d'Indy, in the C-minor Symphony (with organ) of Saint-Saëns, in Dvořák's "New World," and in others. None, perhaps would consciously affiliate themselves with Beethoven—in this respect, at least—but it is through Berlioz that they, too, have become a link in the chain of the thought-provoking power of music to arouse a retrospective association.

For Berlioz, Beethoven was far more than an "influence." He was the master architect of tonal viaducts and sonorous arches from whom one so eagerly attentive, so readily receptive as Berlioz could derive the means of creating structural innovations of his own. Not only what he derived from his predecessor, but also what he passed on to his inheritors defines Berlioz as a prime mover in the prime line of continuity that flowed from Beethoven.

6

As to Berlioz's relationship to the other great force of the first half of the nineteenth century, it is no less interesting if wholly different. His high regard for the qualities of Chopin as he experienced them in the early 1830's has already been cited (pp. 53, 57). Their further contacts in the decade and a half that remained of Chopin's life were increasingly rare and artistically nonproductive. In the early days of

[6] Barzun: *Berlioz*, I, 247.

mutual struggle (1834), Berlioz blithely addressed him as "Chopinetto" when inviting him to share a day in the country with Hiller and Liszt.[7] He enjoyed Chopin's assistance in making a four-hand piano version of the *Les Francs-Juges Overture* in 1836.[8] But with passing time, each went his own way, circles widened, paths did not cross, and eventually they had no relationship at all. Chopin's Paris was the world of the salon and the country estate, the drawing room and the château, where music was directly communicated from maker to consumer. Berlioz's Paris was the demi-world of intrigue and self-promotion, of conflicts with authority and its entrenched control of the means he needed to reach his audience. The difference in the patterns of their existence emerges from a reply by Berlioz to a request from the *Gazette musicale* for an article in 1838. Midstream in the composition of *Benvenuto Cellini*, the composer-critic answered: "If I have to live on bread and water until my score is finished, I don't want to hear a word about criticism. Meyerbeer, Liszt, Chopin, and Kalkbrenner have no need of my praise . . ."[9]

Unerringly, Schumann synthesized the distinctions of his two great contemporaries when he wrote, apropos of the *Symphonie fantastique*, in 1835: "As orchestral music, the symphony [of Berlioz] takes the place of a Chopin concerto in pianoforte playing, though the works cannot be compared with each other."[1] Would that Schumann had pursued his thought beyond the mere conclusion, to a statement of the reasons why "the works cannot be compared with each other." It would have saved laborious effort by others, as well as enriching us with thinking of his quality. The indisputable fact is that for all of Chopin's devotion to nothing but piano music and all of Berlioz's attraction to everything but piano music, each was fulfilling a purpose, performing an indispensable part in the working out of music's continuity at a crucial time of development and change. Some might view it as a wise economy of Nature that each was spared the inclination to do badly what the other could do well.

In the intangibles that made up their qualities as men and artists, Chopin and Berlioz were sufficiently polar for all to recognize their differences. Chopin was a social being who craved companionship and an immediate response to his latest creation. Berlioz, in the admirable image of Newman, ploughed "his own lonely furrow . . ."[2] which he

[7] W. J. Turner: *Berlioz, the Man and His Work* (London: J. M. Dent and Sons; 1934), p. 186.
 [8] Ibid., p. 202.　　　　　[9] Ibid., p. 206.
 [1] Schumann: *Music and Musicians*, I, 245.
 [2] Ernest Newman: *The Life of Richard Wagner* (New York: Alfred A. Knopf; 1937), III, 294.

seeded with a melodic growth peculiar to him. If one could define in a sentence the terminal effect of these intangibles it would be that Chopin created a substance that gave many who followed what they needed to feed on and grow, whereas Berlioz projected an infinite variety of procedures that others could adapt to their own purposes.

There was, however, a tangible element whose presence or absence in the works they created was of far-reaching consequence. Its presence in the music of Chopin permitted the bulk of it to be readily absorbed by public and professionals alike. Its absence from the music of Berlioz was responsible for no small part of the resistance he encountered among all but a minority of enthusiasts. Transferred to the part of his functioning which entered into his critical judgments, it had, by my reckoning, an inherent if nonvolitional part in his reaction to *Tristan* and all that it portended for the future of music.

7

It GOES BACK, curiously enough, to the seemingly insignificant detail that Berlioz was not reared on the piano, never learned to play it, and wrote nothing of consequence for it. But the seemingly insignificant can be intensely suggestive if it sets the individual apart from the mass, the more so when the "mass," the wide range of composers before and after him, is made up of other highly distinctive individuals. Wagner was certainly no pianist: he lamented his inability, in later years, to play Bach fugues and his dependence on others for that pleasure. Nevertheless, he was reared on the instrument, conditioned to it, and enjoyed owning the best he could borrow or induce a manufacturer to lend him. As a student, Berlioz, too, found possession of a piano useful —but by his own words the best use he could make of it was to "crash out some chords on it."[3]

Earlier in the same text, Berlioz dealt with the circumstances: "My father did not wish me to learn the piano . . . I daresay he thought that if I learned the piano I should devote myself too passionately to it, and become more absorbed in music than he wished or intended me to be. I have often felt the want of this accomplishment, and it might have been of the greatest use to me: but when I consider the appalling number of miserable musical platitudes to which the piano has given birth, which would never have seen the light of day had the authors been confined to pen and paper, I feel grateful to the happy chance which caused me to compose freely and in silence, and has thus de-

[3] Berlioz: *Memoirs* (Knopf edition, 1932), p. 44.

livered me from the tyranny of the fingers, so dangerous to thought, and from the fascination which the ordinary sonorities always exercise on a composer, more or less. Many amateurs have pitied me for this deprivation, but that does not affect me much."[4]

For Berlioz, the "happy chance" permitted the song in his mind to take wing, birdlike, uncaged by the black and white bars of the keyboard. For Chopin, the keyboard was a ladder, leading to destinations otherwise unattainable. But, all other pros and cons aside, Berlioz's conditioning unquestionably put him in a category aside from virtually all others in at least one respect: he was not exposed to the discipline of "equal temperament" in which all his contemporaries, and most other creators for decades to come, were reared.

The term embraces the compromise devised to enable the players of pre-tuned, keyboard instruments—the organ as well as the clavier, clavichord, piano, etc.—to move freely from one key to another. Essentially a matter of mechanics in which a slightly mistuned ("tempered") tone between C and D, say, serves as both C sharp and D flat, it had far-reaching consequences hardly foreseen by those who devised it. Immediately, string players, who can subtly differentiate between one and the other when playing alone or with other strings, had to sacrifice this refinement in order to live harmoniously with the pianists who accompanied them. In like respect it has influenced the intonation of the orchestra when it performs with a piano soloist: its members must "pull down" their sharp tones, slightly "push up" their flat ones to stay on the same plane as the unchanging C sharp-D flat of the piano. (In such a work as Beethoven's Concerto No. 5, where the orchestra has a lengthy *tutti* involving such a half step, the conductor must expend special effort to make sure that the final chords[5] come out on the E flat that is sounded immediately afterward by the piano.)

Inevitably, the compromise begot results far from the intended ones. Bach's demonstration, in his *Well-Tempered Clavier*, that all the keys, sharp and flat, were accessible on such an instrument, proved the mechanical point beyond contradiction. But the mechanical latitude brought into being an artistic liberty previously unknown. Rather than merely making a desirable end possible, the means produced other, unsuspected possibilities of tonal combinations and juxtapositions.

In the first wave of exploration came vastly more complicated modulations, or means of connecting one key to another. At earlier times, the approved procedure was to move decorously, one step at a

[4] Ibid., pp. 13–14.
[5] First movement, measures 259–60.

time, through closely related tonal neighbors, around what is academi-
cally called the "circle of keys." A first deviation was through the
"pivotal" modulation, in which a tone common to two keys took the
place of a chord sequence. By Schubert's time, compositional practice
had progressed (primarily through the influence of Beethoven) to the
freedom of construing a "tempered" tone as common to sharp key and
flat key though they were otherwise far apart on the "circle of keys."

A memorable, easily identifiable example occurs in the B-flat (opus
99) Trio of Schubert, in which, at a strategic point in the first movement, the cello hovers on the tonic tone of B flat. Suspense and uncer-
tainty are converted into delight when Schubert construes the B flat
as A sharp, and takes the music into the "remote" key of F sharp
(of which A sharp is the third). He has taken advantage of the "enharmonic" sound of B flat-A sharp, their interchangeable character
as the root of one chord or the third of another, to charm the ear into
a relationship it does not normally expect or casually accept without
the sense of surprise intended by the composer. The device might be
likened to a tonal escalator, moving the listener several steps at a time
around the "circle of keys."

In the harmonic schemes of others, Chopin especially, more than
one tone was exposed to this kind of double meaning, leading the
composer farther afield in key relationships and the juxtaposition of
them. To a degree, this could be compared to a musical pun, in which
a likeness of sound is employed to convey a difference of meaning.
But, even as good puns are hard to make, reflecting taste as well as
ingenuity, so a truly satisfying enharmonic change calls for discretion
in addition to impulse.

Camille Saint-Saëns stated his view thus: "From the time that the
tuning established the present system of sharps and flats and permitted
one to play in all keys, the spirit of the clavichord was on its way . . .
This spirit became the conquering tyrant of music by its unlimited
propagation of the heresy of enharmony. From this heresy sprang all
of modern music; it has been too fertile for regrets, but it is, nevertheless, a heresy destined at some time in the distant future to succumb
to the same process of evolution that created it."[6]

As the references to Schubert, Weber, Chopin, et al. suggest,
enharmonic change, or "enharmony" as Saint-Saëns calls it, became
a particular resource of composers who were also pianists. The relationship to the hand-and-keys aspect of Chopin mentioned earlier is obvious.

[6] Camille Saint-Saëns: *Portraits et souvenirs* (Paris: Société d'Éditions Artis-
tiques; 1899), pp. 21–2.

But even some who were not primarily "piano" composers—Vieux-temps, Bruch, Dvořák, Wagner—regarded the device affectionately and took pride in the results they achieved by means of it.

But not Berlioz. Among his many harmonic preferences, the en-harmonic was low on the list. He was not unaware of its serviceability in certain circumstances, but he construed both the serviceability and the circumstances in his own way. Tovey alludes to this in a discussion of *Harold en Italie*, when he says: "There, then, let Berlioz lie: the whitest liar since Cyrano de Bergerac. (This sentence is a completely Berliozian enharmonic modulation.)"[7]

In terms of their harmonic functioning, the two great innovators could be set apart thus: Chopin was an exquisite (as he was in many phases of life)—subtle, diverse, infinitely adept at drawing fine lines of distinction through chromatic shadings, enharmonic parallels, even to the complete omission of connections in pursuit of the elision, to previously unimagined relationships and refinements. Berlioz was wild, unexpected, prideful of his originality even when it was excessive, rarely mindful of the art of knowing how far to go too far. His harmonic texture was like homespun, tough, durable, and a little bit harsh to the touch; Chopin's was like silk, pliable, long-lasting and, for the most part, suave.

Berlioz conveyed his concept of harmonic originality when he wrote (among other aphorisms in À *travers chants*): "Natural gift alone can make the great harmonist; yet a knowledge of those groups of tones which form chords (generally recognized as agreeable and beautiful) and the art of regularly connecting them is taught everywhere with success."[8]

A seemingly concise single-meaning statement, this contains several key words which, when further evaluated, tell us what Berlioz was thinking even more than what he was saying. The first, of course, is "great." Not "good" or "fine," but "great." Greatness is a product of "natural gifts alone." Next is "knowledge," which can be taught (not "discrimination" or "originality," which cannot). And it is clear, from his choice of the tepid term "regularly," that he is not overimpressed with what can be taught.

The net of it is that Berlioz is really describing his own harmonic sense as it existed *before* he entered the Conservatoire, in *Les Francs-Juges*. Much as this tells us about Berlioz the pioneer of instrumenta-

---

[7] Tovey: *Essays in Musical Analysis*, IV, 74.
[8] Included in Hector Berlioz: *Memoirs*, ed. William Apthorp (New York: Henry Holt and Company), p. 363.

tion, it tells us just as much about Berlioz the harmonic individualist. He is not in rebellion against the ground plan of keys and modes, the foundation of tonality and its interrelated supports that make up the house of music as he knew it. But he did not feel obliged, in building Casa Berlioz, to put each pillar in the place where established practice called for it to be put, or to connect every staircase to every landing just as they always had been connected. If he did not fancy escalators (enharmonic change), he might be said to have been partial to sunken landings and sharp ramps.

The musical equivalents could be extracted and exposed as they exist not only in *Les Francs-Juges*, but also through the *Carnaval romain Overture*, *Roméo*, and *Les Troyens*. But that would diffuse rather than concentrate purpose. More important is his statement, made well before chromaticism had become a fact of musical life: "The abuse of appoggiaturas, which denatures every chord, gives to the harmony a vague coloring . . . weakens the force of certain dissonances . . . or else augments it to the point of discordance . . . seems to me one of the most unbearable affectations of the Parisian school . . ."[9] Written of Hérold's *Zampa* in the early 1840's, this bears the ring of the same objections that he voiced to *Tristan* twenty years later.

What, then, of the contention (advanced by Barzun, among others) that when Wagner wrote *Tristan*, he "reproduced," if he did not "borrow" or "steal," certain chromatic ideas of Berlioz's own kind from *Roméo*? This, it seems to me, is an instance of confusing what appears on the printed page and what is heard by the ear. In *Roméo*, in one of the most beautiful phrases Berlioz ever invented, over a pungently mixed chord that opens and closes like a temptingly fragrant but possibly poisonous flower,[1] he nevertheless adheres firmly to tonality rooted in an organ point A all the time. A parallel-sounding mixture in Act III of *Tristan*—the outcry of Tristan on the words "*Ach! Isolde! Isolde! Wie schön bist du!*"[2]—leads to something else altogether (see pp. 108, 109). It is instructive to note that when Verdi invoked the same kind of resource for Desdemona's "*E son io l'innocente*" in Act IV of *Otello*,[3] the superficial suggestion of *Tristan* is basically much closer in formulation (with its organ point F) to Berlioz and *Roméo*.

In a continuation of the observations previously cited, Saint-Saëns says: "What, then, will survive of our present-day work? Perhaps only

[9] Barzun: *Berlioz*, II, 180 *n*.
[1] Broude Brothers score, p. 109 (No. 39).
[2] G. Schirmer piano score, p. 263.
[3] Ricordi miniature orchestral score, p. 355.

Berlioz: Roméo et Juliette, Jardin de Capulet

the music of Berlioz, who, never having learned to play the piano, had an instinctive objection to enharmony. He was in that the exact opposite of Richard Wagner, who was enharmony personified, forcing its principles to their extremities. The critics, and the public in their wake, have put Wagner and Berlioz into the same category: this misunderstanding will be the wonder of future ages."[4]

Thus, what was characterized as "thought-provoking" some pages

4 Saint-Saëns: *Portraits et souvenirs,* pp. 21–2.

Wagner: Tristan und Isolde, *Act III*

earlier has provoked enough thought to lead incontrovertibly to a conclusion: Berlioz's distaste for the idiom of *Tristan* was related neither to antipathy induced by Wagner's personality nor to the wholly human frailty of resistance to the Coming Man by one whose day was fading. It was related, clearly, to a lifetime's conditioning, which he could neither deny nor evade. Indeed, having found a basis for objection to it in the Eighth Symphony of Beethoven (an equivocal interchange of C sharp and D flat), he was prompted to remark of his idol: "All this is very curious."[5] Thus, the red rag to the bull and enharmony to Berlioz had something in common.

[5] Hector Berlioz: *Beethoven's Nine Symphonies* (London: William Reeves; 1913), p. 99.

8

It is almost needless to say that these investigations into the sources and the stimuli of Berlioz are intended neither to deny nor to decry his sizeable place in music, but merely to define it. But it will be said anyway. In the aftermath of his rejection of the *Tristan* prelude—which gave great comfort to Wagner's detractors—it would have been reasonable for its composer to be deeply offended. Disappointed rather than disgruntled, Wagner solaced himself by writing a letter answering some of Berlioz's contentions (in the same article about "music of the future," a phrase that, he politely reminded the critic, he had not invented).[6] In a letter to Liszt shortly afterward, he enclosed a copy of a letter he had sent to Berlioz, complimenting him on an article he had just published on *Fidelio*. Wagner also intimates that it was the influence of Mme Berlioz which had made her husband "ridiculous." Nevertheless, says Wagner: "In the world of the present, only we three belong together—you, he, and I."[7]

Certainly this was a valuation at maximum from one not over-disposed to idle praise. It puts in a bracket with Liszt, his benefactor and in some respects his salvation, a man who had been to a degree an antagonist and, more recently, his deprecator. I would not put any stress on Wagner's "fairness" in making this evaluation. The stress, rather, should be on the immensity of Berlioz's accomplishment, which clearly entitled him, as musician to musician, to no less than the greatest recognition of which Wagner was capable—equal rank with Liszt and himself.

This adds pertinence to the comment, just about forty years later, by Claude Debussy. Writing of Berlioz as one who "never had any luck," he continues: "Musicians are alarmed at the liberties he takes with harmony—they even call them blunders—and with his 'Go to the devil' style. Are these the reasons which make his influence on modern music negligible and leave his own, in a way, unique? In France, with the exception of Gustave Charpentier, I can find hardly a trace of his influence, and even there only in a superficial sense . . ."[8]

Presumably the reference to Charpentier relates to the early works

[6] Ernest Newman: *The Life of Richard Wagner*, III, 19. Newman identifies the phrase as the coinage of a journalist of Cologne (Dischoff) in misunderstanding Wagner's term "art work of the future."

[7] Ibid., III, 21.

[8] Claude Debussy: *Monsieur Croche* (New York: Viking Press; 1928), p. 177. The comment was prompted by Raoul Gunsbourg's stage production of *La Damnation de Faust* at Monte Carlo in 1893.

that are little known today (the *Impressions of Italy*, for orchestra, various settings for voice and orchestra) rather than to *Louise*, which was not performed until after Debussy made his comment. But the deeper stress seems to be on "imitation" rather than influence, and not at all on continuity as conceived here.

For if it were, Debussy would have to reckon with himself, to some extent at least, as one in the continuity of Berlioz. Not, certainly, in such flamboyant use of the orchestra as is considered typical of Berlioz, but at least in terms of such a subtle stroke of sonority as the antique cymbals in *L'Après-midi d'un faune* (which had been practically a creation out of limbo by Berlioz for the "Queen Mab" Scherzo of *Roméo*) or the suggestive power of music-heard-over-the-water in *Fêtes*, with its echoes of the *Carnaval romain*; or, most consequentially, in the rise and fall of prosody in *Pelléas*, after the example of scansion of French for musical purposes which Berlioz had pioneered.

If, in Debussy's phrase, Berlioz's music was "in a way, unique," his contributions to continuity were also unique. There was a first, immediate impact on a few—Gounod and Saint-Saëns, Liszt, Wagner, and Verdi—even before his music was known to many. There was a second, even more influential effect of his thinking through Berlioz's singular (if not "unique")[9] service in making his practice the preachment of others through the *Treatise on Instrumentation*. Berlioz himself prepared the English text at the invitation of Alfredo Novello in 1855,[1] and it came into widespread use almost at once.

Among those who were nearest to Berlioz in mind and spirit—the "you and I" of Wagner's letter to Liszt—the consequences of Berlioz were as considerable as one chooses to make them. As early as the *Francs-Juges* and *Waverley* overtures, Berlioz was making of his brass the proclamative voice so typical of Liszt; and the influence of the *idée fixe* has already been noted. Could the *Dante Symphony* have come into being without *Harold en Italie*, the *Faust Symphony* without the *Damnation of Faust?*

Wagner's acknowledgment of the debt he owed to Berlioz is clearly on the record. Where he deals in generalities, we may make note of such specifics as the use of the trombone in the *Tannhäuser* overture[2] and

[9] A prior instance of a celebrated composer formulating his practices in a published text was the *Treatise on Harmony* of Jean-Baptiste Rameau (1722), which in Berlioz's opinion was "a treatise on harmony solely for those who already know harmony." Berlioz: *Memoirs* (Knopf edition, 1932), p. 11.

[1] *New Letters of Berlioz*, ed. Jacques Barzun (New York: Columbia University Press; 1954), p. 141.

[2] In sending the score of the *Tannhäuser* overture to Berlioz, Liszt observed: "You will find something of yourself in it." See Julian Tiersot: "Hector Berlioz and Richard Wagner," *The Musical Quarterly* (New York), III, 3 (July 1917), 479.

the vivid figurations of the violins above it; the dark coloration of the second act of *Lohengrin*; and the whole instrumental conception of *Roméo* as a revelation of what the orchestra could do for the purposes of *Tristan*.

It is in the latter respect that the stream of continuity brought Wagner closest to the flow of Berlioz. Gerald Abraham made the appropriate distinction between procedure and substance decades ago in his statement: "The parallel [between *Roméo* and *Tristan*] lies, of course, in the similarity of tone colour and in general treatment rather than in any particular melodic resemblance."[3] When he comes to a passage with a note-for-note similarity,[4] Abraham remarks: "It cannot

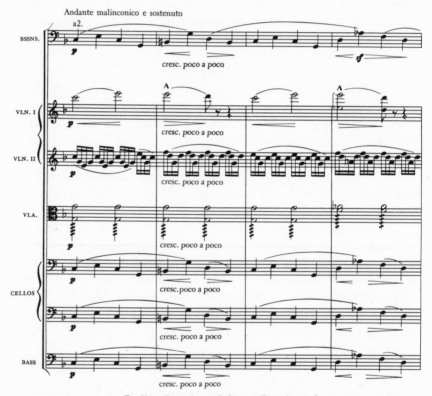

Berlioz: Roméo et Juliette, Roméo seul

be mistaken as the germ of the chief theme of the . . . love duet of Act II of *Tristan* and hence also of the *Liebestod*." He comments

[3] Wagner and Berlioz: *Music and Letters*, London, July 1924.

[4] *Roméo Tristesse*. Broude Brothers orchestral score, p. 46 (five measures before No. 18).

further: "While Berlioz . . . was content with the mere repetition of his decidedly commonplace theme, Wagner, with a stroke of genius, added a little three note pendant which transfigured it into the immortal tune so familiar to everyone." The greatly lightened texture of the

Wagner: Tristan und Isolde, *Act III*

Tristan instrumentation (by contrast with the *Ring* as it existed up to that time), the affecting use of such instruments as the English horn (for Marke's monologue and the mournful introduction to Act III, the combination of strings and distant horns early in Act II), the emphasis on the low strings—doublebasses in particular—all these are

Berlioz: Absence (Nuits d'été, No. 4)

derivations from *Roméo,* with which, by the time he came to write *Tristan,* Wagner was amply familiar.

Whether or not he was also familiar with Berlioz's *Nuits d'été* is not documented. But it is a temptation to believe that Wagner was, at least, acquainted with *"Sur les lagunes,"* a product of 1856. In this "Sailor's Lament," which paints the emotions of a bereaved sailor contemplating the fate that has befallen him ("to journey on the sea without love"), there is an uncanny suggestion of the opening of Act III of *Tristan.* Here, too, there is anguish, an absent love—a state of mind expressed in Théophile Gautier's image of "the immense night" which "spread like a shroud"—that could be likened to Tristan's own.

Tune detecting might make a match of Berlioz's C-D flat-E flat-F with Wagner's G-A flat B flat-C (in the prelude to Act III of *Tristan*), even to the provocative parallel of whole and half steps. But a sense of continuity is conveyed by more fundamental values: the mood of desolation embodied by the low strings in minor, their interweaving with the voice above the staff and the woodwinds between (substantially the texture in Tristan when Kurvenal's voice enters after the shepherd's mournful piping).

Wagner: Tristan und Isolde, *prelude to Act III*

V

Berlioz at Home
and Abroad
(À Travers Champs)

T HE WHOLE OF *Les Nuits d'été* could be used as a modulation,
pivotal or enharmonic, for a consideration of Berlioz's place in
the continuity of French composition (that place which, to
Debussy's way of thinking, was less than consequential). A relatively
minor work in contrast with the size and scope of *Roméo* or *La Damnation de Faust*, a trifle beside the monumental *Troyens*, the cycle of five
settings of texts by Gautier has rarely been excelled by anyone for
perfection of workmanship, total identity of vocalized words and in-
strumented texts, or melodic intensity combined with harmonic justice.
If Gounod's *Faust* (which was introduced in 1859 but did not become
an audience favorite until it was revised, with ballet, for the Opéra ten
years later) marked a new birth of interest, world-wide, in French
opera, that rebirth must be reckoned as having been born under the
star of *La Damnation* on some *nuit d'été*.

Nor can it be forgotten that Gounod's next most popular work to
Faust is *Roméo et Juliette*. Of his sometimes forgotten hero worship for
Berlioz, Gounod has left explicit testimonial in his own words:[1]

[1] *Letters of Berlioz* (London: Remington and Co.; 1882), II, 7. (Preface by
Gounod.)

Berlioz was one of the profoundest emotions of my youth. He was fifteen years my senior and was thirty-four years of age at the time (1837) when I, a lad of nineteen, was studying composition at the Conservatoire under Halévy. I still remember [this would, by the date of publication, have been forty-three years later] the impression then made upon me by Berlioz and his works, rehearsals of which frequently took place in the concert-room of the Conservatoire. Hardly had my master Halévy corrected my lesson than I was off in hot haste to ensconce myself with this weird, passionate, convulsive music, which unfolded to my gaze horizons so new and so vivid in colour. One day, among others, I had been present at a rehearsal of the symphony *Roméo et Juliette*, then unpublished but on the eve of being brought out by Berlioz for the first time in public.[2] I was so struck with the breadth of the grand *finale* of the reconciliation of the Montagues and the Capulets that I carried away with me in my memory the whole of the superb phrase put into the mouth of Friar Lawrence: "*Jurez tous par l'auguste symbole.*"[3]

A few days later I called upon Berlioz, and sitting down at the piano, I played the entire phrase. He opened his eyes and, looking at me fixedly, said: "Where the devil did you get hold of that?" "At one of your rehearsals," I replied. He could scarcely believe his ears.

One can imagine that Berlioz listened with greater disbelief some years later when he heard the introduction to the "*Veau d'or*" in Gounod's *Faust* performed to much the same colorful phrase (in the same key) that precedes the scene in Auerbach's Cellar in *La Damnation*.[4] This, however, was done by Gounod not in a spirit of innocent amusement, but in helpless bemusement that the idea was his own. Faust is a tenor for Gounod, as he was for Berlioz; Méphistophélès is also a bass-baritone in both instances. For Marguerite, Berlioz preferred a mezzo, Gounod a soprano. However, the tune preferred by the peasants outside Faust's study in the opening scene of the opera strongly suggests that Berlioz's *Harold* had passed that way ("Serenade in the Mountains of the Abruzzi" [see pp. 120, 121]).

Here was artistic consanguinity as well as continuity, a sharing of like ways of doing things whose results impelled Berlioz to speak highly of Gounod's work when it was new and the public not yet habituated to it. Certainly Berlioz could not have conceived the most popular parts of *Faust* any more than Gounod could have imagined the most sophisticated sections of *La Damnation*, which the just gods reserved

[2] November 1839.
[3] Broude Brothers orchestral score, p. 226 ("The Oath").
[4] Pages 86–7 of miniature orchestral score published by Costallat et Cie.

Berlioz: La Damnation de Faust, *Scene 6*

Gounod: Faust, Act II

Berlioz: Harold en Italie, *second movement*

to Berlioz alone. It is, however, constantly necessary to keep in mind everything relating to priority and sequence (original conception 1829, final realization 1846) in assigning to *La Damnation* everything that Berlioz put into it. Of all the Berlioz scores now well known, this is the prime exemplar of continuity-in-reverse, full of "borrowing" from those who came after him, of devices familiar from works most persons come to know long before they acquire a taste for *La Damnation.*

Among them are not merely the orchestral colorations that make the name of Faust synonymous with Gounod rather than with Berlioz (a backward progression like one of Berlioz's typical harmonic sequences), but also the prototype of all student and soldier choruses to come (from Offenbach to Romberg), a stage band which plays fanfares that are close kin to those heard from Puccini's street scene in *La Bohème* fifty years later, a thesaurus of orchestral devices in the "Dance of the Sylphs" and the *"Menuet des feux-follets,"* and a "Ride to the Abyss" that invents not only the Ride, musically, but the Abyss as well. This is a far deeper, more ominous chasm than the Wolf's Glen in Weber's *Der Freischütz* (which may very well have gestated the thought to which Berlioz gave birth), and lies very close to Mussorgsky's *Bald Mountain.*

The consolation for those who would set the historical record

Gounod: Faust, Act I

straight is that no one could pre-empt credit for the total conception, which belongs to Berlioz, or deprive him of the distinction rightfully his for such an exquisite detail as *"D'amour l'ardente flamme."* In his own contribution (unintentionally, of course) to this survey, Léon Vallas contends that this striking invention, with English horn obbligato, has "close kinship with cerain songs of Schubert, from which it is derived," songs he does not identify.[5] Perhaps the allusion is to

[5] *Grove's Dictionary of Music and Musicians,* 5th edn., I, 663.

"*Gretchen am Spinnrade*," which is also *Faust*-and-Goethe-derived. If so, this merely suggests anew that one man's trickle may become another man's torrent.

Among later composers who, unlike Gounod, were not near-contemporaries of Berlioz, and therefore absorbed his abundance from a greater distance, mention might be made of Saint-Saëns. As a student of seventeen, he heard the *Requiem* performed at St.-Eustache in 1852, and talked about it for nearly seventy years, until his death in 1921. Whether, eventually, he found more that was musically congenial in Wagner or Liszt (being a composer for the stage as well as for the piano and the orchestra, he was in the stream of all their innovations), Saint-Saëns profited first of all from the example of Berlioz, who took a liking to his younger colleague. They did, indeed, develop a relationship of sufficient cordiality for Saint-Saëns to venture a rebuttal of Berlioz's opinion of *Tristan*. In another phraseology underlying the reasons previously mentioned (p. 108) for this antipathy, Saint-Saëns wrote: "Berlioz detested *Tristan und Isolde*. As I could speak to him without reserve, I made no bones about challenging his opinion and expressing the admiration which the general conception and a large part of the work of the great Richard inspired in me. Then it was that his profound antipathy to the enharmonic dissonances and modulations was brought home to me in full force . . ."[6]

The wide-ranging impulses of Berlioz entered, in varying degree, into the thinking of the very young Fauré, whose early songs are tinged with the subtle effects of *Les Nuits d'été*, composed a few years before. And if one can listen to Dukas's *Sorcerer's Apprentice* with anything like an uncluttered ear, the echoes it rouses as it approaches a climax are those of the "*Ronde du sabbat*" in the *Fantastique*, whose 6/8 meter has served for several similar evocations of the grotesque. Whatever its own seaworthiness, the operatic hulk of *Les Troyens* has been plundered for treasure by composers as various as Delibes (for *Sylvia*) and Ravel (for *Daphnis et Chloé*). The "Royal Hunt and Storm" was created for orchestra and chorus (though it is not often performed that way). It projects more than a few devices utilized by Ravel for *Daphnis et Chloé*, which was likewise written for orchestra and chorus (a mode of performance becoming increasingly common). And where the creators of such *grandes machines* as Honegger's *Le Roi David* and *Jeanne d'Arc aux bûcher* or Milhaud's *Christophe Colomb* might have found their example save in Berlioz, only they could say.

[6] Julien Tiersot: "Hector Berlioz and Richard Wagner," *The Musical Quarterly* (New York), III, 3 (July 1917).

2

So FAR, THIS CITATION of continuity from Berlioz has been almost exclusively in terms of Parisians who encountered his innovations at first hand (a category to which Wagner, though not born a Parisian, belongs) or were exposed to them after his death. But in addition to these, there were the others who clustered about *la ville lumière* like moths, attracted by the prospect of making their fortunes (as Wagner was), or to further already flourishing careers (as Verdi did). Several were fortunate to find an even more precious reward than financial return—creative stimulation that made them something other than what they had been previously.

Verdi's first Parisian exposure came just ten years later than Wagner's. It had, however, another character altogether. Wagner was virtually unknown, without assured prospects, and eventually was reduced to hack writing (music as well as prose) to sustain himself and his wife. Verdi was barely more than passing through on the way to the production of *I Masnadieri* in London in 1847. He returned for a brief stay, received an offer to convert *I Lombardi* for the French stage under the name *Jérusalem*, and settled down to make Paris his home for the better part of two years.[7] That could, in some ways, be likened to Wagner's time in Zürich.

On the earlier side of this residence are a dozen works, of which, besides the youthful *Nabucco* and *Ernani*, only *Macbeth* (in the revision of 1865) is still performed with some regularity. On the later side, after the forgotten *Stiffelio* (recast as *Aroldo*), begins the remarkable succession of *Luisa Miller*, with its instrumental enrichment of the vocal line, on the way to *Rigoletto, Il Trovatore*, and *La Traviata*, which propelled Verdi into world-wide prominence. His experience in Paris, musical as well as personal (he became re-acquainted with Giuseppina Strepponi, who shared his roof from 1850 on and became his wife in 1859), certainly had a part in the greater scope and broader scale, orchestrally in particular, of these later works.

How much of Berlioz was heard by Verdi during this time is undocumented. He was not a correspondent save for specific cause, and musical experience was not often such cause. He did not write an autobiography, as Wagner did, and thus left no comparable documentation of the forces to which he was exposed. But by comparison with its

[7] *Grove's*, VIII, 734.

predecessors, *Rigoletto* is a work in which the orchestra is employed with far more purpose. There is also a hint of a device to which Berlioz was partial as early as the *Francs-Juges Overture*. That is the power inherent in a short phrase repeated on an ascending scale step and becoming constantly shorter. No one acquainted with *Rigoletto* has to be reminded of how well that device serves Verdi as the frenzied search of Rigoletto for his abducted daughter is depicted in the orchestra.

To dwell on *Rigoletto, Il Trovatore,* and *La Traviata* as representative of "sophisticated" use of the orchestra may strike some (accustomed to the "big guitar" characterization) as ludicrous. But the powerful impact of the trombone in *Rigoletto*, the divided strings in *Traviata*, the raw power in certain climaxes of *Trovatore* were halting steps in a direction that eventually carried Verdi in giant strides to the orchestral abundance of *Aida, Otello,* and *Falstaff*.

During Verdi's next visit to Paris, between 1853 and 1855, he made the acquaintance of Berlioz, and endured Berlioz's biting characterization of himself as one of those "monkeys, orangutans, constantly grinning puppets who make operas like those of Bellini, Pacini, Rossini,"[8] before earning his praise for the "immense sorrowfulness . . . magnificently expressed" of "*Ai nostri monti*"[9] on the way to being carried to heights of esteem in the columns of the *Journal des débats* for *Les Vêpres siciliennes* of 1855. Said Berlioz the critic: "In *Les Vêpres*, the penetrating intensity of the melodic expressiveness, the sumptuous, wise variety of the instrumentation, the vastness and poetic sonority of the concerted pieces, the hot color that shines throughout, and that strength—impassioned but difficult to explain—which forms one of the characteristics of the Verdian genius, communicates to this opera an imprint of grandeur, a species of sovereign majesty more distinguishable than in this composer's earlier products."[1]

One would not have known that Verdi was present at the *première* of *L'Enfance du Christ* in December 1854 had he not mentioned it in a letter dated many years later. It was written from Genoa in April 1879 to Ferdinand Hiller on the occasion of a concert at which "a little bit of Berlioz was performed, and was a great fiasco! Poor Berlioz now has become fashionable, he who was so badly treated in the past. I knew him well, and heard *L'Enfance du Christ* for the first time, performed under his direction, I think at the Salle Herz. Certainly it has very beautiful things! elevated aspirations and twisted manifestations, confused and without natural development . . ."[2]

[8] Franco Abbiati: *Giuseppe Verdi* (Milan: Ricordi; 1959), II, 357.
[9] Ibid., II, 199.   [1] Ibid., II, 300.   [2] Ibid., IV, 75.

In sequence thereafter came the first version of *Simon Boccanegra* (1857) and *Un Ballo in maschera* (1859), followed by *La Forza del destino* (1862) and the revised *Macbeth* (1865). By the time of *Don Carlo*'s production in 1867, Verdi's conception of the ways in which orchestral color and the weight of a choral ensemble could be marshaled for dramatic purposes had broadened enormously. It, too, was written for the Paris Opéra, where pageantry was not merely *en vogue*, but *de rigueur*. It was Verdi's subtle triumph to satisfy this need by means of such a grisly scene as the *auto-da-fé* without compromising dramatic truth or the dignity of his subject. What is more, through the dark colorations of the trumpet, tuba, and trombone and the ominous tread of the bassoon as the heretics are led to the stake, Verdi evokes the cruelty and malevolence of the whole epoch. The purposes are Verdi's, but the means are Berlioz's.

By the time that *Aida* was first performed in Paris in 1876, Verdi's greatly expanded use of the orchestra was readily recognizable and, for the most part, misattributed to the influence of Wagner. A more sophisticated opinion was expressed by Vincent d'Indy (then twenty-six), who, in rating it a "Meyerbeerian-Wagneroid bore," also described "its tendency to Berliozian orchestration."[3]

The enrichment of Verdi's soil by the chemical elements of Berlioz is even more conspicuous in the "Manzoni" Requiem, written between 1868 and 1874. In expressive power and vividness of musical imagery it is the only work of its type to merit mention in a sentence with Beethoven's *Missa solemnis* and Berlioz's *Requiem*. How much the thinking of the latter entered into its formulation goes beyond Verdi's demand, at one extreme of sonority, for the largest possible drum (in the *Dies irae*) and, at the other, for the soaring voice of the tenor (in the *Ingemisco*) in the same register and the same inflection that Berlioz wrote for it in his *Sanctus*. It embodies, as well, the tone, the atmosphere, and the profundity of its French predecessor. Verdi, with his sense of practicality, did not request four brass bands at corners of the auditorium; but he paid Berlioz the compliment of reproducing, in his *Dies irae*, trumpet fanfares very similar to those which had first resounded through Les Invalides in 1837.[4] Jacques Barzun notes that they are "in the same key—though Berlioz begins in the major—in the same rhythm, with the same triplets and the same dominant seventh chords . . . [see pp. 126, 127, 128]"[5]

[3] Martin Cooper: *French Music from the Death of Berlioz to the Death of Fauré* (London: Oxford University Press; 1951), p. 76. The source is not specified; it may have been a letter.

[4] Broude Brothers orchestral score, p. 19.

[5] Jacques Barzun: *Berlioz and the Romantic Century* (Boston: Little, Brown and Company; 1950), II, 281 *n*.

(*continued*)

Berlioz: Requiem (Dies irae)

Verdi: *Requiem* (Dies irae)

If anything, Verdi grew closer to the continuity of Berlioz as his life advanced through *Aida* and the Requiem, the revisions of *Boccanegra* and *Don Carlo,* to the crowning achievements of *Otello* and *Falstaff.* Here, indeed, he met Berlioz on the common ground of Shakespearean enthusiasm which produced the Frenchman's *Roméo* and *Béatrice et Bénédict.* This made them closer musical kin than perhaps any other pair of their generation. From first violent outburst to last commiserating chord, *Otello* is full of the kind of orchestral imagery which Berlioz pioneered and in which he reveled. The serpent that crawls through the orchestra as Iago cautions Otello to beware the green-eyed monster·jealousy, the trombones that thunder his Credo, the trumpets that evoke the martial side of Otello, the English horn that weeps for Desdemona in *"Salce! salce!"*—all are Berlioz-born and Berlioz-bred. In *Falstaff,* the quicksilver glint of the orchestral texture no less than the distant horns of enchanted Windsor Forest are flights of fancy caught on the wing from the fairies and lovers of the forest near Verona.

Verbally, the kinship is closest to open acknowledgment in a letter from Verdi to Arrivabene in 1882. In it the elderly Italian, commenting on the new spurt of interest in Berlioz's music in Paris a decade after his death, remarks: "Berlioz was a poor, sick man who raged at everyone, was bitter and malicious. He was greatly and subtly gifted. He had a real feeling for instrumentation, anticipated Wagner in many instrumental effects (the Wagnerites won't admit it, but it is true). He had no moderation. He lacked the calm and what I may call the balance that produces complete works of art. He always went to extremes, even when he was doing admirable things. His present successes in Paris are in good part justified and deserved; but reaction is even more largely responsible. When he was alive they treated him so miserably! Now he is dead: Hosanna!"[6]

3

A SIMILAR CHORD of sympathy vibrated in the soul of another composer visiting Paris at about the same time. Writing to P. I. Jurgenson in 1879, Tchaikovsky observed: "Last Sunday I had a real musical treat. Colonne conducted one of my favorite works—Berlioz's *Faust.*

---

[6] *Verdi: The Man in His Letters,* ed. Franz Werfel and Paul Stefan (New York: L. B. Fischer Publishing Corporation; 1942), p. 363.

The performance was excellent. It was so long since I had heard any good music that I was steeped in bliss, all the more because I was alone, with no acquaintance sitting by my side. Poor Berlioz! As long as he was alive no one wanted to hear about him. Now the newspapers call him 'the mighty Hector' . . ."[7]

Tchaikovsky was far from the first Russian composer to include a work of Berlioz among his "favorites." The entry of Berlioz into the continuity of Russian music long predated 1879 and almost predated the birth of Tchaikovsky himself in 1840. It forms a singularly absorbing episode in the extensive chapter of Berlioz's part in the continuity of music.

It might be said to have begun as early as 1830, when Berlioz, a Prix de Rome winner after earlier unsuccessful efforts, was living at the Villa Medici and frequenting the Caffè Greco. It was there that he first met Mikhail Glinka, in whose life he was destined to play a part. By extension, anything significant to the life of Glinka was significant to the life of the Russian music to come.

Though only a year older than Glinka, who was then twenty-five, Berlioz possessed accomplishments far beyond those of his Russian friend. Glinka was St. Petersburg-conditioned to Italian opera (for which Berlioz's scorn was already well developed), but he could claim no musical distinction beyond a few piano lessons with John Field and a collection of student efforts at composition. There was no opportunity then for Glinka to hear any works of Berlioz, but he could file their friendship for future reference.

Before Glinka left Italy (in 1833), he conceived the idea of a Russian opera on a Russian subject utilizing Russian folk music, to which he was strongly attached. When it came into being (1836) as *A Life for the Tsar* (current Soviet usage prefers the title *Ivan Susanin*, after its leading male character), Glinka had to withstand abuse both for the attachment and for its results in his music. Some connoisseurs accustomed to the elegant superficialities of the Italian works favored in St. Petersburg disparaged it as "music of the coachmen" (probably because a coachman's song appears in the score).

Substantially Italian in design, if Russian in spirit (its overture suggests Schubert or one of the Italians whose style Schubert sometimes imitated), *A Life for the Tsar* was followed, in 1842, by *Russlan and Ludmilla*. Even those whose knowledge is confined to the much-played overture are aware of the dash and vitality it contains, with its vivacious

---

[7] *The Life and Letters of Peter Ilich Tchaikovsky*, ed. Rosa Newmarch (London: John Lane, The Bodley Head; 1906), p. 335.

opening for the brass and the tune in the strings which rises to a tri-
umphant climax. Those who penetrate to the tenor aria in Act II, with
its suggestion of the false Dimitri in *Boris,* or to the mezzo aria later
on à *la* Mussorgsky's Marina, or to the ballet music in Act IV, which
defines the Oriental idiom so successfully exploited by Rimsky-Korsakov,
become acutely aware that the common characterization of Glinka as
"the father of Russian music" is no mere figure of speech. How far that
paternity prevailed may be read in Montagu-Nathan's observation: "The
music of Kaschei's approach in 'The Fire-Bird' and that of the Chinese
Emperor in [Stravinsky's] 'The Nightingale' is instinct with the spirit
of Chernomor's march in 'Russlan and Ludmilla.' "[8]

Glinka: Russlan and Ludmilla (*Chernomor's March*)

[8] M. Montagu-Nathan: *Glinka* (New York: Duffield and Company; 1917),
p. 12.

Though acclaimed a "genius" by Liszt[9] on a visit to Russia in 1842 and honored by the latter's performance, on a tour the following year, of a transcription of the same Tchernomor's March (Liszt's German title was *Tscherkessenmarsch*), Glinka was hardly held in high esteem at home. For a variety of reasons, personal and domestic as well as professional, he left Russia in 1844. The prime European attraction for most Russians, even then, was Paris, where Glinka reacquainted himself with Berlioz and improved his knowledge of the work his friend had done in the eventful years since their earlier meeting.

The results were conveyed in a letter from Glinka to his Russian colleague, the poet-dramatist Nestor Kukolnik, dated Paris, April 15, 1845:

> The most precious acquaintance I have made here is, without doubt, Hector Berlioz. Learning to know his works, so discredited by some, so admired by others, was one of the principal objects I had in mind in coming to Paris. Luck favored me. Not only have I heard some Berlioz music in concert and even in rehearsal, but I am now on intimate terms with this composer, to my mind the foremost of our time (and in his genre, of course) and have become his friend, as far as is possible with a fellow as eccentric as he. This is my opinion of him:
>
> In the realm of fantasy, no one has such colossal invention: and his musical combinations possess, among all their other merits, the quality of true novelty. Breadth in ensemble, abundance of detail, a compact harmonic tissue, powerful and until now unheard-of orchestration are the attributes of Belioz's music . . . Among his pieces which I have heard, here are those which I prefer: the overture to the *Francs-Juges*, the Queen Mab scherzo from *Romeo and Juliet*, the march of the pilgrims from *Childe Harold*,[1] and the "Dies irae" and "Tuba mirum" from the Requiem. All these pages have produced an indescribable impression on me. At the moment, I have at home several unpublished manuscripts by Berlioz which I am studying with unmixed pleasure . . .[2]

After detailing the reaction of Parisians to several works of his own ("An enormous article by Berlioz appeared in the *Débats* which will prove to you that my amour-propre as a composer should be fully satisfied"), Glinka continues: "From the artistic point of view, the study of Berlioz's composition and acquaintance with the Paris public have led me to some important conclusions. I have resolved to enrich

---

[9] *Letters of Liszt* (New York: Charles Scribner's Sons; 1894), II, 353.
[1] *Harold en Italie.*
[2] *Composers on Music,* ed. Sam Morgenstern (New York: Pantheon Books, Inc.; 1956), pp. 131–3.

my repertoire with some concert pieces for orchestra which will take the form of picturesque fantasias, and health permitting, I shall write much . . ."

The results of Glinka's resolve were several and world-famous. Outstanding were the products of a long-contemplated venture to Spain: the *Jota aragonesa* (earliest enduring orchestral fantasy on Spanish folk songs and prototype of Rimsky's *Capriccio espagnol* and Chabrier's *España* as well as Ravel's *Rapsodie espagnole*) and the equally charming if less well-known *Summer Night in Madrid*. Surpassing both in direct musical consequences was the unique *Kamarinskaya*.

It was of this last work, based on Russian folk music for a wedding ceremonial (a "song" at moderate tempo and a faster "dance"), that Tchaikovsky wrote to Nadejda von Meck in July 1880:

"How astonishingly original is his *Komarinskaya* [the spelling is Tchaikovsky's], from which all the Russian composers who have followed him (including myself) continue to this day to borrow contrapuntal and harmonic combinations directly they have to develop a Russian dance tune! This is done unconsciously: but the fact is, Glinka managed to concentrate in one short work what a dozen second-rate talents would only have invented with the whole expenditure of their powers . . . [see p. 135]"[3]

To labor continuity from Berlioz to Glinka should hardly be necessary, so clearly is it reflected in Glinka's deeds as well as his words. But hardly of less moment is Tchaikovsky's casual reference to the later borrowings from Glinka as "unconscious." Intensely conscious of his own indebtedness to others (see p. 37), he was human enough as well as sufficiently perceptive to grant that the historic process could operate below the threshold of consciousness with no less productive result. The components in the instance of *Kamarinskaya* may be summarized as follows: it blends Berlioz's love of low strings and percussion, solemn brass chords of the *Francs-Juges* sort and high woodwinds with a fugued development of the dance which parallels many such passages in Berlioz overtures. Unlike the music of some others responsive to Berlioz's procedures, the substance remains Glinka's own.

Glinka's misgivings about his health (his promiscuity was legend, if his syphilis was not[4]) were only too well-founded. He died in 1857 with little of consequence added to the works already enumerated. However, he endowed Russian music with even more than the influence of

[3] *Life and Letters of Tchaikovsky*, p. 377.
[4] Richard Anthony Leonard: *A History of Russian Music* (New York: The Macmillan Co.; 1957), p. 53.

the works he wrote. When Berlioz made his first visit to Russia in 1847, it was "by the instrumentality of Glinka."[5] And it was Glinka who fostered the talents of Mili Balakirev, progenitor of the "Mighty Handful" (or "Five") and instigator of Berlioz's second visit to Russia in 1867.

4

THAT SPAN OF TWO DECADES was exactly the crucial period in which the character of Russian music for decades to come was determined. On the occasion of his first visit to St. Petersburg, on March 17, 1847,[6] Berlioz conducted his *Carnaval romain Overture*, the first two parts of *La Damnation de Faust*, the "Queen Mab" Scherzo from *Roméo et Juliette*, and the finale of *Symphonie funèbre*. He then went to Moscow for similar programs, returning later to St. Petersburg for performances of *Roméo*, the *Symphonie fantastique* and *Harold en Italie*.[7] Not only the influential critic Vladimir Stassov, but also such prominent persons of the aristocracy as Count Michael Wielhorsky and General Alexis Lvov (conductor of the Imperial band as well as composer of "God Save the Czar") were left with a warm admiration for Berlioz and a strong desire to further his ideas.

As chance would have it, the instigator of this development was not in Russia. After his visit to Spain, Glinka settled (1847) in Smolensk to profit from the ministrations of a married sister during one of his periodic illnesses. However, news of Berlioz's success was conveyed to him in a letter from Prince Odoevsky, who had published an article extolling Berlioz the day *before* his concert: "Where are you, friend? Why are you not with us? Why are you not sharing our joy and pleasure? Berlioz has been 'understood' in St. Petersburg! ! Here, in spite of the scourge of Italian cavatina, which has well-nigh ruined Slavic taste, we showed that we could still appreciate the most complicated contrapuntal music in the world. There must be a secret sympathy between his music and our intimate Russian sentiment. How else can this public enthusiasm be explained?"[8]

.The public enthusiasm may have been a passing fancy, but the influence among musicians lingered. The first of the new group was Mili Balakirev, then only ten, but already possessed of such talent that

---

[5] *Life and Letters of Tchaikovsky*, p. 87.
[6] Hector Berlioz: *Memoirs*, tr. R. and E. Holmes (New York: Alfred A. Knopf; 1932), p. 427.
[7] Ibid., p. 440.
[8] *Life and Letters of Tchaikovsky*, p. 88.

Glinka: Kamarinskaya

his mother took him to Moscow from their home in Nizhny-Novgorod to study with a pupil of John Field. Her death soon afterwards caused Balakirev to digress from concentration on music to general studies and a university education. However, his musical impulse continued to flourish and he composed a fantasy on themes from A *Life for the Tsar* which brought him to the attention of its creator in 1856. "He is going to be a second Glinka," the first Glinka pronounced, seeing to it that young Balakirev met all his friends, including Stassov.

Glinka did not live to witness the outcome of his prophecy, for he soon afterward left for Berlin, where he died in 1857. But his encouragement doubtless strengthened Balakirev's decision to devote his life to music and to share his enthusiasm with others less advanced. Almost at once (1857) he met his first disciple, an army officer of twenty-two. César Cui, in turn, met Modest Mussorgsky, also an army officer, but even younger than himself, at the home of Alexander Dargomijsky. Cui brought Balakirev and Mussorgsky together, thus initiating a teacher-pupil relationship. In 1861, Balakirev found his third recruit, the seventeen-year-old midshipman Nikolai Rimsky-Korsakov. Now a grown-up twenty-six, Balakirev assured Rimsky, as he had Mussorgsky, that harmony and counterpoint were not really essential studies and were time-consuming. He suggested that his naval friend should start by writing a symphony and offered him, as a guide to scoring it, Berlioz's *Treatise on Instrumentation*.

Needless to say, it was not by such easy-going methods that Rimsky-Korsakov developed the knowledge and the experience to produce, nearly fifty years later, the classic successor to Berlioz's *Treatise*, his own *Principles of Orchestration*. But it was at least a map for the first part of the long journey, a guide to the terrain he would have to travel until he reached, by dogged step-by-step application to everything young Balakirev thought unnecessary, a destination of his own.

It was in Balakirev's circle, in company with Mussorgsky and Cui, that Rimsky absorbed the music of the masters in piano-duet form. Chopin and Mendelssohn rated rather low, Mozart and Haydn were old-fashioned and naïve, but Berlioz was "highly esteemed."[9] When they reached the development section of a symphony by Schumann or Mendelssohn, Mussorgsky would say: "Now the musical mathematics begins."[1] The group was completed in 1862, when Mussorgsky brought in the twenty-nine-year-old chemist and self-styled "Sunday composer," Alexander Borodin.[2]

As the individual members of the group went their individual, productive ways, one thing remained common to them: they wanted to write music reflective of their own background and heredity. Both the individual ways and the common background were embodied in a program selected by Balakirev for the first Pan-Slavic meetings in 1867.

---

[9] N. A. Rimsky-Korsakov: *My Musical Life* (New York: Alfred A. Knopf; 1923), p. 18.
[1] Victor I. Seroff: *The Mighty Five* (New York: Allen, Towne and Heath; 1948), p. 110.
[2] Ibid., p. 77.

It included Glinka's *Kamarinskaya*, Dargomijsky's *Kozachok*, Rimsky's *Serbian Fantasy*, and his own *Fantasy on Czech Themes*.

A work not known to present-day listeners, the *Fantasy on Czech Themes* provides a curious example of Glinka's influence overflowing national boundaries and of Russian music profiting from the tidal resurgence. It was through the intercession of Glinka's married sister (p. 134) that negotiations looking toward the first performances of his operas outside of Russia were initiated with Prague. It was to further these arrangements that Balakirev went to Prague in June 1866. The outbreak of the "Seven Weeks' War" disrupted theatrical activities, and Balakirev went back to Russia. By the time he returned to Prague in January of the following year, *A Life for the Tsar* had already been presented, and rehearsals for *Russlan and Ludmilla* were well advanced, both through the enterprise "of the composer Smetana, who was then an opera house conductor."[3] It was during this second visit that Balakirev concluded the *Fantasy on Czech Themes*, which had come into being out of his continuing involvement with Glinka.

There was, however, a collateral result of even greater consequence. How long before this Smetana had become acquainted with Glinka's music, I have not been able to discover. All I can discover is the implicit evidence in both of Glinka's operatic masterpieces of procedures and preferences in Smetana's *Prodaná Nevěstá (The Bartered Bride)*, the source from which flowed the impulses that watered the soil of a native Czech music. The many likenesses in Smetana's zestful masterpiece to *Russlan and Ludmilla* in particular begin with the bustling overture and continue with the treatment of the leading voices, female as well as male. In the latter category there is a direct parallel between the famous patter song of the bass Farlaf and the "bartering" of Smetana's Kezal (one of the choicest parts in the repertory of the operatic bass). Similarly the chorus and orchestra are combined in ways decidedly characteristic of Glinka. It is well known that *Prodaná Nevěstá* did not have, at its first performance in May 1866, anything like the musical dimensions known today. It was originally in two acts, with the musical numbers connected by spoken recitative (in the *Singspiel* tradition). Besides lacking connective musical tissue, the score lacked the big choral passages at the beginning of Act II and several of the dances that are now among its most favored episodes. It was not until 1870 that the score emerged in its definitive shape.

Candor compels the notation that, if Glinka's example influenced Smetana's thinking, it was not volitional or a result of admiration.

[3] Rimsky-Korsakov: *My Musical Life*, p. 70.

Writing from Prague in December 1866, Balakirev characterized Smetana as "the worst sort of intriguer" who "hates Glinka's music and calls it *Tartar*."[4]

The profit to Balakirev from the concert in which he presented his *Fantasy on Czech Themes* went far beyond personal reward. It brought from Stassov in the St. Petersburg *Gazette* the comment: "Let us hope that our Slavic guests will remember how much poetry, feeling, talent and ability the small but already mighty heap of Russian musicians has."[5] It was from "*Moguchaya Kuchka*" ("Mighty Heap") that there arose the English terminology "Mighty Five," by which the pioneering group of Russian composers became known in England and America. It was also as a result of this and other fruitful activities on behalf of the new Russian music that, later in 1867, Balakirev became director of the Russian Musical Society's concerts in succession to Anton Rubinstein.

One of his first important actions was to invite Berlioz to repeat his visit of twenty years before. Now, however, Berlioz was an aging, sickly man of sixty-four (he had barely a year to live), existing only with the help of laudanum, to whom travel was an ordeal. Nevertheless, he divided his time between St. Petersburg and Moscow, as before. In addition to his own *Symphonie fantastique* and the *Benvenuto Cellini* and *Carnaval romain* overtures, he conducted the Third, Fifth, Sixth, and Ninth symphonies of Beethoven[6] and the second act of Gluck's *Orfeo* in St. Petersburg. In Moscow, more than twelve thousand listeners attended a concert by five hundred participants in which the whole of *Roméo et Juliette* was paired with the Offertory of the Requiem. On his return to St. Petersburg, Berlioz gave two more concerts, in which *Harold en Italie* was performed. They were the last in which he ever participated.

In *My Musical Life* (p. 74) Rimsky notes that, though old and ill, Berlioz was "alert at rehearsals," suggesting that he attended one or more. Because of age, fatigue, or disinterest, Berlioz did not meet any of the "Five" except Balakirev, his musical host. He was well aware of the esteem enjoyed by his *Treatise* (especially with Mussorgsky, who was deep in scoring his *St. John's Night on the Bald Mountain* by means of it).[7] When he departed, Berlioz left behind more than memories

---

[4] *The Musician's World*, ed. Hans Gal (New York: Arco Publishing Company, Inc.; 1966), p. 355.

[5] Seroff: *The Mighty Five*, p. 3.

[6] Barzun: *Berlioz*, II, 280. The finale of the Ninth was omitted for lack of adequate vocalists.

[7] Ibid., II, 282.

of his music, the influence of his *Treatise,* and the autograph score of the *Te Deum.* He left a blueprint for the "Mighty Heap" of alternatives to the "musical mathematics" of the Germans, bold new concepts of sonority and color (two respects in which Russian music would come to lead the world), inspiring precedents to encourage all who wished to be themselves, artistically. Indeed, some of what they had first learned to value at second hand from Glinka they had now been fortunate enough to imbibe undiluted at the source.

After Berlioz's death in 1868, Mussorgsky registered his personal evaluation in a letter to Stassov (1872):

"In poetry there are two giants: coarse Homer and refined Shakespeare. In music there are two giants: the thinker Beethoven and the super-thinker Berlioz. When around these four we gather all their generals and aides-de-camp we have a pleasant company: but what has this company of subalterns achieved? Skipping and dancing along in the paths marked out by the giants—but to dare to 'go very far ahead,' this is terrifying!"[8]

In the aftermath of the performance of *Boris,* the composition of *Khovanshchina, Pictures at an Exhibition,* the *Songs and Dances of Death,* and the *Sunless* cycle, Mussorgsky was asked to contribute a statement of self-description to Riemann's *Musiklexikon* in 1880. In his response he stated: "Mussorgsky cannot be classed with any existing group of musicians, either by the character of his compositions or by his musical views . . . Acknowledging that in the realm of art only artist-reformers such as Palestrina, Bach, Gluck, Beethoven, Berlioz, and Liszt have created the laws of art, he considers these laws as not immutable, but liable to change and progress, like the entire spiritual world of man . . ."[9]

5

THE CIRCUMSTANCES WHICH DECREED that Berlioz perform virtually the last acts of his musical life in Russia might be termed lucky—if "luck" is understood as it was defined by Arnold Schoenberg when he wrote: "People generally do not know that luck is a heavenly gift, equivalent to, and of the same kind as, talent, beauty, strength, etc. It is not given for nothing—on the contrary, one must deserve it."[1] Or as a profound

[8] *Composers on Music,* ed. Morgenstern, p. 247.
[9] *The Mussorgsky Reader,* ed. and tr. Jay Leyda and Serge Bertensson (New York: W. W. Norton and Company, Inc.; 1947), p. 416.
[1] Arnold Schoenberg: *Style and Idea* (New York: Philosophical Library; 1950), p. 62.

thinker in another realm[2] came to conclude: "Luck is the residue of design."

The "Mighty Heap" not only had the "luck" to enjoy Berlioz's presence in 1867–8 because they had the enterprise to initiate his visit; they also had the good judgment to realize how suitable to their needs were the vitality and substance of his example. At just about the same time (1863) they were offered the choice of an alternate set of examples when Wagner visited St. Petersburg and Moscow to conduct his own music. There was considerable enthusiasm from the audiences and some members of the press, including his old friend Serov. But the "Mighty Heap" was fortunate enough, or sufficiently "lucky"—in the Rickeyan sense—to realize that what he had to offer was not yet a part of their design. That Wagner, as late as 1880, when all his work was achieved, was not admitted to the company of "artist-reformers" revered by Mussorgsky (see p. 139) extends the period of Berlioz's high esteem in Russia by another dozen years at least.

During the 1868–9 concerts under Balakirev's direction, Rimsky and his associates had the opportunity to hear three movements from *Roméo et Juliette* and parts at least of the second act of *Les Troyens*. (The relevant entry in Rimsky's *My Musical Life*, p. 91, is vague, and may refer only to orchestral excerpts.) Several years later, when Rimsky became inspector of naval bands, he arranged a number of orchestral pieces for the service ensembles, including Berlioz's *Marche marocaine*. In 1875, at the Free Music School of which Rimsky had become the director, Balakirev directed portions of *Lélio*. Two years later, the same series included excerpts from *Les Troyens*, which Rimsky himself conducted, as he did the *Carnaval romain Overture* in 1881.

The practical results of these exposures and absorptions may be found in Rimsky's creation, during the immediately succeeding period, of three of his most characteristic works: the *Capriccio espagnol*, *Scheherazade*, and the *Russian Easter Overture* (all by 1888). Of this time he wrote: "At the end . . . my orchestration had reached a considerable degree of virtuosity and bright sonority, without Wagner's influence, within the limits of the usual make-up of Glinka's orchestra . . ."[3] The year of this reference is 1888, meaning that Rimsky had spent twenty-five years of his career—and an enormously influential twenty-five years—in the continuity of Glinka and Berlioz.

[2] The baseball philosopher, Branch Rickey.
[3] Rimsky-Korsakov: *My Musical Life*, p. 250.

Most of the lasting effects on Russian music attributed to Berlioz derived from his activities in St. Petersburg, the home terrain of the "Mighty Heap." As might be expected, Tchaikovsky was one musician in Moscow who listened with interest to the programs given by Berlioz. He made a point of not leaving Moscow in mid-winter of 1867 for fear that something might prevent his return in time for Berlioz's appearance. Tchaikovsky's accolade was to describe him as "the personification of disinterested industry, of ardent love of art, of a noble and energetic combatant against ignorance, stupidity, vulgarity and routine."[4]

About Berlioz's music, Tchaikovsky's enthusiasm was less inclusive. He rated *La Damnation de Faust* among his "favorite" works (see p. 129), and respected Berlioz as "the true founder of program music"[5] as well as a generative factor in the development of the orchestra, but was not partial to what he described as Berlioz's "ultra romanticism."[6] That there is, nevertheless, clear evidence that Berlioz played some part in Tchaikovsky's development as a musician does not necessarily argue for a discrepancy between his spoken preferences and his subconscious reactions. Tchaikovsky was highly selective in his predilections, with a range of enthusiasms from Mozart and Beethoven (in a letter to Taneyev about his own Fifth Symphony, Tchaikovsky wrote: "In reality my work is a reflection of Beethoven's Fifth Symphony: I have not copied his musical contents, only borrowed the central ideas")[7] to Delibes (for whose *Sylvia* he had vast admiration), and from Schumann (in whom he admired a "vast creative force" at an extreme from the "externally effective writings" of Liszt) to Wagner.

Tchaikovsky's Wagner, however, was not the Wagner of Bayreuth and the *Ring*, two subjects on which his negative views are well known[8] (Tchaikovsky was among those who made the effort to visit Bayreuth for its opening in 1876). Rather, he believed that Wagner's "great musical gift" reached its climax in *Lohengrin*, "which will always remain the crown of all his works." An unconscious expression of his admiration occurred when Tchaikovsky came to write his own Swan drama. Given a receptive ear, with the wind in a favorable quarter of the Scheldt, the familiar phrase with which Lohengrin admonishes Elsa *"Nie sollst du mich befragen"*:

[4] *Life and Letters of Tchaikovsky*, p. 88.
[5] Ibid., p. 330.   [6] Ibid., p. 296.
[7] Ibid., p. 294.   [8] Ibid., p. 344 (letter to Mme von Meck).

Wagner: Lohengrin, *Act I*

could easily bring to mind the hardly less familiar phrase in the prelude to Tchaikovsky's *Lac des cygnes* first heard from the oboe:

Tchaikovsky: Lac des cygnes (*op. 20*), *introduction*

As Wagner had priority in this formulation by some thirty years, Tchaikovsky would doubtless have attributed his impulse to something as unconscious as his assimilation of Glinka's *Kamarinskaya* (see p. 133). In the context of Tchaikovsky's admiration for *Lohengrin* and his distaste for most other works of Wagner, it offers an extraordinary example of something akin to biological selection in the persistence of an idea and its associations.

Though Tchaikovsky's admiration for Mozart did not delude him into either envy or emulation, he was quite capable of valuing his own worth highly. When it was suggested to him that, being in the West, he might seek out Saint-Saëns and enlist his assistance on behalf of the new Russian school and its productions, he replied: "It would be unbearable to have to stand humbly before Saint-Saëns and to be humbled by his gracious condescension, when in my heart of hearts I feel myself *as far above him as the Alps*"[9] (italics in the original). In this letter of January 1878 from San Remo to a fellow member of the Moscow Conservatory's faculty (K. K. Albrecht), who had suggested a concert of Russian music in Paris under Saint-Saëns's patronage, Tchaikovsky said that "a man of temperament, skill, and talent for organization" could do much with a program of works by himself, "Glinka, Dargomijsky, Serov, Rimsky-Korsakov, Cui and Borodin." He ruled himself out as such a person, if only because his talents as a conductor were so inferior.

Tchaikovsky's prophecy took a decade for fulfillment, but when it was fulfilled, the results were historic. The nominee for the task was Rimsky-Korsakov, the occasion the *Exposition universelle* of 1889. He went to take part in a series of *auditions musicales* at the Palais du Trocadéro, directing, on June 22 and 29, those devoted to Russian music.

The first program began, in an appropriate spirit of historical priority, with Glinka's overture to *Russlan and Ludmilla*. It was followed by Borodin's *On the Steppes of Central Asia*, the first movement of Tchaikovsky's B-flat-minor Piano Concerto, and Rimsky's *Antar* symphony. Balakirev's *Overture on Russian Themes* came after the intermission, and was followed by works of Cui (*Marche solennelle*), Liadov (piano pieces), Dargomijsky (*Fantasia on Finnish Airs*), and Glazunov (*Stenka Razin*).

The second program began where the first had left off, with Glazunov's Second Symphony, Rimsky's Piano Concerto, and Glinka's *Kamarinskaya*. Two excerpts from Borodin's *Prince Igor* (Polovtsian March and Dances), Mussorgsky's *Night on the Bald Mountain*, three

[9] Ibid., p. 259.

piano pieces of Balakirev, Tchaikovsky, and Blumenfeld, an orchestral scherzo by Liadov, and, as a grand peroration of all that had preceded, Rimsky's *Capriccio espagnol* were crowded into the second half of the program.

Among the visitors to the Trocadéro were two precocious musicians of fourteen, both students at the Conservatoire: Maurice Ravel and his piano-playing friend Ricardo Viñes. They responded to the new aural sensations not only with the enthusiasm but also with the avidity of youth. Or, as Ravel's biographer Seroff says, the "Oriental sumptousness and the untold riches of their brilliant orchestral coloring were 'pure magic' to Ravel and Viñes."[1] The radiant clamor at the end of the *Capriccio espagnol* remained in Ravel's inner ear until he converted it, years later, into a new, dazzling sound pattern of his own.

For another musician of French birth, the effect of Berlioz's influence in Russia had begun to rise even earlier. Mussorgsky's esteem for the example of Berlioz, as reflected in *Boris*, first became known to Frenchmen through Saint-Saëns, who acquired a score on a visit to Moscow in 1874. It had, says Martin Cooper, "been brought back from Moscow by Saint-Saëns . . . and lent by him to Jules de Brayer."[2] Whatever its impact on either Saint-Saëns or Brayer, it eventually meant much more to a young man who was exposed to its contents soon afterwards. How soon remains a source of contention, for the versions of Claude Debussy's receptivity to this treasure vary. (See p. 276.) It had, in any case, been prepared on the spot, during his time as pianist-tutor in the home of Tchaikovsky's patron Nadejda von Meck earlier in the decade. He had, as a Conservatoire student, served her needs for house music so well in Switzerland in 1880 that she invited him to her Russian estate for similar duties in the summers of 1881 and 1882. His experiences during the second visit included several weeks in Moscow during a period when an all-Russian exposition produced a series of ten concerts, two of them conducted by Rimsky.[3]

In his later years, no longer "Bussykoff,"[4] as he was known to Mme von Meck, but "Claude de France," he wrote of Mussorgsky: "He is unique and will remain so, because his art is spontaneous and free from arid formula."[5] If it was the example of Berlioz, "super-thinker," which

[1] Victor I. Seroff: *Maurice Ravel* (New York: Henry Holt and Company; 1953), p. 28.

[2] Cooper: *French Music*, p. 90.

[3] Victor I. Seroff: *Debussy: Musician of France* (New York: G. P. Putnam's Sons; 1956), pp. 40–50.

[4] Ibid., p. 40.

[5] Claude Debussy: *Monsieur Croche* (New York: Viking Press; 1928), p. 41.

impelled Mussorgsky to go "very far ahead" (see p. 139) in the direction of music that was "spontaneous and free from arid formula" and later aroused Debussy's own sense of exploration and enterprise, how does this relate the latter to his great predecessor twice removed? More closely, certainly, than he could have possibly suspected when he described Berlioz's part in the continuity of French music as "negligible."

VI

Wagner and Wagnerism

I

THE "EDDIES AND WHIRLPOOLS" that swirled about the confluence of Berlioz, Liszt, and Wagner generated cross-currents that opened up new channels for the flow of music-to-come, set up the impulse that took Berlioz into the Russian stream, and, eventually, brought his powerful influence back to France and the West generally through the "Mighty Heap." While these forces were gathering, so was the push of Wagner, dammed up for a decade and a half behind the wall of his exile from Germany, but finally liberated in the mid-sixties.

Doubtless it would have flooded over, sooner or later: it was much too elemental a force to be held in check perpetually. But two circumstances contributed to making it sooner rather than later. One was revocation of the decrees excluding him from travel in Germany (he was after 1861 barred only from Saxony, which is to say, from Dresden); the other was Ludwig II's accession to the throne of Bavaria (March 1864). One of Ludwig's first acts thereafter was to send a messenger in quest of Wagner (in Stuttgart). The famous consequence was to assure Wagner's artistic and financial future, with Munich as the base of his activity until he forfeited his welcome there and went to live elsewhere with Cosima.

Thus, what had been sober fact about Wagner's work since *Lohengrin* to such intimates as Liszt, Bülow, Tausig, and Klindworth became

almost all at once intoxicating reality to anyone with the wit to recognize it and the enterprise to seek it out. The long interchange of
thought and experience that had flowed from Liszt to Wagner and
back again through their letters virtually ceased. It was as if both recognized that the time for meditation and mutual encouragement had
passed, that the need was now for the action that would make the
world aware of what had been happening. Each became the center
of a separate musical universe: Liszt in Rome, from where his influence
radiated in all directions, Wagner in Munich and then Bayreuth, where
he finally created the means for exerting his influence on those who
came from all directions.

More miraculous still was the inner resource that extended and
renewed that influence as long as Wagner lived. Rather than abating
when the accomplishment of the long planned *Meistersinger* was followed by completion of the *Ring*, the incentive of *Parsifal* tapped even
deeper, previously unsuspected reservoirs of thought and impulse. Thus,
for a period of nearly two decades—from the first performance of *Tristan
und Isolde* in 1865 to the revelation of *Parsifal* in 1883—the provocative concern of much of musical Europe was: What is Richard Wagner
doing? During the whole last decade of the period, when the *Ring* was
being prepared for sequential performance and *Parsifal* was being
created, nothing new was produced by his opposite number in Italy.
Between the *première* of *Aida* in 1872 and the first performance of
Otello fifteen years later, Verdi occupied himself with revisions of *Don
Carlo* and *Simon Boccanegra*, but was otherwise musically silent.

Even those whose style was fully formed by 1860 and whose mode
of expression carried them into other areas could not ignore Wagner's
existence or do their work without reacting favorably or unfavorably.
In the second category were such men as Joachim and, more reluctantly,
Brahms, who joined in a manifesto denouncing the "new trends" in
1860. Whether Verdi was responsive to the influence of Wagner or to
such a common progenitor as Berlioz will always be debatable. The
allegations of such influence in *Don Carlo* have already been mentioned
(p. 125). They were renewed when *Aida*, with its richly textured
orchestral writing and motival elements, was first produced in Cairo in
1871, causing Verdi to write to Giulio Ricordi: "On top of all that, I am
an imitator of Wagner! ! ! A fine outcome after thirty-five years to wind
up as an imitator! ! !"[1] In vain might Verdi protest the sweeping pronouncements of those disinclined to seek fine distinctions. The pre-

[1] *Verdi: The Man in His Letters*, ed. Franz Werfel and Paul Stefan (New
York: L. B. Fischer Publishing Corporation; 1942), p. 310.

sumption was already at large that anyone who gave the orchestra a bigger share of importance than had previously prevailed in Italian or French opera must, necessarily, be subservient to Wagner.

The true course of the continuity in which Wagner was a generative element actually went in a rather different way. At first it showed itself in superficial response to his procedures, in the appropriation of his technical means, and sometimes in fatuous imitation of his "system." It would take some time for the credulous to realize that there is no music in a system, but only in a man. But those who were in need of stimulation took it as it came. Then it became a favored enthusiasm of the young, who swallowed its procedures, fed upon its precepts, were nourished by its substance, and, thus gorged, delivered ill-digested imitations. Eventually there were those who came to Wagner's literature as one more among the nearly limitless resources of music, to be utilized to a greater or lesser degree, according to needs, inclinations, and affinities.

By contrast with such an earlier innovator as Chopin, who conveyed much the same stimuli to all those who responded to his example, the Wagnerian accomplishment was so great, its production sustained over so long a time, and its energy directed into so many diverse expressions, that a "contemporary" could even react strongly to one aspect of it and no other. Dvořák, for example, was absorbed by the language of *Tannhäuser*, but not much else. Tchaikovsky, as has been noted, went as far as *Lohengrin*, but no farther. Even earlier in his selection of a point of reference was Max Bruch. I have not heard him described as a Wagnerite (though he is, because of his *Kol Nidrei*, sometimes mistakenly thought of as Jewish). He was a student in his teens in Frankfurt-am-Main under Hiller, then in Cologne with Reinecke, while Wagner was an exile in Zürich. But in some matter he became infected with the vocabulary of *Der fliegende Holländer*, to the extent of making its idiom the starting point for his best-known work, the G-minor Violin Concerto written in 1865. There are shadowy suggestions of this beginning all through Senta's Ballad (which, as it happens, is also in G minor). It comes into sharper prominence in Act II, when Erik becomes part of the action and Senta sings: *"Ach! was die Ruhe."*[2]

This embodies a variation on Axiom II, as stated on page 32. This is less an instance of one composer's atypical becoming another's typical through "anticipation" of a later man's mode of expression than an instance of a stylistic gambit abandoned by one composer and reclaimed for his own use by another. By the time Wagner attained full

[2] Adolf Fürstner miniature score, p. 382.

Bruch: Violin Concerto No. 1, G minor (op. 26)

Wagner: Der fliegende Holländer, Act I

command of his abilities, this kind of youthful "typical" no longer served his needs: but it suited those of Bruch well enough.

At the other extreme of the composers in Wagner's continuity from Dvořák, Tchaikovsky, and Bruch were such later musicians as

Bruckner, Strauss, Mahler, and Schoenberg (to mention but a few), who rejected much but were deeply attached to one or more specific works. By the time of late Rimsky-Korsakov and early Stravinsky, it is possible to characterize one composer as essentially in the continuity of the *Ring,* another as a descendant of *Tristan,* a third and fourth as responsive to *Parsifal* only. A scale for weighing influence has yet to be invented, but the scales of musical history suggest to me that only Beethoven contributed more to those who followed him than Wagner did.

2

AS FAR AS I HAVE been able to determine, the first direct reference to the *Tristan* idiom in the music of another (outside the interrelated trio grouped by Wagner as "you, he, and I") dated from the mid-sixties. It can be found in the least likely of places: Ambroise Thomas's overture to *Mignon.* I refer to a passage in the slow introduction typical of the French overture. Its purpose, it seems to me, is to establish a distant, far-off atmosphere, from which the pleasantries that follow can come as a more than ordinarily welcome relief.

What Thomas reached for, with its sharp tang somewhat sweetened by an infusion of his own simple syrup, is the G sharp-A-A sharp-B sequence in measures 2 and 3 of the *Tristan* prelude.

This might have come to Thomas's attention any time between the concert of 1860 at which the *Tristan* music was first performed in Paris and the date of *Mignon's première* in November 1866 at the Opéra-Comique. The sequence is heard once in a low register, then repeated an octave higher (the same procedure pursued in Wagner's prototype at measures 11 and 12, 13 and 14), before being resolved innocuously in the comforting lower register, *à la Mignon* rather than *à la Tristan.* Having served its seasoning purpose, the borrowed flavoring is returned to the shelf from which it was taken (see p. 152).

If this allusion to a French response to Wagner seems paradoxical, it should not be so regarded. It is altogether expectable that the French, who invented the term, should be in the *avant-garde* of his following. Among those attending the first performance of *Das Rheingold* in Munich in 1869 was Camille Saint-Saëns, who had outlived his beloved Berlioz, as he would outlive Wagner, Liszt, Brahms, Mahler, and even Claude Debussy (then aged seven). He might have encountered among the attendants one described as "the Russian Wagner" by Hans von Bülow in a letter to the "German Wagner," then at Triebschen."[3]

[3] *Letters of Hans von Bülow* (New York: Alfred A. Knopf; 1931), p. 238.

Wagner: Tristan und Isolde, *prelude*

This was the composer-critic Alexander Nikolayevich Serov, who had become, in his own words, "Wagner mad"[4] after a visit to Germany in 1858. (He was one of those who welcomed Wagner on his visit to St. Petersburg in 1863.) Both by expressions of opinion and the example

[4] *Grove's Dictionary of Music and Musicians*, 5th edn., III, 711.

Thomas: Mignon, *overture*

of the works he composed, Serov sought to persuade the "Five" that their objectives were unworthy. They were neither deterred by the first nor impressed by the second.

Saint-Saëns returned to Munich for the performance of *Die Walküre* in 1871, congratulating himself on "being alive" to participate in such momentous events. In his symphonic poems—whether *Phaëton, Danse macabre,* or *Le Rouet d'Omphale*—Saint-Saëns was clearly a Liszt-Berlioz kind of composer, but in his many operas (of which *Samson et Dalila* is but the best-known) Wagner is, certainly, a presence.

Georges Bizet has often been represented as the arch instance of extreme opposition to Wagnerian practices, very largely because of Friedrich Nietzsche's need to set up an Avignon pope after his falling out with the Triebschen one. Bizet was, rather, both emotionally and musically mindful of Wagner's enormous attraction, as he made clear in a letter to Mme F. Halévy in 1871. Said the thirty-three-year-old Bizet: "This man [Wagner] is the nineteenth-century German spirit incarnated . . . The charm of his music is inexpressible. Here are voluptuousness, tenderness, love . . ."[5] But, added Bizet in a prophetic vision of what he would accomplish in his own way with some Wagnerian innovations (motives, and a varied palette of orchestral colors) a few years later in *Carmen:* "In spite of my admiration, if I thought I was imitating Wagner, I would never write another note. A fool imitates. It is better to do inferior work of one's own than to copy someone else's." If it was by means of such hard thought that Bizet achieved his progress from *Les Pêcheurs de perles* to *Carmen* (passing, on the way, through the phase of *Djamileh* in 1872 and the charges of "Wagnerism" it aroused),[6] it characterizes him as one of the more aware participants in the community of continuity.

It was through Saint-Saëns, whom he accompanied to the first Bayreuth Festival in 1876, that Vincent d'Indy (then twenty-five) had his first, lasting exposure to Wagner. It was also through Saint-Saëns, at the Conservatoire, that Gabriel Fauré had his indocrination in the works not only of Wagner, but also of Liszt. Initiation was not infrequently followed by imitation, a particularly notable instance being Fauré's *Ballade* (opus 19). It was written, Joseph Marliave said, "under the impression of the Forest Scene in *Siegfried.*"[7] Its implications were fulfilled a year after its original composition for piano alone, when Fauré re-scored it (1881) in the concertolike form with orchestra in which it is now known. In the incidental music he composed for *Shylock* (a comedy by Edmund Haraucourt based on *The Merchant of Venice*), Venice and Cornwall have a common meeting ground in derivations from *Tristan.* By the time of *La Bonne Chanson* (1892), however, Fauré had found his way to an idiom distinctively his own.

The lure of the "New Thing" drew Henri Duparc, then a pupil of César Franck, to Munich for the full *Ring* cycle in 1879. He was accompanied by Emmanuel Chabrier, then devoting more of his time to a job in the civil service than to music. All that changed, however, before the Munich season ended. It included a performance of *Tristan* which affected Chabrier so profoundly that he resigned from the civil

---

[5] *Composers on Music,* ed. Sam Morgenstern (New York: Pantheon Books; 1956), p. 240.

[6] *Grove's,* I, 737.

[7] Martin Cooper: *French Music from the Death of Berlioz to the Death of Fauré* (London: Oxford University Press; 1951), p. 82.

service and entered the Conservatoire. In the variety of works he composed in the brief span of ten years before he suffered a mental breakdown, the Wagnerian attraction expressed itself most compulsively in the opera *Le Roi malgré lui*. The title has a measure of irony, for it was Chabrier's aim to become "a composer, but not a Wagner." Cooper describes the opera as "strongly colored with Wagnerian harmonic progressions and Wagnerian orchestral timbres,"[8] to which Chabrier had succumbed in spite of himself. Adolphe Jullien, in his biographical sketch of Chabrier in *Grove's Dictionary*, attributes "the tragic mental breakdown from which he suffered for some time before his death" to his "Wagnerian taste," which was "so much at variance with his own disposition."[9]

That a comparable cause was responsible for the cessation of Duparc's compositional flow has not, to my knowledge, been alleged. Everything he wrote dates from the first thirty-seven years of his life (he wrote nothing after 1885, though he did not die until 1933). He was, in any case, a disciple of the *"enharmonie"* so vigorously rejected by Berlioz, developing an extraordinary refinement in the use of the materials with which he worked. According to Cooper, "Duparc's lyrical and dramatic style came from the fertilization by Wagner of a natural lyric gift." In his judgment, "Enharmony is at the root of Duparc's style, but enharmony in the Lisztian sense . . . or even more frequent, in the manner of *Tristan* (*Soupir* and *Extase*), and not in the manner of Franck."[1]

Franck, of course, took a trend toward the work by which he is best known (beginning with *Les Éolides* in 1875) only when the fresh, seductive language of chromaticism came under his complete control. Despite the fact that he inscribed a score of *Tristan* with the single word *"Poison"* or the subdivision of *enharmonie* into one tendency or another, the Franck sonata for piano and violin (a product of his later years) as well as the D-minor Quartet, the symphony, and the *Variations symphoniques* have, at the base of their Franckincense, more than a trace of *essence de Wagner*.

Another who passed through his own *crise de Wagner* was Ernest Chausson. A recipient of a law degree at the University of Paris (1877), he encountered the irresistible at the same Munich festival of 1879 which exerted a determining effect on the other E.C. (Emmanuel Chabrier). Chausson, too, gave up the career for which he had been

[8] Ibid., p. 40.   [9] *Grove's*, V, 148.
[1] Cooper: *French Music*, pp. 62–3.

destined by parental decree and enrolled at the Conservatoire, where his masters included Franck and Massenet.

In 1880, Chausson visited Germany again, this time with consequences that can best be conveyed in his own words. In a letter to his "godmother," Mme Saint-Cyr de Rayssac, from Munich, dated October 10, 1880, Chausson wrote:

> I have heard Tristan, which is marvelous: I don't know any other work which possesses such intenseness of feeling. As pure music it is splendid and of the highest order; as a way of understanding the musical drama it is a revolution. Gluck already had a presentiment of it, but since then people have hardly thought about it. Wagner has taken up his work, has enlarged and transformed it, and created a new art which will inevitably overturn the old molds of opera . . .[2]

A man essentially of small skills, Chausson first showed his innate musicality in some fine songs of opus 2, dating from 1882. As his aspirations expanded, so did his frustrations: endeavoring to express himself operatically on a subject entitled *Hélène* in 1884, he assured his correspondent (the same Mme de Rayssac): "I have done all I could in order to avoid being too Wagnerian." But, a little later he was complaining: "Add to that [the other difficulties of the work] the red specter of Wagner that does not let go of me. I reach the point of detesting him . . ."[3]

Along with creating more excellent songs, chamber music, and the inimitable *Poème* (many will share Debussy's view that "Nothing is touched more with dreamy sweetness than the end of this *Poème*"),[4] Chausson was drawn again and again to writing for the stage, almost as compulsively as a drug addict succumbs to his destructive habit. He spent years working on a treatment of the Arthurian legend (*Le Roi Arthus*), always in fear that it would be found too close a relative to *Tristan*. Writing in early 1885 to Paul Poufaud, he observed: "The greatest defect of my drama is without doubt the analogy of the subject with that of Tristan. That would still not matter, if I could only successfully dewagnerize myself. Wagnerian in subject and Wagnerian in music, is that not too much altogether?"[5] Perhaps it was as well that *Le Roi Arthus* was not produced until 1903 (in Antwerp), four years after Chausson's death. Cooper's verdict that it is "impeccably Wag-

---

[2] Jean-Pierre Barricelli and Leo Weinstein: *Ernest Chausson, The Composer's Life and Works* (Norman: University of Oklahoma Press; 1955), p. 11.
[3] Ibid., p. 27–8.   [4] Ibid., p. 178.   [5] Ibid., p. 66.

nerian from beginning to end"[6] would have confirmed Chausson's worst fears.

Cooper's excellent survey, which traces its subject from the death of Berlioz in 1869 to the death of Fauré in 1924, provides more frequent mention of Wagner than it does of any French composer. Indeed, it parallels Barzun's mention, in his mammoth study of Berlioz, of his subject's part in the continuity of music in his own land. The difference is, however, that Barzun looks wherever he can to find the influence of Berlioz, whereas Cooper finds the influence of Wagner wherever he looks. For this stretch of time, at least, Wagner was so inextricably woven into the pattern of French musical thought that the latter cannot be discussed without reference to the former. To have a "Wagner period" was almost as obligatory for the rising French generation as to grow a beard or fall in love. As Cooper well phrased it, "To be in opposition and to be Wagnerian were almost interchangeable terms."[7]

Even if one were no more "in opposition" than Jules Massenet, who had been practicing what D'Indy observantly described as *"l'érotisme discret et quasi-religieux,"*[8] the invitation to share the fashion was scarcely resistible. Massenet found, in motives and orchestral interplay, a source of the strength that added much to his name when *Manon* was produced in 1884. He also added to his name the questionable distinction of being called "Mlle Wagner," though, on balance, this may have seared less than his earlier designation *"la fille de Gounod."* Cooper's summation is apt: "Any deep understanding or assimilation of Wagner's idiom was plainly unthinkable for Massenet: but, like Puccini later, he was anxious and able to adopt any device which could give his music more modern colour and a more piquant flavor, without affecting its fundamentally conventional and popular character."[9] If, as Romain Rolland caused Jean-Christophe[1] to say, there is "the Massenet that slumbers at the heart of every Frenchman," then some part of the Wagnerian component in him must have been transmitted also.

For all that the residual repertory shows little evidence of it, this was a time of intense operatic creativity in Paris, much of it *wagnérienne.* Some who participated in it—Saint-Saëns, Chabrier, Chausson, Massenet—have already been mentioned. Others included Lalo, Ernest

---

[6] Cooper: *French Music,* p. 66.
[7] Ibid., p. 54.
[8] Ibid., p. 42. D'Indy attribution: *Grove's,* V, 623.
[9] Ibid., p. 43. [1] Ibid., p. 117.

Reyer (who, as a youth, was very close to Berlioz), and D'Indy. The compositional career of D'Indy is now recalled for such orchestral works as the *Symphony on a French Mountain Air* and the *Istar Variations*, but he also invested considerable time in the creation of a French *Meistersinger* (for the concert hall) entitled *Le Chant de la cloche*, a Parsifalish *Fervaal*, and an equally Wagner-influenced *L'Étranger*.[2]

Further cataloguing would be pointless, for the Wagnerian tide had now (1890) reached flood stage and crested in France. Its momentum had carried Debussy, then twenty-six, to Bayreuth in 1888 and again in 1889. It was also in 1889 that Gallic emotional response to the appeal of Wagner attained its highest pitch. In the emotional continuity of Chabrier and Chausson as well as the musical continuity of Wagner, the gifted but short-lived Guillaume Lekeu fainted at the end of the *Tristan* prelude and had to be carried from the Festspielhaus.[3]

Among those who had been exposed somewhat sooner to the Wagnerian virus and were now beginning to hear, as well as see, somewhat more clearly, the recession had already set it. As the cultists became entrenched with their official publication, the *Revue wagnérienne*, and snobbish regulations were propounded for qualifying as a member of the True Faith (1884), the more humorful French expressed themselves in ways that came naturally to them. Chabrier shattered the solemnity with his *Quadrille sur les principaux motifs de Tristan et Yseult* (for pianoforte duet) in 1887, to be echoed by the gales of laughter aroused by Erik Satie's parodistic *Le Fils des étoiles* in 1891.

That this alteration of emphasis coincided with the introduction of Russian music to Paris on a large scale[4] in the *Exposition universelle* concerts of Rimsky-Korsakov in 1889 (see p. 143) was not wholly accidental. Twenty-five years is the customary measurement of time for a generation, and just about that period had elapsed since the first "mention" of *Tristan* in the *Mignon* overture of 1865. Not only for the teen-aged Ravel, but also for the older Satie and Debussy, the greater simplicity, the more extroverted expressions of the Russians provided a new source of identity and interest. There was, also, something natively French in it which may have been Russified, but could, and would, be repatriated.

It would be reasonable to assume, from the foregoing pages, that

---

[2] Ibid., p. 118.

[3] Ibid., p. 56. (Author is quoting Paul Landormy.)

[4] Jules-Étienne Pasdeloup, conductor of the pioneering *Concerts populaires*, included works of Mussorgsky and Rimsky-Korsakov in his programs of 1878.

the Wagnerian debacle at the Opéra's production of *Tannhäuser* in 1861 had long since been reversed, that his works were as familiar to the French public as they were to the composers. Factually, as may be deduced from earlier citations, there was little source of stage experience for them in France. The Wagner performances on which the composers nourished their enthusiasm were almost wholly in Munich or Bayreuth. In the concert hall, the enterprising Pasdeloup was no less mindful of the interests of Wagner than he was of those of Berlioz or Mussorgsky and Rimsky-Korsakov. In the concerts he conducted at the Cirque d'Hiver, the *Tannhäuser*[5] overture was performed amid "wild commotion" in March 1865. However, when he ventured the *Meistersinger* overture in 1870 it was "hooted from beginning to end." (The Franco-Prussian War was a fresh memory.) He tried again in 1873 with the funeral music from *Götterdämmerung*, but with no greater success. At length, in 1879, he won a real triumph for Wagner, with the first act of—*Lohengrin*.[6]

Between 1869, when *Rienzi* was given under Pasdeloup's direction at the Théâtre-Lyrique, and 1887, no Wagner opera was performed in full in Paris, though New York had by then heard *Tristan, Meistersinger,* and the *Ring* on stage and much of *Parsifal* in the concert hall. And then it was not at the Opéra (where what is universally known as the "Paris" version of *Tannhäuser* continued to be excluded), but at the Théâtre-Eden. The work was—*Lohengrin*. Says Louis Reynaud:

"This performance was an apotheosis, and on the next day Paris had a new idol, Wagner. His name was on everybody's lips. This infatuation approached the limits of frenzy . . . Scenes took place which until then had been the mark of religious fanaticism."[7] Still, the major works of Wagner became realities to Parisians only at a measured pace: *Walküre* in 1893, *Fliegende Holländer* and *Meistersinger* in 1899, *Siegfried* and *Götterdämmerung* in 1909. It was not until 1911 that the *Ring* was performed in sequence for the Paris public. *Parsifal* was staged as soon as practicable, when the restriction that had limited its presentation to the Bayreuth Festspielhaus was rescinded in 1914 by Wagner's heirs.

Typically, and not unexpectedly, by the time Wagner became an obsession with the French public, he had ceased to be a stimulus for the composers—consciously, at any rate. What was *dernier cri* for the

[5] Adolphe Jullien: *Richard Wagner* (Boston: J. B. Millet Co.; 1892), II, 416.
[6] Ibid., II, 417.
[7] *L'Influence allemande en France au XVIII et au XIX siècle.* Quoted by Jean-Pierre Barricelli and Leo Weinstein in *Ernest Chausson*, p. 16.

the masses was *passé* for the upper classes, a not altogether uncommon distinction between those who are "in," aesthetically, and those who are "out." Unmistakably, however, the taking to heart of Wagner, and specifically of *Tristan,* by the French composers who matured between 1865 and 1885 is a phenomenon rarely matched by any other work in the affections of so supersensitive a coterie of musicians. None of them shared Berlioz's aggravated antagonism to *enharmonie;* and many of them derived sustenance, impulse, or direction for their own work from the experience.

Even when the tide of fashion had passed and the accomplishment of Wagner was subject to a gigantic and unreasoning reaction, the affection remained. In the secret heart of more than a few, it continued to vibrate long afterward, if only in such a wry cross-reference as may be found in the middle of Debussy's *Golliwog's Cakewalk.* Only one who had served, and survived, an apprenticeship to the sorcerer could make a joke of his countrymen's obsession, a sound trait of national humor widely recognized. The Frenchman's head still ruled his no-matter-how-susceptible heart.

3

OR, PERHAPS, IT IS AN INSTANCE, on a national scale, of an encounter that could be likened to Byron's formulation:

> Man's love is of man's life a thing apart;
> 'Tis woman's whole existence.

In this parallel, the French would play the male part in the love affair with Wagner, with the composer's own compatriots (those from the Elbe to the Danube who speak the same language) in the female role.

Taken altogether, the Wagnerian communication to the French, if more immediately persuasive than it was to any others elsewhere, tended toward the superficial rather than the profound. Chausson was disturbed and distressed to discover how deep his Wagnerism ran, but he managed to do the best work of which he was capable. Massenet appropriated as much of Wagner's procedure as served to make his music *à la mode,* but he was wise enough not to burden himself with its substance. Duparc, Chabrier, Franck, and D'Indy took Wagner into their continuity in varying degrees and with diverse results. None, however, suffered so violent a reaction that he was impelled to overthrow the existing language and set up a new-sounding one of his own, with its guarantees of individuality. That remained for one who was, so he thought, acting on behalf of "German music" and was nominally at least Wagner's compatriot.

Such a development was, however, still some years in the distance, when the Wagnerian tide began to rise in Central Europe. At first those who profited from the liberating effect of Wagner's example were primarily composers for the concert hall—Dvořák, Bruckner, Mahler, Wolf, and Richard Strauss. Whereas the French affair was mostly with *Tristan* and its idiom, the German inclination ranged more broadly. As previously indicated (p. 148), the overpowering attraction might be to one work and in much smaller degree to any other, or to a single period of Wagner's life's work and to nothing before or after it. Eventually there came to be a kind of continental divide separating those who were responsive only to *Tristan* and those whose attraction was to everything but *Tristan*. All the influence on the *Tristan* side flowed in one particular current; that on the other side sought out many different channels to pursue and wholly different streams of thought to rejoin, regenerate, and redirect.

The omission of Johannes Brahms from the group of composers cited above may appear, merely, a natural consequence of his known dislike for some of Wagner's music. However, there is much to prove that Brahms did not consider himself the "leader of the opposition," as some of his more fanatical supporters did. His awareness of Wagner's work was both keen and appreciative, his reaction to it a special case that merits some exposition of its own.

Unlike Verdi, who once wrote to a correspondent: "In my home there is almost no music, I've never gone to a music library or to a publisher to look at a piece of music . . . ,"[8] Brahms was a lifelong devotee of the works of others, from Johann Sebastian Bach to Johann Strauss, and not excluding Richard Wagner. He cherished the original manuscript of the revised Venusberg scene from *Tannhäuser*, which had been given to him by Karl Tausig (who had acquired it from Cornelius, who had had no more authority to give it away than Tausig had). Brahms resisted several suggestions from mutual friends that he return the manuscript to Wagner. When the latter finally made a direct request for its return, Brahms offered to exchange it for a full score of *Die Meistersinger*. This not being available (1875), he finally settled for a *de luxe* edition of *Das Rheingold*, autographed.[9]

[8] *Verdi*, ed. Werfel and Stefan, p. 261.
[9] Ernest Newman: *The Life of Richard Wagner* (New York: Alfred A. Knopf; 1937), III, 471.

Brahms was a lifelong collecter of manuscripts, and his attachment to the revised Venusberg scene may be attributed by some to an unwillingness to part with a property of some value. But his attitude toward his older contemporary was steadily objective, and selective. He never visited Bayreuth, but he sent a wreath to the bereaved family at Wagner's death. Something about his attitude may be derived from his letters (though one has the impression, now and then, that he is tempering his views to avoid offending such known anti-Wagnerites and dear friends as Clara Schumann and Elisabeth von Herzogenberg). Much more can be gathered from Brahms's comments to a musican he thought well of and wanted to have think well of him. This was Georg Henschel, a frequent vocal soloist with Brahms before he became the first conductor of the Boston Symphony Orchestra. They spent a holiday together on the island of Rügen in the Baltic Sea in July 1876, and Henschel later published his recollections of their conversations.[1] Prompted by Henschel's expressions of admiration for the first act of *Walküre* and for *Siegfried*, Brahms replied: "Certainly these are fine things . . . what you have hummed [the Renunciation of Love theme] is no doubt beautiful; and when Siegmund . . . pulls the sword out of the tree, that's fine, too: but it would, in my opinion be *really* powerful and carry one away if it all concerned, let us say, young Bonaparte or some other hero who stands nearer to our sensibilities."[2] When Henschel questioned Brahms on his possible attendance at the first Bayreuth Festival later that summer, the latter pleaded: "It's too expensive." Brahms added that he had heard *Rheingold* and *Walküre* "repeatedly" in Munich, and that Bayreuth would "greatly interest" him. But he resisted the temptation both during Wagner's lifetime and after his death.

Later in their stay at Rügen, *Götterdämmerung* was a subject of discussion. Henschel relates that he brought the score to their meeting place on the beach, and Brahms crossly queried: "*Why* did you bring it to me?" (Henschel vows: "He had particularly asked for it.") "The thing interests and fascinates one," Brahms observed, "and yet, properly speaking, it is not always pleasant. With the 'Tristan' score it is different. If I look at that in the morning, I am cross for the rest of the day . . ."

Not being quite sure what Brahms meant, Henschel later asked Brahms's friend and biographer Max Kalbeck for clarification. He was

---

[1] Georg Henschel: *Personal Recollections of Johannes Brahms* (Boston: The Gorham Press; 1897).
[2] Ibid., p. 37.

told: "We know from personal experience that Brahms, although warmly acknowledging the many musical beauties of the work, had a particular dislike for 'Tristan.' " When Henschel left with the intention of visiting Bayreuth for the opening festival, Brahms asked him to write: "I know you will rave about it and I don't blame you. I myself must confess that 'Walküre' and 'Götterdämmerung' have a great hold on me. For 'Rheingold' and 'Siegfried' I do not particularly care. If only I knew what became of the Ring and what Wagner meant by it! Perhaps the Cross?"

It is know that Brahms referred to himself as "the best of all Wagnerians," a remark some have been tempted to interpret humorously. It is more likely that Brahms meant it quite literally, to judge from a comment passed on by Richard Heuberger, who, as a young composer in the 1870's, frequently visited Brahms: "Those understand *nothing* of the real Wagner who are led astray by him. Wagner's is one of the clearest heads that ever existed in the world."[3]

Likewise Brahms, where intoxication on the elixir of Wagner was concerned. He was so solidly formed in the continuity of Beethoven, Schumann, and Schubert (the last also came later) at so early a point in his career that no external influence could deflect him from the direction in which he moved throughout his life. There were, to be sure, reactions to stimuli he encountered along the way—newly discovered works of Schubert, including the B-minor Symphony, previously unpublished music of Bach and Mozart—but they were, for the most part, those to which, in a sense, he was pre-conditioned.

A conspicuous reaction to musical stimulation is cited by Hans Gal.[4] In the immediate aftermath of Robert Schumann's attempt to drown himself in the Rhine in 1854, Brahms heard Beethoven's Ninth Symphony "for the first time" (in Cologne). Says Gal: "The feelings of his lacerated soul and the chaotic mood of catastrophe which he sensed in the first movement of the Ninth Symphony gave rise to an eruptive inspiration: the opening theme of the D-minor piano concerto . . ." It is a curious, revealing incident in the whole chain of continuity that the D-minor Concerto itself entered powerfully into the development of a later composer, thus asserting the parental influence of Beethoven twice removed (p. 186).

After a long, sometimes arduous application to the orchestral music of Brahms, I can instance not more than two passages that suggest

[3] Florence May: *Life of Brahms* (London: William Reeves; 1905), II, 518.
[4] Hans Gal: *Johannes Brahms, His Work and Personality* (New York: Alfred A. Knopf; 1963), p. 111.

an unconscious reproduction of some typical expression of Wagner. One may be heard in the second movement of the Symphony No. 4, some eleven measures before its end. Here, at the beginning of the coda, where a moment of quiet is desired, the voice of Brahms speaks with the tongue of Wagner as the low strings sustain an organ point, the violins whisper in tremolo thirds, and the clarinets above them, also in thirds, bring to mind Brünnhilde and *Götterdämmerung* (after Siegfried's departure).

The other instance relates much more to procedure than to substance, and thus may have been quite purposeful. It comes at the peroration of the *Academic Festival Overture,* and, with its brass and percussion flourishes, arouses a resonant recollection of the *Meistersinger* overture. It could also be said that as both works are in C major, and Brahms chose to solidify everything that had preceded with a plagal cadence (the fourth, or F-major chord, to the tonic, C) as Wagner had (measures 8–7–6–5 before the double bar), the resemblance could hardly be avoided. At the same time, he may have been *predisposed* to the effect from familiarity with *Die Meistersinger* (see pp. 164–167).

At the only other point at which they overlap—the slow movement of Brahms's opus 5 Sonata and the phrase to which Hans Sachs sings the words *"Dem Vogel, der heut' sang"*[5] in Act II of *Die Meistersinger* —it is clearly the voice of *Das deutsche Volkslied* that resounds in both (see p. 168).

4

IN THE CASE OF ANOTHER COMPOSER, born nearly ten years before Brahms, the list of allusions is as long as it is fascinating. Anton Bruckner is perhaps unique among all those who come and go in this chronicle in the extent to which he was physically and emotionally attached to the man he also considered his spiritual mentor. He earned his place among the most devout of Wagnerites by such acts of faith as the dedication of his Third Symphony to the *Meister,* repeated pilgrimages to Bayreuth, and the adoption, for symphonic purposes, of the *Wagnertuben* almost as soon as they had been created for the *Ring* orchestra, even before he glorified the memory of his idol in the adagio of his Seventh Symphony. These, however, were only a few of the manifestations that entered into the complex process by which Bruckner's musical personality was molded.

Though he was only nine years Wagner's junior, Bruckner revered

[5] G. Schirmer piano score, p. 217.

(*continued*)

Wagner: Die Meistersinger, *overture*

(continued)

Brahms: Academic Festival Overture

Brahms: Piano Sonata No. 3, F minor (op. 5)

Wagner: Die Meistersinger, Act III

him as one might a towering figure of a prior generation. Bruckner was still a church organist in Linz, taking lessons in composition at thirty-five, when Wagner completed *Tristan* in 1859. He did not, indeed, fall under the Wagnerian spell until he was nearly forty and had ventured his first orchestral work, an overture in G minor which suggests a Schumann-Mendelssohn orientation. Even Beethoven's symphonies were not a meaningful reality to Bruckner until he heard the Ninth for the first time in 1867.[6]

It is to another source that one must turn for the idioms and concepts that entered into the kind of symphonist that Bruckner became.

[6] J. F. Redlich: *Bruckner and Mahler* (London: J. M. Dent and Sons; 1955), p. 79.

That is the church music which was his primary, almost his exclusive, concern between 1848, when he became organist in the Stift (Seminary) of his native St. Florian, and 1868, when he left a similar but much more important position in Linz to become teacher of theory and organ at the Conservatory in Vienna.

Unlike almost all other symphonists in the long line from Haydn to Brahms (always excepting Berlioz), Bruckner was not conditioned in his early musical development by innumerable exercises in the disciplines of sonata form (sonatas, quartets, etc.). Rather, he wrote psalms, Masses, and Magnificats, either *a cappella* or with organ and orchestra (the means depended, of course, on the forces available for a given occasion). It is, perhaps, for this very reason that when he was impelled toward the creation of symphonies, the results were as different, in their way, from those of his predecessors as those of Berlioz were from those of *his* predecessors.

Among the Masses of Bruckner's immediate pre-symphonic period, there is particular interest in the D-minor of 1864 and the F-minor of 1867–8. Both are sizeable creations in the symphonic-Mass sequence of Haydn, Mozart, Beethoven, and Schubert (there is no reason to suppose that he knew the *Grande Messe des morts* or any other work of Berlioz). The first followed immediately on his hearing *Tannhäuser* in 1863, an experience that he considered one of the most influential of his life. It was performed in Linz under the direction of his mentor (Otto Kitzler), who followed it, a year later, with *The Flying Dutchman* and *Lohengrin*. The first effect on Bruckner was not so much toward emulation as to liberation from the "scholastic chains" of Sechter and others, a confirmation, through Wagner's "extended use of chromatics and enharmonies," of impulses that Bruckner had suppressed through deference to his teachers.[7]

Through the blessed virtue of hindsight as well as the comparative analysis made possible by recordings (and scores) one can see in the later portions of the D-minor Mass (beginning with *"Et resurrexit"*) the shape of Bruckner's symphonic movements to come. Were the vocal parts of the *Benedictus* to be consolidated with the instrumental, and the whole performed by an orchestra, the result would be very close to some of his later symphonic movements. In it are many of the devices—the build-up through repetition of a short phrase, the sudden pauses and dramatic contrasts of volume, the approach that proves to

---

[7] Werner Wolff: *Anton Bruckner, Rustic Genius* (New York: E. P. Dutton; 1942), pp. 45–6. The quotations are derived from Max Auer: *Anton Bruckner, sein Leben und Werk* (Vienna: Musikwissenschaftlicher Verlag; 1934).

be only an approach and not a climax—whose understanding is essential to an understanding of Bruckner's personal sense of structure.

As Redlich makes clear in his invaluable commentary, there are excellent reasons why the first three symphonies in the sequence of nine may be called Bruckner's "Mass symphonies." They are transitional not only in spirit and texture, but also in thematic content. No. 1 draws on the E-minor Mass; No. 2 chooses elements from the F-minor Mass (No. 3), as well it might, for it contains much distinguished music. No. 3, the earliest of Bruckner's symphonies still performed with some frequency, attains a point in the first movement which "finally trails off mysteriously into a quotation from the 'Miserere' section of the D minor Mass."[8]

Clearly these are elements hitherto regarded as alien to the symphonic continuity (save, perhaps, as Mendelssohn cites hymnal matter in his "Reformation" Symphony). But they do not, by any means, exhaust the varied, unusual factors that entered into Bruckner's concept of the symphony. There is, as early as the first, in C minor (begun in 1865), an opening movement of a macabre march character (prophetic of a mood that Mahler was to make his own twenty-five years later). The same work contains a scherzo with the hammering rhythmic insistence so characteristic of scherzos in later Bruckner symphonies. Were these strokes of startling originality self-generated by the modest-mannered organist, or do they warn of Bruckner's familiarity with musical sources not commonly associated with him? Between 1857 and 1861 Bruckner went repeatedly to Vienna for lessons with Sechter. Whether he heard such works as Schubert's C-major ("Great") Symphony and Beethoven's *Missa solemnis* during these visits, one can only conjecture. But a recently published letter[9] from Bruckner to a correspondent interested in his study years defines the number of these visits as "one or two" a year, each lasting "six to seven weeks," which would permit much extracurricular listening. Dangerous as it would be to derive conclusions from conjectures, it would be even greater folly to assume, as sure evidence of Bruckner's impulses in the 1860's and 1870's, passages that appear in works he revised twenty years later.

The issue, in any case, is not how Bruckner came to be what he was at the beginning of his artistic journey, but how he arrived at his eventual destination. Among the forces that propelled him on his way, one of the most powerful, without question, was the Wagner orchestra

[8] Redlich: *Bruckner and Mahler*, p. 57.
[9] *The Musician's World*, ed. Hans Gal (New York: Arco Publishing Company; 1966), p. 327.

itself. In my view, Bruckner did not turn to the Wagner orchestra for purposes of writing symphonies: he turned to the symphony because it was—for one lacking any disposition to the opera house—the one, the only, way he could make use of the intoxicating sound on which he had become quite drunk.

As Bruckner's acquaintance with the works of Wagner broadened and deepened (he was a regular attendant at the *premières* beginning with *Tristan* in 1865), so did his enthusiasm for this fantastic sound source, this super organ. He poured into the symphonies not only the ideas and procedures he had devised for his sacred music, but also the devotional impulse itself (No. 9 bears the inscription "To the dear Lord"). Indeed, after the symphonic sequence began in earnest, Bruckner wrote only two large-scale sacred works with orchestra, both (the *Te Deum* of 1881–2 and the Psalm CL of 1892) at the urging of others.

Lack of knowledge-in-depth of Bruckner's listening experience in the years prior to his exposure to Wagner is one reason for treading warily where "influences" and lines of continuity are concerned. Another relates to the special character of the Bruckner-Wagner relationship. It is, in many instances, questionable whether, in reproducing a segment of Wagner's thought or pursuing a line of his procedure to the point at which it almost becomes quotation, Bruckner is rendering homage consciously or unconsciously.

Both impulses, one is inclined to think, enter into the Third Symphony, whose majestic opening phrase for the trumpet won Wagner's permission for Bruckner to dedicate the work to him. In the first version (1873), Bruckner indulged in a number of quotations from *Tristan* and *Walküre*. They disappeared before the revision of 1876, which provided the text performed at the *première* in Vienna the following year. But it would have been quite impossible to delete the reminiscences of the *Tannhäuser* Bacchanale, the brass fanfares à *la Lohengrin*, or the ascent to Valhalla in the last movement without destroying important pillars on which the work rests.

What this first of regularly performed Bruckner symphonies tells us about the six symphonies to follow is at once dependable and misleading. As in almost all his first movements, the Bruckner of the D-minor may be described as a composer of magnificent beginnings. He was compulsive in exposition and commanding in peroration; but the expanses between are sometimes interminable not merely for the length of time they occupy, but also for the tedious pace at which musical ground is covered. Rather than being developed, the basic thought is mauled and mulled, rolled about and kneaded, but rarely given new direction, fresh purpose, or stimulating re-appraisal. Too often one has the feeling that the mere sounding and resounding of the choirs of the orchestra connote, to Bruckner, the kind of interest his predecessors felt obliged to provide through organic growth.

This point becomes of absorbing interest at the moment (measures 590–600 of the first movement) when Bruckner introduces an ostinato on the notes, D, C, B, B flat, A. This crawling, serpentine figure around

Bruckner: Symphony No. 3, D minor, first movement

the key tones of D minor does well enough what Bruckner wants it to do: to generate a kind of excitement desirable at that point. But it fails to do what Beethoven achieved with much the same pattern when he originated them for a similar point in the first movement of his D-minor Symphony (measure 513): to convey, out of what had preceded, a sense of organic growth, to make these notes the inevitable, logical, exalting fulfillment of the whole grinding process of structural evolution.

Either the choice of D minor for this Third Symphony or the

Beethoven: Symphony No. 9, D minor, second movement

trumpet call on the tones of its tonic chord might be cited as evidences of Bruckner's response to the great work of Beethoven which he had heard for the first time a few years before. They could also be described as accidental likenesses or coincidences. But it is quite clear from the reference to Beethoven's ostinato that Bruckner was calling upon a work of his greatest predecessor to aid him *in tiefer Not.*

This may be the first instance in Bruckner of his response to a work whose enormous influence on Berlioz, Wagner, and Brahms has already been cited, but it was far from the last. Indeed, as Bruckner proceeded with tenacity and determination to repeat the symphonic process (as he understood it) time and time again, it becomes unmistakably evident, in conjunction with his orientation to church music and his intoxication with the Wagner orchestra, that the Holy Ghost of Bruckner's trinity was the Ninth Symphony of Beethoven. It took Bruckner a decade and more (between the conception of his Third Symphony in 1873 and that of his Eighth in 1884) to overcome the attraction to Beethoven's substance and to absorb the lessons of procedure suitable to his own substance.

It has been said of Tchaikovsky that he wrote three symphonies—bearing numbers 4, 5, and 6. It could be said of Bruckner that he, too, wrote three symphonies—bearing numbers 7, 8, and 9. The opening of No. 7 is as much if no more "a magnificent beginning" than that of No. 3, but it comes to vastly greater results for the simplest of reasons. It takes its departure from the Beethoven impulse in Bruckner by means of a *theme* rather than, as No. 3 does, from the Wagnerian disposition to a *motive*. The difference is, of course, that a theme can be developed whereas a motive can only be altered or transformed. Now, when he subjects a phrase to a violent curtailment (as at the end of the exposition in the first movement), it sounds like the tread of Bruckner in full stride rather than the fluttering of Isolde's scarf.

As well as tending to work more with themes that can be developed than with motives that can only be altered or transformed, the last three symphonies show better judgment on Bruckner's part as to what constitutes a proper *Gesangsperiode* (his own term for what had been conventionally characterized as the second "lyrical" subject of a sonata allegro movement). It is no longer a trivial appendage to a majestic opening statement, but an idea qualified to participate in a build-up that mounts in meaning as well as in volume. At the beginning of the adagio, when he uses the three *Wagnertuben* for the first time, Bruckner proves himself worthy not only of their Wagnerian associations, but also of their expressive implications. The lilting melody that follows the opening statement is clearly designed to fulfill the function of a similar acceleration in the adagio of Beethoven's Ninth, but the treatment of it is Bruckner's own (as Beethoven's response to what was described as "the Mozart effect" on p. 18 was his own). As if to solidify

Bruckner: Symphony No. 7, E, adagio

Beethoven: Symphony No. 9, D minor, ~~scherzo~~ adagio

his sense of singularity, his feeling that he now can use the means of Wagner to speak the language of Beethoven with the tongue of Bruckner, he brings in a reference to the *"Non confundat"* motive from his *Te Deum*[1] in a brilliantly sonorous proclamation of identity.

The scherzo of the Seventh Symphony is easily the best of those written up to that time by Bruckner. It is tight, compact, and, above all, laid out in a thematic pattern that lends itself perfectly to interplay and overlapping of the kind for which Bruckner's contrapuntal skills were ideally suited. Bruckner's purpose in the finale, clearly, is to make a merger of all that has preceded, in a final rounding-out of the symphonic sequence that would embody all the implications of Beethoven's "Rejection" section of No. 9. He comes within a shout of his goal, but it is the shout's repetition rather than realization that thwarts the listener of the expected fulfillment—or, at least, thwarts *this* listener. For, at the very end, the columnar files of brass fanfares welcome us not to Brucknerland, but to a suburb of Valhalla.

Several things of immeasurable importance happened to Bruckner between the completion of No. 7 in 1883 and the composition of No. 8 between 1884 and 1887. He heard *Parsifal* for the first time, being among those privileged in 1883 to attend the rehearsal before the first performance (his enthusiastic applause was silenced by Wagner himself).[2] Later that year, Wagner died in Venice. Finally, almost at the end of 1884, Bruckner's Seventh Symphony was performed in Vienna, and for the first time (at sixty) he had something to be described as a popular success.

Each happening had its influence on the Eighth Symphony. In the aftermath of the *Parsifal* experience, his requirements included eight horns; the harp was admitted to his symphonic community; and other areas grew commensurately. He now had the confidence born of being the Wagner disciple with the longest, strongest claim to the rank of successor and public endorsement of the right to make such a claim. Finally, he conceived a structural change that brought him closer to the inner logic as well as to the outer compulsion of Beethoven's Ninth Symphony than any predecessor had approached.

This was the interchange of sections by which the scherzo of the Eighth became the second movement of the symphonic sequence and the adagio the third, an order of succession pioneered by Beethoven in his final symphony. This may seem a procedure of but limited sig-

[1] Redlich: *Bruckner and Mahler*, p. 99.
[2] Erwin Doernberg: *The Life and Symphonies of Anton Bruckner* (London: Barrie and Rockliff; 1960), p. 86.

nificance, but it brought about several important consequences for Bruckner. The first was to draw tighter the circle of his affinity with Beethoven. It symbolized, for anyone who cared to draw the analogy— as I am drawing it here—that he now felt himself able to accomplish the emotional transition from the depths to the heights without the intermediation of the "earthly" scherzo (the analogy Berlioz used in trying to explain why the Funeral March in the *"Eroica"* was followed by a scherzo). Moreover, it set his great gift for spinning a long, leisurely lyric sequence in a position where it had maximum effect. Finally, it renewed his interest in the challenge of the symphonic structure and showed greater confidence in his ability to dominate it.

Perhaps he would have closed the circle even more tightly had he gone a step farther and followed his adagio with a choral finale. There is some sentiment to the belief that this was part of his intent in his own uncompleted Ninth. That is the position of those who interpret a marking of *Te Deum* on the manuscript's incomplete finale as indicative of vocal participation. Others[3] point to the presence in the sketch of a quotation from his existing *Te Deum* and surmise that Bruckner meant to relate the other content of the movement to a monumental proclamation of *Te Deum laudamus* as instrumental counterpoint. In this way he would make unmistakably graphic his emotional attachment "To the Dear Lord," to whom the Ninth is inscribed.

Death intervened before Bruckner could complete his plan, whatever it may have been. It is now customary to conclude the work with the third movement—which, through the alteration of plan introduced for the Eighth and perpetuated for the Ninth, has exquisite applicability. With the scherzo again second, what comes to the ear last in Bruckner's final symphony is not a tempestuous effort to shout the Lord's praise in a voice louder, almost, than any man could discipline, but the consoling murmur of faith, dying away in as profound an adagio as he ever wrote. Why, within it, Bruckner chose to embody a quotation from Wagner's *Faust Overture* is at best a rhetorical question: no answer is known. But it is at least a possibility that Bruckner knew from Wagner himself, if not from the privately published *Mein Leben,* that the *Meister,* too, owed a monumental debt to the Choral Symphony and its creator (see p. 67).

At the end we are left not in a suburb of Valhalla or, as in No. 8, on a plateau overlooking Parsifal's Montsalvat, but in Brucknerland itself, where the composer's quest for identity and his obedience to the compulsions of continuity had led him not only to create a work of

[3] Redlich: *Bruckner and Mahler,* p. 104.

Bruckner: Symphony No. 9, D minor, adagio

profound beauty, but also to evolve thoughts such as one which "strongly affected the aural imagination of a whole generation of Austrian composers during the first quarter of this century."[4]

5

ALMOST AT THE SAME TIME as Bruckner was resolving the problem of his identity *vis-à-vis* the influence of Wagner, forces were coming into existence that would carry the influence of Wagner to those who could not go to Bayreuth itself. (That is to say, the influence of Wagner as contained in those works which were, as yet, beyond the resources of most theaters elsewhere.) The mechanism was the formation of the Angelo Neumann Opera Company in the early 1880's to tour the *Ring* through Europe.

Its birth had several, rather than merely two, progenitors. One was Wagner's need to raise money to proceed with a repertory of his works at Bayreuth after the introductory *Ring* of 1876; another was the composer's desire to have the young tenor Georg Unger perfect his performance of Siegfried through repetition; a third was the ambition of Angelo Neumann, a Herald in the *Lohengrin* performances of 1862 in Vienna and director of the Leipzig Opera since 1876, to produce the *Ring* in the city of Wagner's birth.

His approach to Wagner for loan of equipment from Bayreuth for the purpose was sympathetically received. For a series of reasons, it

4 Ibid., p. 102.

was spring 1878 before a beginning could be made with *Das Rheingold* and *Die Walküre*. A large share of the credit for success of the venture went to Bayreuth's energetic young "second conductor," Artur Nikisch, then thirty-three. As plans went forward for the performance of *Siegfried* and *Götterdämmerung* later in the year, the Leipzig management heeded Nikisch's urging to take on another of the young musicians clustering around Wagner as copyists, *répétiteurs*, etc., Anton Seidl.[5]

From the success of the Leipzig venture emerged a plan for presentation of the *Ring* in Berlin in 1880 and, finally, the larger scheme for a grand "Wandering Wagner Opera Company"[6] in which Nikisch and Seidl were joined as conductors by another celebrity-to-be, Felix Mottl. London followed in 1882, then Rome, Brussels, Amsterdam, and Prague (but not Paris). The composer's death in 1883 decreed a pause, but neither interruption nor cessation of the work to which Wagner attached so much importance and from which solid earnings flowed.

With older artists replaced and newer ones added, the wanderers wandered on: to Budapest, to Königsberg, to Trieste. Then came an interlude as Neumann, who had established a solid reputation as an *entrepreneur* as well as a theater man, took time out for new duties in Bremen. Also, as he writes: "Each town where we had given the 'Nibelung' now eagerly clamored for the rights to presentations"[7] on its own. Neumann was also involved with a project to establish a German opera theater in Prague (when Anton Seidl, his first conductor, left in 1885 to begin his famous Wagnerian work at the Metropolitan in New York, the replacement Neumann hired was Gustav Mahler, then twenty-five).

But Neumann could not ignore one persistent request. That was to organize a Wagner company for a tour of Russia. When this was finally arranged in 1889, his other conductorial discoveries were busy elsewhere. But there was, active in Prague, the thirty-nine-year-old Karl Muck, who agreed to go along. Many of the choral and orchestral performers at the Maryinsky Theatre in St. Petersburg were German, and they put themselves out to impress the visiting celebrities from "home." In Neumann's opinion, the result of the two cycles at the Maryinsky in March 1889 "compared most favorably with Bayreuth."[8] A visit to Moscow followed in April.

A sampling of opinion from the musicians who listened and learned in the cities visited by the Neumann companies between 1878 and

[5] Angelo Neumann: *Personal Recollections of Wagner* (New York: Henry Holt and Company; 1909), pp. 70–5.
[6] Ibid., p. 193.   [7] Ibid., p. 193.   [8] Ibid., pp. 311–12.

1889 would add immeasurably to the scope of this inquiry. It does not, as far as I have been able to discover, exist. But the impressions of one important listener at the performances in St. Petersburg do exist, and can be cited. Writing in *My Musical Life*, Rimsky-Korsakov recalled the visit of 1889 in these words: "All musical St. Petersburg was interested. Glazunov and I attended the rehearsals, following them score in hand. Muck—an excellent conductor—rehearsed Wagner's works with great care. Our orchestra strove with all their hearts and surprised Muck with their ability in quickly grasping and mastering whatever he demanded." Then, he adds: "Wagner's method of orchestration struck Glazunov and me, and thenceforth Wagner's devices gradually began to form a part of our orchestral tricks of the trade."[9]

Several details in Rimsky's remarks prompt comment. One: the enthusiasm nurtured by Berlioz a score of years before had given rise to musicians now sufficiently sophisticated to appreciate Wagner's additions to their craft. Two: these perceptions had developed since the visit of Wagner himself in 1863. Three: the full appreciation of Wagner's contribution came not from looking at the score alone, but from consulting it in conjunction with the sound of the music.

In his refreshingly candid recollections, Rimsky cites (on the same page) the manner in which this newfound knowledge was put to use: "The first application of Wagner's orchestral methods and of an increased orchestra [in the wind choir] was made in my orchestration of the Polish dance from *Boris Godunov* for concert performance." Noting that Mussorgsky had originally treated it for strings alone in a simulation of Lully and had then recast it when it failed to make the effect he desired, Rimsky says: "Yet in its music, the Polonaise was characteristic and beautiful: for this reason I undertook to turn it into a concert piece, the more so as *Boris Godunov* was no longer on the boards. I linger on this intrinsically lesser opus of mine because I attach importance to it as being my first essay in the new field of orchestration that I had entered therewith."

And, as affirmation of the alteration in taste noted above, Rimsky writes that among others to whom the Wagnerian experience was decisive was "V. V. Yastrebtsev, an ardent admirer of mine. During the first years of our intimacy he was also a violent Berliozist. Subsequently this passion of his died down considerably and gave way to a worship of Wagner."[1] This was the enthusiast to whom Rimsky confided the

[9] N. A. Rimsky-Korsakov: *My Musical Life* (New York: Alfred A. Knopf; 1923), p. 251.
[1] Ibid., p. 263.

remark "In Chopin you will find many of the real roots of contemporary music" (page 62).

Attracted though he was to the new resources of Wagner and eager as he was to make their procedures part of his own, Rimsky had pressing business of other sorts to take his mind from composition in 1889. This was the *Exposition universelle* in June at which (pp. 143–4) the musicians and musical public of Paris were aurally dazzled by the sunburst of Russian orchestral sound embodied in the works of composers from Glinka to Glazunov. But even as the French were gathering sources of new momentum from the Russians, so the principal Russian, Rimsky-Korsakov, was deriving new stimulus from a German.

It was to carry his career to a commanding climax, not only in the creation of such operas to come as *Mlada, Tsar Saltan*, and *Le Coq d'or*, but also in broadening the knowledge he was able to impart to those who came to study with him or who absorbed his wisdom at second hand through the *Principles of Instrumentation* (begun in 1896, published in 1908, the year of his death). Among the former were such successors to the "Mighty Heap" as Liadov, Ippolitov-Ivanov, Gretchaninoff, Glazunov, and Stravinsky.

Thus, through time, circulation, and combination, those impelling forces of continuity which had come together thirty or so years before in violent action and reaction were now diffused and separated. Through their effect on those who added substance of their own to the procedures of others, or *vice versa,* new, refined strains of continuity had come into being. The old projection of affinities which suggested that Chopin and Berlioz were in opposition, or that a choice had to be made for Wagner and against Brahms gave way to fresh appraisals and new attitudes in which one could be "for" Chopin as well as Brahms, or for both Wagner and Berlioz, or even Brahms and Wagner. Whether induced by accident or cultivated by plan, absorption of one led to susceptibility to another. As time passed, it became increasingly apparent that what nourished interest in youth also fed curiosity in adolescence and enlarged the mental appetite in manhood. This, in turn, enabled the fully formed adult to formulate his own combination of tastes, develop his own fulfilling mental and spiritual diet, and pass on the result of his selective judgment to others in a cycle whose rhythm of action and reaction now extended over more than a century.

VII

Strains and Mutations

I

THE EMPHASIS AS WELL AS the sentiment conveyed by Rimsky's words leave no doubt that in the aftermath of the St. Petersburg experience of 1889 he became a partisan of Wagner. But it is equally clear that he was more absorbed by the procedures of Wagner than by his substance. What he referred to as "tricks of the trade" were so many, enticing, and useful that the opportunities they suggested to an experienced composer—particularly one of Rimsky's methodical turn of mind—were unlimited.

For another composer equally enticed by Wagner—especially one younger and lacking such a substance of his own to exploit as Rimsky possessed—the problem could well be otherwise. What it amounted to, really, was whether one who was magnetized by Wagner's procedures could avoid being mesmerized also by his substance. For one such unique exception as Humperdinck, who made the happy misstep of stumbling on so suitable a folk subject as *Hänsel und Gretel* and of realizing it completely in mostly Wagnerian terms, a dozen were unable to resist a trend to the heroic. Elementary "logic" argued that large-scale resources dictated the choice of subject matter on an equally grandiose plan.

The first to venture the enticement and achieve an enduring result was Bruckner. Fortunately, Bruckner had the biggest of possible subjects to absorb him: earthly strife, celestial bliss. From the start, music for him was a means to the fulfillment of a religious conviction. When he discovered that there was, on earth, Richard Wagner, he did not forget that there was, in Heaven, *der liebe Gott*.[1] Indeed, the dedication of his Symphony No. 9 "To the Dear Lord" is simplicity itself beside the earlier inscription of his No.3[2] to

> That incomparable, world-famous, sublime
> Master of Poetry and Musical Composition
> Mr. Richard Wagner
> with the most profound respect
> by Anton Bruckner.

The words were hardly too elaborate to convey his indebtedness to the one who made Bruckner's veneration of the other more embracing. When he could not make Wagner's orchestra part of the house in which he worshipped (the Church), he willingly followed it into the one in which it flourished best (the concert hall), satisfied that it would serve his purpose there no less well, perhaps even better. Thus, rather than expressing the orchestra through his religious impulse, he expressed his religious impulse through the orchestra.

How could another, with different impulses and other convictions, arrive at a satisfactory solution of his own? Only with difficulty, by a process of trial and error through which he could be proved worthy or unworthy. If this sounds strangely kin to the philosophical formulation of *The Magic Flute*, it is merely a reminder that neither the dilemma nor the means of solution was wholly new. Very likely the possibility of a successful outcome would relate to the elements one selected or was selected by. Volition might be usurped by a helpless attraction to something one could not master unless—as with Berlioz's attraction for Gounod, or Wagner's for Humperdinck—it was rationally appraised and realistically reduced in scale.

The first German composer of consequence to develop during the high noon of Wagner's prominence was born almost as the clock struck eleven, in the pivotal year of 1864. He was, furthermore, born not only at a time of intellectual division and aesthetic dissension but, literally, into it. The son of the Munich Opera Orchestra's most distinguished virtuoso of the French horn, Richard Strauss related with relish the

[1] J. F. Redlich: *Bruckner and Mahler* (London: J. M. Dent and Sons; 1955), p. 98.
[2] *The Musician's World*, ed. Hans Gal (New York: Arco Publishing Company; 1966), p. 325.

description of his father Franz by no less a sage than Richard Wagner: "Old Strauss is an unbearable fellow, but when he plays his horn, one cannot be cross with him."[3]

What made Franz Strauss, by the measure of Wagner, a crusty dissident, made him, in the interests of a musical son, an ideal *pater familias.* Quick to recognize and encourage his son's extraordinary talents, father Strauss knew where and how to see to their furtherance. From the start, he applied the level and T-square of a high professional standard as his frame of reference. Within it there was no place for the slipshod, the meretricious, or the merely dilettantish—qualities, after all, that he deplored in the one he would refer to scornfully as "the swindler of Bayreuth." Such a father's influence (and perhaps no parent other than Leopold Mozart had so immediate an effect on the development of a creative offspring) guaranteed obeisance to the accomplishments of those who had preceded him, which is to say, a strong indoctrination in the sequence of continuity.

It has become customary to accept as reasonably reliable, especially in the light of the elderly composer's aphorisms on the subject, Strauss's declaration of his "lifelong devotion to Mozart." Doubtless such a disposition was always latent in him, and it eventually became a part of his compositional discipline (portions of *Der Rosenkavalier, Ariadne, Arabella,* etc.). But the early works that are still occasionally performed tell another story, or stories.

In the Serenade for Thirteen Winds of 1881, which first aroused Hans von Bülow's interest in the youth who was to become his prized protégé, the household god is not Mozart (despite the likeness of the instrumentation to that of the great B-flat Divertimento, K. 361), but Mendelssohn. Both in density and flow, the sound has more kinship to the resonance-soaked interludes of the incidental music to A *Midsummer Night's Dream* than to anything else that comes to mind, unless it is a way of cresting a musical wave and causing it to shatter in a splash of sparkling sonority which Strauss was to remember and improve upon in the Act III trio of *Der Rosenkavalier.*

As the abundantly able youth rushed on, in his late teens, to the expression of the ideas flooding his mind, the link of continuity drew him closer to contemporary sources without, so to speak, crossing party lines. In his engrossing study of the composer, Norman Del Mar refers to an unpublished Concert Overture in C minor (1883) in terms of "the Max Bruch G minor violin concerto, a work which was to lend

---

[3] Richard Strauss: *Recollections and Reflections,* ed. Willi Schuh (London: Boosey and Hawkes; 1953), p. 128.

ideas to Strauss on more than one occasion in later life."[4] If so, it was indication of a susceptibility to a Wagnerian idiom, if but the early one of *The Flying Dutchman*.

A next source of stimulation, and a decidedly longer-lasting one, was Johannes Brahms. This was an inevitability not only because of the parental proscription of Wagner, but also because of the close affinity which bound the young Strauss to Bülow. Since those days of the 1850's in which Bülow had been Wagner's confidant, circumstances had made of him something of a displaced artistic person, come to rest (literally) in the camp of Brahms. It was Bülow, at the time of Strauss's apprenticeship to him in Meiningen, who rehearsed its orchestra in the Fourth Symphony of Brahms before its author came to conduct the *première* in 1885.

Strauss's E-flat Concerto for French horn (first performed under Bülow's direction in the same year) builds its introduction on the pattern of the similar section in the Brahms Violin Concerto, then only half a dozen years old. Many flourishes in the horn part proclaim Strauss's prenatal conditioning and prophesy the prominence its strong masculine voice would have in his later tone poems and operas. When the sentiment is not Brahmsian, it is Mendelssohnian. Its most "modern" touch, perhaps, is the recurrence of the opening horn theme, in an altered form, as the main subject of the finale.

A chance attendance at a rehearsal in Leipzig of Brahms's *Gesang der Parzen* in 1885 filled Strauss with the impulse to create a choral work of his own. He was drawn not only to the same poet, Goethe, for the text of the work known as the *Wanderers Sturmlied*, but also to the same formulation for six-part chorus. It is hardly remarkable that the outcome, in the words of Del Mar, is a work "full of a thousand and one touches of pure Brahms in the figuration, the orchestral layout and, above all, in the harmonic scheme . . ."[5]

Perhaps the Brahmsian involvement is strongest in what has always appealed to me as the most likeable as well as the most enduring of the works that preceded those which made Strauss's name world-famous a few years later. This is the *Burleske* for piano and orchestra, whose striking theme (on four timpani) is quoted in a letter from Strauss at Meiningen to his father (dated November 7, 1885). Describing the work as a scherzo with a *Pedalpauken*, Strauss notes that it will be for piano solo and orchestra. By the following February it had grown

[4] Norman Del Mar: *Richard Strauss* (New York: The Free Press of Glencoe; 1962), I, 13.
[5] Ibid., p. 35.

to be both a *Burleske* and a "piano concerto," which its composer hoped Bülow would sponsor as soloist. However, the virtuoso who had received the dedication of Tchaikovsky's B-flat-minor Concerto a decade before, when Nicholas Rubinstein had declared it "unplayable," now, in his turn, found Strauss's *Burleske* "unplayable" (its stretches, the composer later revealed, exceeded Bülow's reach[6]). It was not until the young Eugène D'Albert came upon it in 1890 that it was performed for the first time.

Without doubt, the *Burleske* shows a young musician of extraordinary gifts, magnetic personality, and startling command of musical materials, on the verge of doing something earthshaking. Unfortunately, Strauss was a musician of quite other inclinations by the time the *Burleske* had its first performance and was not disposed to be voluble concerning its title. In any case, the pre-*Don Juan* Strauss's earthshaking was accomplished with means very similar to those of the first piano concerto of Brahms, especially as it approaches the climax of the first movement (measures 21 from the end, to the double bar [see pp. 187, 188]). Del Mar cites the D-minor Ballade (opus 10) by Brahms (on the Scottish ballad "Edward") as the source of the opening *Pedalpauken*, an observation made by James G. Huneker many years before.

In any case, the Concerto, Ballade, and *Burleske* are tied in a tight D-minor knot, in the midst of which is the (also) D-minor Symphony No. 9 of Beethoven (see p. 162). This association may have been, and doubtless was, far from Strauss's mind as the work took shape, but it is an absorbing instance of the tangled web that allusion spins. What was much closer to his mind, clearly, was the lightly sensuous, always elegantly musical throb of 3/4 time as it was manipulated by Johann Strauss, Jr. Here in the *Burleske* is the first manifestation of the easy mastery of such material which was to play so sizeable a part in the spell cast by *Der Rosenkavalier* twenty-five years later.

The addition just then of the manner of "the laughing genius of Vienna"[7] to Strauss's range of resources was by no means inexplicable. The works of Johann Strauss were a particular enthusiasm of Bülow, who gave his friend from Munich one of the most memorable evenings of his young life by playing endlessly on the piano from "a beautifully bound collection of all the Strauss waltzes." It was then, Richard Strauss later (1925) recalled, that he "really got to know and to love the whole realm of his [Johann Strauss's] wisdom."[8]

As Strauss assigns the experience to Meiningen, which Bülow had left by November 1885, the evening must have been just before the

---

[6] Strauss: *Recollections and Reflections*, p. 137.
[7] Ibid., p. 77.   [8] Ibid., p. 77.

Brahms: Piano Concerto No. 1, D minor, maestoso

composition of the *Burleske*. Without the seed thus planted and the flowering that followed, the *Burleske* might never have happened, and *Der Rosenkavalier* might have been deprived of some of its most characteristic moments.

Strauss: Burleske

2

STRAUSS DERIVED MUCH from the presence of Bülow in Meiningen, but that "much" was matched, if not exceeded, by an influence that emerged after Bülow's departure. This was a friendship with Alexander Ritter, who later wrote the prose "poem" associated with *Tod und Verklärung*. At this time merely one among the number of violinists in the string section of Bülow's orchestra, the fifty-two-year-old Ritter was a singular segment of continuity in himself.

His mother was the Julie Ritter who befriended Wagner in Dresden, contributed generously to his financial support in Switzerland, and earned the honor of being mother-in-law to the composer's niece Franziska when "Sascha" (as Wagner addressed him in their correspondence) married her in 1854. A violinist by training, Ritter had settled in Weimar, where he participated in the exciting events organized by Liszt during the 1850's on behalf not only of himself and of Wagner, but also of Berlioz. During his wife's operatic career (she was Flosshilde in the first *Rheingold* [1869] and a Valkyrie in the initial *Die Walküre* [1870]), he lived in various German cities but retained a close contact with Wagner. He had turned to running a music shop when Bülow, who had been a daily companion in their youthful days of mutual enthusiasm for Wagner, rescued him with an offer of a place in the Meiningen orchestra (an act that did not immunize Bülow from Ritter's occasional reminders of his "apostasy").

Ritter was keenly attracted to young Strauss, who later said: "The greatest event of my winter in Meiningen was my acquaintance with Alexander Ritter . . . He invited me to his house, where I found the spiritual stimulus which was the decisive factor in my further development."[9] This was by no means limited to generalities. It ran rather specifically to areas of musical thought and inclination which had hitherto been officially off-limits to Strauss. Says Del Mar: "Ritter lost no time in inviting him to his house and acquainting him with the programmatic works of the modern school."[1]

The new trend became apparent almost immediately, when Strauss departed on a trip to Italy after resigning his Meiningen post (1886).

[9] Ibid., p. 138.
[1] Del Mar: *Richard Strauss*, pp. 39–40.

Before the journey was well begun (which is to say, half done), he was advising family and friends of his musical response to the new surroundings. As the trip was a direct result of his meetings with Brahms in Meiningen (at the time of the *première* of Symphony No. 4[2]), and as he was thoroughly acquainted with Mendelssohn's "Italian" Symphony (No. 4 in A) as well as Berlioz's *Harold en Italie*,[3] Strauss was honoring a choice cross-section of antecedents in the work he called *Aus Italien*.

From this distance it is clear that the tribute was rather more specific than Strauss intended it to be. The opening of the work, describing the Campagna, is curiously akin to the opening of *Harold*, not only in its slow pace, but also in a hovering between G and G minor (both works are in G). The grade of melody he invented for *Aus Italien* is not very good Strauss, with the result that in his stroll through the ruins of Rome (p. 81 of the miniature score), he seems to have Brahms as his companion, up to and including the "dying fall" from the end of the Third Symphony. Perhaps the most prophetically Straussian impulse *Aus Italien* contains is the rich impasto of sound with which he depicts Sorrento. It shows, also, a trend to a kind of note-picking melodic formulation—a swoop from a high tone to a low one, a leap over an octave to a neighboring tone that thus becomes a ninth rather than a second—practiced by few predecessors other than Berlioz. The concluding "*Neapolitanisches Volksleben*," in which Strauss made the glorious mistake of supposing Luigi Denza's *Funiculì-Funiculà* to be a folk song, is a tarantella akin to the finale of Mendelssohn's "Italian" Symphony. *Aus Italien* takes another trend when it gathers material from earlier movements in a summation suggestive of Berlioz's similar procedure in *Harold en Italie*.

The overriding reality of Ritter's influence on Strauss is that, by turning his thoughts to such a poetic or pictorial, even programmatic, concept as *Aus Italien* embodies, he was catering to the strongest, deepest impulse in the composer's aesthetic disposition, the Word. For, with negligible exceptions, virtually any music of consequence achieved by Strauss during a creative life of more than sixty years (1882–1946) was either in direct conjunction with a text—songs or operas—or the outgrowth of a verbal suggestion—tone poems. In the wide range of the world's literature (including some parts of it specifically created for him by Hofmannsthal, Zweig, Clemens Krauss, etc.), Strauss found the fuse

[2] Ibid., p. 40.
[3] In his *Briefe an die Eltern*, ed. Willi Schuh (Zürich: Atlantis Verlag; 1954), p. 71, Strauss describes a rehearsal he had conducted in Meiningen.

to ignite his own enormously flammable facility, to regenerate his impulse when other stimulation faltered. And finally, in what may well be his last work of sustained quality, it is a prolonged, sometimes playful, sometimes heated, consideration of the relative importance of "word" and "tone" (*Prima la musica e poi le parole?*) which provides the "argument" of *Capriccio.*

I date the predisposition to 1882 not because of any unknown masterpiece recently come to light, but because of a known masterpiece rarely traced to its time of origin. This is the flavorsome *"Zueignung"* ("Dedication"), justly admired as one of Strauss's most beautiful songs, but rarely identified as the first published (opus 10, No. 1) of his nearly one hundred and fifty. Nor was this merely a happy accident. The same group of his eighteenth year (1882–3) also includes the eloquent *"Allerseelen"* and the still-performed *"Die Nacht."*

The inclination being clear, it remains to be judged how large a part it would have played in Strauss's functioning without Ritter's fertilizing influence or its equivalent. Not, to my way of thinking, nearly so large a part, certainly not at so early a point in his development. In turning Strauss's thoughts to sources of musical continuity that he had not encountered previously—Liszt as well as Wagner—Ritter made possible a new blend of strains and mutations which not merely favored Strauss's innate impulses, but contributed mightily to their furtherance.

For the while, however, the search for a substance to absorb the procedures he was capable of disposing led Strauss into error as well as trial. In the aftermath of *Aus Italien,* he was attracted to *Macbeth,* somehow overlooked by such musical exploiters of Shakespeare as Berlioz, Tchaikovsky, and Liszt. Certainly its tough-fibered mixture of ambition and envy, hatred and remorse could withstand the ultimate in realistic auralization of which Strauss was capable. But even in the revised edition used for its first performance in 1890, *Macbeth's* musical substance (distinctly Brahmsian, after an opening in the mood of Beethoven's Ninth) wars with its procedure (emphatically Wagnerian). Little wonder, then, that in its first form (1887), *Macbeth* remained "silent and buried in my desk," in the composer's words to Bülow in a letter of August 24, 1888.

In this revealing document, in which Strauss speaks his mind even more candidly than he does in his music, he refers, with disappointment, but without distress, to Mottl's refusal to perform the earlier F-minor Symphony. For, he continues: "From the F minor Symphony onward I have found myself in a gradually ever-increasing contradiction between the musical-poetic content that I want to convey and the ternary sonata form that has come down to us from the classical composers." To Strauss's subtly comprehending mind, "A link-up with the Beethoven of *Coriolan, Egmont,* the *Leonore* III Overture, of *Les Adieux,* above all with late Beethoven, whose complete *œuvre,* in my opinion, could never have been created without a poetic subject, seems to me the only course for the time being by which an *independent further* [Strauss's italics] development of our instrumental music is yet possible."

Perhaps Strauss was capable of so clear an intellectualization of his artistic problem because he had, already, arrived at a profoundly satisfactory solution of it. For, in the same paragraph in which he describes *Macbeth* as lying "silent and buried" in his desk, he says: "Perhaps Don Juan will join him soon." It was, rather, the other way around. When the last E-minor chord of *Don Juan* had died away at its first performance in Berlin before the next year was out, there was no doubt that in this orchestral drama Strauss had taken a stride beyond the perimeter of instrumental expression achieved by Wagner in his music dramas. In the same stride, he had caught the world's attention and guaranteed its interest in anything he had written before or would write for years to come.

Of the first importance in *Don Juan,* through materials more consistently his own and a method that was a composite of many predecessors', was the propagation of Strauss's concept of the orchestra as a protagonist of and in itself. Born in the mind of Berlioz and nursed through adolescence by Liszt, the brainchild had been reared to vigorous manhood by Wagner. In the latter's concept of the *Gesamtkunstwerk,* it was but one element (if a sometimes irrepressibly assertive one) in a complex of voices, words, scenery, lights, and action. Years before, Grétry had created a memorable image by complaining that "Mozart placed the statue on the orchestra and the pedestal on the stage."[4] If so, Strauss completed the cycle by taking the orchestra out of the pit altogether and making it both pedestal and statue on a stage of its own in the concert hall.

The resemblance of Strauss's procedures in *Don Juan* to those of Liszt in his best tone poems is clear enough, but he improved on the model in more than enough ways to differentiate invention from imitation. First, and of supreme importance, was his skill in evolving an opening theme that lent itself superlatively well to the

[4] Hector Berlioz: *Memoirs,* tr. R. and E. Holmes (New York: Alfred A. Knopf; 1932), p. 78.

function it was meant to serve. I say "evolving" rather than merely "creating" because it combines with certain mingled elements of rhythm, stride, and dynamics (which caused Tovey to term it "Berliozian"[5]) an improvement on the kind of brass flourish with which Wagner prefaces Act III of *Lohengrin*.

In the letter to Bülow previously quoted, Strauss continues: "I consider it a legitimate artistic method to create a correspondingly new form for every subject, to shape which neatly and precisely is a very difficult task but for that reason the more attractive." For the purpose of *Don Juan*, which dictated something very much like the first movement of a symphony (sonata allegro form), this theme and its successors were ideally evolved. As he came to the creation of a rondo (*Till Eulenspiegel*), a theme and variations (*Don Quixote*), and even a total symphonic sequence in a single movement (*Ein Heldenleben*), the thesaurus of thematic material he commanded served him hardly less well.

He was well served, too, by his absorption in the procedures of his predecessors. In *Don Juan*, as has been suggested, Strauss went beyond the merely rhapsodic or improvisatory structure of Liszt to evolve a well-balanced sequence that had impressive design as well as content. With it he combined the orchestra as a source of narrative power not merely comparable to, but derived from, Wagner's use of it for Siegfried's Rhine Journey or the funeral music of *Götterdämmerung*. One may sense what is in the back of Strauss's mind when the initial impulse runs down and some outside assistance is required to get him back to the next point of self-generating momentum (pp. 58–74 of the Novello and Company miniature score). It is a transition cut out of the Wagnerian cloth, but styled to his own needs. At the first of the work's biggest climaxes (p. 88), not only the cloth but also the design and stitching are identical with the model in the first act of *Götterdämmerung*. However, Brahms is neither scorned nor rejected either. What Tovey characterizes as "a melody of intense repose"[6] in G, led by the oboe (first heard at p. 44 and recalled later), owes both the generative phrase and its underlying harmonic color to a thought invented by Brahms when he was writing the *andante moderato* of his A-minor String Quartet (opus 51, No. 2) fifteen years before (measures 59-60 [see p. 194]).

[5] D. F. Tovey: *Essays in Musical Analysis* (London: Oxford University Press; 1935), IV, 157.
[6] Ibid., p. 158.

Brahms: *String Quartet, A minor (op. 51, No. 2)*, andante moderato

Strauss: Don Juan *(op. 20)*

None of this should be construed to mean that there was not a heady brew of Strauss's own distilling in *Don Juan*. In the span of but half a dozen years he had achieved the astounding feat of inverting the proportions of familiar to unfamiliar in the music he was writing. Gradually, from a mere flavoring of personal quality in the Serenade, opus 7, he had achieved a quantitative strengthening in the *Burleske* and *Aus Italien*. It was not until *Don Juan* that the proportions were finally reversed, with the traces of others now the off-taste in a mixture predominantly his own.

For a while to come, however, some dilution would remain as Strauss soaked himself more and more in the Wagnerian essence. At first (1889) an assistant at Bayreuth, then a conductor there in his own right (he had the responsibility for the first *Tannhäuser* ever to be given at a Bayreuth Festival, in 1894), Strauss attained rank as a singularly eloquent interpreter of *Tristan*. Much later in life he confessed that at the age of seventeen "against my father's orders . . . I had positively wolfed the score of *Tristan* as in a trance . . ."[7] It took him a full seven years (from 1881, when he was seventeen) to digest the substance of *Tristan* and to reproduce a part of it through his own artistic bloodstream, in *Tod und Verklärung*.

In addition to achieving his stated objective of creating "a correspondingly new form for every subject," Strauss achieved an unstated objective—to evolve a new blend of strains and mutations for each new subject. In *Don Juan*, as cited, the point of departure is Wagner, especially the Rhine Journey, with a cross-pollination from Brahms. In *Tod und Verklärung*, the point of departure strikes me as an episode deep in Act III of *Tristan*. The wounded knight has sunk back from one of his outbursts of delirium, and Kurvenal poses the anxious question: "*Bist du nun todt? Lebst du noch?*"[8]

It is there, in the *pianissimo*, barely audible, chords breathed by stopped horns and bass clarinet in 12/8 meter, that the suggestive nuclear element may be found for Strauss's successor to *Don Juan*. It provides the atmosphere as well as the substance of its opening. He extends it harmonically (with a fleeting suggestion of Liszt's *Orpheus*) while adding what Lawrence Gilman described as a "complaining phrase" from Wagner's *Eine Faust-Ouvertüre*.[9] Once the

---

[7] Strauss: *Recollections and Reflections*, p. 132.
[8] G. Schirmèr piano-vocal score, p. 259.
[9] Lawrence Gilman: *Orchestral Music* (New York: Oxford University Press; 1951), p. 460.

primary associations have been made, it is clear to the ear that the invalid is lying not in the "necessitous little room" of Ritter's prose poem, but under the "great lime tree"[1] specified by Wagner for Kareol in Act III of *Tristan*.

Strauss: Tod und Verklärung (*op. 24*)

[1] Robert C. Bagar and Louis Biancolli: *The Concert Companion* (New York: McGraw-Hill Book Company, Inc.; 1947), p. 694.

Wagner: Tristan und Isolde, Act III

Strauss fares well enough on his own with the generative thought, adding to it the massive brass passages which convey the sick man's "idealism" (and are later associated with his "transformation"). The harmonic thought it exploits and the modulatory manner it pursues have become identified with early Strauss, but the colorations were first mixed by the late Brahms in the *Alto Rhapsody*. Strauss's treatment of the opening sequences is reasonably related to the material with which he is working, but the development is in the musically incongruous manner of *Tannhäuser* rather than the more suitable vein of *Tristan*.

The "sundry poor passages" of which the pitiless Bülow complained to Strauss after hearing the work from the composer's hands at the piano must certainly have included the Hagen-ish horn phrase (Act II of *Götterdämmerung*) on the trombone (at a point associated with the menace of Death) which precedes the next statement of the big brass theme. There is, over-all, the sturdy Strauss orchestral craftsmanship on the level of *Don Juan*, but it is such allusions as the foregoing (plus an echo of Siegfried discovering Brünnhilde on her rock which serves as a bridge along the way) that leave some with the feeling that *Tod und Verklärung* is yeasty and half baked (meaning that it fails to rise) by comparison with the works on either side of it.

In many ways, however, *Tod und Verklärung* rates Bülow's description of it in a letter to his wife (November 13, 1899) as "a very important work."[2] It demonstrates Strauss's ability to organize the orchestra on another plan and to another sonorous outcome than in *Don Juan*, as the instrument of quite different psychological suggestions. Some might say that it shows the breadth of Strauss's knowledge rather than the depth of his originality; but that, too, has its place in stylistic evolution.

3

THE APPEAL OF THE WORD in its most elementary musical context—sung—and the entree to the opera houses of Germany that Strauss enjoyed through his ability as a conductor as well as his merits as a composer drew him almost compulsively toward his next objective: creation of an opera. But to mention that its name, *Guntram*, was created for its hero from a combination of Gunther and Wolfram is to say as much as is necessary for the purposes of this investigation.

Guntram's completion and production (interrupted by a stubborn illness that had Strauss traveling in the warm Mediterranean countries for more than a year in 1892-3) deterred him from another large-scale orchestral project until the summer of 1894. Though a successful operatic resolution of the problem posed by *Guntram* was beyond him at this time, he was adding steadily to a related aspect of his art with the composition of such songs as "*Ruhe, meine Seele,*" "*Cäcilie,*" "*Heim-*

[2] Ibid., p. 694.

liche Aufforderung," and *"Morgen."* With the right collaborator, he might even have realized his intention of writing a one-act fantasy for the stage on the subject of an old German folk tale. The lack of such a collaborator turned his thoughts from the opera house to the concert hall for a treatment of Till Eulenspiegel.

Here again Strauss validated his personal commitment to "create a correspondingly new form for every subject." For *Till* is a gigantic, good-humored rondo whose like (in extent or detail) had never been imagined for the orchestra before. (Those who are tempted to advance the claims of Paul Dukas's *L'Apprenti sorcier* will find that *Till* was at large and racing through the concert halls of Europe two years before the Sorcerer and his Apprentice made their bow in Paris in 1897.) Besides fulfilling his intent, Strauss continued to sustain my contention that he was drawing on a different source of continuity for each of these epoch-making works.

With *Till* it is almost certainly Berlioz. Strauss's acquaintance with the great French innovator's works was as extensive as a composer's need be, and as intensive as a conductor's could be. Bülow, of course, was partial to Berlioz (the program of 1884 in which he introduced the Strauss *Serenade* also offered two Berlioz overtures), and the disciple followed the master's practice at Meiningen. There has been prior mention of his preparation of *Harold en Italie.* Soon enough the *Symphonie "phantastique"* (as Strauss spelled it) entered the list of the works he was preparing to conduct,[3] and he endorsed *Les Troyens* for its *Klang-zauber* when he heard a famous performance of it under Mottl at Karlsruhe in 1887. Not long afterward, the whole of *Benvenuto Cellini* was in Strauss's operatic repertory, as were a cross section of the overtures (*King Lear, Rob Roy,* and the *Carnaval romain*) and the *Fifth of May* cantata.

All of this leaves no doubt of his acquaintance with such models for Till's grotesqueries as the transformation of themes in the Witches' Sabbath, or the overtone of macabre humor (in the March to the Gallows) which Strauss found so appealing for Till's mock trial and execution. A specific instance may be cited in the recurrence of the drum roll and brass chords invented by Berlioz for the closing measures of his March at the apex of Till's mischief-making (p. 90 of the Eulenburg miniature score). Like much other orchestral *diablerie, Till* is written in the 6/8 meter that Berlioz propagated for the purpose in the *"Songe d'une nuit de Sabbat."* With nearly a century's experimentation to enlarge his stock of proven values, Strauss commanded (in 1895) a deftness of orchestral detail even greater than the composer of the

[3] Richard Strauss: *Briefe an die Eltern,* p. 116.

Fantastique had had. There is no reasonable doubt whose example had served him best.

With this deftness of detail and intense sophistication of style there is a balancing strain of folkish humor, an engaging simplicity and warmth in the "Once upon a time" spirit in which the work begins, which complement each other ideally. Indeed, they coexist as well only in Humperdinck's *Hänsel und Gretel*. That it was, of all possible conductors, Strauss who prepared and presented the *première* of Humperdinck's masterwork at Weimar in December 1893 cannot be excluded from the stimuli and conditioning which found their way into *Till* the following year. (There are some comparable folk usages in the early works of Mahler, whom Strauss met as early as 1887, but performances of these were rare occurrences before, approximately, 1895.)

By the time he had completed *Also sprach Zarathustra* (first performed in November 1896) and *Don Quixote* (introduced on March 8, 1898), there was little question that Strauss had evolved a style distinctively his own. Indeed, *Till* was barely launched and the next works were already waiting their turns for performance when Strauss was absorbed in a project in which the composer, no less than the orchestra, was the protagonist. In this exercise in self-appreciation, Strauss was finally free of a primary involvement with a continuity of moribund "immortals." He was responsive to and conscious of a living continuity of his own, as conveyed in the famous section of *Ein Heldenleben* titled "The Hero's Works of Peace."

As itemized in the helpfully circumstantial thematic index assembled by Del Mar,[4] *Ein Heldenleben* contains citations from all six earlier orchestral dramas, the opera *Guntram*, and two songs. The ease or difficulty of recognition relates to the familiarity or obscurity of the theme cited, but there is no doubt that Strauss, at thirty-four, had earned the right to proclaim his own place in the continuity of which he was so well aware, and to which he owed so much. With it went all the appurtenances of mastery: the unleashing of a power which would virtually determine the life direction of a younger composer ("What roused me from torpor, like a clap of thunder, was the first performance at Budapest in 1902 of *Also sprach Zarathustra*," Béla Bartók is quoted as saying[5]), and would infiltrate the practices of sundry others (Mahler,

---

[4] Del Mar: Richard Strauss, p. 177.
[5] Serge Moreux: *Bartók* (London: Harvill Press; 1953), p. 25. The same page contains a description of Bartók's early addiction to *Ein Heldenleben*, which he played in concerts to show his virtuosity as a pianist.

Schoenberg, Stravinsky, to mention only the most notable "survivors");
the acquisition of a full-fledged disiciple (Erich Wolfgang Korngold,
born in 1897); and the status, before he was forty, of a "legend in his
lifetime."

4

PARADOXICALLY, HOWEVER, in freeing himself from a "primary" involvement with the continuity of the past, Strauss engaged another, even
more difficult to escape—the continuity of his own creation. In *Heldenleben,* of course, the allusions are overt and purposeful, as consciously selected for specific consequence as Wagner's quotation of
a phrase from *Tristan* to make a dramatic point in the Workshop
Scene of *Die Meistersinger.* But in those that followed the *Symphonia
domestica* (1903), the reproduction of means and methods evolved
by himself is sometimes as hopeless a form of imitation as Dvořák's
reproduction of the means and methods of Wagner or Brahms.

This raises the interesting possibility—the first time it has arisen
in this study—of a composer in whose mind the conscious and the
unconscious have become transposed. It seems clear that, by the
time of the *Symphonia domestica* (which followed *Heldenleben* by
five years), Strauss's citations of predecessors were generally knowing
and volitional. It was quite otherwise when he reproduced a texture,
melodic phraseology, or emotional gesture of his own (leap of an
octave up, swoop of a ninth down, a G. P.—Grand Pause—for
dramatic effect, an equally sudden digression to another mood without bridge or modulation, etc.).

A point of transition might be cited in *Ein Heldenleben* itself,
where, amid all the conscious quotations of self, he draws on another
kind of *Helden's Leben.* It comes in the appearance, at a strategic
point of the Hero's retreat from the World, of an ascending scalewise
figure marked *ausdrucksvoll.* It forms a counterpoint to a broad
E-flat invention of Strauss, or perhaps it should better be said that
it is Strauss's invention which becomes a counterpoint to this beautiful expression. Together they create an effect which prompted Philip
Hale to say that this was music "worthy of Beethoven in his supreme
moments of rapt meditation."[6]

And well it might be, for the ascending passage is borrowed from
the finale of the *"Eroica,"* where it performs an ennobling function

[6] Gilman: *Orchestral Music,* p. 386.

in the sustained variation (*poco animato sostenuto*) just before the movement's end. Willfully or otherwise, it came to Beethoven by way of Mozart, who used much the same underlying thought to embellish a moment of lofty sentiment uttered by Sarastro during *"In diesen heil'gen Hallen"* in *Die Zauberflöte.* In both earlier instances it is associated in the composer's mind with a state of being

Beethoven: Symphony No. 3, E flat, finale

on a super-terrestrial plane. This very much suits Strauss's purpose, which is to glorify his hero (himself) as Beethoven did the one to whom the *"Eroica"* was originally inscribed (Bonaparte). I should be as much surprised to learn that Beethoven was aware of his Mozartian allusion as to discover that Strauss was unaware of his Beethoven-Mozart reference.

Strauss: Ein Heldenleben *(op. 40)*

There need be no speculation about Strauss's awareness of his other reference to the *"Eroica,"* in the *Metamorphosen* of 1945. It is, from the start, "in the clear," neither encoded nor disguised, plainly suggested by the *"Marcia funebre"* of the *"Eroica."* At its final citation it is labeled "*In Memoriam.*" Such involvement with the listener's sense of historic relationships was common with Strauss. These relationships flourish more abundantly than elsewhere in the high-spirited *Ariadne auf Naxos*, where a humorous reference to the *commedia dell'arte* characters is set off by a theme associated with the clowns in Mendelssohn's *Midsummer Night's Dream* music; the trio of Najade, Dryade, and Echo warbles in a manner much like that of the Rhinemaidens, and even the tread of the Giants in *Das Rheingold* is purposefully reproduced. The intellectual charade is carried a step farther in the incidental music for *Le Bourgeois Gentilhomme* (the performance of Molière's play was originally intended to include *Ariadne*). For good historical reasons, Strauss reproduced almost in toto the *Menuet* written by Lully for the first production of *Le Bourgeois Gentilhomme*, also the entrance of Cleonte (both Straussified, of course). But one must listen more carefully, or be forewarned, to discern that the meal of M. Jourdain is served to a citation of the Rhine motive (appropriate to the district where the wine originated) and that the bleating of sheep from *Don Quixote* accompanies the meat course (lamb). Other self-quotation may be found in *Intermezzo* (where the *Symphonia domestica* is invoked) and, least forgettably of all, in "*Im Abendrot*" of the *Four Last Songs*.

All the evidence shows, thus, that Strauss was generally aware of what he was doing when he had recourse to the invention of others, if not always when he was quoting himself. Considering his youth when he first became world-famous (mid-twenties) and the steady productivity of his next twenty-five years, the marvel is not how much he repeated his methods or stylistic traits during this fruitful period, but how little.

There is no written statement of intent or manifesto of purpose before his composition of *Salome, Elektra,* and *Der Rosenkavalier* to parallel the declaration of 1888 to Bülow that he intended to find a "correspondingly new form" for each of the orchestral works he would compose. But, with or without it, there is every indication that what he sought was a "new musical atmosphere" for each subject he would treat operatically. The measure of his success is not primarily the continued interest each work has for today's audiences (the Puccini operas retain such interest, even though parts of *Bohème, Butterfly,* and *Tosca* are readily interchangeable). It is, rather, contained in the creation of a sound vocabulary distinctive to each subject, as Wagner created one vocabulary for *Tristan*, another for *Die Meistersinger*. To a considerable extent, Strauss had the necessary resources within himself to achieve this result: but when needed, he also had a shrewd awareness of where to search out what he required.

In *Salome*, Strauss's dissatisfaction with the conventional kind of "exotic" idiom carried him in the direction of polytonality (of the sort related to Chopin's bitonality rather than the kind already conceived by Charles Ives for *Three Places in New England* in 1903). His travels in the Near East in 1892–3 were also productive of useful results, as interpolated into a discussion of the proper interpretation of Salome herself: "Anyone who has been in the East and has observed the decorum with which women there behave will appreciate that Salome, being a chaste virgin and an oriental princess, must be played with the simplest and most restrained of gestures . . ."[7] When he chose to, Strauss could use tonal combinations almost as adroitly as a painter mixes a tint of his choice: the straightforward, diatonic pronouncements of Jokanaan identify him as a man of the Church even as the register for which they are written identifies him as a blood brother of Wotan and the Wanderer.

In *Elektra*, the idiom as well as its utilization is substantially different, far more granitic, harsh, and somber. As befits the subject matter, which is much more extroverted and emotionally varied than that of *Salome*, there is much more emphasis on extended vocal line, especially after the "Recognition" scene. And the orchestra broods rather than gleams, a sounding likeness of the scene itself (the somber courtyard of the Palace in Mykena for *Elektra* shows another shade of theatrical possibility than the moonlit terrace of Herod's palace in Palestine for *Salome*).

As for *Der Rosenkavalier*, its procedures have little in common with either *Salome* or *Elektra*. The musical idiom is self-determined by its Viennese locale, the *patois* of which Strauss had learned to paraphrase in *Burleske*. Some literal-minded critics complained, when *Rosenkavalier* was new, that such waltzes as Strauss's (whether Johann Sr., Johann Jr., or Richard) were an anachronism in the time of Marie Therese, the Marschallin. The objections have faded along with resistance to the "immorality" the work embodies.

What relates these works to the total operatic literature of which they are now a part is on a rather more sophisticated level of continuity. That is the utilization of prior means for present ends, as the concept of Jokanaan for the *Heldenbaryton* kind of voice brought into being for the Wotans, or Herod as a kind of Loge gone mad. Woven into the texture of polytonality Strauss evolved for *Salome* is a chromatic

[7] Strauss: *Recollections and Reflections*, p. 151.

figure (when Jokanaan descends defiantly into the cistern) that Del Mar[8] associates with Act III of *Siegfried,* as well as a melting cadence that emanates from *Parsifal.* But the taut, steel spring frame as well as the tense skein of sound stretched over it substantially Strauss's own.

In *Elektra,* the affinities assert themselves only after repeated hearings and rehearings. Thus, the coloration of voice and orchestra borrowed from a section of Brünnhilde's Immolation for Elektra's "*Allein! ganz allein,*" the resonant range of Orestes' pronouncements and their kinship to the Wanderer's music in Act II of *Siegfried,* the likeness to Leonore's (in *Fidelio*) defiant "*Töt' erst sein Weib!*" in Elektra's inciting "*Triff noch einmal*" (same number of syllables, similar speech rhythm), and the mind-shattering impact of the final dance conveyed by orchestral means similar to those imagined by Wagner for the world-shattering finale of *Götterdämmerung.*

By the time of *Der Rosenkavalier* (which was a much closer collaboration with Hofmannsthal than *Elektra* had been), Strauss was counseling his partner on how to shape a scene or sequence to ends of proven productivity for the musical theater. Thus, for Act II, he suggests: "It would be very nice if for the second act you could write a contemplative ensemble passage, to follow the moment when some dramatic bomb has just gone off. . . . Examples: Act II of *Lohengrin,* the great ensemble, known as the 'dark broodings.' The *Meistersinger* quintet. Also *Barber of Seville,* end of Act I."[9] Whatever Hofmannsthal's response to this suggestion, Strauss remembered his own prescription for dramatic contrast when he came to write the celebrated trio of *Der Rosenkavalier.* What he needed here was not musical matter per se, for he had accumulated an abundance of it by this point in the opera. His need, rather, was for a manner of evoking an atmosphere suitable for the concluding phase of the opera, after the hurly-burly that had preceded it—or, to cite his own words, for converting a moment "when a dramatic bomb has just gone off" into a scene in which "everybody is lost in contemplation." The likeness to the *Meistersinger* quintet (horn support in the background, as well as the crossing voices) begins to emerge on page 494 of the Boosey and Hawkes *Studienpartitur.* It continues to build steadily from page 494 on, beginning with Octavian's "*Marie Theres', wie gut Sie ist.*" Once launched on ways provided by Wagner, Strauss is quite capable of guiding his craft to a safe harbor of his own. A collateral circumstance may be

8 Del Mar: *Richard Strauss,* p. 261.

9 Strauss-Hofmannsthal: *A Working Friendship,* tr. Hanns Hammelmann and Ewald Osers (New York: Random House; 1961), p. 33.

noted in Samuel Barber's *Vanessa*, which reaches its emotional climax in the quintet of Act IV. This too is "contemplative" in the Straussian sense, but it tends to be imitative rather than generative because it settles for the solution provided by Strauss rather than achieving a further projection, on Barber's part, of Wagner's initiative.

Whether one subscribes to the premise that Strauss's decline began immediately after *Der Rosenkavalier* or considerably later, there would be general agreement that this trio marks the high point of his life's creative effort. He came close to equaling it in some moments of *Ariadne*, *Die Frau ohne Schatten*, and *Capriccio*, but never with such complete success at so strategic a dramatic moment. In the works after *Rosenkavalier*, the lapses from the highest level are more frequent, the descents more precipitous, the striving for a musical solution to a dramatic problem more conspicuous. Clever craftsmen that they were, both Hofmannsthal and Strauss were aware in their later work together of difficulties beyond those that ordinarily beset librettist and composer. A particular instance may be cited from a letter of September 1916 in which Strauss writes to his co-worker: "Your *cri-de-coeur* against Wagnerian 'note-spinning' has deeply touched my heart and has thrust open a door to an entirely new landscape . . . I promise you that I have now definitely stripped off the Wagnerian musical armor . . ."[1]

It was, of course, not a matter as simple as "putting on" or "taking off" the "Wagnerian musical armor," and one suspects that Strauss knew better than to believe that the conditioning of a lifetime could be foresworn by a mere declaration of intent. He strove mightily, through one stratagem and another, to find a way out of the dilemma into which he had been led by his own success. The problem, basically, was to find a further extension of the language he had evolved from the strains and mutations of the continuity to which he was insuperably joined.

There were many appealing things he could do by skill alone (as in *Ariadne*), or by way of diversion (*Intermezzo*), or by a supreme effort of the will (*Die Frau ohne Schatten*), or by a sentimental *Nachblick* (*Arabella*), but there was one thing he could not do, and did not do. That was to find his way out of the tonal labyrinth whose depths he had penetrated more deeply than any other. Many subtle schemes occurred to him by way of escape: an extension and subtilization of the side-slipping harmonies (more specifically, the *enharmonies*) which first appear in the early tone poems; more artful

[1] Ibid., p. 262.

evasions of the cadence than even Wagner had devised in his quest for "endless melody"—those cadences which Strauss realized to be among the major barriers to progress on the main path of musical development; a reversion to simplicity when all the many means of complication known to him resulted only in works which were more Straussian, not more distinctive.

In old age, it almost seemed that in the chromatic involution and tonal convolution of *Metamorphosen* Strauss had fashioned the key to unlock the door, had found the thread of thought to lead him out of his mental confinement. But this insuperably happy ending to an amazing career was denied to him in a work which, for all the promising beating of wings, resolutely refuses to take flight. He personally, and music impersonally, had to settle for the warm afterglow of his youthful fire in the *Four Last Songs*, as affecting a swan song as ever a composer conceived. Strauss-like to the end, he recalled, for *"Im Abendrot,"* his personal place in music's continuity with a citation of a phrase from *Tod und Verklärung*, written more than fifty years before.

5

WHAT STRAUSS TRIED and failed to do has a counterpart in the efforts of others born during his lifetime and come to musical maturity with his rich-textured vocabulary added to the other accumulations of the past. As his productivity began as early as 1882 and remained a factor of musical life until 1948, this takes in all of those (born for fifty years on both sides of the dividing line of the centuries) who addressed themselves to the common problem: how to combine the strains and mutations of the past into a new blend, personally ordained, that would convey individuality, sustain continuity, and endow the tonal language with new shades of meaning.

It took in one born four years before Strauss, who had not only a longer but also a considerably harder struggle to make his name known in the world of composition. By Straussian standards, recognition was painfully slow in coming to Gustav Mahler. (The work generally recognized as his best, *Das Lied von der Erde*, was not even performed during his lifetime.) Yet, by an odd inversion of values, the esteem for his work in the intellectual-professional community tends to rise ever higher. With some, his graph, on a rising curve, may by now have passed Strauss's, on the downward swing. This would have relatively little to do with their status among music lovers generally, but would relate, rather, to the sustenance and suggestion for the musical mentality which Mahler's work contains and Strauss's no longer offers in equal measure.

The simple phraseology of the difference between them (during the fifty years in which their lives overlapped) was that Richard Strauss was a composer who also conducted, whereas Gustav Mahler was a conductor who also composed. Nor was Mahler by any means uncommon in possessing such a "hobby," at a time when the creations of conductors who composed (Weingartner, Max von Schillings, Mottl, and Bülow, among others) were sufficiently numerous to be grouped in a category of their own—*Kapellmeistermusik*.

In the mature years of his life, Mahler raged against the turn of events that compelled him to devote so much of his time to conducting other people's music rather than to writing his own. In his view, this was primarily the fault of the jury for the Beethoven Prize of 1881, which had failed to favor him with its award when he was twenty-one. Lacking the recognition as well as the cash, he was forced to make his way as a conductor, from a subterranean starting point (a spa company in Bad Hall, Austria) along such stepping stones as Ljubljana, Olmütz, and Kassel before attaining the relative prominence of Prague, Leipzig, and Budapest on the way to Hamburg, Vienna, and New York.

There is some doubt that Mahler's recollection of the competition is accurate (he long attributed his failure to the presence of Brahms on the jury) or that winning the prize would have brought him an audience at once. As for the occupation to which he turned, even so prodigiously successful a composer as Richard Strauss found conducting a natural outlet for part of his musical nature. From what might be called a standing start, Mahler raced on to become head of the Budapest Opera at twenty-eight and director of Vienna's Opera on the Ring before he was forty. Such progress speaks of more than a reluctant pursuit of survival. Musical performance was a necessity of his being which, in combination with an unquenchable appetite for self-improvement, carried him to scarcely imaginable heights. It could be agreed that some of what he conducted irked Mahler and that there was, eventually, too much of it. But it is also apparent, from the new documentation of his career by Henry-Louis de La Grange, that conducting gave Mahler an insight into structural and textural values that intimately affected his own music.[2]

[2] Henry-Louis de La Grange: *Gustav Mahler, His Life and Times* (to be published by Doubleday & Co., New York).

If Mahler had a legitimate complaint, it could be that his primary prominence during his lifetime as a conductor tended to mask his primary significance for posterity as a composer. From this confusion of identities arose an easy opportunity to condemn Mahler as a dilettante, who wrote music "on the side." Even one who was as closely associated with Mahler as Arturo Toscanini was at the Metropolitan expressed surprise when he heard William Steinberg conduct a rehearsal of *Das Lied von der Erde* at La Scala in the early fifties. "I didn't know Mahler wrote anything that good," Steinberg quotes him as saying (Carla Toscanini, who overheard their comments at the dinner table, queried: "Is that Mahler the conductor?").

As the enthusiasts for his music were limited to a few conductors (such as Strauss, Weingartner, and Mengelberg), there was relatively little opportunity for it to exert a contemporary effect (as Strauss's did almost at once) save when Mahler conducted it himself. In Vienna, where the impact of the man's day-to-day functioning over a ten-year period (1897–1907) was compulsive even in the absence of regular performances of his music, Mahler compacted a force that expressed itself for years to come. The action and reaction he aroused in such determinative figures of the next decades as Arnold Schoenberg, Alban Berg, and Anton Webern would have given Mahler a monumental place in continuity even if his own music were of lesser consequence.

Few musicians other than Berlioz and Wagner illuminated their time so much by what they *were* as what they did. Much more than his younger contemporary, Strauss, who was born to comfort and swiftly promoted himself to luxury, Mahler typifies the unadvantaged musician at war with a materialistic world, with no weapons at his disposal save talent, resolution, and unrestricted ambition.

By unremitting effort and a capacity for labor hardly less than that of Sisyphus—with whose lot he sometimes affiliated himself[3]— Mahler achieved the incredible feat of writing a dozen orchestral scores of staggering size (if variable quality) and more than a score of fine songs while pursuing a backbreaking career as a conductor. The sheer output of physical effort cost him his life at fifty-one, but it also earned him the enduring esteem he craved. Essentially, it was the fulfillment of a personality pattern that led him, from youth, to mourn the bitterness of life's brevity rather than to savor the sweetness of its length.

The tensions and counterpulls that characterize Mahler's yearning to be a composer-conductor rather than a conductor-composer are intimately characteristic of the cross-hatchings and dichotomies that blur

[3] La Grange: *Gustav Mahler*, ms. p. 1,106.

the lines of the total picture he presents. By birth and orientation he should have been a Czech composer in the continuity of Smetana and Dvořák, both of whom he admired. By taste and predisposition, he was a supremely gifted songwriter, who earned a place in the same wing of the musical Pantheon—if on a slightly lower level—as that of his friend Hugo Wolf. That he became, instead, a composer who ranged from the intimate lyric expressions of *Aus der Jugendzeit* and the *Lieder eines fahrenden Gesellen* to the dithyrambic proclamations of *Veni, Creator Spiritus* in the Eighth Symphony and the epochal adagios of the Third and Ninth symphonies doubtless resulted from the strains and mutations that entered into his gravitation to Vienna at fifteen (from his birthplace in Moravia) rather than to Prague.

To a degree, Mahler paralleled the progression of one with whom his partisans are reluctant to have him affiliated—Anton Bruckner. The easy ignorance with which society (or musical journalism) creates a single individual called Haydnmozart or Debussyravel decreed the conjunction of Bruckner and Mahler as a symphonic Gog and Magog long ago. But the much-needed clarification to establish their separate identities should not lead to the extreme of disassociating them altogether. A simpler solution would be to pursue such a process of elimination as the following:

BRUCKNER AND MAHLER

Identities?	No
Opposites?	Hardly
Affinities?	Decidedly

Whereas Bruckner brought his country manners and rustic impulses to Vienna (from Linz) when his character if not his art was fully formed, Mahler came to the metropolis as a youth, with both character and art malleable and unformed. The childhood fascination with sound which had found expression on an accordion was converted into sufficient pianistic skill, through studies at the Conservatory, to master a Chopin ballade or a Schubert fantasie. From forming his early memories of folk music into polkas and *Ländler*, he progressed to more ambitious ventures into composition. Along the way he spent a year attending Bruckner's lectures, which have caused some to cite him as a pupil of Gog (or Magog) and others to denounce this ascription heatedly as fraudulent. Whatever he may or may not have learned in

Bruckner's classes, he learned a good deal from his study and conducting of Bruckner's Masses; from making, with a fellow student, a transcription for four hands of the Third Symphony; and from hearing the performance of others as circumstances permitted. He was in no more realistic sense a pupil of Bruckner than Beethoven was a pupil of Haydn, but he was no less responsive to the example of his older contemporary, an aware and conscious participant in the musical continuity that he represented.

In the absence of such a frame of reference as was parentally provided to Strauss, Mahler was forced to evolve his own scheme of values from his enthusiasms, good and bad, to find his way unaided and mostly unguided. Losing the Beethoven Prize of 1881 may have forced Mahler into a hard school of servitude—what he called "this hell of the Theater"[4]—but it is a certainty that the great and not so great music he mastered as he mastered the art of conducting cultivated his impulses, sharpened his ear, and furthered that rarefied sense of orchestral color which beams a light, prismlike, through his musical universe. In more than a manner of speaking, the hard school became the university from which he graduated with honors (in tonal refinement) and a doctorate (in musical pathology). Difficult as it was, by comparison with some musicians to whom the command of musical materials came much more easily, the mere problem of achieving self-expression made what Mahler wrote ever more an expression of self.

It has been noted on several occasions earlier in this survey (especially with Berlioz) that an "immature" early work sometimes tells us more about a composer and his essential artistic disposition than a mature later one. Fortunately Mahler's self-esteem rated *Das klagende Lied* of 1880 higher than the Beethoven Prize jury did, and he preserved it despite their rejection for an award. Unfortunately, it does not exist today exactly as it did then, for he took it up again in 1898 to produce the form in which it is now occasionally performed.

However, by the word of the reliable Redlich, the "revision of 1898" of *Das klagende Lied* was "concerned for the most part with the dotting of i's and the crossing of t's and the addition of a profusion of expression marks to what was an already perfectly organized score."[5] Donald Mitchell, in his more recent text, supports this view by saying: "Parts I and II of the cantata we know today correspond very nearly to Parts II and III of the original (1880) version . . . the revisions

---

[4] La Grange: *Gustav Mahler*, ms. p. 109.
[5] Redlich: *Bruckner and Mahler*, p. 174.

were much less far-reaching than has been assumed hitherto."[6]

Whatever may have been contained in the discarded first part, the sections that endure serve perfectly to isolate the earliest evidence of the underlying "fault" (in the geological sense) in Mahler's nature, the schism between the lyric and the dramatic, the simple and the grandiose, the natural and the affected. Here, arrayed in two evenly divided halves, are the essentials of the man-to-be, conveyed in an unmistakably graphic and revealing way. To appreciate the relationship they bear to his later works, it is desirable to know something of their occurrence in this one.

As we know it today, *Das klagende Lied* ("The Song of Lament") embodies a retelling in Mahler's own strophic verses of a Grimm fairy tale known as "The Singing Bone." It relates the suitably barbaric, as well as bardic, legend of a minstrel whose travels through a forest bring him upon a whitened bone, which he fashions into a pipe (or flute). The sad strain it yields comes to have a dramatic result when his wanderings take him to a court where a wedding is about to be celebrated. Bidden to perform, the Minstrel puts the flute to his lips, whereupon it tells the tale of a knight who slew his brother, made off with his young widow, and proclaimed himself king. As the culprit tries vainly to silence the "Singing Bone," vengeance strikes the castle, which crumbles, as the guests flee in terror with their host and the bride-to-be falls to the floor.

The remarkable thing about *Das klagende Lied* as heard today is not the expectable amount of others that it contains, but the unexpected amount of essential Mahler that emerges from it. This relates not only to what he does supremely well in creating a mood for the forest of Part I, but also to what he does clumsily in tracing the happenings of Part II from the Minstrel's arrival to the catastrophic outcome.

Part I, with its opening atmosphere of *Der Wald* ("The Forest"), puts Mahler in the continuity of Bruckner's world of horns and hunters (Symphony No. 4), where Weber and Wagner had wandered before him. The echoes aroused by the horns are not wholly those of others, however. A marchlike motive such as he would write many times in the future (even to the distinctive upper sweep on the shortened first beat of the measure) takes its place among the ideas he manipulates behind the setting of the text. One of them, in a ghostly reminder of Berlioz's *Symphonie fantastique* (in which it appeared for the first

[6] Donald Mitchell: *Gustav Mahler, the Early Years* (London: Rockliff; 1958), p. 174.

time in an orchestral work), is the traditional *Dies irae*. Through Mahler's deft and insinuating setting of this portion of the text runs a musical impulse of warm appeal, especially notable for the one thing that is given, but cannot be taught: the ability to invent musical ideas both shapely and individual. The idiom is clearly that of the *Volkslied* as practiced by Karl Löwe, but Mahler speaks it with an accent of his own.

In the shift to Part II, with its wedding music and steadily more dramatic situation, the transition in artistic values is as drastic as the change of locale from outdoors to indoors. We are, almost at once, caught between the blare of trumpets and the ruffle of drums for the wedding of Lohengrin and Elsa (offstage in Act III), and the chorus of vassals who greet Gunther and Brünnhilde for their similar ceremony in Act II of *Götterdämmerung*. With the reappearance of the story-telling element in the voices, Mahler's personal note also returns, but the reliance throughout on Wagner's orchestral procedures is almost compulsive.

What reveals itself strikingly in these pages of 1880 is, for me, the following: Mahler's strong impulse to lyric sentiment and treatment of words carried him to a fulfillment both purposeful and personal even at this early point of his career. It is when he ventures from the lyric to the dramatic, from the intimate and personal to the epochal and dithyrambic, that there arise those aspects of the whole which leave some listeners mistrustful, disaffected, and unconvinced. However clear this may be to them, the results were all of a piece for the composer, even after a lapse of a dozen years. Writing to his friend Natalie Bauer-Lechner shortly after his rediscovery of *Das klagende Lied* in 1893, Mahler exclaimed in gratification: "The 'Mahler' whom you know was all revealed there at a single blow."[7] Writing a few years later to the same correspondent, he awards *Das klagende Lied* the accolade of "Mahlerian."[8]

Whatever the path Mahler might have taken had *Das klagende Lied* achieved its prize-winning purpose, the one he did follow led, within a few years, to the accomplishment of some of his most characteristic vocal writing. Included were the charming *Aus der Jugendzeit* songs (with piano) of 1882, and the *Lieder eines fahrenden Gesellen* (with orchestra) of 1885. In the latter, especially, Mahler's mating of his own texts (which parallel by more than a little the poems of Wilhelm

[7] La Grange: *Gustav Mahler*, ms. p. 430.
[8] Ibid., ms. p. 562.

Müller made beloved by Schubert) with folk-flavored settings of simple sincerity proclaims the fervent lyricist who would write the later *Kindertotenlieder* and the *Wunderhorn* songs. Here, too, one may observe the first evidence of Mahler's remarkable instinct for what might be called "natural" counterpoint (to distinguish it from the noninstinctive, unnatural, contrived kind), of which Schubert was such a master, the whole of the "Unfinished" Symphony being a particular example. I refer to the free, harmonious interplay of ideas that seem to arise in spontaneous association with each other. Out of this facility, refined and subtilized, emerged some of Mahler's most marvelous moments of expressivity (especially in *Das Lied von der Erde*).

Given the time, the places in which he worked, and the temperament with which he was born, it was beyond the law of probability for Mahler's impulses to confine themselves to small means and easy solutions. The challenge of the impossible was, in my view of his intrinsic nature, a strong spur to Mahler's will to achieve. Working with the orchestra almost daily, learning its resources and still unexploited means tempted conductor-composer Mahler to the command not merely of the biggest apparatus that Wagner had devised, but also of the additions to it by Strauss as well as Bruckner. With the temptation also went the dilemma that had confronted them: to find subject matter suitable to the means. Lacking Bruckner's drive for religious fulfillment or Strauss's flair for the theatrical, Mahler found a comparable source of subject matter in the philosophical and the cosmic—man's place not merely on earth (or in Bruckner's Heaven), but in the universe itself. In turn came works of a size to be described by such names (approved or unapproved) as "The Titan" (Symphony No. 1), "Resurrection" (No. 2), "Giant" (No. 6), and "The Symphony of a Thousand" (No. 8).

Splitting apart the elements in Mahler's artistic personality may hardly be as challenging as rending the atom, or bear with it such consequence to mankind, but it has its fascinations nevertheless. What was evident in the two parts of *Das klagende Lied* remains a factor, present or latent, in all the large-scale works he wrote thereafter: a lyric impulse that carried him to lofty surges of highly personal expression, a compulsion to dramatic gestures which, as often as not, sank him in an abyss of the commonplace. With the enlarged means went problems of extended design which, in turn, presented perilous possibilities of repetition, dullness, and aural satiety. And with all his affection for mammoth utterance, there abided a love for intimacy of detail and clarity of texture which could hardly be called ideal housemates.

6

How MAHLER RECONCILED the warring elements within his nature and achieved a substantial share of the ends to which he aspired is an absorbing study in music's continuity and its own urge to assert itself. It may seem an unwarranted liberty to assign a life force or impute a power of determination to such an abstraction as "the continuity of music." However, it is no abstraction when it becomes the day-and-night concern of one who lived the musical life as intensely and with such absorption as Gustav Mahler lived it. Not only in the works he composed, but also in those he studied to conduct, and many more which he studied but did not conduct, Mahler became as much an instrument of the forces to which he devoted his life as the men under him were instruments of his will.

He had, as we have seen, a typical strain of his own from the beginning. There was the perilous possibility that it could be subdued, submerged, or even destroyed if it were subject to the typical strain of some other, mightier composer, one such as Wagner or Brahms. The drama of Mahler's achievement derived from the persistence with which he labored at his task till he achieved a double triumph: to survive the impact of continuity in his joint role as creator and re-creator, and to add something meaningful to the resources of music as he had found them.

It was, in the first place, essential for Mahler to determine how and in what way the Word would function in his formulation of musical expression. From the first, it was evident that the conjunction was not merely close, but inseparable. *Das klagende Lied* and the *Lieder eines fahrenden Gesellen* were so urgently in need of expression that Mahler wrote his own text for both. This problem of verbal supply was largely solved in 1888 when he came upon *Des Knaben Wunderhorn,* a famous collection of German folk poetry (by Brentano and Arnim). As time passed, he added, as need decreed, from the works of Klopstock, Nietzsche, Rückert, and eventually Goethe and Li-Tai-Po.

To an extent this parallels Strauss's liberation by the Word, but with a distinction at once more specific and more subtle. Whereas the Word merely provided Strauss with subject matter, it provided Mahler with a frame, a perimeter, a source of formal discipline otherwise often lacking in his writing. Strauss used the Word (text or programmatic idea) as a probe to start the music flowing within him. With Mahler, it was the vessel to shape or contain a musical impulse that already existed. Thus it was not the subject of his musical formulation, but the object of his emotional fulfillment. He was, as the *Lieder eines fahrenden Gesellen* demonstrate, writing *Wunderhorn* songs even before he knew the collection existed. As he wrote to his favorite correspondent (Natalie Bauer-Lechner) in 1893: "At one time, when I did not suspect even the existence of the *Wunderhorn*, I had 'seen' it in spirit . . ."[9] As a further instance of Mahler's awareness of his own natural inclinations and talents, a letter of 1897 to the critic and musical aesthetician Arthur Seidl[1] is revealing: "When I conceive a large musical picture, I always reach a point at which the 'word' is necessary to me as a bearer of my musical idea. It must have been that way for Beethoven with his Ninth, but it was then impossible to find the texts he needed, for at bottom, Schiller's poem could not express what was 'unheard-of' in the spirit . . ."

The question might then be reasonably raised: If Mahler fared so successfully with words, why did he desert them as often as he did? The answer, in my view, would be that, being as intensely human as he was (a man of impulse rather than of calculation), Mahler was prone to miscalculation. One of them was the belief that he could write as good music without words as with them. My conception of the pure, the unadulterated, the indispensable Mahler is *Das Lied von der Erde*, which leaves no alternative but to pursue the path that led to it, through difficulties and despite detours. As Mahler threads his way through the continuity of which he was a part and draws others into the maelstrom after him, it tends to become clear that outer judgment and inner impulse did not always cooperate harmoniously. Fortunately for us, as well as for him, Mahler belonged to that select class of artists whose inner life eventually takes command of their fallible judgment. At times it even turned his heart or emotional impulse in the right (profitable) direction when his mind urged him toward a wrong one.

Before taking Mahler to task for failing to do what others, before and after, have done under the banner of "Symphony," it might be well to establish clearly what he understood by the term which he employed no less than ten times. When the question arose in 1895 (the symphonies No. 1 and 2 were complete and No. 3 was on the way), he answered: "The fact that I call it a symphony doesn't signify

---

[9] La Grange: *Gustav Mahler*, ms. p. 430.

[1] *Not* the conductor Anton Seidl (1850–98) as given in *Composers on Music*, ed. Sam Morgenstern (New York: Pantheon Books; 1956), p. 310. This version from La Grange: *Gustav Mahler*, ms. p. 561.

very much, as it has nothing in common with the usual form. The term 'symphony' to me means to build a world with all existing means."[2]

Mahler attempted the God-like task of building "a world" ten different times, and both the form and the content were different each time. No. 1, for example, bears an outward likeness to the traditional symphony: allegro, scherzo, slow movement, finale. Nominally, the subject is Jean Paul Friedrich Richter's *The Titan*, but factually it is the spirit of music as Mahler knew it at twenty-seven which is invoked in the Schumannesque beginning with a falling phrase A-E, F-C, D, B.

In the fullness of time, this phrase will be transformed into the perorating chorale of the finale, but it is almost immediately unmasked, at the beginning of the movement proper, as the highly quotable song from the *Lieder eines fahrenden Gesellen: "Ging heut' Morgen über's Feld."* This is an expression of delight in pastoral surroundings, as satisfactory a solution of Mahler's dilemma as Haydn's quotation of his own melody from the second movement of the "Surprise" Symphony is in Simon's *"Schon eilet froh der Ackersmann"* early in *The Seasons*. It launches him, on a device of well-tried utility, into the midstream of his purpose almost at once, while bearing with it the hidden sail which will, when unfurled, carry him to his destination.

It also bears with it an instance of the kind of "false continuity" that beset Berlioz: the possibility of confusion with a *better-known* but *later* use of the same notes. When Mahler's Symphony No. 1 was first performed in New York (and America) in 1909, one of his critics observed: "Just precisely why the composer should announce to us once or twice in the course of the movement that he is going back to Maxim's is inexplicable . . ."[3] The reference is to the part of the *Fahrenden Gesellen* song which is associated with the words *"Tau noch auf den Gräsern hing, sprach zu mir der lust'ge Fink,"* which unquestionably

Lehár: The Merry Widow, Act I

[2] La Grange: *Gustav Mahler*, ms. p. 508.
[3] W. J. Henderson in the New York *Sun*.

Mahler: Lieder eines fahrenden Gesellen, *No. 2*

has the conformation of Prince Danilo's *"Dann geh' ich in's Maxim"* in Lehár's *Die Lustige Witwe.*

What the critic could hardly know was that Mahler's tune had been written twenty-five years before, when Lehár was only fifteen, with his most famous creation still twenty years in the future. It raises the possibility, at least, that a suggestion of the same phrase in the "Intermezzo" of Bartók's Concerto for Orchestra[4] is an allusion to a source other than the obvious one, that his mind was on Mahler rather than Lehár.

[4] Boosey and Hawkes miniature score, p. 72.

Bartók: Concerto for Orchestra, Intermezzo

It is also worthy of note that, in his first symphonic undertaking, Mahler strikes out for the ultimate expressive challenge: a sequence in which the scherzo is second and the slow movement precedes the finale. That this formulation was suggested by Bruckner's choice of it for his two last, and greatest, symphonies is at most debatable: Mahler was well versed in the great work in which Beethoven pioneered the practice. Indeed, Mahler conducted the Ninth Symphony as early as 1886 in Prague, not only on short notice (when its scheduled conductor, Karl Muck, was suddenly called away), but also without a score.[5]

In this instance, however, the conformation of the slow movement is much more according to early Mahler than to late Beethoven. He makes striking use of *"Frère Jacques"* as the motive for a macabre march, in which muted doublebasses and muffled timpani have a prominently funereal part. Even more arresting is the intrusion (p. 81 of the Universal Edition miniature score) of a cheap strain of dance music,

Mahler: Symphony No. 1, D, third movement

[5] Gabriel Engel: *Gustav Mahler, Song-Symphonist* (New York: Bruckner Society of America; 1932), p. 50.

the first appearance of this characteristically Mahlerish kind of grotesquerie. It should be noted that it is marked *"Mit Parodie,"* which refines its grossness to, at least, the intentional (see p. 221). Whether a passing allusion to a phrase typical of Grieg (the most common association would be with "Anitra's Dance" in the *Peer Gynt* music) is also purposeful may be left to individual judgment.

Grieg: Peer Gynt *Suite No. 1 (op. 46), No. 3*

Mahler selects well from his own store of melodic material in utilizing *"Die zwei blauen Augen"* from the *Lieder eines fahrenden Gesellen* for the trio, a welcome interlude of sunshine before the bleak cloud of the dead march closes in again.

Up to this point, it seems to me, Mahler had been working well within his capacities as a first symphonist to produce a work as creditable in that context as Schubert's first, or Dvořák's, or Weber's, if not as good as Schumann's. In his striving to produce something like the summarizing climax of the Brahms C-minor—a first symphony of another, vastly superior character—Mahler had nothing so borrowable as a song of his own. For the chorale built from the motive heard at the outset, he has recourse, rather, to the *Lohengrin* trumpets of *Das klagende Lied* as preface to a *Götterdämmerung* kind of clamor.

A revealing word on the First Symphony was spoken by Mahler himself several years later (1894) when Richard Strauss, official head of the *avant-garde* as it was then constituted, put the prestige of his position in Weimar to the advantage of pathbreaking works. Among them was Mahler's First Symphony, which Strauss performed in 1894 in its final, amended form (when the composer conducted it in Budapest in 1889, an andante occupied the place later assigned to the *"Frère Jacques"* march). The composer-conductor, in a spirit of camaraderie, suggested to the conductor-composer an alteration or two that he thought would strengthen its effect. Mahler's reply was that the First Symphony "was as a skin cast off and left on the way."[6] The image aptly suggests something he had grown out of, as much part of a phase of his prior being as the snake's shedding.

Strauss's fame began so much earlier than Mahler's and his life lasted so much longer that today it hardly seems credible that there was a time when they were contemporaries on an outwardly parallel course. Strauss was one of the first to perceive Mahler's qualities as a composer, and he performed several valuable services on Mahler's behalf. For his part, Mahler recognized that he benefited not only from Strauss the conductor, but also from Strauss the composer. In the letter to Seidl previously quoted, Mahler observed: "I should have had the appearance of a monster with my works if Strauss's success had not prepared the ground . . . For me it was extraordinary luck to find among my contemporaries such a comrade in combat and creation . . ."[7]

As well as comprehending the practical advantage of such a "contemporary," Mahler had a formidably acute awareness of the difference between Strauss's artistic objectives and his own. He clearly defined the distinction between the outwardly parallel and the inwardly opposed when, calling upon his contemporary reading, he continues: "Schopenhauer used the figure of speech of two miners, each digging his tunnel, who start from opposite sides of the mountain and finally meet underground. That seems to me to describe perfectly my relation to Strauss."

How comprehensively Mahler meant this image to be applied, he did not then say. However, it was one to which he frequently reverted, according to Alma Mahler, who quotes him (in the context of their relationship beginning in 1901) as saying: "Strauss and I tunnel from opposite sides of the mountain. One day we shall meet."[8] With or with-

[6] La Grange: *Gustav Mahler*, ms. p. 459.
[7] Ibid., ms. pp. 560–1.
[8] Alma Mahler: *Gustav Mahler, Memories and Letters* (New York: The Viking Press; 1946), p. 87.

out the hopeful addendum, it strikes me as not merely a picturesque but also an uncannily accurate summation of their common quest for a satisfactory solution to a common dilemma.

Strauss's side of the mountain found him tunneling from vertical chord formations connected by tentacles of parts (voices) toward subtle, unexpected alterations of customary practice which would bring him out on a fertile valley of fresh possibilities. Mahler's probe was more along the lateral lines of "natural counterpoint," of which harmony was a by-product rather than a precondition. Reduced to fundamentals, it might be stated that Strauss sought to disguise the old relationship among the known resources of music, whereas Mahler was drawn to the possibility of finding new relationships among the unknown. Perhaps Mahler's prediction of a "meeting" would have been proved correct had he continued to compose as long as Strauss did, but the final engineer was the hand of Fate rather than the wit of man.

7

THE SECOND, THIRD, and fourth of Mahler's symphonies are customarily known as the "*Wunderhorn*" symphonies because each of them includes a setting of a poem from that collection (as the first calls upon material from the *Lieder eines fahrenden Gesellen*). In a larger sense, however, they are affiliated with two other characteristics of the First Symphony: the schismatic division between the lyric and the dramatic, and the attraction to the Ninth Symphony of Beethoven as containing the key, somehow, to the kind of symphony Mahler aspired to achieve.

In the First Symphony, Mahler had endorsed Beethoven's procedure of placing the slow movement third in the sequence; in the Second, he added the concept of a vocal finale, which, by the accident of Bülow's death and public funeral in Hamburg, became a setting of Klopstock's *Auferstehen* (Mahler acknowledged, in a letter of the period, "I had had for a long time the thought of using the chorus in the last movement, and only the fear that this might be considered an imitation of Beethoven made me hesitate . . .")[9] In the Third Symphony, the slow movement takes not merely the position pioneered by Beethoven, but also, as its thesis, his procedure. In the Fourth, the same great *adagio cantabile* of the Ninth governs Mahler's thought as he strives for a new direction at a turning point in his own *poco adagio*.

Each work also contains a fair share of other allusions, intentional or not, to works of his predecessors, allusions that exhaust some listeners, exalt others. In either case, they place Mahler firmly in the con-

[9] R. Bagar and L. Biancolli: *The Concert Companion*, p. 406.

tinuity of those who had prepared the ground he now cultivated. Is the opening of No. 2 a reminiscence of the "Storm" in *Die Walküre*?

Wagner: Die Walküre, *prelude to Act I*

Mahler: Symphony No. 2, C minor, *first movement*

Two of Mahler's admirers disagree (La Grange says yes; Neville Cardus says no). Unquestionably Wagnerian, in my judgment, is a phrase a little farther on (p. 28 of the Universal Edition miniature score).

The difference of this from other examples of allusion is simple: Mahler has taken an atypical thought of Wagner and, in the classic way defined in Axiom II (p. 32), has put it to a use that will eventually become typically his own. There are two further factors of interest. The *Siegfried Idyll*, from which it stems, is perhaps Wagner's most sophisticated example of "natural counterpoint." It is also the work cited by Gabriel Engel as forecasting Mahler's "transparent style of instrumentation, prophetic of the modern chamber-symphony language . . ."[1]

Further to distinguish between the generative and the repetitive, one may cite, in the first category, another use of the *Dies irae*; the appearance of an ostinato bass very much like the one borrowed by Bruckner for his Third Symphony (see p. 172) from the first movement of Beethoven's Ninth (in Mahler it appears on p. 13 of the miniature score, and in more determined form on p. 49); interruption of the tranquilly devout mood of the "*Urlicht*," this work's *Wunderhorn* poem, by an angry orchestral outburst which, as Mahler "freely acknowledged,"[2] derived from the famous dissonant chord that precedes the bass recitative in the same No. 9; and a paraphrase of a section of Schubert's C-major Symphony (measures 233–50 of the slow movement) which helps him through a critical phase of his own prelude to "*Auferstehen*" (p. 165 of the Universal Edition miniature score [see pp. 227, 228–229]). In the category of the repetitive is the likeness of the opening phrase of the "*Urlicht*" to a key thought in Brahms's German Requiem, remarked by none other than Brahms himself.[3]

Needless to say, what assures the appeal of Mahler's Second Symphony to contemporary audiences is not the average listener's unawareness of these adulterants—I find much of it impressive *with* the awareness—but the size and scope of the capstone he put upon his structure with all its borrowed blocks. It seems to me inconceivable that Mahler could have worked as he did, under conditions of stress and, literally, on borrowed time, without invoking everything that thronged his mind, old as well as new. In a letter of a few years later (1900) to Bauer-Lechner he put the matter quite bluntly: "Now I must work without

[1] *Thompson's International Cyclopedia of Music and Musicians*, 8th edn., p. 1073 (Engel's article on Mahler).
[2] Redlich: *Bruckner and Mahler*, p. 189.
[3] La Grange: *Gustav Mahler*, ms. p. 588.

an instant's relaxation during these short weeks, sometimes creating at any price, even when I am weary and out of sorts, solely in order to reach the completion, which infinitely increases the effort and cannot benefit my work."[4]

Schubert: Symphony No. 9, C, first movement

[4] Ibid., ms. p. 983.

(*continued*)

Mahler: Symphony No. 2, C minor, "Auferstehen"

What remains inconceivable is how, despite this additional obstacle, Mahler persisted in crowding the largest possible expressions into the shortest available time of creation. He had barely left the Second Symphony behind when he moved on to the mammoth challenge of the Third. Originally intended to be smaller in scope than its predecessor, it came to require eight French horns and a post horn among its one hundred and thirteen instrumentalists, as well as a contralto soloist and two choral groups. (The six movements by which it is now known originally had a seventh, which was detached and utilized in the Fourth Symphony when Mahler realized that the whole work had become unmanageable.)

For much of its length the Third Symphony is remarkable not alone for its scope and generally affirmative mood but also for the brilliant highlights and artful shadows of its orchestral colorations. It is altogether a more subtle, variously tinted creation than either of its predecessors, consistent in its striving for that single quality which Mahler cherished above all others: clarity. Doubtless the ever-expanding range of his activities as a conductor contributed to this refinement and radiance. Writing to Bauer-Lechner during the period of its composition (1896), he observed: "It's no use, in these matters, to form abstract ideas not corresponding to reality."[5] "These matters" were such concerns as having everything "heard just as I myself heard it with my interior ear," even to using the D string of the violin for "singing, tender, exalted passages" and the G string for "sorrowful and more sonorous episodes" when the same scale steps were performed.

This growing awareness of how to employ "each instrument in the right place and for its own qualities" would, of itself, have made the Third Symphony absorbing. What makes it unforgettable is the great slow movement with which it ends. The first intimation of the motivating impulse comes with the unfolding plot of thematic sequence: a broad subject of the langsam opening is succeeded by a rather quicker-moving one; both, in turn, are subject to variations. This very nearly duplicates the procedure of the *adagio molto cantabile* of Beethoven's Ninth, where the plan goes A, B, A1, B1, A2 and then A3—A3 being the almost unendurably extended coda in which music merges into a transport of emotion suspending time. With Mahler, the sequence is A, B, B1, A1, B2, A2 and then A3—A3 compounding into one of his most sonorous climaxes everything that had preceded it.

What Mahler evolved, at a distance of seventy-odd years, can be seen as an instance of continuity at its most compelling. But how he

[5] Natalie Bauer-Lechner: *Erinnerungen an Gustav Mahler* (Leipzig-Vienna-Zürich: E. P. Tal and Co.; 1923), p. 51.

had derived it would doubtless have startled him even more. The scheme to which he was responsive—very consciously, of course—is launched with an idea derived, altogether unconsciously, undoubtedly, directly from another great work of Beethoven: the superb *lento assai* of the last quartet (opus 135, in F):

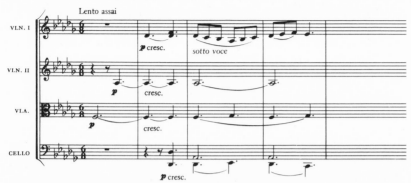

Beethoven: *String Quartet No. 16, F (op. 135), lento assai*

What draws the parallel even closer is the identical position of the notes on the staff, separated by only flat and natural signs. Beethoven, writing in D flat, begins with the tonic tone, goes down the scale to A flat, then up again to F, and comes to rest on E flat. Mahler, writing in D, begins with that tone and goes down to A and back up to F sharp before settling on E. (The note values differ, as Beethoven's meter is

Mahler: Symphony No. 3, G, langsam

6/8, Mahler's 4/4, but the action of the lower voices is much the same.)[6]

Here, then, is an illuminating example of a composer building not only on, but also with, the past. Once launched on this reverie of Beethoven, Mahler draws upon a rich range of the linguistic resources that had been accumulating for nearly a century (Schubertian, Schumannesque, Brahmsian) to dream a vision of his own tonal aesthetic at its most expansive. The difference between the fragmented "allusions" previously remarked and this transformation of a predecessor's germinal concept into a growth of his own is a graphic demonstration of the difference between a half-swallowed recollection and a completely di-

Wagner: Siegfried Idyll

[6] La Grange: *Gustav Mahler*, ms. p. 542, mentions that one of Mahler's diversions during his Hamburg years was playing chamber music and listening to it being performed by members of the opera orchestra (and others) in the circle in which he moved.

gested assimilation. Through the organic change that resulted, Mahler produced a surge of eloquent music quite unlike anything to be found in those who supplied its components—Beethoven or Bruckner, Schubert, Schumann, Brahms, or Wagner (whose young Siegfried, as limned in the *Idyll* (see p. 232) joins in at an exquisitely appropriate place).

Mahler: Symphony No. 3, G, langsam

Four years passed before Mahler addressed himself to the symphonic process again, a lapse of instrumental activity usually attributed to the press of work which began in 1897, when he became director of the Vienna Opera. But it is at least possible that an awareness of the height he had achieved in bringing his Third Symphony to its mountain-topping conclusion made him hesitate to try again just then.

In any case, when he found the time and the impulse to plan another symphony, it was on a quite different scale and in another vein. The Fourth ends with the *Wunderhorn* setting originally intended for

No. 3 ("*Wir geniessen die himmlischen Freuden*"), a fact that has caused most commentators to put it in a bracket with its two antecedents. However, No. 4 is playable by as few as eighty-seven players, trombones and tubas are omitted from the scoring, and it requires but a single vocal soloist. In it Mahler has composed his "*Pastorale*," a conclusion prompted by more than Bruno Walter's reminiscence[7] that its ideas flowed from Mahler's walks in the Vienna countryside beloved by his predecessor.

Intellectually, the neighborhood it favors is that frequented by Schubert rather than Beethoven, but the sense of the sun and its heat, the earth and its life-renewing power is pervasive. Through it courses that abundance of melodic thought and richness of feeling which characterize Mahler's art at its most ingratiating. That he did not undervalue either is abundantly evident from his own words on the subject: "Melodic invention is one of the surest of all the signs of the divine gift; if a man is given it, it seems that one can bet on him as in lottery, with very good chances of success . . . whoever has not received the prize from Heaven in his cradle will not receive it later and by chance."[8]

Though Mahler arrays himself in the guise of Schubert from time to time in the first movement, his own gait and stride are consistently present. Remarkably, several years later Mahler made irritated reference to having duplicated in this movement ideas belonging to "a symphony of Brahms and a piano concerto of Beethoven." They have eluded me, even with his verbal clue.[9] Schubert's spirit hovers almost visibly over the *Ruhevoll* (*poco adagio*) which, faithful to Mahler's most revered model, follows the scherzo. It begins with an ostinato which clearly says "Who is Sylvia?" to anyone who knows that superbly composed song. Unlike the adagio of the Third Symphony, where Beethoven is in the blood of Mahler as well as in the bone of his structure, the ideas that emerge from his nuclear thought are wholly Mahler's own. The procedure is, again, by variations, but this time by a scheme self-evolved rather than derived from Beethoven's. The momentary dependence on a source outside of himself is at number 4, where a fresh breath of impulse is needed, and the oxygen is provided from the cellos in a phrase very close to the *andante moderato* of Beethoven's slow movement (p. 129 of the Eulenburg miniature score). Thus refreshed, Mahler is on his own way again.

That way, by the end of the Symphony No. 4, had clearly carried

---

[7] Quoted in the annotation of his Columbia recording.
[8] La Grange: *Gustav Mahler*, ms. p. 899.
[9] Unless one is the brief horn solo (measures 328–30), akin to the principal theme of Beethoven's Fourth Concerto (also in the key of G).

him to a destination of his own: the tight command of a technique of expression, both in its emotional concept and in its realization for the orchestra, personal to him. In effect, by crossing strains and grafting mutations, he had succeeded in growing his own fruit on roots belonging to others.

8

THUS, BY THE TIME Mahler had numerically equaled the symphonic output of Brahms, he had also achieved a body of work which established him as a master of his endowment as defined in the early songs and the even earlier *Das klagende Lied*. Indeed, in the Third and Fourth symphonies, Mahler had achieved the not inconsiderable feat of playing to his own lyric strength and suppressing his weaker inclination to the dramatic. This might have been a source of gratification, even of satisfaction, to another, but for Mahler at forty, it was but a way point. It was his special distinction, sometimes prizeable, sometimes self-defeating, always to see another, higher objective than the one he had attained, to strive on, toward something elusive and distant, whether it was within the possibility of achievement or not.

It was precisely at this point (1901) that Mahler felt impelled to move on from the objectives with which he had been absorbed till then and strike out along new lines. There are, for example, no more *Wunderhorn* songs, either as independent settings or as parts of larger works. Friedrich Rückert became his favorite poet, not only in the tender texts that are the basis for the *Kindertotenlieder,* but also as the source of such evocative lyrics as *"Ich atmet' einen linden Duft"* and *"Ich bin der Welt abhanden gekommen."*

To say that between 1902 and 1905 Mahler was absorbed with the creation of orchestral music would be to borrow the Brahms kind of understated reference to his Second Piano Concerto as "tiny." He was, rather, obsessed with it. In the space of four summers, he finished the Fifth Symphony, which had been begun in the previous year, and pressed on to the Sixth and Seventh. Such productivity from a Brahms, who devoted all his days to composition, would have taxed credulity. For one whose mind and strength were absorbed with other things between October and May, it was nothing less than frantic.

In the sequence of the nine, the symphonies numbered 5, 6, and 7 have a place akin to that of Nos. 1 and 2. In addition to the musical objectives Mahler achieved within each work, the sequence as a whole carried him to a new plateau of expressivity. In the earlier instance, that plateau means symphonies Nos. 3 and 4; in the latter it was Nos. 8 and 9, and the great work between them, *Das Lied von der Erde.* The haste in composition which marred parts of the earlier symphonies (especially the finale of No. 2) strikes me as unpleasantly evident in Nos. 5, 6, and 7.

Indeed, Mahler achieves his purpose most successfully in the adagietto of the Fifth, which is but eight minutes in length and utilizes nothing more than string choir and harp. Here Mahler writes music of utmost purity, in a serene, assured approach toward his prized goal of tonal transparency. What I previously described as the *"Siegfried Idyll progression"* makes another appearance, here in association with the kind of scoring that produces an iridescent play of color through the individual use of each instrument. Amid all the congested resonances of the Fifth, the simple formulation of the adagietto, with its conjunction of string figures and harp arpeggios, bears truest promise of eloquent things to come.

Despite the increasing frequency with which Mahler has been performed since 1950 in the United States and England, symphonies Nos. 6 and 7 remain all but unknown to the general public. It is not wholly without relevance that they have the least general interest. Both have been picked over by specialists in the lore of Mahler, and cherished by musicians as sources for later manifestations of the Viennese trinity (Schoenberg, Berg, and Webern) in such combinations as celesta, harp, cowbell, and solo violin in the first movement of No. 6, or the use of a metal plate struck by a hammer in its finale. As an absorption from another source, one may note the first prominent appearance in Mahler of the intertwining string passages introduced by Tchaikovsky in the finale of the *"Pathétique"* (violas over violins, first violins below seconds, and cellos between). This gives a new sonorous cast to a much-used range of the tonal spectrum.

In the Seventh Symphony, however, the interests are of rather another sort. It bears the title "The Song of the Night," but it might be better described as Mahler's conception of a divertimento (if anything whose playing time is nearly two hours can be described by so lighthearted a name). At the center of the five-movement sequence is a scherzo, preceded and followed by sections titled *"Nachtmusik."* The first and final movements are among Mahler's most elaborate.

Throughout, the emphasis is on the glorification of the commonplace. This, of course, had crept into every one of his previous symphonies at some point, but not as a guiding principle. Now it provides the prevailing mood and tone, a coloration parodistic, perhaps even satiric. Much of it is done with extraordinary point and deftness of incongruous detail, as if exclusively designed to serve some future admirer, a Shostakovich say, as a paradigm of grotesqueries. Indeed, the last bumptious pages, with their timpani fanfares, cymbal clashes, and brass proclamations of a theme from movement one, are almost a caricature of Mahler's own style as it might be rendered by a Bartók.

Assuming that one listens to it for the sake of what had preceded (and might follow) rather than for itself—it is much too repetitiously tedious to award pleasure as well as reward curiosity—the Seventh is liberally spotted with colors, contrasts, devices, and procedures that carry the art of sound-combination much beyond anything Mahler had previously achieved. Whether it is the violins in the highest possible register and the basses far below them, or the birdlike conversations of the clarinet, oboe, and horn in the first *Nachtmusik*, or a pizzicato punctuation marked *fffff*[1] for basses and cellos (produced by drawing the string [on B flat] so far away from the fingerboard that, when released, it produces an ear-popping clatter), or such a delicacy as mandolin and guitar vying with each other for inaudibility, or glockenspiel matching irreconcilable "beats" (vibrations) with a cowbell—the Seventh is a thesaurus of the odd and the unusual in musical effect. Mahler, who had striven for so long to master clarity in the usual was now, it would seem, driven to assert similar domination of the unusual.

It is perhaps significant of the real utility of such sound-values that they have come to their most prominent, lasting use in the works of Webern—on a scale, to paraphrase Schumann on Schubert, of heavenly brevities. With all the manpower of the oversized orchestra at his disposal and the command of a tonal vocabulary matched by few composers at any time, Mahler finds little to convey but such impractical musical jokes as might have been done delightfully in rather less than half the length of time he utilizes.

In a larger view, all this was perhaps a needful part of Mahler's special kind of quest, a further probe into the mountain in which progress was slow, resistance hard and grinding. There is some suggestion in the Mahler literature that both works gave him an inordinate amount of difficulty in revision and alteration, even some worrisome thought that he was losing the impulse to write in a fresh, compulsive way. Discussing No. 7, Redlich writes: "In the Seventh Symphony . . . an alarming thing becomes apparent for the first time in Mahler's

---

[1] Is there another *fortississississimo* in the range of music? Mahler perhaps acquired the idea for this directive from Tchaikovsky, who cautions his players to reduce their effort from *pp*, *ppp*, *pppp* to *ppppp* thirty measures from the end of the "*Pathétique*."

career as a composer: the self-repetition which was destined to mar the last two symphonies . . ."[2]

If Mahler was beset by a psychic problem, it was one in which the conscious was rescued from the path it was pursuing by the intercession of the subconscious. In his last three symphonies Mahler had forgotten what he had confided to Arthur Seidl about the importance of the Word . . . or else he had determined to prove that he could create an instrumental cosmos without intervention of a text. Whether by accident or by coincidence, by soul-searching or by a vigilant instinct for self-perpetuation, his subconscious, in the course of his "year-round reading," guided him to the Latin hymn *Veni, Creator Spiritus* by the eighth-century monk Hrabanus Maurus. The result was much like the liberating effect of encountering Klopstock's "*Auferstehen*" at Bülow's funeral—a rush of response in which the whole of the first section of the mammoth Eighth Symphony was sketched in a frenzied three weeks.

In its verses is embodied a stirring invocation to the Holy Ghost to bestow "the gifts that from the Spirit flow." When Mahler's imagination was seized by the suggestions of this subject, he decided to couple it with the closing scene of Part II of *Faust*, for reasons he explained to his wife in a letter several years later: "That which draws us by its mystic force, that which every created thing . . . knows with absolute certainty as the essence of their being, that which Goethe, here again using an image, calls the Eternal Feminine, i.e., the resting place, the goal, in opposition to the striving and the struggling toward the goal (the Eternal Masculine), you are quite right in calling it the force of Love . . ."[3] However he chose to explain it to himself, the compelling influence of this verbal partnership with Hrabanus Maurus and Goethe was to relieve Mahler of his obsession with the orchestra, to reveal anew (even to himself) his ordination to the relationship of tones and words. Together they set in motion the thoughts and emotions that produced his two greatest works.

9

SUCH WORDS APPLIED TO *Das Lied von der Erde* would not surprise even the dissident music lover, for it is universally esteemed by partisans and detractors alike as the supreme production of Mahler's creative life. But bracketing the Eighth with it may strike even some of his most

[2] Redlich: *Bruckner and Mahler*, p. 202.
[3] Alma Mahler: *Gustav Mahler, Memories and Letters*, p. 258.

ardent admirers as quixotic. This, I am convinced, relates in large part
to an absence of information on which to base a positive judgment
rather than to the possession of experience on which to found a negative one. Performances of the Eighth are at best infrequent—New York,
for example, heard the complete score in 1966 for the first time in more
than thirty years—and the printed score is but a blueprint of an un-
imaginably complex tonal structure. The by-product of Leonard Bern-
stein's venture—the first reasonable facsimile in recorded form—may
provide more clarification of its content than all the words written and
printed about it since it was created in eight weeks of 1906 (with time
taken out by Mahler to conduct *Le Nozze di Figaro* at Salzburg!).

When the listener accomplishes, by whatever means or combinations of them he can command, a comprehension of the musical content
of the Eighth Symphony, its crucial place in the whole of Mahler's
accomplishment is unmistakable. It is a kind of gigantic outward thrust
of sound, a flying buttress on which depended the body of what was
to come. That it happens to embody, also, the most grandiose requirements of any piece of music ever written (with the exception of the
first score of Schoenberg's *Gurrelieder*) is not so much a condition of
its quality as a cause of its neglect.

In the two parts of the Eighth are encompassed, for still another
time, the same tendencies-in-opposition to the lyric and the dramatic,
the reflective and the hortatory, the active and the passive which were
remarked as early as *Das klagende Lied* of twenty-five years before. In
this two-part structure, the order of occurrence is inverted, dramatic
before lyric. Here it is the hymn that drives Mahler almost beyond the
limits of human execution—repeated high C's for the choristers are but
a symbol of the strain that is put upon them—in order to satisfy his
sense of dramatic suitability.

What justifies his demand and carries the work forward against all
obstacles—indeed, against the strongest resistance of the coolest-headed
listener—is the stunning coherence of the contrapuntal texture and the
coruscating brillance of the orchestra's embellishments (a neo-Baroque
concept well before either "Baroque" or "neo" had made their appearance on the world stage of musicology). Implementing the instrumental
skills he had extended and enlarged in the Sixth and Seventh symphonies is a vast expansion in his command of counterpoint. Through
close study of Bach's motets,[4] the "natural counterpoint" for which he

4 The Neue Bach Gesellschaft, founded in 1900, included Mahler among its
members, and its productions of 1901 were of special influence on him. La Grange:
Gustav Mahler, ms. p. 1087.

so long had had a sound instinct was now complemented by a sure hand in the manipulation of more formal devices.

It is this combination of orchestral wisdom and contrapuntal witchery which imparts to the hymn a sound quite unlike anything written before or, for that matter, since. Mingled with his sure sense of purpose in plotting a subject that lends itself to imitations and over-lappings is an instrumental *brio* that drives the music onward in a series of vaulting thrusts that carry through discursive episodes as well as main fugal formations. Here, it could be said, Mahler has succeeded in crossing the learning of Bach's *Kunst der Fuge* with the energy of Beethoven's *Grosse Fuge* to evolve a structure as much his own as the combined sound of voices and instruments which reverberate within it.

In the quieter, more retrained second part, Mahler reaches even greater heights of eloquence. Constant adherence to a verbal pattern provides not only the subject of his discourse but also the form and design of its expression. In a retrospective projection of a Lisztian principle of unity, the basic theme of the long movement is derived from the opening phrase of the preceding hymn (the notes to which the words "*Veni, Creator Spiritus*" are sung). Transformed to the needs of a *poco adagio* (as the second part is marked, by exception to Mahler's common preference for German terminology), it serves as a *basso ostinato* above which Mahler embroiders some of his most fanciful melodic traceries. Some commentators have likened the treatment of the final "*Alles Vergängliche ist nur ein Gleichnis*"[5] to Liszt's formulation of the same words in his *Faust Symphony*; others attribute to it a "deep affinity" with the "*Auferstehen*"[6] of Mahler's own Symphony No. 2. But it is, in either case, preceded by nearly a hundred and twenty-five pages of orchestral writing which reach out into areas of expression and sensibility not previously accessible even to Mahler.

It is noteworthy, for example, that the concept of mass in Part I is succeeded by a treatment decidedly soloistic in Part II (affecting instruments as well as voices). For the first time in a Mahler symphony, solo male voices appear in Part II, with increasing prominence for the tenor as the work develops. The alto sound which added so much to sympohnies 2 and 3 is herein restored to its position of prominence, with the alternation of tenor and alto permitting Mahler to write some of his most beautiful passages of contrast as well as of collaboration. As the section develops, it tends more and more to such fanciful com-

[5] Dika Newlin: *Bruckner, Mahler and Schoenberg* (New York: King's Crown Press; 1947), p. 195.
[6] Redlich: *Bruckner and Mahler*, p. 216.

binations as piccolo, harmonium, celesta, and harp, as well as to the first suggestion of a pentatonic scale in Mahler (p. 161 of the miniature score).

As he strives for a conclusion worthy of the whole—in which, as is so often the case with Mahler, the reach exceeds the grasp—he pushes his contrapuntal lines to harmonic combinations of striking originality. At the words *"zum Dienst erbotig,"* the pattern of relationship is so intricate that one part must be expressed as A flat, another as G sharp.[7] At this point *enharmonie* is no longer a harmonic abstraction: it is a physical fact. Finally, it is toward the end of the whole movement (pp. 212–13) that the echoing sound of *"Ewig"* takes hold of Mahler for the first time, not to relinquish its possessive, obsessive power for months to come.

The physical events of those next months, preceding the creation of *Das Lied von der Erde,* are well known, for they are as frequently reproduced as his most frequently performed work is heard. The Mahlers' first-born daughter (Maria Anna) died of diphtheria at the age of five, and in the aftermath of this tragedy, a doctor's examination disclosed that Mahler's heart was seriously deficient, his active life a dangerous strain on its limited capacity. Other than orchestrating the Eighth Symphony, he wrote little music during the summer of 1907. Despite these grievous happenings, and with a full knowledge of his precarious health, he signed the contract that took him to America as a conductor at the Metropolitan. It was his hope to earn enough money, in the next few years, to relax his strenuous pattern of performance, perhaps even to become a full-time composer.

On the other hand, the development of the musical means to make *Das Lied* what it is has not been so frequently discussed. Like certain works by other composers—Berlioz, for example—*Das Lied* becomes a familiar part of the average music lover's experience before he knows much else of Mahler. It is thus all too easy to regard it as the most characteristic vein of his expression rather than as, in many ways, the least. Even those who know a fair range of Mahler's earlier works may conclude, from the subtlety and perfection of its coloration, that the language came to him as a happy, spontaneous response to the eloquent, bittersweet words with which it is mated.

But close attention to Part II of the Eighth Symphony leads inescapably to the conclusion that the musical language of *Das Lied* was not invoked or evoked, invented or revealed, but evolved. Without such an awareness, the power and resource to set the Chinese verses of Li

[7] Page 197 of the miniature score, number 188 of the conductor's markings.

Tai-Po (as rendered in German by Hans Bethge) must seem a miraculous dispensation from a benign divinity. With such an awareness, it is abundantly evident that the power was achieved, not bestowed, that it proceeded from Mahler's own labors, and that, like most things of deceptive simplicity, it was the product of the hardest kind of manual labor. That, of course, is the backbreaking effort that went into symphonies 6 and 7 (unsatisfactory as they may be in their several ways) and that begins to yield a residual matter of exceptional purity and malleability halfway through Part II of the Eighth Symphony. Revealingly enough, it begins to show itself at the words *"Kein Engel trennte,"*[8] which mark the first appearance in Part II of the alto (or mezzo) whose sound is so much a part of *Das Lied*. At moments one has the uncanny illusion of hearing a new, previously unfamiliar part of *Das Lied* (with chorus). They soon pass, as Mahler pursues what is more relevant to Goethe than to Li-Tai-Po, but the link exists for whosoever cares to connect it.

The special phenomenon of *Das Lied* is that its sound was arrived at wholly by Mahler's inner ear, unaided by either worldly approval or professional endorsement of the experimental work that had preceded its composition in 1908. The Eighth did not receive its first performances until September 1910 (in Munich). But it was the intellectual muscle that Mahler developed to move the mountains of sound it contains which enabled him also to shift the grains of tonal sand on which the gradations of meaning in *Das Lied* rest.

Providentially, Mahler's initial impulse to set several of the poems as individual songs (in the manner of the *Wunderhorn* excerpts and Rückert's *Kindertotenlieder*) was superseded as he entered deeper into the world of imagery created by Li-Tai-Po. His next thought was to connect them by interludes. Out of this evolved the final, continuous texture of voice and instruments, in which the tenor has the first words but the last "word" is delivered nonverbally by the instrumental ensemble.

It is not without significance that Mahler achieved his finest expression in a vein of vocal lyricism that he had commanded as early as the *Lieder eines fahrenden Gesellen*. What he had added in the intervening years was the skill to make every instrument of the orchestra an equal embodiment of his poetic purpose. Out of his absorption with such an ideal as the *Siegfried Idyll* he had developed the tonal draughtsmanship to make a thin line of violin sound stand out against the sustained tone of the oboe and to select the right combination of wood-

[8] Page 121 of the miniature score.

winds to sound an A flat against which the voice on A natural is perfectly, prismatically, and pragmatically adjusted for just the shade of shimmering contrast desired. Here there is nothing in the least tentative, uncertain, or experimental. The text is exposed through the focus of the voice: both are immediately, permanently "fixed" in the mixture of sonorities in the orchestra. A somewhat larger ensemble than he permitted himself for the *Kindertotenlieder*, yet a very much smaller one than he required for the Eighth Symphony, enables him to achieve any dynamic result, from the most extensive to the perimeter of inaudibility.

Unlike those earlier, less completely realized expressions in which a modest beginning leads almost inevitably to an immodest conclusion, the tumult with which *Das Lied* begins is rarely invoked thereafter. The sound level rises and falls according to the sentiment of the word, but when it reaches its almost unbearably poignant crisis in the "*Abschied*," it sinks lower and lower, not even speaking the final "*Ewig*" the listener expects, but allowing him to imagine it as the vibrations in the orchestra die away.

Where *Das Lied* undoubtedly takes a unique place of its own in music—which is also to say in the continuity of music—relates not to melody, rhythm, or even orchestral color, right as it is in all these values. It is contained, rather, in the harmonic gold that Mahler has mined in his probe into the mountain, a new, responsive kind of metal which enables him to realign the familiar intervals and scalewise steps in a subtle, newly meaningful way. To some extent, this is derived from the pentatonic scale, which Mahler uses as a kind of aural incense to perfume the sound of the familiar Western instruments with the aura of their Eastern counterparts. But vastly more is inherent in his own, ever more refined sense of voice-leading applied to the scale he evolved for this work (D minor, with the raised sixth resulting in B natural rather than B flat). With his rich feeling for "natural counterpoint" strengthened by his ever-increasing command of the more intellectual kind, Mahler is able to carry forward two, three, or four lines of interest simultaneously.

This may result in a progression in which E flat is substituted for the expected B flat, swinging open a door of escape from the confinement of the traditional cadence. Or it may yield, finally, a new resolution for what I have called the *Siegfried Idyll* progression. This occurs on page 112 of the miniature score. As Mahler guides several crossing lines to unexpected destinations, he imparts a stretch and reach to its terminal elements by which it becomes a new thing and wholly his own.

Throughout *Das Lied*, and especially in the *"Abschied,"* there is an increasing tendency in a direction that is not atonal (without a key center) or bitonal (with two centers), but toward what I would call untonal. Each section has, assuredly, a key center, but the old lines of procedure by which the composer was restricted to combinations related to that center have now been breached altogether. Mahler assumes, as his natural right, access to any harmonic pigmentation that suits his purpose, without even such an intermediation as the enharmonic. But with the right he recognizes the obligation to order what he offers to the listener with the logic of a mosaic rather than to challenge him to produce his own discipline from a pastiche. That is to say, the individual bits and pieces are composed into an intelligible design, which seems to me the least that can be asked of a composer.

Thus it is possible for an old "join" to be adapted to the needs of a new design, as at that critical moment when Mahler launches his unburdening *"Die liebe Erde"* (p. 148) with a breadth and in a manner strongly suggestive of *"Ist auf deinem Psalter"* in Brahms's *Alto Rhapsody* (see pp. 245–6, 247). But it is beautifully retooled to convey his own characteristic workmanship, with a shade of meaning as individual to him as his signature. Or one can hear an echo of Fricka in the setting of *"Er stieg vom Pferd"* (p. 139), but before it becomes more than an echo, the inflection turns in Mahler's direction and it is all quite different. Again, a few pages later, when a passage in C (*"all, über all"*) finds the vocal line dropping down from C to B to B flat in substantial duplication of a typical trait of Schumann (*"Du Ring an meinem Finger"* in *Frauenliebe und Leben* illustrates it well), Mahler clings to the B flat in the voice part but moves an interior line in a way that makes it a freshly beautiful thing all over again. It is through such subtleties, refinements, and innovations that Mahler justifies his right to sing again of *Der Vogel*, *Der Frühling*, and *Der Lenz*, and make the expression as well as the sentiment timeless.

10

THE DESCRIPTION of Mahler's last three works as "a trilogy of farewell" is a favorite among commentators, and understandably so. It is a convenient metaphor, appealing in its brevity and presumably in its meaning. But, as in the earlier grouping of the Second, Third, and Fourth as the *"Wunderhorn"* symphonies, it may imply more than it really means. As in the case of the *Vier letzte Lieder* of Strauss, the terminology

is one that hardly would have occurred to the composer himself. Men
of fifty-one, even as sickly as Mahler was in the years of *Das Lied,* the

(*continued*)

Mahler: Das Lied von der Erde

Ninth, and the uncompleted Tenth, are not in the habit of writing their own obituaries or accepting an inevitability a day sooner than they must.

Das Lied is an undoubted act of renunciation, which is quite different from resignation. It does not assert Mahler's inability to engage in further struggle; it says, rather, that he is withdrawing from that part of the struggle in which he no longer finds himself an active participant. With *Das Lied* he executed a receipt marked "paid in full" for all the things of the world he had enjoyed and cherished, taking leave of them in music that makes him one with the masters he adored and to whom he devoted his life. But he did not take leave of music as either a public vocation or a private avocation.

What followed, in the Ninth Symphony and the uncompleted

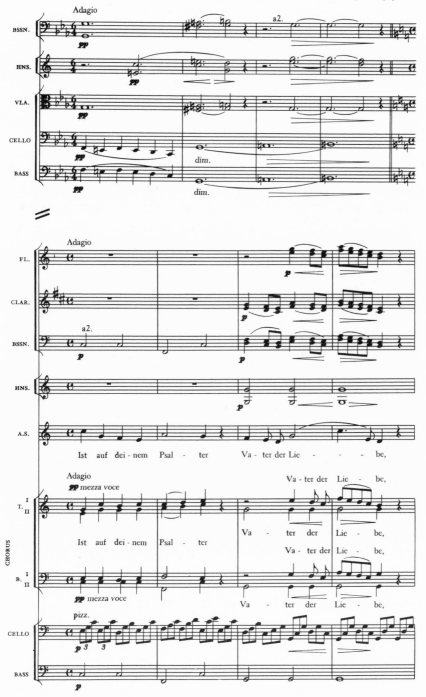

Brahms: Alto Rhapsody (op. 53)

Tenth, was not so much farewell or renunciation as meditation and speculation. The Ninth, especially, is full of meditations on the resources and possibilities of the musical compound he had labored so long to make his own, its possibilities both for greater complexity and for more simplicity. Rather than restricting himself to the mixture as before, he colored it with materials from a source he had barely exploited before: the harmonic fabric and instrumental tints of *Parsifal* (especially in movement one). Now and then there is also evidence that Tchaikovsky's *"Pathétique"* had come into his mind and lodged there.

For all of its lack of cohesion or of a steady level of quality on anything like the plane of *Das Lied*, the Ninth is absorbingly beautiful in detail and, in the concluding adagio, in sum. It is hardly surprising that Mahler takes up his new task where he had left off the old one, even to the first A in the cello as a link to the A in the flute with which *Das Lied* ends. As momentum accumulates after the languid beginning, so does interest in Mahler's discovery of new ways to vary the stratification of thought into the multiple lines of interest which had absorbed him for years.

On page 25 of the first movement, for example, there are three separate planes of action: one, of a fanfare character, is concentrated in flutes, oboes, and clarinets; a second, of a more driving rhythmic disposition, utilizes a blend of bassoons and low strings; the third, building into an impassioned melodic line, is in the high register of the violins (seconds as well as firsts). These are not so much contrapuntal, in the old sense of being "against" each other, as they are concurrent. Stated in physical terms, though they are sounded simultaneously in time, they have an individual identity in space, each occupying an aural *locus* of its own, with free, unencumbered access to the listening ear.

Here, it seems to me, Mahler has pushed his probe through the center of the mountain, opened the "way out" for which music had been seeking for so long. He has, in fact, drawn a blueprint of the way in which music could regain a direction it had lost when confronted by the huge upthrust of the Wagnerian accomplishment—which could very well have been the "mountain" Mahler had in mind when he used Schopenhauer's image. In a way, Mahler's course was parallel to, if it did not actually intersect, the line of thought Beethoven pursued in his last quartets. (Those, too, are much more elaborately stranded than their predecessors.) However, with the restriction of the medium in which he was working, Beethoven could implement his initiative only within the color chart of four stringed instruments, and his tonal orientation drove him inevitably toward established points of harmonic rest. Mahler had at his disposal all the chromatics, in a color sense, of a huge orchestra with which to exploit a freedom from terminal constraint which led, repeatedly, to new destinations.

It remains a probe rather than a breakthrough for the simplest of reasons—Mahler had other things on his mind, such as getting on with a four-movement symphony. Following a *Ländler*-like scherzo, which is a look backward beyond both *Das Lied* and the Eighth Symphony, Mahler addresses himself to a *Rondo-Burleske* that is perhaps, of all the movements in the Ninth, the most generative of the continuity-to-come. It is an expression, in even more mirthless laughter than before, of the parodistic tendency that characterized the *"Frère Jacques"* march of the First Symphony, parts of the Fourth and Sixth, and much of the Seventh. That he is able to weave ever more overlapping, jagged lines of sonority into a jostling interchange without leaving the ear befuddled or confused is a dividend on his life-long investment in the development of clarity. Individual instruments, choirs, and sections are assigned suitable places in the total tonal range so skillfully that what is written can be heard and what is not meant to be heard is not written. It is from this example, it seems to me, that many of the best-sounding passages in the mature orchestral writing of Bartók (Concerto for Orchestra, Music for Strings, Percussion and Celesta, among others), Hindemith (Metamorphoses on a Theme of Weber, *Mathis der Mahler*), and Shostakovich (various movements of the Fifth and Sixth symphonies, specifically) took their point of departure.

In the adagio finale, Mahler attains an emotional liberation rarely equaled since the hymnal exaltation of the concluding movement in his Symphony No. 3. This time he draws on his own melodic capital rather than borrowing from the bank of Beethoven as he had a dozen years before. Interest is compounded by profit from the traits of Tchaikovsky's *"Pathétique"* which Mahler had made his own (such as the use of the bassoon and contrabassoon for melodic purposes in their lowest, most sonorous registers, or the interweaving of the strings above and below their normal range to enhance the prominence of a particular line). In a single measure, the span of the first violin may arch upward from the lowest A to the highest before coming to rest halfway between (p. 167[9]). Or, a little later (p. 170), the violas plunge from B natural above the staff (adjacent to the tenor's "high C") to E flat below it, then dart up to a G flat that dissolves into a spatter of sound

[9] All references are to the Universal Edition study score.

cascading (E flat, C, A, G, E flat, C, A) down to a low G flat, where it finally comes to rest. Both of these are combined with a wide-ranging, octave-spanning kind of melodic writing rather than the stepwise (vocally derived) patterns of earlier composers.

No less exploratory is a point of contrast (p. 172) for woodwinds (the thought of the movement is expressed, predominantly, through the strings). Here there are *four* different key signatures concurrently: four sharps (E major) for flute, oboes, bassoons, and strings; five sharps (B major) for the English horn; five flats (D flat) for the clarinet in E flat, and six flats (G flat) for the clarinet in B. To be sure, some of this apparent contradiction relates to Mahler's way of dealing with such transposing instruments as the clarinet and English horn. The net of it is to have A sharp (in the English horn) and D (in the clarinet) moving to G sharp and C without the expectable sense of conflict because each can be perceived aurally as an individual horizontal element rather than as parts of two vertical elements in opposition.

At another point in this movement (p. 167) Mahler introduces what appears to be a foreign key into a chordal formation only to "make it right" a measure later when it becomes the tonic element of a new digression. In a far more sophisticated way, as befits the accretion of auditory resource over the decades, this is precisely the kind of aural mystification practiced by Chopin, just as the distribution of discordant elements through the wide range of the orchestral gamut to produce a new concordance extended Wagner's initiative in *Tristan*. Neither Chopin nor Wagner might recognize himself as mirrored in Mahler's reflection. But any ear conditioned to their modes of thought can adjust to Mahler's adaptations of them, given the will, the interest, and, of course, the opportunity.

Unless one believes implicitly in the premise that there is a divinity that shapes our ends and that unprecedented results are the product of happy accidents, it is a temptation to speculate why, of all composers, it was Mahler who carried out these implications of preceding music. It could well have been related to a reason suggested earlier (p. 212): conducting the music of others as much as he did "cultivated his impulses, sharpened his ear, and furthered that rarefied sense of orchestral color which beams a light, prismlike, through his musical universe." If one is inclined to counter that Strauss, too, did a considerable amount of conducting but did not profit accordingly, the rejoinder could be in terms of a previous distinction: one was a composer-conductor, the other a conductor-composer.

To have achieved so much that is productive of pleasure in his perfectly realized works and that is provocative of interest in even his imperfectly realized ones should be sufficient to make a cycle of any man's musical life. In the imperfect no less than the perfect, Mahler closed a circle of continuity from his reception of it through his absorption and transmission of it. But there remains a further expression of Mahler's mentality not to be characterized either as perfect or imperfect, but as productive of pleasure and profound interest nevertheless. That is the uncompleted Tenth Symphony, which, since his death in 1911, has passed through two phases of public revelation. The first was the publication, in 1951, of two movements in which Mahler's intentions could be realized from the "short score" or detailed draft that he habitually wrote before laying out the full score. In the second, more recent phase, such musicologists as Deryck Cooke and Joseph Wheeler have produced "performing versions" of the other three movements from their interpretations—not without exercising debatable alternatives—of Mahler's mass of sketches.

From this abundance of posthumous material, my attention has been magnetized by the one movement of the Tenth which Mahler advanced to near completion in a full score[1] (though an unrevised and not wholly sequential one). As befits a man of Mahler's meditative, speculative turn of mind in these last years, it is an adagio that

Mahler: Symphony No. 10, adagio

[1] Redlich: *Bruckner and Mahler*, p. 228.

he labored to bring as near to fulfillment as possible in the last summer of his life (1910).

To Redlich, the octave-spanning thematic impulse with which Mahler begins the movement he intended to stand first in the sequence of the Tenth is curiously kin to the opening of the final movement (also adagio) of Bruckner's uncompleted Ninth[2] (see p. 178).

Bruckner: Symphony No. 9, D minor, langsam

This is a good example of Axiom IV of this subject: *The obvious source is not always the true source.* It strikes me that both composers were rather more mindful of Wagner's *Faust Overture,* the basic theme of which follows just such a ground plan ("middle" D to upper D, E flat down to lower E flat, then D, C sharp, upper C sharp, C natural down to lower C, the phrase ending on B natural below "middle" C). What Mahler's conditioning prompted him to do, and which neither Wagner's nor Bruckner's enabled them to do, was to spin out a texture from the nuclear thought, rather than "developing" it in the manner of his predecessors.

The germ phrase is heard first (shortly after an opening recitative

[2] Ibid., p. 231.

Wagner: Eine Faust-Ouvertüre

by the violas) on middle A sharp, upper A sharp, the C sharp above, then the G double sharp a tenth below.[3] Nine measures later it is answered by almost an exact inversion. From this concept of image and reflection emerges the pervasive scheme of the movement, the several sections of which are set off from each other by references to the recitative-like statement previously noted. It should not surprise anyone familiar with Mahler's musical mentality that his objective would be to combine the theme and its inversion into a single texture, concurrent rather than contrapuntal, coincidental rather than simultaneous. This he does midway through the forty-four pages of score (p. 24), meanwhile adding instrumental interest to a pattern that was initially for strings alone, suffusing his ideas in a mingling of orchestral spray and harmonic mist that makes for an interplay as fanciful as anything he ever created.

Whatever Mahler's emotional state as he organized this expression —and there is an interjection of brass (first at p. 32) that is all but vocal in its rejection of impending doom—his mental functioning was of a sophistication that remained unique half a century later. It still remains unique as a directive to those who conceive their mission to be the expansion of the musical language within an evolutionary pattern.

[3] Page 2, miniature score, Associated Music Publishers.

I I

EVEN WHILE MAHLER was hammering his tunnel through "the mountain" in a straight line of evolutionary thought, the combination of strains and mutations which would produce the next revolutionary upheaval was fermenting, even fomenting. Indeed, one could say "where" as well as "while," for it was happening in such proximity to Mahler that he could be termed its spiritual father, if he was in no other way directly related to it.

Improbable as it may seem, the world's introduction to the name of Arnold Schoenberg was prepared under the roof of the Vienna Opera while Mahler was absorbed with his triple identities of administrator, executive artist, and creative being. The intermediary was Arnold Rosé, who had almost as many identities as his celebrated brother-in-law (Rosé's wife was Mahler's sister, Emma). As concertmaster of the Opera orchestra, he automatically was concertmaster of the Vienna Philharmonic, and leader of a famous quartet bearing his name. It was while Rosé and a group of associates were preparing the first performance of *Verklärte Nacht* on March 18, 1902, that Mahler dropped into the studio in the opera house where the rehearsal was in progress.[4]

There were other lines of connection between them. When Mahler married Alma Schindler in March, 1902, he also married into a circle of painters, poets, musicians, and writers who were her friends by birthright (her father was a prominent painter). Among them was Schoenberg, whom she had met as a fellow student of composition under the tutelage of Alexander von Zemlinsky. Even then, she later recalled, "Nobody who entered the charmed circle of Schoenberg's spirit could resist his intellectual pre-eminence or the force of his logic."[5] Lack of recognition did not deter him from observing with lofty disdain, when he was asked whether he was going to the first performance of Mahler's Fourth Symphony (January 12, 1902): "How can Mahler do anything with the Fourth when he has already failed to do anything with the First?"[6] An expression of Schoenberg's characteristic love for paradox,

4 Newlin: *Bruckner, Mahler and Schoenberg*, p. 224.
5 Alma Mahler: *Gustav Mahler, Memories and Letters*, p. 73.
6 Ibid., p. 75.

it was also characteristic of the "girlish passion," of the "love vexed by hate" for Mahler which he confessed in a notable letter of tribute on the older man's fiftieth birthday (dated July 5, 1910).[7]

Well before that, however, there had come a schism of the generations, a separation of understanding, an interruption of intellectual contact as absorbing to the historical-minded as any previously cited: Haydn's incomprehension of the young Beethoven, Berlioz's bafflement by the *Tristan* prelude, Bülow's confession of mystification with the Second Symphony of Mahler himself. It came about at the first performance of Schoenberg's *Kammersymphonie* No. 1 in 1907, not long before Mahler's first departure to America. As a gesture of support for Schoenberg and a rebuke to those who left the hall while the work was in progress, Mahler made an angry request for silence. At the end, he applauded vigorously from a place of prominence near the stage. But he had to confess to his wife: "I don't understand his music, but he's young and perhaps he's right. I am old and I daresay my ear is not sensitive enough."[8]

As Mahler was then forty-seven and Schoenberg thirty-four, it could hardly have been a matter of age alone. Together with fundamental differences of intellectual disposition and artistic aspiration, one must reckon with exposure at different times to different elements in the vast heritage of music. The fourteen years that separated the two put in a rather different relationship the influence exerted on them by the three dominant musicians of Schoenberg's formative period—Wagner, Brahms, and Richard Strauss.

Vienna-born though he was, Schoenberg grew up without even minimal exposure to its official musical life the Bohemian-born Mahler had experienced at the Conservatory. His first school was at home, then in the café. Both his parents were musical, his father an amateur of the violin, his mother enough of a pianist to qualify as a teacher. It was under such circumstances that Schoenberg first learned the violin, then taught himself the cello (among those with whom he played chamber music was the young Fritz Kreisler). Music was primarily an avocation while he attended the Realschule. At the age of seventeen he went to work in a bank, but destiny intervened to resolve the problem posed by his lack of interest in finance: the bank failed in 1895, when Schoenberg was twenty-one.[9] He had by then become acquainted with Zemlinsky and made some ventures into composition. Zemlinsky found him

[7] Ibid., p. 275.   [8] Ibid., p. 101.
[9] H. H. Stuckenschmidt: *Arnold Schoenberg* (New York: Grove Press; 1959), p. 19.

a job as conductor of a workers' chorus, which provided a meager source of income while Schoenberg pursued his (and Mahler's) favorite occupation—self-improvement, musically.

For a musician of such limited background to produce so superb an example of craftsmanship as *Verklärte Nacht* after barely four years of serious effort as a composer must be reckoned among the most remarkable manifestations of talent known to musical history. It proceeded from a background, both before and after the bank, in which music had been an intense, if undirected, interest. Like some others who grew up at the time (Artur Rubinstein is one), he responded to the attraction of Wagner no less than to that of Brahms, though this meant crossing party lines and mingling with partisans exclusively devoted to one or the other.

One consequential influence may be dated from 1883, when Vienna finally heard *Tristan und Isolde* for the first time. Had it been introduced a decade earlier, as in Weimar and Berlin, Schoenberg might possibly have taken it in stride as the enthusiasm of his elders. Now, as he entered his teens in the mid-1880's, it was the all-important "New Thing," redeemed at last from the scandal of 1862-3 (when it had been abandoned after seventy-two rehearsals) and all the more enticing for having been so long inaccessible.

Whatever the circumstances, Schoenberg and his fellow students immersed themselves in this new experience, playing a game which went far beyond the quotation of obvious themes or excerpts. They "delved deeper and deeper into the structure of the work, seeking for new melodies"[1] with which to baffle those less enterprising. *Tristan* was but one work of Wagner which Schoenberg heard twenty to thirty times while growing up.[2]

A comparable attraction to the music of Brahms was intensified by the composer's physical being as the senior presence on the Viennese musical scene. The youthful Schoenberg shrank in awe when the bearded, stocky figure actually selected a seat next to his own at the rear of a concert hall. The slightly older Schoenberg cherished a life-long regret that Brahms did not live to pass judgment on *Verklärte Nacht* when it was completed in 1899.[3]

It might possibly have paralleled what Mahler said of the *Kammersymphonie* in 1907, though perhaps for different reasons. Toward its well-known Wagnerian assimilations Brahms very likely would have

[1] Newlin: *Bruckner, Mahler and Schoenberg*, p. 210.
[2] Stuckenschmidt: *Arnold Schoenberg*, p. 18.
[3] Newlin: *Bruckner, Mahler and Schoenberg*, p. 211.

expressed the same feeling of being "cross for the rest of the day" which he had conveyed to Henschel about their prototypes in *Tristan*. Toward the superbly interwoven texture of the string sextet (a kind of sound for which Brahms had demonstrated his own affection in two memorable works) he doubtless would have been more partial. Both speak in unmistakable terms of Schoenberg's commitment, at that time, to the continuity of Brahms.

This may strike some as surprising, for on its first, fifth, or tenth hearing it is the vocabulary of the work which dominates the attention, with the chromatic idiom and closely knit melodic texture of *Tristan* (and their extension in *Parsifal*). It is only after these have been accepted for what they are and closer attention is directed to the structural means by which they are supported and tied together that there emerges a larger involvement with Brahms than is commonly recognized.

Doubtless the reason is that Schoenberg's Brahms is not the Brahms of the best-known symphonies and concertos. Rather it is the Brahms of the A-minor and C-minor quartets, with their soloistic mode of writing for the individual instruments. This is expanded, in the later phases of the work,[4] to utilize the layout and interplay of the even more demanding string writing that Brahms conceived for the A-minor Concerto for violin and cello with orchestra. Intermingled with these elements are others suggesting the string writing of Grieg (*Zwei elegaische Melodien* of 1886) and Dvořák (serenade, sextet, etc.). Schoenberg's attraction, even this early, was primarily to what might be generically termed German music, with a periphery perhaps extending to Grieg and Dvořák.

Schoenberg had scarcely seen the old century out with *Verklärte Nacht* (1899) before he was pressing on to welcome the new one with the *Gurrelieder*, based on texts of Jens Peter Jacobsen. Sketched between February 1900 and May 1901, the work was not completely orchestrated until a decade later (1911). It is without question the most immodestly demanding composition in the orchestral literature, especially in Schoenberg's first version. This asked for ten French horns, seven trumpets, eight trombones, six timpani, four harps, five solo voices, a narrator, three four-part male choruses, and an eight-part mixed chorus, as well as violins divided into ten parts and violas and cellos each pursuing eight different parts.[5]

By the time it was first performed in 1913, both the mental and emotional atmosphere of *Gurrelieder* had ceased to exist for the com-

[4] Miniature score, Dreililien Berlin-Lichterfeld Edition, pp. 41–3.
[5] Stuckenschmidt: *Arnold Schoenberg*, p. 27.

poser, who had gone on to far, far different things. It was a relic of a relatively remote period of his musical thinking, a brontosaurus of a composition beside which Mahler's Eighth Symphony was a quite practicable matter. Through the influence of Richard Strauss, who saw the "short score" of the *Gurrelieder* in 1901, Schoenberg received a stipend from a charitable source as well as an appointment to the faculty of the Stern Conservatory in Berlin. Both were intended to assist him toward completion of his great project, but he returned to Vienna not long afterwards.

Stuckenschmidt says of the *Gurrelieder* that it would be "unthinkable without Wagner's example."[6] This is, on the whole, a restrained assessment. As heard today, *Gurrelieder* strikes the ear as quite a different matter than *Verklärte Nacht*, in which the devices of several predecessors are creatively combined. In his setting of Jacobsen's poems, Schoenberg passes in review the wide range of Wagner's musical cosmos, restating various sections of the *Ring* and *Tristan*. When an urgent need for music suitable to the supernatural, the mystical, or the recondite arises, it is the tritone of *Parsifal*[7] (most characteristically associated with Gurnemanz's "*Das ist Karfreitagszauber*" in Act III) which is invoked. In the later phases of the scoring, the world's progress in this science (and art) during the first decade of the century can be detected. The Strauss of *Salome* comes into play, as does the Mahler of the later works. But the first allegiance is to the first Richard.

In addition to gaining Schoenberg a sponsor, *Gurrelieder* provided him with the impulse for an immediate, more manageable project while the larger one was taking shape. At Strauss's suggestion, he took Maeterlinck's *Pelléas et Mélisande* as the theme of his next work. The probability is that Strauss had a stage treatment in mind (Debussy's setting was not performed until April 1902), but Schoenberg decided otherwise. He took not only the theme but also the style of treatment from his benefactor, writing the equivalent of a four-movement symphony that flowed on, in the manner of a Strauss tone poem, without interruption.

In the view of Dika Newlin, *Pelleas und Melisande* is evidence that "the influence of Strauss upon him preceded that of Mahler . . ."[8] Thus, in a quest for a manner of his own, Schoenberg had moved forward more than a little from Wagner and Brahms. In Strauss he found a source of new precepts and fresh resources not only orchestrally, but

---

[6] Ibid., p. 28.
[7] Page 265, Universal Edition, piano-vocal score.
[8] Newlin: *Bruckner, Mahler and Schoenberg*, p. 221.

also in the harmonic refinements embodied in *Don Juan* and *Don Quixote*.

A page-by-page analysis of *Pelleas und Melisande* would be pointless, for it is very possibly one of the least distinguished works by any composer with a world-wide reputation. Reference can be made, however, to a few points at which the influence of Strauss is close at hand. At number 12 of the Universal score, for example, the atmosphere of scoring for woodwinds, particularly the use of the flute, is that of *Tod und Verklärung*. At number 30, where a big climax is required, the tonal approach is very much like that striking moment in *Don Quixote* (p. 36 of the Eulenburg score) when the hero's mental control gives way and he discovers his knightly mission.

But beyond all others, the attachment to Wagner remains profound and unshakable. Golaud's forest rustles very much like Mark's, and the shattering of Wotan's spear by Siegfried's sword accompanies a moment of dramatic crisis at number 22. There are also clear aural references to the manner of Scriabin, though I have seen no direct evidence that Schoenberg had, as of 1902, been exposed to the Russian's music.

On his own, Schoenberg evolved a fair share of individual touches in *Pelleas*, mostly in the realm of orchestral sonorities. One may be noted at number 59, where harp tremolandos are used in a distinctive combination with descending thirds in the flutes over sustained chords in the bass strings. Another is the use of a trombone glissando, up and down, to intensify the ominous sound, in the scene in the vaults, of muted timpani, flutter-tonguing of the flutes, and cellos *sul ponticello*. Also indicative of the later, fully developed Schoenberg is a crawling kind of chromatic "melodic line" which occasionally makes its appearance (number 51 is an example).

That none of this suited Schoenberg's sense of style or mission is suggested by his turn to still another mode of expression in the aftermath of his meeting with Mahler. In the manner of the latter's *Wunderhorn* settings and *Kindertotenlieder*, Schoenberg's next project was a setting of six songs with orchestra. In this seldom-heard product of 1904 (published as opus 8) two of the texts are taken from *Des Knaben Wunderhorn*.

This, too, passed, to be followed by the major effort of a new string quartet. This is the D-minor, opus 7, the first in Schoenberg's sequence of four published quartets. As its workmanship and sure sense of procedure suggest, this was no tentative, maiden effort in a challenging mode of composition. Prior to the *Verklärte Nacht* of 1889, he had

written a quartet that was privately performed in 1897 but not published, and, even earlier, at least one other quartet that was neither
performed nor published.

Here another source of continuity is invoked, for Schoenberg made
no secret of using the development section of the opening movement
of Beethoven's *"Eroica"* as the model for his own development.[9] This
is combined with the Lisztian conception (particularly in the B-minor
Sonata) of a single continuous movement in which all the divisions of a
customary sonata, quartet, or symphony are included. That "ideal,"
Miss Newlin says, "is here definitively fulfilled."[1] It was, she continues,
Schoenberg's belief "that his style of string-quartet writing (as represented in the development from First to Fourth Quartets) is the continuation of tendencies inaugurated by Beethoven in those late quartets,
especially in the *Grosse Fuge*. In fact, he once said that certain portions
of the latter work could easily pass as his own composition if presented
to the average musical audience under his name." Miss Newlin terms
this a "good-natured exaggeration," but the implication is: how like
Schoenberg Beethoven was, rather than how like Beethoven Schoenberg
could write.

This much having been said about the elements of the past which
Schoenberg recognized as present in his opus 7, it remains to be added
that there were others of interest as well. The launching of the quartet,
the interrelationship of parts, and the restatement of the opening theme
almost at once with an altered pattern of inner voices are distinctly
Brahmsian (C-minor Quartet, opus 51, No. 1). The harmonic texture
is richer; the whole technique of dissembling tonal orientation by means
of passing tones, altered intervals, and by-passing of normal resolutions
is masterfully manipulated. The flow of idea is impressively sustained
through the varying moods of its considerable length. Sometimes this is
aided by a reference to one of Beethoven's "middle" period quartets (E-
flat, opus 74, or F-minor, opus 95), the *Aus meinem Leben* of Smetana[2]
(a work which Schoenberg knew well and admired[3]), or the Schubert
D-minor,[4] but most often the soundest reliance is upon his own impos-
ing brain power.

Crowning Schoenberg's aspiration to mastery is the convincing
climax he achieves after forty uninterrupted minutes of music. Altogether, opus 7 was by far his most successful venture (up to that time)

[9] Ibid., p. 227.
[1] Ibid., p. 227.
[2] Page 56 of the miniature score of opus 7, Verlag Dreililien.
[3] Newlin: *Bruckner, Mahler and Schoenberg*, p. 211 *n.*
[4] Scherzo section of opus 7.

to extend the musical language as he found it and to lengthen the continuity of tonal music. It was also close to his last, for his next consequential product, aside from some songs and several incomplete beginnings, was the *Kammersymphonie*, opus 9, to which Mahler found his ears insufficiently sensitive.

12

IT IS, OF COURSE, possible that Mahler was listening for more than was, or is, there. It might also have gone better for Mahler had he known a secret now visible to anyone who studies the score. The opening chordal structure is based on intervals of fourths, rather than the conventional structure of thirds with "added" tones. The construction C-F-B flat-E flat-A flat is heard almost at once, and the first stated theme, which follows immediately, is its echo a fifth higher[5] (G-C-F-B flat-E flat). In quick succession come groupings of chords based on a descending sequence in the wholetone scale, even more adventurous harmonic sideslips and cadential evasions than those propounded by Strauss. Perhaps even with this forewarning, Mahler might not have found his ear attuned to what Schoenberg was about in the Chamber Symphony (he may have been no more partial to fourths than Berlioz was to *enharmonie*), but he would at least have known the reason for his dissatisfaction.

The reference to chords in fourths, wholetone scales, and harmonic evasions should leave little doubt about just what Schoenberg was doing in the Chamber Symphony. This was, merely, to combine the most advanced practices of Scriabin, Debussy, and Strauss into an idiom characteristically his own. So far his quest was for diversity, not revolution. His objective was to achieve the fogged progression, the unexpected resolution, the anticonventional cadence, the elisions and evasions that disguise tonality but do not deny it. As with those contemporaries to whom reference has been made (Scriabin's system had attained an advanced expression in the *Divine Poem* of 1903, Debussy had moved on from *Pelléas* to the completion of much of his piano music by 1906, and Strauss was looking for a subject to succeed *Salome*), there is no inclination to pretend that this gravitational pull does not exist. Even less was there a disposition to argue that it could be suspended by individual fiat (which would be akin to Einstein proclaiming the repeal of Newton's law of falling bodies). F major beguiles us here, A minor there, and the end is clearly in a Schoenbergian E major (that

[5] Stuckenschmidt: *Arnold Schoenberg*, p. 38.

is, with a blast of C sharp on the horns added to E-G sharp-B).

This permits, or perhaps it would be better to say it does not exclude, the possibility of a reminiscence of Dvořák's "American" Quartet (opus 96) at number 6 (its derivation from an Indian source suits the wholetone surroundings admirably); a reversion to the idiom of *Tristan* (the Shepherd's piping of Act III, on p. 91 of the Chamber Symphony score); and adaptations of Mahler's "planes of sonority" at several points (pp. 27–8 among others). Mahler's place in the Schoenberg firmament was, at this time, becoming ever more firmly fixed. Indeed, he wrote Mahler a letter in July 1906 to announce the completion of the Chamber Symphony. Shortly before, another letter[6] had expressed Schoenberg's profound admiration for a work of Mahler which he had just heard. Its title is not specified, but its reference, on June 14, 1906, to "today" suggests that Schoenberg may have attended a "reading" rehearsal of the Symphony No. 6 prior to its first performance in Essen later in the year.

For all its mixture of elements and loss of direction from time to time, the Chamber Symphony moves ahead relentlessly, powered by the single-mindedness of a man determined not to be denied his objective. Not the least of its interests is the sonorous breadth and variety that Schoenberg achieves with an instrumental ensemble numbering less than twenty. With the omission of the trumpet and the addition of English horn, bass clarinet, and contrabassoon, it is exactly the combination used by Wagner for the original version of his *Siegfried Idyll*. Quite clearly Schoenberg's perception of the suggestions contained in Wagner's charming work was different from Mahler's.

By the measure of the Chamber Symphony, the Second Quartet (written in 1907, first performed in 1908) is a work of great delicacy, clarity of purpose, and refinement of style. It differs from the Quartet No. 1 in demanding far less virtuosity from the players. But its Brahmsian bent is no less profound. This time the suggestion is not so much of Brahms's quartet as of his Quintet in B minor for clarinet and strings. At the outset, Schoenberg takes as his own a principle of Brahms for which he had great admiration:[7] to alter the opening theme rhythmically at its first repetition—a mode of procedure to which he gave the name of "developing variations."[8] This refinement also puts Mahler as a link in the stylistic chain from Brahms to Schoenberg, as it is

[6] Alma Mahler: *Gustav Mahler, Memories and Letters*, p. 232.
[7] Arnold Schoenberg: *Style and Idea* (New York: Philosophical Library; 1950), p. 94.
[8] Ibid., p. 185.

very much in accord with the thinking he expressed in a conversation with Natalie Bauer-Lechner: "According to my belief there should be no plain repetition, but all should go forward developing."[9]

In harmonic conception as well as tonal fulfillment, the Second Quartet is decidedly purer, much more consistent in texture than the Chamber Symphony. Chords of the fourth are banished, the trend to the wholetone scale is more pronounced, and a sense of tonality prevails to the extent of a recognizable F sharp minor at the beginning and end of the first movement, a no less palpable F sharp major for the conclusion of the whole work. It is, altogether, a more relaxed, less consciously "purposeful" production than the Chamber Symphony.

Perhaps this is related to Schoenberg's success in finding elements of interest and distinction which do not require an unusual vocabulary for their expression. One, midway in the scherzo, is a delicately canonic allusion to the old Viennese drinking song "*Ach, du lieber Augustin.*" Schoenberg's use of it "reminds us," Miss Newlin writes, "of the bitterness of '*Frère Jacques*' (or '*Bruder Martin,*' as the Germans would have it) in Mahler's first symphony."[1] Another is the pioneering use, in a string quartet, of the human voice to make a quintet of the finale.

Miss Newlin's reference to Schoenberg in terms of Mahler is eminently reasonable, for the change of manner in the scherzo is indeed Mahlerish. But one question lingers in the aftermath of experiencing this willful touch of the commonplace in the midst of its sophisticated surroundings. Was it a sheer accident that, of all the hundreds of folk songs he might have chosen, Schoenberg's selection happened, just happened, to be "*Ach, du lieber Augustin*"?

It is impossible for those acquainted with the Mahler-Schoenberg lore and the relationship of the two men to ignore the possibility that the particular tune was chosen for a particular reason. It is well known that in 1910 Mahler was beset by a domestic crisis. His famously beautiful wife was being wooed by the architect Walter Gropius, a man much younger than himself. To resolve the tensions that had arisen between himself and Alma, and to determine if there was a way in which their marriage could be saved, Mahler arranged an interview with Sigmund Freud. The result of their meeting (in Leyden, Holland, where the psychiatrist was working at the time) was eventually published in a biography of Freud by Ernest Jones. Among the many insights into Mahler's personality which this consultation produced, one bears musical significance. It relates to a familiar, indeed highly characteristic trait

[9] Bauer-Lechner: *Erinnerungen an Gustav Mahler*, p. 165.
[1] Newlin: *Bruckner, Mahler and Schoenberg*, p. 235.

in his compositions: the juxtaposition of the rarefied with the common-place. As Jones paraphrases him: "Mahler suddenly said that now he understood why his music had always been prevented from achieving the highest rank through the noblest passages, those inspired by the most profound emotions, being spoiled by the intrusion of some com-monplace melody. His father, apparently a brutal person, treated his wife very badly, and when Mahler was a young boy there was a specially painful scene between them. It became quite unbearable to the boy, who rushed away from the house." At that moment, however, a hurdy-gurdy was grinding out a popular Viennese air. In Mahler's view, as Jones relates it, "the conjunction of high tragedy and light amusement was from then on inextricably fixed in his mind . . ."[2]

The Viennese air, as might be surmised, was "*Ach, du lieber Au-gustin.*" What better way of evoking an association than for Schoenberg to make the allusion directly? This presumes that Mahler had related the circumstances to Schoenberg even before recalling them in his conversation with Freud. This, according to the reader's disposition, is probable or doubtful, but not impossible. (The closeness between them is suggested by Mahler's inviting Schoenberg to visit him at Maier-nigg during the summer of 1906. Schoenberg had to beg off because it was a fourteen-hour train trip from Upper Bavaria, and his wife was pregnant.) The thought lingers that the choice of the folk song was related to a "secret program" (for both quartets) which Schoenberg never revealed.[3]

There need be no such speculation about Schoenberg's use of two Stefan George lyrics in settings for the soprano voice in the quartet's finale. They served precisely the same function as Mahler's use of "*Auferstehen*" in the Second Symphony, the Nietzsche and *Wunder-horn* texts in the Third and Fourth symphonies. They added to the instrumental resources the power of the "Word," the catalyst that Mahler recognized as the potent ally of Beethoven in the Ninth Sym-phony, and the source of new stimulation to his own imagination when all else had been exhausted. It was an adaptation, for Schoenberg's own purpose, of a procedure practiced by two predecessors for whom he had profound regard: Beethoven and Mahler.

As a reward, Schoenberg found in his innovation a mode of pro-cedure, a source of impulse and stimulation which opened a whole new world of possibilities for him. In the settings of "*Litanei*" and "*Entrück-*

[2] Ernest Jones: *The Life and Work of Sigmund Freud* (New York: Basic Books, Inc.; 1955), II, 79–80.
[3] Newlin: *Bruckner, Mahler and Schoenberg*, p. 235.

ung," Schoenberg is freer of fetters, more nearly unleashed from the restrictions of the tonal system, closer to being adrift on the blue waters of a bottomless sea of sonority than in any earlier creation. What saves him from drifting altogether out of contact with the listener is the anchor of words. They maintain a course, provide a factor of attention when the other elements of context (and continuity) have been abandoned.

Finally, and this must be noted as a deep source of purpose for one of Schoenberg's "intellectual pre-eminence" who was noted for "the force of his logic" (p. 254), his newfound manner of treating words provided him with that priceless distinction of *singularity*, of being unlike any other predecessor, which he obviously craved. After numerous false starts and some true achievement, he had discovered that the way to be most like Schoenberg was to be wholly unlike anybody else. If the means could not be found within the same ideological frame, then a new frame could be devised. If this meant throwing out not only the baby with the bath water but the old tub itself, then the tub would have to go too.

In the period succeeding the Second Quartet, the drift away from the shore of tonality becomes ever more pronounced. As a conscientious master of his craft as well as a profound student of the guiding principles of those who had journeyed before him (Schoenberg was, in these years, also doing the groundwork which produced his *Harmonielehre* in 1911), he took the offshore soundings with care and purpose. The movement was not too far at a time, and was made with no commitment to a single mode of procedure. The sequence was:[4]

YEAR	WORK		SOURCE OF TEXT
1908	Three Piano Pieces	opus 11	
1908	*Das Buch der hängenden Gärten*	opus 15	(Stefan George)
1909	Five Orchestral Pieces	opus 16	
1909	*Erwartung*	opus 17	(Marie Pappenheim)
1909	*Die glückliche Hand*	opus 18	(By the composer)
1911	Six Piano Pieces	opus 19	
	Herzgewächse (undated)	opus 20	(M. Maeterlinck)
1912	*Pierrot lunaire*	opus 21	(Albert Giraud)

The image could be extended to express the means by which Schoenberg steered his offshore course. Certainly it was not by a com-

[4] As documented in Josef Rufer: *The Works of Arnold Schoenberg, A Catalogue of His Compositions, Writings and Paintings* (New York: The Free Press of Glencoe; 1963).

pass related to the polar opposites, major and minor. It was, rather, by dead reckoning on a fixed star of instinct.

He was most assured when working with a text that provided a direction of its own. It is hardly accidental that, of the eight works (or groupings of works) cited above, only three are wordless. It could be added that the famous Five Orchestral Pieces bear descriptive titles; according to the composer's diary, however, the titles were devised in response to a request from Peters, who published them.[5] Of the two sets of piano pieces, the last of the six in opus 19 was sketched on the day of Mahler's funeral, May 19, 1911.[6] Schoenberg's grief is conveyed in a tolling of bell-like sonorities.

Taken together, the works begun during this four-year span (some of them were not finished until later) are impelled by a vitality of thought and a power of imagination far beyond anything Schoenberg had previously achieved. It is as if the liberation from Wagner's, or Brahms's, or Richard Strauss's domination had given him fresh zest and motivation. There are vestigial remains of continuity in certain phases of them: the liquid mixtures suggestive of late Mahler in the second of the Five Orchestral Pieces; exploration of his "planes of sonority" in all of them; chord formations in support of the voice in *Das Buch der hängenden Gärten* which could be returned, as written, to *Tristan* (but which have no link or connection to what precedes or follows); inflections of the vocal line in *Erwartung* and *Die glückliche Hand* which might arouse recollections of *Salome* and *Elektra*, though in neither case is there anything remotely Straussian in the totality; a coloratura kind of *Sehnsucht* in *Herzgewächse*, which is written for a soprano with the range of "Blonde in the *Seraglio* (to low G sharp) extended a minor third higher to high F'''"[7] (a truly Schoenbergian thought).

But in *Pierrot lunaire*, the unquestioned masterpiece of Schoenberg's first forty years, the realization as well as the impulse were wholly his own. It is as significant a departure in the vocal realm as Stravinsky's *Le Sacre du printemps* was to be in the orchestral, and it begot a comparable quantity of artistic offspring. Born barely eight months apart (*Pierrot lunaire* was first performed in Berlin on October 16, 1912, *Le Sacre du printemps* was introduced to Paris and the world on May 29, 1913), both have passed the test of half a century's usage with no loss of respect for the wholeness of purpose each embodies.

[5] Ibid., p. 34.
[6] Stuckenschmidt: *Arnold Schoenberg*, p. 57.
[7] Robert Craft in the commentary for Columbia ML 5099.

In a way, Schoenberg invented not merely the purpose of *Pierrot lunaire,* but also an important part of the means by which it is achieved. This is the singer-speaker who performs the *Sprechstimme* through which the texts of Giraud are conveyed. Through successive steps from the narrator-speaker of the *Gurrelieder* finale to the solo peformer of *Erwartung,* Schoenberg created a new instrument of vocal communication. From the slender means of such a voice and an instrumental quintet, he endowed *Pierrot lunaire* with a world of tonal imagery as stylistically sufficient unto itself as the *Pierrot* of Picasso, which is sometimes used in visual association with it.

Along with the realization of his own purposes in this remarkable series of creations (from opus 11 to opus 21), Schoenberg set in motion the means for later fulfillment of his two most distinguished disciples, Alban Berg and Anton Webern. To the drifting song-speech of *Erwartung* and *Die glückliche Hand* may be traced the impetus for certain vocal values in Berg's *Wozzeck* and *Lulu.* The procedural was added to the substantive by Schoenberg's use of a fugato for one section of *Pierrot lunaire,* a passacaglia for another, a canon for a third. This could well have been the basis for the ground plan of *Wozzeck,* in which, among other procedures, an invention, a fugue, and a sonata movement are utilized. It is the measure of the artistic accomplishment of both that in neither case is it necessary for the listener to be aware of the formal means used for the tonal ends. How many listeners to *Siegfried* are aware that its concluding love duet is a rondo?

Instrumentally, the schematics[8] of Webern's later, best-known works, with their emphasis on instrumental texture, color, and sonority, are substantially defined by the Five Orchestral Pieces. These may, perhaps, be no more than the elements, as Field provided Chopin with "no more" than the elements of the nocturne, but they put into motion a mode of procedure, a syntax of speech (however fragmented) from which Webern evolved a vocabulary of his own.

Thus the path that Schoenberg pursued from 1899 to 1913 ran parallel to the highway traveled by his predecessors. From a beginning as a man of talent dependent on the examples of his chosen affinities, Schoenberg proceeded by some short and some long steps to a new point of departure. From here he went on to claim high ground of his own and to cultivate it productively. He had, in more than a figurative sense, effected a change in music's direction by unhinging from the frame of *enharmonie* the chromatic means that Wagner had devised

[8] Using that term as it is applied to the technical data descriptive of an amplifier or other electronic device.

for *Tristan.* In so doing, he had dissociated it from a chordal base, thus freeing its resources of color, of accent, of vocal intervals and instrumental combinations from the confinement of a closed cadential system. For almost any other composer, this would have been a deep and abiding satisfaction. But Schoenberg was not "any other composer." He was, like Mahler, drawn by the challenge of the impossible. The difference was, however, that Schoenberg wanted to succeed regardless of cost.

13

IN THE AFTERMATH of *Pierrot lunaire,* Schoenberg wrote no music of consequence for nearly a decade. He made some beginnings, but they were not carried to completion. He was, during World War I, occupied for many months with military service in a rather senseless utilization of capacity which conformed to the rationale of a senseless time. When he was finally discharged in October 1917, he organized a Seminary for Composition[9] whose participants included Hanns Eisler, Rudolf Kolisch, Rudolf Serkin, Eduard Steuermann, and the theoretician Josef Rufer. And, of course, he pondered on his extraordinary succession of works and what it connoted.

At this time of schism in Schoenberg's productive life, it may be recalled that he was, within himself, a man divided. The reference is not to any ordinary schizophrenia, but to the subtler, no less profound division of creator and theorist. Perhaps it was the penalty of his demanding innovations that his creations brought him small, if any, financial return. None save *Verklärte Nacht* attained even moderate frequency of performance, and its royalties (because of a nonproductive copyright) were meager. It was thus in a time when Strauss became wealthy from his royalties and Stravinsky built a legacy of valuable properties that Schoenberg, out of both need and inclination, turned to teaching for subsistence.

Fortunately for Schoenberg, as well as for those who were drawn to him, teaching satisfied an inner impulse, as conducting did for Mahler. It provided an outlet for his compulsion to organize, to propound, to schematize. What was unwelcome, if perhaps inevitable, was the flowing together of the two impulses, the coalescing of the separate parts of his being into one. The creative urge turned ever more to the formulation of a method, and the impulse to schematize or to organize and propound took over the direction of his compositional career.

In the works Schoenberg composed up to and including *Pierrot*

9 Stuckenschmidt: *Arnold Schoenberg,* p. 75.

lunaire, his musical instinct dictated a line of procedure for which his richly furnished musical mind found a means of fulfillment. The heart decreed and the mind concurred. In the years that immediately followed, the mind became ever more domineering about its share of the partnership, determined to seek out the whys and wherefores of the instinct. He was not content that in a certain episode of *Verklärte Nacht* he had done a beautiful and striking thing. He brooded upon it until "one night unable to sleep after a performance of the work [years after its composition] he thought the music through and through again, and suddenly hit upon the idea which (though he had not realized it when composing) is the true structural basis of the work's profound inner logic."[1]

This had to do with a complicated relationship of enharmonic tones, in which G flat becomes F sharp and certain things "logically" ensue. To those familiar with the manner in which Schoenberg's mind functioned, it is a fair certainty that the discovery of the "reason" for what he had done gave him as much satisfaction as the creation of the beautiful and striking thing itself (perhaps even more). One doubts that Wagner really brooded over the tonal context of the *Tristan* prelude, worried whether it was in A minor or not. Had he been so obsessed, he might have stopped right there and gone no farther. To the world's benefit, he did not make a dogma of his procedure or impose it on others. He did not even make the heated, chromatic world of *Tristan* a sanctuary in which he took refuge. He turned immediately to the creation of a wholly different atmosphere for *Die Meistersinger,* in which, if anything, there is a surfeit of C major, and in which the conscious introduction of the *Tristan* idiom (in the Workshop scene of Act II) comes as an intrusion from another world.

Schoenberg, obviously, was as much interested in how his mind functioned as in what it produced. It was in the aftermath of the developments that culminated in *Pierrot lunaire* that he began to take apart his inner mechanism to see, if possible, what made it perform as it did. He went beyond such *a posteriori* reasoning as kept him awake in Barcelona that night pondering on the logic of *Verklärte Nacht* to propound, *a priori,* how a new mode of writing could be devised that would solve all stylistic problems, answer all emotional needs. It would negate tonality, doing away once and for all with a key center and thus ending the tyranny of the cadence. It would also, of course, confer the not inconsiderable benefit of eliminating comparison with any preceding music. Here, it seems to me, Schoenberg achieved such a fusion of the

[1] Newlin: *Bruckner, Mahler and Schoenberg,* p. 214.

creative and the didactic as he rarely had attained in his music. The new method would replace with a rule of thumb the sensitive choice that had made *Pierrot lunaire* and its predecessors what they were. It would, in short, make a doctrine of a discovery.

The development of his *Method of Composing with Twelve Tones Which are Related Only with One Another*[2] has been summarized, explained, and expounded in numerous studies by various disciples. But the best exposition of all remains Schoenberg's own, as conveyed in a letter (1937) to Nicolas Slonimsky. He associates it with "some movements of the 'Suite for Piano' which I composed in the fall of 1921. Here I suddenly became conscious of the real meaning of my aim: unity and regularity, which unconsciously had led me this way."[3]

To his pupil Josef Rufer, who subsequently published a comprehensive exposition of the method,[4] Schoenberg phrased the discovery in somewhat more cosmic terms. While walking with Rufer during the summer of 1922, which he spent with a group of pupils in Traunkirchen[5] Schoenberg confided: "I have discovered something which will guarantee the supremacy of German music for the next hundred years."[6] Aside from the irony in the turn of events which made unwelcome in Germany itself the man who conceived himself to be the savior of "German music," the exclusivity of Schoenberg's objective strikes me as self-demonstrably defeating.

The pattern of this survey as it has now revealed itself is, clearly, that the "German" music of Wagner profited no less from the innovations of the "Polish" Chopin than the "Italian" music of Verdi did from the orchestral explorations of the "French" Berlioz. If, indeed, there is in the long line of masterpieces which caused this book to be written one which was exclusively the creation of a "national" impulse it escapes recognition. Glinka, father of Russian music, was propelled by Berlioz. Beethoven paid tribute to Cherubini, an Italian. Even Bach, before whom all Germans genuflect, studied and assimilated the ideas of Vivaldi, an Italian. It was left for Schoenberg to narrow, confine, and reduce the base of his musical thinking from the international to the national and, in so doing, to exclude so much of everything that

[2] Schoenberg: *Style and Idea*, p. 107 (his capitalization).

[3] Nicolas Slonimsky: *Music Since 1900* (3rd edn., New York: Coleman-Ross Co.; 1949), p. 680.

[4] Josef Rufer: *Composition with Twelve Notes* (New York: Macmillan Company; 1954).

[5] On the Traunsee in the Salzkammergut. It is described in Virginia Creed's *All About Austria* (New York: Duell, Sloan and Pearce; 1950) as "a favorite retreat of deposed royalty."

[6] Stuckenschmidt: *Arnold Schoenberg*, p. 82.

had contributed to music's greatness in the two centuries before.

Of the purity of his motives, there need be no question. Winston Churchill has testified that the hardest lesson of his public life was to recognize that a stupid man might be capable of a brilliant suggestion; conversely, that a brilliant man could be brilliantly, profoundly wrong (as, for example, he himself was in his Gallipoli campaign). Whatever Schoenberg thought he was doing, he was confining the art he loved, not liberating it. For some little gain—such as relief from comparison with all preceding music—there was enormous loss. In his own words: "Little is given, but much is taken away."

The argumentative basis is sound: "The ear has gradually become acquainted with a great number of dissonances, and so has lost the fear of their 'sense-interrupting' effect,"[7] Schoenberg says in reviewing the developments of Wagner, Strauss, etc. Perhaps it was some other hand than Schoenberg's which wrote the word *gradually*, for no such concept of gradualism is incorporated in TMOCWTTROWOA (to produce a manageable, twelve-letter symbol for Schoenberg's twelve-tone method). It was immediate, now, here, at once: a break, complete and irrevocable.

To avoid the error that might result from paraphrase and to prevent a prejudicial emphasis that might result from a restatement of Schoenberg's principles at third hand, I present them as contained in Stuckenschmidt's words: "The law which is obeyed by all twelve note disciples and before which the differences of methods vanish is this: no note shall be repeated before the other eleven notes have been used . . ."[8] Stuckenschmidt continues: "The most important factor in Schoenberg's 'Method' is the principle of the supremacy of the row (or series). From this pre-determined sequence of the twelve notes which is not departed from in the course of the composition" is evolved the total content of the movement. As it became evident to Schoenberg that the thematic identity which provided an indivisible factor of attention in almost all earlier music had been largely sacrificed in his, he evolved the concept of serialism. That is, to such "relatively primitive" forms of the technique as equal spacing of intervals or beginning each line of a setting with the next note of the series (as in the Serenade, opus 24) were added the inversion of the row (upside down), the retrograde form (reversed), the upside-down-backward statement of the same "basic shape" (as some commentators prefer to render Schoenberg's term *Grundgestalt* into English), as well as all the more familiar devices

[7] Schoenberg: *Style and Idea*, p. 104.
[8] Stuckenschmidt: *Arnold Schoenberg*, p. 83.

of counterpoint called upon in *Pierrot lunaire*—canon, fugue, *cancrizans* (crab canon)—in their full unrecognizability.

The Method thus consists of two separate but closely related elements: the twelve-tone discipline itself, in which any sense of a tonal center is proscribed through the ban on recurrence of a tone before all the others have intervened (immediate, rhythmic repetition of any note was permissible *within* the twelve-note span); and the mechanics of the serial elaboration. Improbable as it may seem, some part of the impulse from which the serial concept evolved was related in Schoenberg's mind to Johannes Brahms, customarily considered the negation of adventurousness. As his essay titled "Brahms the Progressive" indicates, Schoenberg did not share that view. In his teaching,[9] he frequently alluded to the concept of "developing variations" previously mentioned.[1]

Out of this observed tendency toward motivic alteration in others, Schoenberg moved toward the belief that such subtle changes of the position, contour, and rhythmic definition of each "basic shape" could be employed to sustain a lengthy movement or—as has been ventured in *Moses und Aaron*—a whole opera. There thus emerges a fascinating duality of character in his Method as it finally matured: one element (the rigor of nonrepetition) which was arbitrarily decreed, and one element (the mode of its elaboration) which was, in part at least, historically derived, and thus a part of continuity.

Schoenberg stated his own case *vis-à-vis* others in a verbal foreword to his choral creation of 1925 entitled *Satires*. The objects of his scorn were people who "pile on discords like gluttons (thus wishing to pass as 'moderns') but do not have the courage to draw the consequences of them. The same applies to those who make a selection of discords according to 'good taste' but cannot give any reason why their own cacophony should be allowed and that of others forbidden; also to those, who without 'going too far' don't explain why they go as far as they do; and finally to the pseudo-tonalists, who think that they can allow themselves everything that dislocates tonality, providing that on occasion, good or bad, they can make their profession of faith as tonal composers by means of a common chord."[2]

With or without regard to other sense in this statement, it is perfectly clear that Schoenberg, in setting forth the terms and condi-

---

[9] Telephone conversation with Richard Hoffmann, at Schoenberg's home in Brentwood, August 26, 1964.
[1] Page 262.
[2] *Grove's Dictionary of Music and Musicians*, 5th edn., VIII, 518.

tions in accord with which music should be composed by his Method, was establishing his own reasons why his "cacophony should be allowed and that of others forbidden" (to cite his own terminology). It is evident that he craved the distinction of being both Prometheus and Solomon: to be the one man in history whose formula for stealing divine fire should have the sanction of a legal code (self-invented). It did not work, not even for Arnold Schoenberg.

If he devised anything, it was a new way of writing music, not a way of writing new music. It might, in every smallest detail, make sense, but it did not necessarily make music, save as it existed in the individual himself. Even Schoenberg, who was in the fruitful years of the Second Quartet, the Stefan George songs, the Five Orchestral Pieces, and *Pierrot lunaire* a profoundly original free creator, became, as expositor of his Method, hemmed in by a mode of construction which rendered choice and instinct subordinate to restriction and formula. The great distinction between Schoenberg's dictates and the means evolved by historical change is relatively simple. His is a system of negation, not of affirmation, in which one is indoctrinated in what *cannot* be done before aspiring to do something in spite of it. His method is restrictive; history's is permissive.

With Schoenberg's Method, music arrived at an extremity of evolution, however contrived the end product, from the long sequence of events herein detailed. But it was only an extremity, not *the* extremity. Running parallel to it chronologically but counter to it aesthetically was another line of descent which requires for its exposition a return to a motive unrecalled since page 159 of this rondo on historical themes, but now ready for its place in the recapitulation.

VIII

Shoots and Deviations

I

THE CHAIN OF CONTINUITY by which a mode of thought, a means of solving a musical problem is passed from hand to hand, or perhaps it would be better to say from mind to mind, asserts itself in the least suspected ways, the most unexpected places. Hector Berlioz, while rejecting *Tristan*, wrote music that had an impact on Mussorgsky. Saint-Saëns, who was able to hear something in *Tristan* which Berlioz did not, found no great interest in a score of *Boris* he brought back to Paris from Moscow. But it aroused the interest of a fellow-musician, Julian de Brayer, who came upon it in a visit to Saint-Saëns's apartment.[1] His enthusiasm was eventually communicated to Debussy, who did not,[2] at first encounter, appear to be greatly taken by it (see p. 144). In later circumstances, Debussy responded warmly to the works of Mussorgsky, especially to his songs.

Born Claude-Achille Debussy, known by preference in a youthful period as Ach. de Bussy, he eventually styled himself Claude Debussy, *musicien français*, after earning the accolade, in Gabriele d'Annunzio's phrase, of being called Claude de France.[3] In some respects, Debussy was as much a non-Germanic composer as Schoenberg was a non-Gallic one. However, this was when he was a much younger musician, and

---

[1] The year was 1876, not 1874, as Brayer later recollected. Saint-Saëns did not return from Russia until January 1876. See James Hardin: *Saint-Saëns and His Circle* (London: Chapman and Hall; 1965), p. 143 *n.*

[2] Edward Lockspeiser: *Debussy: His Life and Mind* (New York: The Macmillan Company; 1962), I, 48.

[3] Oscar Thompson: *Debussy, Man and Artist* (New York: Dodd, Mead and Company; 1937), p. 231.

the period of isolation did not last nearly as long as the one in which Schoenberg took a rather mystifying pride.

The published works of Debussy run back as far as the *Nuit d'étoiles* of 1876, when he was fourteen, and so durable a product as the much-sung *"Beau soir"* dates from only two years later. This suggests a man who found his vocation very early, so early that it is sometimes forgotten that he was precociously gifted as a pianist, winning honors at the Conservatoire in his early teens for proficiency as an instrumentalist. Almost immediately, as the dates indicate, the impulse to composition asserted itself, but the precedence of his pianistic abilities should not be forgotten. They not only led him to the use of the instrument in ways varied and subtle beyond those of almost any of his contemporaries, but also provided him with ready access to an enormous range of musical experience ranging from Couperin to Chopin to Wagner.

It was this skill which qualified him to serve, during summer vacations from the Conservatoire, as household pianist for Nadejda von Meck (the "Beloved Friend" of the Tchaikovsky correspondence). Debussy was seventeen when he was first recommended to serve her in Switzerland. In the following two years the invitation was renewed with wider consequences: he traveled to Russia for the summer months to serve on her estate as family tutor and member of a trio that she maintained.

Inevitably, he became well indoctrinated in the music of Tchaikovsky. Proximity to Moscow permitted Debussy to spend some weeks there during a period in the summer of 1882, when the All-Russian Exposition provided a series of ten concerts, two of them directed by Rimsky-Korsakov. Thus Debussy's exposure to Russian music preceded by at least a half dozen years the revelation that came to Ravel in the summer of 1889, when Rimsky conducted a similar series of programs at the *Exposition universelle* in Paris.[4]

There were no Russian summers after 1882, as Debussy bent himself to advancing his compositional career by winning a Prix de Rome. The work with which he succeeded in 1884—*L'Enfant prodigue*—is occasionally performed today and is regarded by some as retrogressive, in originality and personality, by the measure of several earlier works. Lockspeiser, for example, describes it as "deliberately produced for this occasion, a work in the style of the acknowledged masters of the day, Lalo, Guiraud and also Delibes . . ."[5] But, among these manifestations of a will to win so strong that Debussy tempered his own inclinations,

---

[4] See p. 143.
[5] Lockspeiser: *Debussy: His Life and Mind*, I, 67.

one also finds in the likeness of the "*Air de Lia*" to the Chevalier des Grieux's "*Ah! fuyez, douce image*" (in *Manon*) a bit of Massenet.

In time, after his irksome stay at the Villa Medici, came Debussy's attraction to Wagner. Some of it can be heard in *La Damoiselle élue* (of 1887–8) and there are also traces of the *Tristan* idiom in the *Cinq poèmes de Charles Baudelaire*, completed in 1889. It is generally contended that Debussy's encounter with Mussorgsky's mode of thought turned him away from Wagner: the absence of any clear documentation, however, leaves at issue the time when this might have occurred. A new shaft of light is beamed from Igor Stravinsky's recollection of a visit to Debussy sometime after June 13, 1911 (the date of the first performance of *Petrouchka*, and Stravinsky's reference to the meeting as coming "shortly after"). Stravinsky recalls, ". . . we talked about Moussorgsky's songs and agreed that they contained the best music of the whole Russian school. He said he had discovered Moussorgsky when he found some of the music lying untouched on Mme von Meck's piano [which is to say, between 1880 and 1882]."[6]

At the other end of the parenthesis of time assigned to Debussy's response to Mussorgsky is Lockspeiser's statement "It was not until 1896, according to this version [relating to Debussy's *lack* of response to *Boris* when Brayer directed his attention to it in 1889], that, following the lecture recitals in Paris of Pierre d'Alheim and Marie Olenine, Debussy became aware of Moussorgsky's genius."[7] Somewhere in between is the date assigned to a photo of Debussy and Chausson together at the piano, with the score of *Boris* on the music rack (see p. 292).

It is not impossible, of course, that all the statements are true: that Debussy recollected, years later, seeing the music of Mussorgsky on the piano of Mme von Meck; that he was not greatly taken by *Boris* when he first looked at it (one answer he gave, according to his friend Robert Godet,[8] was that, lacking the ability of relating the music to the Russian text, he could not reach a sound judgment); and that his interest was not truly aroused until 1896, by which time he had completed his string quartet and much of the *Prélude à L'Après-midi d'un faune*.

It is, indeed, Lockspeiser's contention that the first Russian to draw Debussy into his continuity was Tchaikovsky. "Something more than an echo of the famous Scherzo [Symphony No. 4] is surely to be

[6] Igor Stravinsky and Robert Craft: *Expositions and Developments* (Garden City, N.Y.: Doubleday and Company; 1962), p. 158.
[7] Lockspeiser: *Debussy: His Life and Mind*, I, 48.
[8] Ibid., I, 48.

discerned in the Scherzo of Debussy's Quartet, similarly remarkable for its *pizzicato* writing. As for *Romeo and Juliet,* we cannot fail to hear something of it in *L'Après-midi d'un faune,* namely in the horn writing voluptuously hovering between two notes in both the love scene of Tchaikovsky's work and in the central section of *L'Après-midi d'un faune.*"[9] In another phase of his study, Lockspeiser alludes to the "Forest Murmurs" in Wagner's *Siegfried* as "a true Impressionist evocation of nature in music by which, around 1893, Debussy was surely influenced in the central section of *L'Après-midi d'un faune.*"[1]

Whatever the detail of when and how, it is an inescapable, substantial fact that Debussy was sensitive to the musical atmosphere about him—in a way, say, that a Brahms was not—and that the more he inhaled of it, the more he tended to exhale a combined by-product of his own. In the earliest songs and piano pieces there is a kind of generalized Frenchness in which traces of Duparc or Chausson are not absent, merely less readily recognizable than an allusion to Fauré's "*Après un rêve*" in "*Beau soir*" (measures 20–1, and again measures

Fauré: Après un rêve (op. 7, No. 1)

22–3). By contrast with many other participants in the continuity of

Debussy: Beau soir

9 Ibid., I, 59.   1 Ibid., II, 19.

which he became so generative a part, Debussy rarely responded to his sources in their way. In common with other truly creative composers before and after him, Debussy was more often than not attracted to the atypical in the music that interested him. This, again, distinguished the act of propagation from the merely mechanical one of imitation (as stated in Axiom II, p. 32).

Nadia Boulanger makes an interesting, if oblique, reference[2] to just this kind of *propagation* in discussing the often-remarked resemblance of the opening measures of the orchestral nocturne titled *Fêtes* to Mussorgsky's *Sunless*. Quoting the two passages, she says: "The passage in question may well represent an unconscious reminiscence, on Debussy's part, of a song with which we know he was acquainted. But the fact still remains that the measures in 'Without Sunlight' are far more characteristic of Debussy's than they are of Moussorgsky's style. They represent, on the part of the latter composer, one of those mysterious anticipations of the language of a future age, of which there are so many examples in musical history and which too often tended to provoke controversies that are more amusing than they are illuminating." If the act of "anticipation" can be construed as applying only to those things which are *acted upon* to another's advantage, the phenomenon is no more "mysterious" than a radio signal, which must have a receiver as well as a sender to be meaningful. It becomes, rather, another of the profoundly generative components of the web that has been woven by musical craftsmen over the decades, from a multitude of differentiated strands.

Had Mme Boulanger's own formidable powers of diagnosis been directed to the total subject, rather than merely to a small part of it, she might have been inclined to reverse her sequence of "amusing" and "illuminating." What might be considered "amusing" is the way in which one manifestation of an outside source may be clearly apparent to its receiver (or "victim," as Mahler noted in connection with his Fourth Symphony) and another escape his awareness altogether. Thus the conjecture of Oscar Thompson[3] that the *Fantaisie* for piano and orchestra written in 1890 was not published in Debussy's lifetime because "some commentators" (identities not specified) were "prompted . . . to liken it to d'Indy's *Symphonie sur un thème montagnard français*." He asks, rhetorically: "Did Debussy, perhaps, discover the dubious resemblance?"

[2] In one of several *Lectures on Modern Music* delivered at Rice Institute, Houston, Texas, in April 1926, p. 167 of the published text.
[3] Thompson: *Debussy*, p. 108.

What prompted *me* to investigate the possibility that Debussy might have known D'Indy's work, which was first performed in 1887 shortly after his return to Paris from Rome, is the likeness of a principal melody of *La Damoiselle élue* (first heard from the flute[4] [see p. 280] and then echoed by the horn) to the opening *cor anglais* statement of the "mountain air" itself in the *Symphonie*. Thompson leaves no doubt that Debussy did know D'Indy's work, and had reacted to it. But presumably, the likeness here, if it occurred to Debussy at all, did not disturb him. It was but one of a complex of ideas he drew upon to produce a composite of his own.

D'Indy: Symphony on a French Mountain Air (*op. 25*)

As the work in which Debussy took a long stride from the ranks of the anonymous *légionnaires* of French music toward a command position of his own, *La Damoiselle élue* rewards a moment's attention. Heard in the sequence of its occurrence, the complex of ideas includes the following:

[4] Number 3 of the Durand and C. orchestral score, miniature version, p. 9.

Debussy: La Damoiselle élue

1 · Five measures after the marking ① a strong suggestion of Wagner's *Siegfried Idyll*, not merely in the rise and fall of a phrase built around a fifth, but also in voice-leading, texture, and contrary motion of the upper and lower parts. It is analogous to, but not identical with, the part of the *Idyll* which made so strong an appeal to Mahler.

2 · A continuation, with a touch of *Tristan,* and a whiff of Grieg (Piano Concerto).

3 · A flute solo, paralleling the *cor anglais* of the D'Indy *Symphonie.* Debussy's is in 12/8, D'Indy's in 9/8.

4 · First appearance of the chorus, not unlike the offstage voices in *Parsifal* or perhaps its prototype, the chorus in Berlioz's *Roméo.*

5 · More D'Indy, developed and expanded.

6 · And more.

7 · Reversion to the *Siegfried Idyll* strain.

8 · Ninths, clarity, lack of doubling are key elements.

9 · "*Alors*" is the word of the solo voice. "*Azaël*" was its counterpart in the Massenet-tinted *L'Enfant prodigue.*

10 · The elaboration takes Debussy into a trend of his own, from which emerges a descending, horn-flavored figure very much like the end of *L'Après-midi* (not to be born for another half-dozen years).

11 · Expanded, intensified.

12 · More so.

13 · A parallel to (2), this time more akin to Fauré.

14 · Mixture—*Siegfried Idyll* in the voice, while inner line (viola) gives shadowy suggestion of the opening of *L'Après-midi*.

15 · Recitative-like statement, for solo voice.

16 · Expanded.

17 · Works toward the sound of Mélisande.

18 · Woodwinds and wavy string patterns bring a picture of meadows (*Parsifal*'s) to mind.

19 · Gurnemanz peeps in.

20 · He is more of a presence.

21 · The Good Friday afternoon becomes the Faun's.

22, 23 · An odd intrusion of Franck (descending figure starting high in strings).

24, 25, 26, 27 · A mingling of prior elements.

28 · D'Indy again.

29 · Expanded.

30 · String tremolos suggestive of *La Mer*-to-come, broadens into "pre-echo" of *L'Après-midi*.

31 · Arpeggios.

32 · For a "mystic" effect, close intervals (augmented thirds?) of *Ring* background, or possibly from Act III of *Parsifal*.

33 · D'Indy idea is finally in the *cor anglais*, where it was, originally, in his *Symphonie*.

The ending is neutral.

The overwhelming evidence from these and other works of the period before Debussy attained his stylistic identity is that, like many of his distinguished predecessors, he selected, rejected, weighed, and accepted what was useful to his purpose with a degree of discrimination almost Mozartian (see p. 10). The commentary by Mme Boulanger to which reference has already been made continues: "The origins of Debussy's harmonic style are to be sought elsewhere: in Liszt, Chabrier, and Fauré rather than in Moussorgsky. The affiliations between Liszt's harmony and the harmony of Debussy are real but somewhat obscure and are most apparent, perhaps, in one or two mutually characteristic ways of connecting triads. The free and expressive manner in which Fauré uses seventh chords is prophetic of Debussy's similar and later use of chords of the ninth. The following cadential formula, almost an obsession with Chabrier, occurs in one form or another again and again

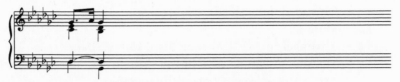

Chabrier: cadence formulation

in the 'Préludes,' making the impression of reminiscence unavoidable." Of course, to one less familiar with Chabrier than such an authority as Mme Boulanger, the effect might seem intrinsically Debussyan. For that matter, for an ear untuned to *Tristan*, *Parsifal*, and the *Siegfried Idyll*, so might some of the most attractive moments of *La Damoiselle élue*.

For the later E. Robert Schmitz, longtime student and interpreter of Debussy's piano music and author of a particularly perceptive book about it, the generative forces in the keyboard music included the following:[5]

> Chopin, via Madame Mauté de Fleurville, and early piano lessons.
> Massenet, Gounod, as part of the Conservatoire days.
> Fauré, and the exquisite art of modulation and poetic inspiration.
> Pre-Raphaelism and Wagner, around the era of the Prix de Rome and Villa Medici days.
> Symbolist poets: a long relationship extending from student days through adulthood.
> The expositions of 1889 and 1900: the lure of the Orient, and the wonderful all-Russian festivals conducted by Rimsky-Korsakoff.
> Moussorgsky: 'Boris Godounov' and the songs.
> Satie, and experimental harmony.
> The clavecinistes: Rameau, Couperin, Scarlatti, their clarity of patterns, their conciseness of form.
> J. S. Bach: the divine arabesque, contrapuntal dissonance, and organ style.
> Palestrina, and modal plasticity.
> Mozart, in his sensitive use of ornamentation, and the appoggiatura.

It will be seen from the foregoing that Schmitz makes no mention at all of Liszt, to whom Boulanger assigns primary importance, whereas she omits reference to Satie. This is in no respect a matter of "oversight" or lack of comprehension: it is a by-product of the sizableness of the subject, and of the aspects of continuity in it to which one assigns major or minor importance. It was in the aftermath of his exposure to Wagner *and* Mussorgsky, D'Indy *and* Liszt, Satie and *cie* that the recognizably

---

[5] E. Robert Schmitz: *The Piano Works of Claude Debussy* (New York: Duell, Sloan and Pearce; 1950), p. 40.

distinctive traits of Debussy began to polarize and affect the swing of his magnetic personality.

Thus if there was Mélisande already in his first songs and particularly in *La Damoiselle élue* (where she appears as a kind of foster-sister to Marguerite, Manon, and, perhaps, Eva Pogner), of Pelléas there was hardly a trace (much less so of Golaud, Arkel, and Yniold) until after his absorption of Mussorgsky's *Nursery Cycle* and the Pimenn scene of *Boris*. Certainly the closely calculated, delicately inflected harmonic changes of Fauré's *Pavane* (a product of 1888) had suggestions for Debussy. And his friendship with Chausson bore positive results not usually considered mutual.

With a wisdom quite intuitive, Debussy resisted attraction to the common forms of ancestor worship, such as symphonies, concertos, sonatas (a youthful venture with a symphony in the Von Meck days did not produce a lasting result). Thus he was spared involvement with Established (which is to say German) Form, the need for machining structural joints which imposed the "quote direct" upon such others as Dvořák, Tchaikovsky, Mahler, and even Brahms.

Debussy was early indoctrinated in the literature of the piano, and his first published efforts show that he was always at home with the voice and the word. For a while, the compulsion to the Word was as strong in him as it was in such contemporaries as Strauss and Mahler (born between 1860 and 1864, as he was). But he soon found another, and largely unprecedented, stimulus in the Image—whether evoked in sound, as in Mallarmé's *L'Après-midi d'un faune*, or in color, as in Watteau's *Embarquement pour Cythère* (*L'Île joyeuse*). As time passed, the image could be as generalized as *La Mer*, as much an abstraction as *Iberia*, or the product of such an inner vision as "*Des pas sur la neige*," a title that was added postcreatively. But it was clearly out of this disposition to a new intermingling of elements that Debussy formed the particularly malleable mix of *L'Après-midi d'un faune*. In it, the "foreign elements"[6] (foreign in the national as well as the physical sense) to which he had been exposed were, for the first time, almost wholly absorbed.

2

IN HIS PREFACE to the Schmitz study of the piano music, Virgil Thomson declares: "Internationally viewed, as Fred Goldbeck lately pointed

---

[6] Among them the pentatonic scales and gamelan timbres brought to Paris by the Javanese visitors to the Paris World Exhibition of 1889.

out, he [Debussy] is to the musicians of our century everywhere what Beethoven was to those of the nineteenth, our blinding light, our sun, our central luminary." At an opposite extreme of evaluation is the statement of the Italian composer-editor-musicologist Gian Francesco Malipiero: "Debussy represents a digression: this exquisite musician, this super-aristocrat could not be the starting point for a school."[7]

To each of these highly subjective evaluators, Debussy no doubt spoke in the manner attributed to him. For others less disposed to extremes, the weight of judgment would fall somewhere between. There was at least one moment in time when the parabolas pursued by the life work of Beethoven and Debussy intersected. That was embodied in Debussy's statement that it was "more useful to see the dawn rise than to hear the Pastoral Symphony."[8]

This was, in all probability, a riposte to Beethoven's well-known characterization of the *"Pastorale"* as "more an expression of feeling than a painting." But there is more than a little painting, however naïve, in Debussy's view, in the *"Pastorale,"* as there is considerable feeling in *L'Après-midi d'un faune.* In the tonal vocabulary as Debussy evolved it, there was an ever-stronger striving for command of elements that would enable him to convey imagery in tone. Unlike such predecessors as Berlioz, who had a bold if broad command of the imagery suitable to his purpose, or Mussorgsky, whose *Pictures* are truly pictorial, or even Wagner, whose visualizations in tone range from the depths of the Rhine to the heights of Valhalla, Debussy was not restricted to the natural or the supernatural, the bold or the broad, the animate or the inanimate. He achieved a more comprehensive range of visual values than known to any other musician before his time, building with the materials of others as well as those invented by himself. Arthur Honegger put a probing finger on this point when he wrote: "Absolute originality does not exist. Despite the prodigious novelty of his contributions, Debussy had his precursors. Certain of the last piano pieces of Liszt are not so distant from Debussy's *Préludes.*"[9] Possibly the reference would include the 1875–6 collection titled *Weihnachtsbaum* (*Christmas Tree*), which the aging composer dedicated to his granddaughter Daniela von Bülow. Some of the pieces have not only an improvisatory flair but also a compactness of statement and a freshness of sonority de-

[7] *Composers on Music,* ed. Sam Morgenstern (New York: Pantheon Books, Inc.; 1956), p. 434. The source of the quotation is identified as an article published in *Modern Music* in 1929.

[8] Claude Debussy: *Monsieur Croche* (New York: Viking Press; 1928), p. 11.

[9] Arthur Honegger: *Je suis compositeur* (New York: St. Martin's Press; 1966), p. 71.

cidedly Debussyan. (During his Prix-de-Rome days, Debussy visited Liszt and heard the venerable Abbé perform.)

Perhaps the most illuminating comparison that can be made to characterize the new impulse brought to music by Debussy is with Chopin. If the latter could be described (see p. 55) as a short-story writer among composers, then Debussy was certainly the draughtsman, the brushwielder, the master of lights and shades, tints and textures *par excellence.* As Chopin's story-telling urge embraced everything from the short-short to the novelette, so Debussy's impulse flowed into every shape and form from the vignette, the cameo, and the caricature to the water color, the landscape, and the seascape on the largest orchestral scale. It might be said that as his ablest predecessors had striven to use their skills to render an image audible, Debussy had the more challenging compulsion to make, with sound, something one could see.

Certainly it is difficult to speak in other terms of the mature art that expressed itself not only in the orchestral murals of the Nocturnes, *La Mer,* and *"Ibéria,"* but also in the line drawings of the keyboard works. These range from the modestly suggestive *"La petite nègre"* (Émile Vuillermoz dates it to 1879) to its far more adroit, later counterpart "Golliwog's Cake Walk." On a larger scale they take in not only the massive *"Cathédrale engloutie,"* but also the surpassingly seeable *L'Île joyeuse.*

Debussy's acquaintance with the painters of the time, the fecundity and range of their responsiveness to the world about them, their ability to modify and control the medium with which they worked doubtless served him well. Whether consciously or otherwise, he applied much the same learning process to the evolution of his own resources. On a sound base of academic training he contrived a color sense quite his own. He was not inclined to borrow or beg an effect or procedure and use it as he found it. Rather, each was, in turn, mixed with strains from another source, transformed, and reconstituted. When he was working on his *Nocturnes,* he described them, in a letter to Eugène Ysaÿe (in the original conception, a solo violin was part of the scheme) as "an experiment with the different combinations that can be obtained from one colour—like a study in grey in painting."[1]

This called, obviously, for something more than previously known means of tonal characterization, such as Schumann had used in his *Kinderscenen* or Saint-Saëns had improved upon in his *Le Rouet d'Omphale.* The need, in short, was for a spectrum of sonority which could

[1] Edward Lockspeiser: *Debussy* (London: J. M. Dent and Sons Ltd.; 1951), p. 61.

be split up and reassembled like the refractions of light through a prism. Lockspeiser has noted[2] the way in which Debussy combined values of Massenet and Wagner in the early *Printemps* to convey what appealed to him in Botticelli's *Primavera*. But what served Massenet for his *Scènes alsaciennes* had to be refined, reduced—one might almost say, strained—to suit Debussy's purpose in *L'Après-midi d'un faune*.

The marvel is that it was done entirely with muscial materials and in no instance with a sacrifice of tonal beauty. What had been, in the experimental stage, a solitary splash of color (an arpeggio on an augmented chord or a misty ninth to blur the outlines of a straightforward progression) came to comprise the means from which the lights and shades of a whole concept could be elaborated. In the early *"Clair de lune"* of the *Suite bergamasque* (1890), a rootless dominant seventh (achieved in measure 58 by dropping the tonic D flat down to C flat) acts as a subtle "modifier" of the previous musical statement as, say, an unexpected adjective might in a familiar verbal phrase ("the varnished truth"). In the later *L'Île joyeuse*, the alteration of an inner voice from A flat to A natural or A sharp makes for the subtle shading of sense which etches a deeper line of meaning though the repeated principal melodic curve is otherwise unchanged. By the time Debussy came to write the *Douze Études* of 1915 (dedicated "To the memory of Chopin"), he was so versed in such modifications and shadings that he could embellish a simple Czernyish five-finger pattern with a sonorous overlay in which the two coexist independently, the one perceived— almost seen—through the transparent, filmy sound of the other.

It was thus, in fact, that Debussy fulfilled the role in the continuity of Chopin defined in their independent ways by Gerald Abraham, Rimsky-Korsakov, and Boulanger. For it was through such movement of voices (remarked in the opening of the G-minor Ballade; (see p. 48) that Chopin projected the direction of the piano writing to come. (With the response of Debussy to his initiative, it might also be said that Chopin predicted it.) It is well known that late in life Debussy accepted as a labor of love the task of supervising a new edition of Chopin. This brought full circle a lifelong association that had begun more than forty years before (1874), when the ten-year-old Debussy had won a second certificate of merit at the Conservatoire for his playing of Chopin's F-minor (No. 2) Concerto. In the fullness of his absorption with the works of his great predecessor, Debussy came to feel not only a mental and spiritual relationship with Chopin, but also a mystical physical identity with him. According to his contempo-

[2] Annotation for London CS 6079.

rary and sometime interpreter Marguerite Long: "He was impregnated with the spirit of Chopin, inhabited by it."[3] Continuity can have no closer connection.

It is a further comment on the economy of Nature (which abhors waste as it does a vacuum) that Debussy furthered, in a direct line from Chopin and Liszt, an artifice that became inseparable from the proper re-creation of his piano music. Of the art of the pedal, Schmitz writes, apropos of *"Clair de lune"*: "If the performer does not find a way to sustain the vibration of the double third D flat-F (measure 1, seventh beat) so that this resonance may encounter the new harmony G flat-A natural (measure 2, first beat), then the subtle tension has not taken place, its subsequent resolution is meaningless."[4] In Debussy's own words (written to the publisher Jacques Durand in 1915), what he remembered most of hearing Liszt perform in Rome in 1885 was his "use of the pedal as a kind of breathing."[5]

As adapted by Debussy to his purpose, the pedal became not only an adjunct to musical meaning (as projected by Schmitz *vis-à-vis* the early *"Clair de lune"*), but also, eventually, another value of the tonal palette from which he conjured images and with which he cast spells. In the *"Reflets dans l'eau"* of fifteen years later (1905), a whole series of chords, over two measures, is blended into a single sound by the use of the pedal. Mme Boulanger makes a singularly apt comparison in saying that this "recalls the manner in which Monet, for example, gets his complementary tones and shades by a sharp juxtaposition of little daubs of primary colors which are fused and blended by the distant eye. The resemblance between the two methods is so striking that the musical device would almost seem a direct transposition of the technique of one art into the realms of another."[6]

With all his strong strain of originality and his ear for what might be called the unfinished tonal business of his predecessors, Debussy was not averse to acknowledging the innovation of a contemporary when it was suitable to his purpose. As an illustration, perhaps, of Grieg's Law that "contemporaries influence each other" (p. 5), there is little doubt that the appearance of Ravel's *Jeux d'eau* in 1901 (composed, says Rollo Myers "with one eye on Liszt and the fountains in the Villa d'Este")[7] prompted a reaction by Debussy. Its innovation has

[3] Lockspeiser: *Debussy: His Life and Mind*, II, 44.

[4] Schmitz: *The Piano Works of Claude Debussy*, p. 55.

[5] Lockspeiser: *Debussy: His Life and Mind*, I, 22.

[6] Nadia Boulanger: *Lectures on Modern Music* (Houston, Texas: Rice Institute), p. 166.

[7] Rollo Myers: *Ravel, Life and Works* (New York: Thomas Yoseloff; 1960), p. 24.

been described by Nicolas Slonimsky as "the counterposition of two rows of mutually exclusive scales of the white (heptatonic) and black (pentatonic) keys."[8] Such an ingenious composite (Slonimsky's term for it is "massed sonorities") had an obviously enticing utility, and Debussy made productive use of it—in his way, however, not Ravel's. The ultimate outcome was the *Douze Études*, of which Ravel's devoted partisan, Myers, was sufficiently the honest music lover to write: "I think we must admit that Ravel wrote nothing for the piano as profoundly original and rich in purely musical content as Debussy's masterly Douze Etudes."[9] As a kind of crown to all his prior musical glories, it has a special distinction all its own: whatever prompting imagery there may have been for these works Debussy kept wholly to himself. Here "titles" are limited to such barren phrases as "For the 'Five Fingers' " (the single quotes enclosing a reference to Czerny), "For the Double Thirds," and "For Octaves."

Had such an expansion of the language as Debussy found it been confined (in the manner of the one who came ever more to be his life's ideal) to the piano, Debussy's name would have had a significance to resound for decades. But one may question which instrument profited more from his probing mind and ear: the piano or the orchestra. If it could be said, as of 1830, that Berlioz "ventilated" the orchestra (p. 91), it might be suggested of Debussy, seventy years later, that he "aerated" it. This is no more than to say, as one dictionary source defines it,[1] that Debussy exposed it to "the chemical action of air." Like a jet of water aerated by a leap through space from a waterfall or spurted upward under pressure, it descends in a finer, mistier mixture than it had when inert. In musical terms, it took the form of a total sound lightened, de-densified, thinned out from the Wagnerian vogue as it prevailed in the 1880's and 1890's, with doublings diminished, closely grouped wind and brass chords opened up and regrouped, brilliance converted into luminosity.

This did not make Debussy anti-Wagner any more than it made Mahler, who pursued similar objectives, anti-Wagner. It merely made both anti the *commonest* kind of Wagner. The lightly stranded lines of the *Siegfried Idyll* and the "Forest Murmurs" of *Siegfried* itself, the pastel tints of Gurnemanz's meadow in Act III of *Parsifal* contained suggestions apparent to both. Whether there was any interchange of

---

[8] Nicolas Slonimsky: *Music Since 1900* (3rd edn., New York: Coleman-Ross Co.; 1949), p. 24.
[9] Myers: Ravel, p. 155.
[1] *Oxford Concise Dictionary*, 2nd edn., p. 21.

impulse to turn Mahler (in 1896) in a direction already taken by Debussy in *L'Après-midi* of 1892–4 (first performed on December 22, 1894) I do not presently know. In any case, each pursued Wagner's lead to a destination ever more distinctively his own.

With Debussy, it was to the achievement of a many-voiced texture of sound that would be as responsive to its "player"—the conductor—as the piano was to its individual performer. Unlike Ravel, who "orchestrated" (with supreme craftsmanship) many of his best-known concert pieces from earlier piano publications, Debussy thought orchestrally from the first in his three major contributions to the symphonic literature: the *Nocturnes, La Mer,* and the *Images* ("*Ibéria,*" "*Rondes de printemps,*" and "*Gigues*").

Each is an adventure into the dream world where sight and sound are facets of the same experience; each is a masterpiece; and each shows an accretion of means not present in its predecessor. In the manner of the great painters to whom Debussy was devoted, each embodies a "period" in the evolution of the artist's ability to realize his objectives through his chosen medium. With Debussy, the design tends more and more to emerge from the background, so that in "*Ibéria*" there is scarcely any of the haze that softens the outlines of "*Nuages*" and "*Fêtes,*" very little of the mystery or the vapor that hangs between the listener and the tonal picture that is *La Mer.* Some might say that this was, to a degree, inherent in the chosen subject matter: it is more to the point that Debussy chose only subject matter for which he had the means to do justice. "*Ibéria*" is the most brilliant of his orchestral achievements, if not the most expressive, because its subject was the most elusive to render palpable.

Should one be so inclined, several of the constituent elements of the *Nocturnes,* beyond the opening suggestion of Mussorgsky, might be cited. "*Nuages*" tends to invoke the Russians more than was Debussy's need later (a Borodinish touch in the English horn, for Oriental atmosphere; a *Steppes of Central Asia* tinge in the languid flow of a passing vista shows clouds rather than camels in the distance). "*Fêtes*" is rather more localized—Italy, for sure, to judge from the saltarello figure with which it opens, as does Berlioz's *Carnaval romain.* The fine striding tune that follows is one of Debussy's best. When it is time for the invocation of music-heard-over-the-waters, it comes like an echo of Berlioz. "*Sirènes,*" with its wordless chorus, would certainly seem a reaction to the same composer's "Royal Hunt and Storm" in *Les Troyens.*

By the time of *La Mer,* only half a dozen years later, but separated by the gulf bounded by the preparation and performance of *Pelléas,* Debussy's artistic vision had broadened considerably. Strings for the surge and flow of the sea, woodwinds for spray, brass and percussion for the unfathomable depths—all are combined in "From dawn to noon on the sea" with a passion for proportion that might be characterized as either Chopinesque or Mozartian. The magical addition of one choir to another provides not only mass but lightness. All the strings are divided and subdivided, the two harps each have a separate part; there is a place for the muted trombone as well as the solo flute. By contrast, the following "Play of the Waves" is a veritable scherzo: smaller groupings of instruments prevail; there is more of the aerated aspect to the chord formations; and when the play of waves naturally dissolves into spray, Debussy is not lacking for the aural equivalent: harp arpeggios, violin harmonics, a touch of bells and cymbals. In the culminating "Dialogue of the Wind and the Sea," the devices of the preceding movements have a properly coordinate part.

Though infrequently performed, *Jeux* (a composition of 1913 with which Debussy took his only part in the creative ferment of the Diaghilev Ballet) had a musical consequence beyond ordinary public awareness. It carries the technique of *"Ibéria"* a step beyond the calculated fragmentations of that work into new dimensions of timbre and color. An uncommonly large woodwind complement and reinforced percussion give lightness as well as dryness to the sound. There is some suggestion in it of Ravel's *Ma Mère L'Oye* (first performed in its orchestral form in January 1912) and even of Rimsky's *Scheherazade,* but one of Debussy's most eminent fellow composers has declared that *Jeux* "discovers a whole new world of nuance and fluidity." In the further opinion of Igor Stravinsky: "These qualities are French, even peculiarly French perhaps, but they are new."[2] And in a dazzling leap ahead in the concept of continuity (which, of course, was no part of his thinking) he states: "The work's influence on Boulez is therefore natural . . ."

As the *Douze Études* crowned Debussy's piano writing and *"Ibéria"* (or *Jeux*) his command of the orchestra, so another work tied together his feeling for words and music as embodied in a splendid repertoire of songs, choral works, and a single opera. This is the too-seldom-heard *Le Martyre de Saint Sébastien,* for which, to do justice to the text of Gabriele d'Annunzio, Debussy utilized not only an orchestra and chorus, but also a solo soprano and a female narrator. In its artful

[2] Igor Stravinsky and Robert Craft: *Memories and Commentaries* (New York: Doubleday and Company, Inc.; 1960), p. 117 n.

composite of elements, as well as in the sumptuous range of theatrical effects thus made possible, Debussy all but invented a genre of or-chestra-with-chorus-and-narrator which has had a progeny of impressive vitality. Lurking in the background are such works as Berlioz's *Lélio* and Strauss's *Enoch Arden,* but it is improbable that, without De-bussy's energizing intercession, there would have ensued Milhaud's *Les Choëphores* (begun in 1913, two years after the *première* of *Le Martyre*), Stravinsky's *Perséphone,* Honegger's *Jeanne d'Arc au bûcher,* and Copland's *Lincoln Portrait.*

There was, in fact, hardly a major segment of composition to which Debussy, in the twenty-five years between 1890 and 1915, did not make a contribution as distinctive in substance as it was individual in pro-cedure. If there was something hardly imitable in his substance, there was always something to be learned from his procedure. Vaughan Wil-liams made an absorbing contribution to the distinction between them when he wrote: "Any student at a musical school can now reproduce the tricks of Debussy's style and therefore it is now, and only now, that we can discover whether Debussy had something genuine to say . . ."[3] The passage of more than thirty years since those words were published has resolved any doubts about the durability of Debussy's substance.

3

WHAT DEBUSSY CONTRIBUTED to the continuity of music in which he had been formed is, even in the reading of titles and types of works (not to mention assets added, possibilities explored), staggering. Com-pared with the stratagems invented by some of his German contem-poraries to get around the Wagnerian mountain, it might be said that Debussy proceeded according to the logic of imagination rather than the fantasy of reason.

As has been observed, Debussy had his Wagner fever in 1885–8, at very much the same time that Arnold Schoenberg was being exposed to *Tristan* in Vienna. There was some difference of age between them—Debussy was born in 1862, a dozen years before Schoenberg—but con-siderably more in the rate of their development. Whereas Debussy reacted to his Wagnerian exposure (in the manner outlined on p. 276) by accepting it as an element of his total creative experience, for Schoenberg, it was the one, the dominant influence for a consider-able time to come. His reaction was somewhat like that of the alcoholic

[3] Ralph Vaughan Williams: *National Music* (London: Oxford University Press; 1934), p. 13.

who has to take "the cure" by forswearing anything associated with his weakness. From this, eventually, derived the gospel of asceticism which would "guarantee the supremacy of German music for the next hundred years."

With Debussy, as we have clearly seen, the rationale was altogether different. He assimilated into the language as he found it all the diverse elements which gave him pause as well as pleasure—Massenet and Mussorgsky, Wagner and Louis Gottschalk, the gamelan of the East and the ragtime of the West. Thus regenerated, the language emerged refreshed and renewed, cross-fertilized to an extent unapproached since Wagner had taken into his essentially Germanic being the "exotic" elements of Chopin, Liszt, and Berlioz. In a phrase, its roots were ready to blossom anew with resources that would serve others for decades to come.

With Schoenberg, to whose thinking mind such a rationale should have made an early appeal and exerted a lasting influence, the reaction was rather the *emotional* one of negation, self-denial, and, in my view, constriction and retreat. Rather than adding to the vocabulary of his craft, he contracted it; rather than opening new vistas, he turned the intellectual gaze inward, away from the free-flowing means of a common experience toward the rigid formulation of an uncommon one.

As Debussy was the earlier to mature, as well as the more productive, the continuity flowing from him merits first consideration. In the classic manner in which ripples of influence have always spread outward from a point of direct contact—Haydn on Mozart and Beethoven, Chopin on Liszt, Liszt and Wagner on each other—so the first to feel the profound impact of Debussy was his friend and colleague Ernest Chausson. It may be recalled that Chausson was one of those to whom Wagner was an all but crushing force, the one he identified as the "red spectre" haunting his compositional dreams.

It was in the mid-nineties (1893–5) that Chausson became closely associated with his younger colleague, spent many weeks of each summer with him, shared musical discoveries with him. Indeed, a memento of their time together casts some light on just when Debussy was exposed to the score of *Boris* brought from Russia by Saint-Saëns and passed on to Bayer. It is a photo taken on a summer day of 1893 at Luzancy (Seine-et-Marne), showing Debussy at the piano. According to Chausson's biographers: "Since Debussy had become interested in Russian music—especially Moussorgsky—Chausson had sent for the score of *Boris Godunov*, which Debussy played on the piano while Chausson turned the pages for him. The camera has immortalized this scene . . ."[4] There is no sure way, from this reproduction, of identifying the open score.

It was in the aftermath of such artistic interchange that Chausson achieved the liberation of self to write what are, by general agreement, his most enduring works: the Piano Quartet, the B-flat Symphony, and the *Poème* for violin and orchestra. There were no more manifestations of such liberation after 1889 for the grim reason that Chausson died in a cycling accident shortly before the *Poème* had its *première*.

Washing outward in ever-widening circles from the point of first personal contact to the impersonal influence that resulted from publication and performance, Debussy's part in the continuity of others soon became historic fact (if, in several instances, not acknowledged until much later). One of his earliest debtors was Maurice Ravel. In later years Ravel responded to a hearing of *L'Après-midi d'un faune* with tears and the words: "It was when I first heard that many years ago that I understood what music is."[5] He was also quoted as saying that there was nothing in music more beautiful than this work and he thought it the kind of music which might ease the pangs of death.[6]

Thus, whatever the return flow of influence later on, there appears to be little doubt that Ravel was one of the first, if not the first, developing composer—he was nineteen when *L'Après-midi* was first performed—of later note to become part of the continuity of Debussy. If, as Thomson suggests, Debussy was the "sun" and "central luminary" of twentieth-century music, then it was a fulfillment of his image that the first beams should have fallen on a fellow Frenchman.

The rising line of Debussy's ascendancy is absorbing to chart for at least two reasons: the illumination it throws on how quickly such an influence can assert itself; the readiness of others to follow Debussy's response to the visual image. Publicly, there was no great accumulation of opportunities to hear Debussy's works between 1893 and 1902. Yet within half a dozen years of the *première* of *Pelléas* (April 30, 1902), his light was shining so brightly that it had brought into being a whole new musical growth identified as *debussysme*.

The strong morning heat (if not yet, perhaps, the high noon) of its ascension can be identified as to month, day, and year through a controversy that erupted in the Paris musical press.[7] In *La Nouvelle*

[4] Jean-Pierre Barricelli and Leo Weinstein: *Ernest Chausson, The Composer's Life and Works* (Norman: University of Oklahoma Press; 1955), p. 60.

[5] Myers: *Ravel*, p. 98.

[6] Ibid., p. 19.

[7] Victor I. Seroff: *Debussy: Musician of France* (New York: G. P. Putnam's Sons; 1956), pp. 263–4.

Presse of February 26, 1907, his onetime champion Émile Vuillermoz wrote, under the stress of a disappointing Debussy "novelty" (*Jet d'eau*, originally created in 1887): "The master can draw a useful lesson from the works of his impudent disciples . . . If he does not resolutely take his place once more at the head of the contemporary musical movement, the composer of *Pelléas* will find that the younger generation . . . which has grown up around his work is writing *Debussyist*[8] music better than he."

The implication that Ravel—whom Vuillermoz did not identify —was more Debussyist than Debussy was rejected in an article a few weeks later by Pierre Lalo (*Le Temps*, March 19, 1907). This led to further discussions and repercussions of the sort that the French dearly love, especially as it could be sensationalized as "*l'affaire Ravel.*" Through it all, Debussy remained calmly quiet, with the serene self assurance of a man free from concern with his "impudent disciples." "*Ibéria*," with which he was concerned, gave its own answer when it was first performed in 1911.

Almost exactly at the time of *l'affaire Ravel*, Debussy's influence was reaching out beyond Paris to another young musical mind. In Aix-en-Provence, the son of Gabriel Milhaud, studying the violin at the local conservatory, was invited to play in a quartet with the best players the town provided. "In 1905," he later wrote, "we studied Debussy's Quartet, which was such a revelation to me that I hastened to buy the score of *Pelléas*."[9] Thereafter, says Darius Milhaud, "When Wagner's operas were published by Durand at five francs a copy, I brought them all: I don't remember ever having been tempted to play them. But *Pelléas* and *Boris Godunov* always stood by my bedside."[1]

"It was then at the age of eight," Henry Hell writes in his biography of Francis Poulenc, which would put the year squarely at 1907, "that he first heard a work of Debussy, the *Danses sacrées et profanes* for harp and string orchestra, by which he was immediately overcome: the attraction it had for him was in the suggestion of wrong notes. His one desire was to be able to find for himself the intriguing chords of the ninth in this work at the piano. Once awakened, this passion for Debussy was steadily to develop, though he was hardly able to play any of the piano works before he was fourteen."[2]

Typical as these examples were of the strong surge of communication from Debussy to those in the immediate area of his physical being,

[8] Italics in the original.
[9] Darius Milhaud: *Notes Without Music* (New York: Alfred A. Knopf; 1953), p. 16.
[1] Ibid., p. 27.
[2] Henry Hell: *Francis Poulenc* (New York: Grove Press; 1959), p. 2.

related to him by national ties of sympathy, others were no less graphic. Of Manuel de Falla, J. B. Trend wrote: "The turning point in his career was, as he always insists, his journey to Paris and meeting with Debussy in 1907 . . . strange as it may seem, it was Debussy who revealed things in the spirit of Andaluz music which had been hidden or not clearly discerned even by Falla, who was born and bred in Andalucia."[3]

The extent of Debussy's compulsion on the course pursued by Falla (who was thirty-one years old and the composer of *La Vida breve* by the time of his Paris visit) has been dealt with at length, and in the composer's own words, in the Debussy issue of *La Revue musicale* (December 1920). The essence of it, as summarized by Trend, is: "Many of Debussy's works created a marvellous atmosphere of poetry and suggestion: to Falla these came with the force of an *evocación* of his own country and its music, and all his later works (down to *The Puppet Show* and the Harpsichord Concerto) may be regarded as an effort to convey this poetry and suggestiveness with the conviction of one who knows that dreams can sometimes come true. So far he had been expressing the letter of Andaluz music: he began now to realize how Debussy had managed to convey its spirit."[4]

This took the form not of mere poetizing, but of the application to his own works of Debussy's skill in shaping the palpable details— harmonic, rhythmic, melodic, agogic—of music to the heightening of its impalpable spirit. Between *La Vida breve* and *Noches en los jardines de España,* Falla's first major work to be completed after 1907, there is not merely a gulf but a void.

What is immediately apparent in a comparison of the two works is the difference in the texture, trend, and cohesion of the subject matter, Spanish though it is in both instances. In *La Vida breve,* Falla has used the sharp lenses of his ears and the focus of his mind to reproduce, photographically, a vista of Spanish life, in the manner of the Italian verists (the *melos* of the recitative could be as expressive of Mascagni's Sicily as it is of Falla's Spain). In *Noches en los jardines,* Falla has learned to reapply his faculties to render not so much a photographic likeness of his subject as a portrait of its mood, climate, and inner temper. His orchestra has become fuller, richer, less specific, more veiled: suggestion has taken the place of the direct statement that prevailed in *La Vida breve.*

In the *Fantasia Baetica* for piano, which came next in his sequence,

[3] J. B. Trend: *Manuel de Falla and Spanish Music* (New York: Alfred A. Knopf; 1929), p. 51.
[4] Ibid., p. 53.

Falla began to re-express some of the innovations he found in Debussy's *"La Soirée dans Grenade"* (which earned the Spaniard's endorsement of "the real Andalucia"). This was a technique of fragmentation, of interrupting the audible course of a phrase so that it had to be *carried forward in the listener's mind* rather than being baldly stated all at once. In the manner of some painters whom Debussy admired, it was the equivalent of suggesting a visual line of which the completion was left to the viewer's imagination. Had Mme Boulanger directed herself to this further refinement of aural-visual reference, she might have substituted the name of Seurat for that of Monet, which she invoked apropos of *"Reflets dans l'eau."*

In his later works—*El Amor brujo* (written after *Noches*, but performed before it), and especially in *El Sombrero de tres picos*—Falla sharpened considerably his command of such constructive details, including a kind of rhythmic stutter that Debussy had invented for *"Ibéria."* (It occurs just before and after number 10 in the Durand miniature score of *"Ibéria,"* pp. 16–17.) In his turn, Falla evolved his own cherishable traits of individuality, which have passed into the later language of Spanish composition as utilized by Turina, Mompou, Montsalvatge, Pittaluga, and Rodrigo, of the more recent Hispanic company. How distinctive it became need not be the subject of exposition, verbalization, or mere description. When, in a certain moment of his *Pulcinella* ballet score (measures 3-2-1 before ⃞110⃞), Stravinsky chooses to invoke a reference to Falla's *El Sombrero de tres picos*, it is as immediately arresting to the ear as his references, in other works, to Rossini and Tchaikovsky.

Farther east, almost at the same time, the seepage from Debussy came to the surface in the unexpected area of Budapest. As previously noted (see p. 200), Strauss's *Also sprach Zarathustra* had an extraordinary effect on the young Béla Bartók when he heard it in 1902, as a student in Budapest, aged twenty-one. After a number of turnings on the path toward a highroad of his own, Bartók discerned a distant light that attracted him more than any other. Says Serge Moreux: "In 1907 he was to say that French music had been to him what the vision on the road to Damascus was to St. Paul."[5]

Here, again, the witching year 1907! Bartók's attraction was clearly not so much to French music generally as to Debussy's, specifically. Speaking to Moreux some years later (1939), Bartók said: "It was your Debussy, whose music had just begun to reach us [Kodály, who was included in Bartók's plural, published a piano work entitled *Médi-*

[5] Serge Moreux: *Bartók* (London: Harvill Press; 1953), p. 59.

Falla: El Sombrero de Tres Picos

Stravinsky: Pulcinella

tation sur un motif de Debussy in that same inescapable year], who
showed us the path we must follow . . . Debussy's great service to
music was to reawaken among all musicians an awareness of harmony
and its possibilities. In that, he was just as important as Beethoven,

who revealed to us the meaning of progressive form, and as Bach, who showed us the transcendental significance of counterpoint . . ." Reflecting on his own statement, Bartók continued: "Now, what I am always asking myself is this: is it possible to make a synthesis of these three great masters, a living synthesis that will be valid for our own time? . . ."[6]

Even farther east, the penetration of Debussy had been sufficiently swift for his works to come to the attention of Rimsky-Korsakov, who died in 1908 (June 8). Interesting testimony regarding his reaction is provided by Igor Stravinsky: "At a concert where one of the latter's [Debussy's] works was on the program I asked Rimsky-Korsakov what he thought of it. He answered in these very words: 'Better not listen to him: one runs the risk of getting accustomed to him and one would end up by liking him.' "[7] Thus, a linkage of the generations, in which the older innovator of much that had come to be a part of the French musical personality, who discerned in Chopin many of the seeds which had been harvested by Debussy, spoke his guarded appreciation of another innovator to still a third.

4

IDENTIFICATION OF STRAVINSKY with the Debussy stream of continuity may seem, at this distance in time, perverse. Indeed, one may find it written: "From the historical point of view, Stravinsky's music represents a sharp reaction against the subtle and vaporous sonorities of Debussy's impressionism . . ."[8] But there was a long road for Stravinsky to travel from his early, experimental E-flat Symphony (1906–7) to the masterpiece by which he will be longest remembered (though *Le Sacre du printemps* began to germinate barely half a dozen years later). Debussy was with him at many points on this journey, from the potent use of wholetone progressions in *Faune et bergère*, to which Rimsky applied the scoffing term "Debussy-ist" when he heard it in 1907,[9] to the direct equivalent of the opening of Debussy's *Nuages* in the beginning of Stravinsky's *Le Rossignol* and even some details of *Le Sacre* itself. I use the term "equivalent" rather than "imitative" or "assimilative" in remembrance of Axiom IV as set forth on page 43: *The obvious*

[6] Ibid., p. 92.
[7] Igor Stravinsky: *An Autobiography* (New York: W. W. Norton and Company; 1962), p. 18.
[8] Boulanger: *Lectures on Modern Music*, p. 193.
[9] Stravinsky and Craft: *Memories and Commentaries*, p. 57.

source is not always the true source. The "Debussy" in *Le Rossignol*, as well as in *Nuages*, may have been Mussorgsky in both instances (the common ground is the *Sunless* cycle).

In some respects, the interchange between Debussy and Stravinsky might be likened to the Berlioz-Wagner relationship: Debussy was a master while Stravinsky was still a neophyte, and the younger man went on to innovations that far outdistanced his older contemporary's. But the details were of their own special distinctiveness. The French-born Debussy was exposed to a Russian environment with lasting effects while still a student at the Conservatoire. In his turn, Stravinsky became immersed in the artistic atmosphere of Paris at an equally critical point in his own career, as a participant in the great upheaval of the Russian ballet. Debussy without the Russian experience would, one is almost certain, have been something close to the kind of creator he became. Without exposure to Western trends, of which he not merely became a part but on which he also exerted a decisive influence, Stravinsky would hardly have been the same composer. In this case, music would have not merely been different, but poorer.

How insidiously the awareness of Debussy crept into his being may be gathered from Stravinsky's self-query, reproduced from a diary he kept at the time of his work on the first act of *Le Rossignol:* "Why should I be following Debussy closely, when the real originator of this operatic style was Moussorgsky?"[1] The answer—if any, beyond the immemorial inclination of young creators, however gifted, to be "influenced by what they love"[2]—would also take in Stravinsky's indebtedness to a whole alphabet of composers.

It is basic to a comprehension of the special phenomenon represented by Stravinsky that he be identified correctly as a product of Russia's fourth generation of musically gifted individuals. The first, of course, was personified by the pioneering Glinka and his disciple Dargomijsky. From their example sprang not only the "Mighty Five" —almost all of them amateurs of music, and self-educated—but also their opposite numbers, Tchaikovsky and the Rubinsteins. They were instrumental in establishing conservatories, formulating courses of study, developing means of nurturing the abundant talent of the Russias— Little, White, Big, etc.—to productive fulfillment. An immediate outcome was to turn the course of operatic and concert-giving institutions from the propagation of foreign works (Italian in opera, German in

---

[1] Stravinsky and Craft: *Memories and Commentaries*, p. 125.
[2] Stravinsky to Craft, in explanation of Scriabin's *lack* of influence on him: "I never could love a bar of his bombastic music." Ibid., p. 63.

the concert hall) toward the advancement of their own. A direct bene-
ficiary of these developments was Feodor Stravinsky, father of Igor.
He made his debut at the Maryinsky Theater in St. Petersburg at the
age of twenty-six in 1876 and sang a wide variety of non-Russian bass
roles in addition to taking prominent parts in many new Russian works
of his time.

In a way, young Stravinsky could be likened to Richard Strauss in
being the offspring of a professional musician of distinction, and thus
having been indoctrinated in high criteria of musical values from childhood on. Stravinsky Sr. did not look after his son's education with
the attention of Franz Strauss, but opportunities were available, from
piano lessons beginning at nine, to permit his inclinations to develop
unhindered if not warmly encouraged. The university and a career in
law were considered more suitable for a young Russian of his family
position than pursuit of music as a livelihood, but no barriers were
put in the way of his access to the busy musical life of St. Petersburg.
Through a sympathetic uncle, his avenue of approach was to the "intellectual" circles where Brahms, Bruckner, and Wagner were even
more in vogue than the nationalist composers. When his own impulses
began to clamor for expression, his parents permitted him a tutor in harmony.[3] He soon passed on to counterpoint, which interested him more.

At the age of twenty, he made the acquaintance of Rimsky-
Korsakov, through a son of the composer who was a fellow-student at
the University. Rimsky Sr. was far from lavish in praise of the first
work Stravinsky showed him. But he was sufficiently impressed to offer
advice and a promise of personal interest when he should think it in
order. The advice was to stay away from the Conservatory, finish his
studies at the University, and meanwhile work at fundamentals with an
advanced Rimsky student. The advice was accepted, the interest came
in due course, and Stravinsky's future was held in high esteem at the
time of Rimsky's death in 1908.

Thanks to the flourishing musical life of tsarist St. Petersburg,
there was little new at the turn of the century to which Stravinsky did
not have almost immediate access. Pianists, singers, and conductors of
high rank from abroad were steady visitors. Works of Franck, Fauré,
Chabrier, D'Indy, Dukas, Richard Strauss, and Debussy were available
to him for acceptance or rejection, as were, as a matter of course, those
of Liadov, Taneyev, Arensky, Glazunov, etc. Despite the disparagement
of Rimsky, who found Tchaikovsky's music "in abominable taste,"[4]

[3] Stravinsky: *An Autobiography*, p. 13.
[4] Stravinsky and Craft: *Memories and Commentaries*, p. 56.

the latter exerted an appeal for Stravinsky magical beyond all others.

In the works he wrote before the one that made him well-known (*L'Oiseau de feu*), there is ample external evidence of Stravinsky's internal ferment. Included are an early sonata for piano, characterized by the composer himself as "an inept imitation of late Beethoven,"[5] and the *jeux d'esprit* entitled *Feux d'artifice*. The latter is far from inept in its articulation, tonally, of the stimulating effect of a firework display (until the initial impulse runs down and the scherzo is carried forward by references to Dukas's *L'Apprenti sorcier*). Along the way, also, are *Faune et bergère*, to which reference has already been made, and the Symphony in E flat.

Of particular interest among the youthful works is the E-flat Symphony: not because it is a good symphony, but because of what it is besides not being a good symphony. Each of the four movements strives for a distinctive character, and two of them achieve it: the scherzo, which comes second, and the slow movement that follows. Considering Stravinsky's later disparagement of Richard Strauss, it is curious to hear references in the opening of the E-flat Symphony to the sound of *Ein Heldenleben* (a work whose effect Stravinsky later [1962][6] likened to that of an "emetic"). Wagner, in a *Meistersinger*-ish way, also makes an appearance, but it is Tchaikovsky who settles in as house guest.

Both the scherzo and the slow movement are substantially superior to the other two. In them Stravinsky is freed from commitment to the binding limitation of "form," and can pursue with relative freedom his first, enduring inclination as a composer of ballet music. The scherzo is chatty and gay in a woodwindy way, leading to a trio based on a folk song for which he also found a place in *Petrouchka* ("*La vechor moloda*"—"Down the Peter's Road"). Among the elements in the largo are an affectionate reminiscence of the finale of the "*Pathétique*," but the moody minor swath it cuts are largely Stravinsky's own. Before long it takes on the character not only of a *pas de deux*, but of a *grand pas de deux*, complete with drum roll (if not cymbal crash). One distinctive episode before the end rewards attention: an ingenius way of getting from E major to D minor (number 18, p. 101, P. Jurgenson score). In the finale, Stravinsky turns to another balletic mood: the grand company entrance. It goes its way in a friendly, extrovert manner, to a result that is well summarized by V. Yastrabtszev in his *Recollections of Rimsky-Korsakov*: "In the opinion of Rimsky-Korsakov, the

[5] Ibid., p. 28.
[6] Stravinsky and Craft: *Expositions and Developments*, p. 84.

talent of Igor Stravinsky had not yet taken clear shape. Rimsky thinks that the fourth movement of his symphony imitates Glazunov too much, and Rimsky himself."[7]

How long Stravinsky's talent might have taken to assume "clear shape" had Anton Liadov been a more industrious man can only be a speculation. It was Liadov's failure to fulfill a commission for Diaghilev which provided the opportunity for Stravinsky to become a composer for the Ballet Russe in his place. The *Fireworks* score is decidedly more individual, especially in the whirling figures with which it is set in motion, in its overlapping tonal concepts, in its definite if not yet defiant disregard for conventional consonance; and the first act of *Le Rossignol* displays a delightful gift for make-believe. But even the latter would have had a different outcome had not Stravinsky suddenly received the opportunity to work in a wholly different artistic environment than that to which he had been previously exposed.

5

IF THE E-FLAT SYMPHONY projects a disposition and *Fireworks* proclaims a vocation, *L'Oiseau de feu* not only announces a fulfillment but also defines a promise. To appreciate its impact when it was first performed in Paris in 1910, it would be desirable (if impossible) to "hear" the new work as it sounded then—a combination of elements new if not revolutionary, and unfamiliar if not altogether original. In Stravinsky's own words it is "more vigorous than most of the composed folk music of the period, but also not very original. These are all good conditions for a success."[8] If, fifty years later, it continues to be a success, that is not only because the vigor endures undiminished, but also because the elements in it which are "not very original" are, in the main, as unfamiliar to non-Russian audiences of today as they were to those of 1910.

In consideration of the composer's crucial position at a confluence of continuity, it is instructive to have him define for us the sources of *L'Oiseau de feu* as he saw them in 1962: "It seems to me now that the two strains of Rimsky and Tchaikovsky appear in *The Firebird* in about equal measure."[9] Close attention to the music's sound (especially in the complete, original form rather than in the amended, contracted

[7] Igor Stravinsky and Robert Craft: *Dialogues and a Diary* (New York: Doubleday and Company; 1963), p. 103.

[8] Stravinsky and Craft: *Expositions and Developments*, p. 149.

[9] Ibid., p. 146.

suites more commonly favored) will show these and other elements of interest. As Eric W. White has noted,[1] Stravinsky followed Rimsky's lead in *Le Coq d'or* by using diatonic themes for the human elements in the story and "chromatic arabesques of an oriental character" for the magical elements. The derivation of the elements that enter into the "chromatic" concept goes a little bit beyond Rimsky, however.

As with *Fireworks*, the opening seizes the attention for its vigor, boldness of thought, and evocation of the desired atmosphere. As it progresses, it becomes apparent that Liadov's failure to fulfill his commitment to Diaghilev did not wholly exclude his participation in the finished product. It makes its appearance in the music of the Firebird[2] itself, recalling Liadov's facility for suggesting, musically, the grotesquerie in such folk subjects as *Baba-Yaga* and *Kikimora* (both works were well known to Stravinsky).[3]

When the music moves into its lyric phase, other presences assert themselves. Of special interest, perhaps because it is least expected, is a

Wagner: *Parsifal*, Act II

---

[1] Eric Walter White: *Stravinsky: The Composer and His Works* (Berkeley and Los Angeles: University of California Press; 1966), p. 148.
[2] Page 18, Broude Brothers score.
[3] Stravinsky and Craft: *Memories and Commentaries*, p. 61.

string from the bow of *Parsifal* in the episode titled "*Supplications de l'oiseau de feu.*"[4] This affiliation with the Flower Maidens of Wagner's Act II permeates much of the succeeding scene, and includes use of the solo oboe and violin in a manner favored by Wagner (a similar moment in *Parsifal* can be identified at p. 159 of the Universal Edition piano score). What is atypical for Wagner becomes "characteristic" of Stravinsky's *Firebird* vocabulary through alteration of an interior line and other subtle changes.

Stravinsky: The Firebird

Less surprising, perhaps, but no less provocative, is the perpetuation of some initiatives of Mussorgsky, especially the kind to be found in

4 Page 44, Broude Brothers score.

such portions of his *Pictures at an Exhibition* as "Baba-Yaga," the "Ballad of the Chicks," and "The Great Gate of Kiev." Before we reach the final passage of *L'Oiseau de feu* in which, on a chorale borrowed from Russian religious sources, a build-up akin to Mussorgsky's "Great Gate of Kiev" is set in motion, there are other elements from the continuity in which Stravinsky had been reared. Among them are the passage for oboe in the *Ronde de princesse* which has convinced many a listener of Stravinsky's gifts as a melodist (it is, rather, a treatment of the folk tune that had served Rimsky for the slow movement of his Sinfonietta on Russian Themes thirty years before); several references to the "surprise" pianissimo after a fortissimo which Dukas had made his own in *L'Apprenti sorcier;* and repeated outcroppings of the affinity for Tchaikovsky to which the composer himself has made reference. Finally, in that climactic passage itself (which attained another kind of acceptance in the forties, when it became the model for a climax in a popular dance band arrangement), there is a heightening of tension achieved by the rise of a scale step, without bridge or modulation, for the repetition of a prior passage. This can also be heard in a mazurka (opus 19) written by Liadov as early as 1888.

But neither Liadov nor anyone else of whom there is knowledge predates Stravinsky's stinging use of the proclamative brass (horns, trumpets, trombones, and bass tuba) in parallel motion over the organ point on B which embellishes the final cadence;[5] or in the utilization of an ostinato for a kind of hypnotic, lulling effect (in the *"Berceuse"*); or in the projection of a slashing rhythmic onset for the "Dance of Kashchei" in which a fellow practitioner discerned Stravinsky's "true musical nature."[6] For craftsmanship alone, the whole of *The Firebird* remains a work on which a reputation could be based; the high points previously enumerated proclaim a man not merely with a spirit of his own, but also with the aural capacity to hear new sounds and imagine fresh combinations of old ones.

Unlike the subject matter of *Firebird*, which Stravinsky inherited along with an opportunity he was not disposed to reject, *Petrouchka* was a product of his own fancy. It emerged from a piece for piano and orchestra which took on a different form when Diaghilev saw balletic possibilities in what he heard of the incomplete score. Chronologically

[5] Stravinsky had moved in the direction of this harmonic scheme for the end of the third song in *Faune et bergère.*
[6] Alexandre Tansman: *Igor Stravinsky: The Man and His Music* (New York: G. P. Putnam's Sons; 1949), p. 162.

it straddles the first thoughts of *Le Sacre du printemps*, which had come to Stravinsky in 1910, and the completion of *Le Rossignol* (set aside when *Firebird* came his way).

Musically, however, it does more than merely take up where its predecessor had left off. *Petrouchka* draws almost exclusively on the best, the most individual elements of Stravinsky embodied in *The Firebird*, and leaves behind almost everything derived from his Russian predecessors. Like several earlier works of Stravinsky, it begins with a flash of thought that illuminates like lightning on a dark night the subject to be treated. Whereas *Fireworks* and *The Firebird* go on to reveal a Stravinsky somewhat taxed to re-create, without some dependence on others, the landscape thus illuminated, *Petrouchka* shows him in complete command of virtually every detail. It draws on outside sources for its lyric melody (Stravinsky rarely has invented a wholly convincing one of his own), as in two Lanner-like dance sequences, the Russian folk song ("Down the Peter's Road") first heard in the E-flat Symphony, another entitled "Don Juan of the Village," and even a French *chanson* ("*Elle avait une jambe en bois*"). The composer heard it from a hurdy-gurdy outside his house near Nice[7] while the score was in progress, and reproduced it for "atmosphere." Not until later was it discovered to be the composition of one Emile Spencer, whose heirs long continued to collect royalties from each performance of *Petrouchka*.[8]

If *Le Sacre du printemps* detonated a thunderous power that demolished a whole prior mode of musical thought, *Petrouchka* might be described as the fuse by which it was ignited. When it is separated— by an effort of the mind—from the all-too-familiar contexts with which repetition has endowed it, one can perceive in the earlier score not only the source of the later work's convulsive rhythms (as in the chords of pp. 79–80 which follow the appearance of the Blackamoor, through the intensification of the pulse in the "Dance of the Coach-men" at p. 136, to the fusillade of timpani of the Masqueraders on p. 157),[9] but also a new freedom of emphasis in the displacement of metric regularity through such sequences as 3/8, 5/8, 2/8, etc. Not only for their novelty but also for their physical impact, these are the immediately apparent elements of likeness, but they are far from being the only important ones.

[7] White: *Stravinsky*, p. 162.
[8] Stravinsky and Craft: *Memories and Commentaries*, p. 89.
[9] Édition Russe de Musique edition (1911) of *Petrouchka*.

Of equal importance is the almost total rejection of orchestral glitter (or "iridescence" as Arthur Berger aptly calls it)[1] which makes an aural peacock of *The Firebird*. In place of this inheritance from Wagner through Rimsky-Korsakov is a new conception of each instrument as an individual voice of its own. Rather than conceiving his orchestral palette in terms of "Debussyist" combinations, Stravinsky evolved a new composite of his own by a return to pure, primary colors to outline his themes. Save for an occasional, perhaps involuntary reversion to a practice of Rimsky (as in a pattern near the climax of "Masqueraders" which has its source in the *Russian Easter Overture*), such clarity of line is a consistent part of Stravinsky's procedure throughout *Petrouchka*. "Hearing" as acutely as he does, it is no insuperable challenge (though no simple matter, either) for him to imitate the sound of a hurdy-gurdy, a music box, or an accordion by ingenious combinations of conventional instruments. All are famously "present" in the aural imagery of *Petrouchka*, though not in its instrumental personnel.

Complementing this instrumental virtuosity applied to nonvirtuoso ends, and of incalculable importance to the total result, is a new, clarifying system of harmonic values and, even, of tonality. Whereas *The Firebird* was still moist with the wash of chromaticism devised by Wagner for purposes of *Tristan* (and appropriated by almost everyone thereafter), *Petrouchka* took a historic turn away from chromaticism toward a more open connection of diatonic tones and steps. It begins in F and ends in C (or, at least, with measures lacking an identifying key signature), but what happens between, harmonically, is of surpassing historic significance.

The path to which Stravinsky found his way in *Petrouchka* was a long disused one that led back to the kind of polytonality imagined so many years before by Chopin in his mingling of G minor and E flat in the introduction to his G-minor Ballade, and only partially pursued by Debussy (see p. 286). It also took in the 1901 innovation by Ravel in *Jeux d'eau*, whether derived from that source or not. Whereas Ravel had exploited the possibilities presented by a "counterposition of two rows of mutually exclusive scales of the white and black keys," Stravinsky invoked a mingling of chordal values personified by C-E-G in the bass, F sharp-A sharp-C sharp in the treble. In effect he "verticalized" a procedure hitherto restricted to horizontal usage or,

[1] *Stravinsky in the Theater*, ed. Minna Lederman (New York: Pellegrini and Cudahy; 1949), p. 53.

in Alexandre Tansman's neat verbal distinction, effected a "superposition" rather than a "counterposition of elements."[2]

Tansman also identifies a procedure midway between Chopin's and Ravel's on the way to Stravinsky's in *Petrouchka*. It may be found in a work now so intellectually *démodé* as Rimsky's *Scheherazade*, in the first movement of which, Tansman says, the composer "modulates directly from C major to F sharp major by sustaining the dominant, reduced to its tones of the third and the seventh . . ." In this combination of B and F, the latter is considered alternately as "the seventh of the dominant of C, or as its enharmonic, E sharp, the third of the dominant of F sharp major . . ."[3] What is being described is, clearly, another step along the road of ever more remote allusion that the ear had learned to tolerate from the enharmonic innovations of Chopin and Wagner, and to which Berlioz had reacted so violently.

Stravinsky's exploitation of such "superposition" had further technical connotations (related to the tritone, or augmented fourth), which need not be dwelt on here, but which also had an aesthetic implication of supreme importance. That was the affirmation of a new base in tonality, though not necessarily the base of a *single* tonality. Almost at the same time that Schoenberg was striving to evolve a mode of procedure that would *negate* what was confining (to him) in chromaticism, Stravinsky had, in effect, picked his way through that mined field and come out on the other side of it. In the judgment of Stravinsky's ear, more than one center of tonal attraction could be tolerated, endured, perhaps even enjoyed, assuming that a sense of balance and proportion prevailed. In keeping with the directions of thought being independently pursued by Mahler in his planes of sonority and by Debussy in his tonal juxtapositions, it played on the possibility that the ear, like the eye, could adjust itself to more than one center of activity without cowering into confusion or surrendering concentration—an aptitude adroitly exploited by Pablo Picasso.

In Stravinsky's conception, such powers of divided concentration were invoked with greater frequency and over a wider span of perception than had been demanded by any predecessor. Always, however, he preserved the awareness of an inclusive tonal equilibrium, the sense of a theoretical aural horizon—as a plane's pilot preserves an artificial visual horizon to which reference may be made in banks and turns—in which the principle of departure and return prevailed. Thus the ear was being

[2] Tansman: *Igor Stravinsky*, p. 81.
[3] Ibid., p. 165.

educated to a new perception of old values rather than being commanded forthwith to embrace a set of relationships unlike anything it had known before. In other words, it was being enticed rather than coerced, reckoned *with* rather than against.

It could be contended that, in his pragmatic approach to a new co-ordination of elements, Stravinsky had articulated the gist of a new Axiom:

Progress to a point of rest may be delayed, or suspended,
or interrupted, but the eventual destination should never be disavowed.

The propagation of any one of the arresting innovations of *Petrouchka* (rhythmic, instrumental, harmonic) in its successor would have made it a milestone on Stravinsky's road. The amalgamation of all of them into a dramatic and philosophic conception as strikingly original as *Le Sacre du printemps* made it a landmark on the road of music as well. Like such esteemed predecessors as Beethoven's Ninth Symphony, Berlioz's *Symphonie fantastique*, Wagner's *Tristan*, and Debussy's *Pelléas*, *Le Sacre* embodies so much intellectual energy that it continues to function as a pumping station for the main current of music long after its components have been analyzed, evaluated, and, supposedly, absorbed.

It is a mistake, I would say, to assess the response of the first audience to be exposed to it (May 1913) as indicative of poor perception, prejudice, or lack of intellectual fibre. That it aroused, in fulfillment of a long-respected scientific premise, an equal and opposite reaction was, rather, a measure of the force in the work itself. Had it embodied less that was elemental, had it been drawn from a shallower subsurface source of musical currents, it would have long since gone the way of many other "novelties." But its roots are so deep, its heritage is so sturdy, its realization so consummately artistic that it remains an Event each time it is encountered, as much a reminder of the cataclysmic kind of communication inherent in tone as the works with which it has been affiliated above.

From the first hoarse whisper of the bassoon (articulating what Eric W. White has defined as a Lithuanian folk song), *Le Sacre* mingles tones and timbres in a way almost to suggest that there had been no music before. Given the kind of familiarity made possible these days by mechanical reproduction, it is a possibility that some might agree with Arthur Berger that *Petrouchka* is "in many ways as trenchant and prophetic a work" as *Le Sacre*. But, as the lasting impression of the Grand Canyon owes something to its sheer magnitude, so *Le Sacre* projects through the symphony orchestra an order of aural energy, a pulsation of ordered sound, a sensation of elemental happenings more formidable and fundamental then the affecting little drama of Petrouchka, the Ballerina, and the Moor.

Musically, *Le Sacre* also marks an extension, an expansion, even an aggrandizement of the things in *Petrouchka* which are, in Berger's appropriate phrase, trenchant and prophetic. The orchestral tints are drier, dustier, even less "moist" in the Wagner-dewy sense. The harmonic scene, while closely related to D minor, is both varied and austere, with chordal combinations that carry the hammer blows of rhythmic force with the unflinching firmness of tempered steel (they are, for those concerned with their legitimacy, inversions of chords of the thirteenth, says E. W. White). As time lengthens and repetitions accumulate, it is no longer even a lingering sense of revolution that makes an encounter with *Le Sacre* stimulating and rewarding. Rather the revelation of musical satisfaction it contains makes it a ceremonial not only for the Spring of its life, but truly for all seasons.

The arrangement of its innovations as rhythmic, instrumental, harmonic may—according to individual preference—be read in either an ascending or a descending order of importance. By my reckoning, it is certainly the rhythmic which continues to command the greatest esteem among musicians and to exercise the most profoundly moving effect on the lay listener. Building on the insights of Olivier Messiaen, Pierre Boulez has demonstrated that its rhythmic cells "evolve according to highly rigorous patterns."[4] Whether planned in all deliberation or brought into being, as Stravinsky himself has said, by a composer who "heard" and "wrote what [he] heard,"[5] the special distinction of *Le Sacre* is that nothing goes on longer than it can be endured. Tension and its relaxation—the immemorial components of any valid musical experience—are parts of a complementary impulse, in which one element is as wholly conceived and fulfillingly achieved as the other.

As for the virtual obliteration of the bar line (with its system of up beats and down beats) and the substitution of asymmetrical periods for the previously prevalent march of four-measure phrases, Nadia Boulanger has an interesting suggestion of a source:

"Stravinsky's music suggests the old Greek system of rhythm which (instead of taking, as we do, a maximum unity, like the whole note, and cutting it up into various small divisions, e.g., halves, quarters, eighths, etc.) took a minimum unity and multiplied it by any even or odd

---

[4] André Hodeir: *Since Debussy* (New York: Grove Press; 1961), p. 27.
[5] Stravinsky and Craft: *Expositions and Developments*, p. 169.

number: 3, 4, 5, 6, 7, etc. This is precisely what Stravinsky does, for instance, in the last tableau [of *Le Sacre*]. Nor is the example an isolated one . . . . It is illuminating to compare the metre of these themes with the metre of the first few lines of a speech in Euripides' *Hippolytus.* ♩♩ ♩♩ etc."[6]

As these words were written before Stravinsky made his first venture into the treatment of such Hellenic subject matter as *Oedipus Rex, Perséphone,* and *Orpheus,* Mme Boulanger's perception might be considered close to clairvoyant.

However, other, more accessible predecessors than Euripides affiliate *Le Sacre* with worthy antecedents. One becomes increasingly aware, with time and repetition, that in addition to those common sources which appear first in *Petrouchka,* there is more that is fundamentally Russian in *Le Sacre* than its use of folk matter. Its closest kin in spirit is Mussorgsky's *Night on the Bald Mountain,* not only because it, too, mirrors a primitive ritual (the original title was *St. John's Night on the Bare Mountain*), but more particularly because it communicates an amount of violence, restated musically, not to be encountered in any other predecessor known to me. More than once, Stravinsky may be heard echoing, in a formulation of his own, the orchestral colorations that Rimsky-Korsakov had evolved in his orchestration of Mussorgsky's flourishes more than twenty years before. In addition, Mussorgsky's reflective coda evokes the same mystic sense of eternal things as the opening of *Le Sacre,* though without such a smell of the primitive as Stravinsky achieved through the use of the high register of the bassoon.

In the composer's view, however, "*Le Sacre* owes more to Debussy than anyone else, the best music (the Prelude) as well as the weakest (the music of the second part between the first entrance of the two solo trumpets and the Glorification de L'Élue)."[7] In this latter section (pp. 75–86 of the orchestral score) there is, indeed, a reversion to the language of *Nuages* as Stravinskyized for *Le Rossignol.* Had he pursued the subject more completely, Stravinsky might also have cited a reference to *Nuages,* farther on (p. 103) this time in terms of the *cor anglais* playing an almost identical figuration (see pp. 313–14, 315).

Doubtless it was such latent back-references to earlier works, the hidden admixture of the new with the old, that aided *Le Sacre* in its conquest of a world-wide public. It is another affirmation, in a perhaps unexpected context, of Honegger's dictum (p. 285) that "Absolute

6 Boulanger: *Lectures on Modern Music,* p. 184.
7 Stravinsky and Craft: *Expositions and Developments,* p. 163 *n.*

(continued)

Debussy: Nuages (Nocturnes, No. 1)

originality does not exist." It also affirms Stravinsky's unmistakable place in the continuity from which he emerged.

6

PERCEPTION OF *Le Sacre*'s components and acceptance of them as a totality were both still well in the future when its prodigious force and unprecedented propulsion were encountered by an audience for the first time on May 29, 1913. In all the years since, that audience's behavior—it had, after all, come to see a ballet *première* rather than to

Stravinsky: Le Sacre du printemps

participate in a musical revolution—has been cited as an arch-instance of noncomprehension. Why this was less than completely true has already been assessed (p. 310). At the least, it should be mentioned that the reaction of some rather more sophisticated individuals differed in degree rather than in kind when they were exposed to *Le Sacre* privately.

The very first whose reaction is on record appears to have been the late Pierre Monteux, a privileged participant in the first performance of *Petrouchka* who was nominated by Diaghilev to conduct its successor. Monteux writes: "One day in 1912 . . . Diaghilev summoned me to a tiny rehearsal room in a theater in Monte Carlo where the Ballet was at the time appearing. We were to hear Stravinsky run through the score of his new work *Le Sacre du printemps*. With only Diaghilev and myself as audience, Stravinsky sat down to play a piano reduction of the entire score. Before he got very far I was convinced he was raving mad. Heard this way, without the color of the orchestra which is one of its great distinctions, the crudity of the rhythm was emphasized, its stark primitiveness underlined. The very walls resounded as Stravinsky pounded away, occasionally stamping his feet and jumping up and down to accentuate the force of the music. My only comment at the end was that such music would surely cause a scandal . . ."[8]

This was more than the comment of which Debussy was capable when he had a similar experience at about the same time. It was at the home of the critic Louis Laloy, where Stravinsky had brought a four-hand arrangement of *Le Sacre*. "Debussy agreed to play the bass . . . his [Stravinsky's] sight was not improved by his glasses, and pointing his nose to the keyboard and sometimes humming a part that had been omitted from the arrangement, he led into a welter of sound the supple, agile hands of his friend. Debussy followed without a hitch and seemed to make light of the difficulties. When they had finished there was no question of embracing, nor even of compliments. We were dumb-founded, overwhelmed by this hurricane which had come from the depths of the ages and which had taken life by the roots."[9]

Some months later, in a letter prompted by the general feeling of friendship which had grown up between them, Debussy wrote to Stravinsky: "Our reading at the piano of *Le Sacre du printemps*, at Laloy's home, is always present in my mind. It haunts me like a beautiful nightmare, and I try, in vain, to reinvoke the terrific impression. That is why I wait for the stage performance like a greedy child impatient for promised sweets."[1] When that occasion had passed into history and

---

[8] *Stravinsky in the Theater*, ed. Lederman, p. 128.

[9] Lockspeiser: *Debussy: His Life and Mind*, II, 181.

[1] Igor Stravinsky and Robert Craft: *Conversations with Igor Stravinsky* (Garden City: Doubleday and Co.; 1959), p. 52. The date for this letter is given as November 1913, an obvious error, inasmuch as Debussy refers to a *première* that occurred in May 1913. In Stravinsky and Craft: *Expositions and Developments* (p. 162 n.) it is corrected to November 1912. This does not agree, however, with Laloy's attribution of the meeting at his home (as quoted in Lockspeiser) to "a bright afternoon in the spring of 1913." The recollection is contained in Laloy's *La Musique retrouvée*, published in 1928.

Stravinsky had a score of *Le Sacre* to send to Debussy, the latter acknowledged the gift not merely with praise—"a very beautiful thing that with the passage of time will be more beautiful still"—but also with a penetrating observation. It was a statement that could be made only by one who had traveled the same road himself: "For me, who descends the other slope of the hill but keeps, however, an intense passion for music, for me it is a special satisfaction to tell you how much you have *enlarged the boundaries of the permissible* [italics added] in the empire of sound." Here, in a phrase, is a summation of a *composer's* view of what continuity is and how its perimeters are extended.

Also admitted to the privileged circle of pre-performance auditors was Maurice Ravel. He visited Clarens, Switzerland (where Stravinsky was living in the spring of 1913), and there "first saw the score of Stravinsky's newly composed *Sacre du printemps*."[2] He was "enormously impressed" and "realized at once the implications of this (as it seemed to him at the time) revolutionary work and the impact it was bound to have on the course of musical history . . ." On March 3 Ravel wrote to his friend Lucien Garban "urging him not to miss the first performance of *Le Sacre*," and adding: "I think this will be as important an event as the *première* of *Pelléas*."

For his part, Stravinsky has paid Ravel the compliment of saying in his *Conversations* "he was the only musician who immediately understood *Le Sacre du Printemps*."[3] The remark was left unamplified in this source, perhaps because Stravinsky had stated the matter fully in the earlier *Poetics of Music*: "When *The Rite* appeared, many opinions were advanced concerning it. In the tumult of contradictory opinions my friend Maurice Ravel intervened practically alone to set matters right. He was able to see, and he said, that the novelty of *The Rite* consisted not in the writing, not in the orchestration, not in the technical apparatus of the work, but in the musical entity."[4]

Detached from its balletic halter, *Le Sacre* had an unbridled success when it was first performed in a Parisian concert hall (also under the direction of Pierre Monteux) on April 5, 1914. The war, of course, had an effect on its immediate dissemination elsewhere, but musicians generally and composers in particular began to react almost immediately. The first, in all probability, was Serge Prokofiev, who heard it at

[2] Myers: *Ravel*, p. 47.
[3] Stravinsky and Craft: *Conversations with Igor Stravinsky*, p. 67.
[4] Igor Stravinsky: *Poetics of Music* (New York: Alfred A. Knopf, Inc., and Random House, Inc., Vintage Books edn.; 1956), p. 11. Previously, the Charles Eliot Norton lectures for 1939–40 were published in French by the Harvard University Press in 1942 and in English in 1947.

a Koussevitzky concert in Moscow in 1914.[5] Prokofiev had just been claimed by Diaghilev[6] in the latter's never-ceasing quest for new, important talent, and had chosen the story of Ala and Lolli for a project in which the impresario of the Ballet Russe had expressed an interest. It was begun in 1914 and submitted to Diaghilev the following February at a meeting in Milan. When it failed to materialize as a ballet, Prokofiev converted much of its musical content into the *Scythian Suite* for orchestra. A joyously vigorous work that proclaims the immense resources of the twenty-three-year-old Prokofiev, it is, nevertheless, inconceivable without the pathbreaking predecessor by Stravinsky. It is the latter's recollection of Prokofiev's visit (when they renewed an acquaintance that had begun in St. Petersburg) that *"Le Sacre du printemps* was his only subject of conversation. He adored *Le Sacre* and was for many years quite unable to recover from the effect of it."[7]

Inferentially, though I have no knowledge of a direct connection, the rhythmic insistence and orchestral emphasis of Gustav Holst's *The Planets* (especially the section titled "Mars, the Bringer of War") strike me as Stravinsky-related. Holst's score was composed between 1914 and 1916 and first performed in 1918. In turn came the effect of *Le Sacre* on the thinking of Milhaud and Varèse among the French; Bartók (who had his Stravinsky period after his Strauss and Debussy phases); Mossolov, whose *Iron Foundry* is the pulverization of the bare bones of Stravinsky's skeleton; Antheil (*Le Sacre* was automated in his *Ballet mécanique*); Copland; Revueltas (*Sensemaya* is a translation into Spanish from the Russian); Chávez; and to a degree Villa-Lobos. These are instances related to certain specific components of *Le Sacre,* rather than to the effect of the "musical entity" identified by Ravel. Rhythmic energy, harmonic sparseness, instrumental definition were the first factors that could be emulated, adapted, or "borrowed" in initial reaction to its impact. It look longer for the "Ravel effect" to be absorbed, but few composers of the following generation were immune to it.

The linkage of Puccini with Massenet (by Martin Cooper) as a composer who was "anxious and able to adopt any device which could give his music more modern color" (p. 156), is affirmed by the Italian's reaction to the innovations of Stravinsky. The two men became

[5] White: *Stravinsky*, p. 178. The month of the first Koussevitzky performance in Moscow is given as February, which would pre-date Monteux's in Paris.

[6] Israel V. Nestyev: *Prokofiev* (Palo Alto: Stanford University Press; 1960), p. 92.

[7] Stravinsky and Craft: *Memories and Commentaries*, p. 64.

acquainted in the aftermath of the introduction of *Petrouchka* in 1911. Stravinsky recalls[8] that when he was ill with typhus after the *première* of *Le Sacre,* Puccini took the trouble to visit him, though Diaghilev stayed away out of fear of being infected. Puccini admired Stravinsky's talent,[9] but thought his music "horrible" (an opinion conveyed by Diaghilev). Nevertheless, Stravinsky thought that Puccini might have "half-remembered the tuba solo in *Petrouchka*" in writing *Gianni Schicchi* (seven measures before number 78).

A suggestive instance of a Stravinsky thought more than half remembered by Puccini is to be found in the latter's last, most ambitious opera. I owe to the perception of Roman Vlad the analogy between the *"Augures printaniers"* motive of *Le Sacre* and the orchestral background to Liù's *"Tu che di gel sei cinta"* at her dying moments in Act III of *Turandot* (p. 387 of the Ricordi orchestral score [see pp. 320, 321]). Says Vlad: "Puccini took this motif bodily and incorporated it into the aria . . . needless to say first sweetening it and lopping away all trace of its harmonic harshness."[1] This may have been the first but was certainly not the last instance of such adulteration of a Stravinskyan innovation for easier consumption. Popular musicians, radio "background writers," movie underscorers, and, more recently, television sound-effect contrivers have taken as they pleased, always with greater profit to the listener than if they had relied on their own ingenuity.

The one important change of attitude from enthusiasm to indifference of which I have knowledge is attributed by Stravinsky to Debussy. To be sure, nothing could expunge Debussy's earlier words of praise, but it offended Stravinsky that they were replaced by a "later, negative attitude"[2] which embodied "some ambivalence" toward *Le Sacre.* And there is perhaps a too-prophetic vista of a long-term future in Debussy's comment of 1917 (the year before he died) that "Stravinsky himself inclines dangerously toward the side of Schoenberg."[3]

At the least, this disaffection might have been a by-product of Debussy's steadily deteriorating health, which, from 1915 until his death in 1918, required him to be supported by constant doses of morphine. At the most, it could have been a realization that his own remark about a great predecessor might very soon be applicable to himself. Asked in

[8] Stravinsky and Craft: *Expositions and Developments,* p. 157.
[9] Ibid., p. 157.
[1] Roman Vlad: *Stravinsky* (London: Oxford University Press; 1960), p. 31.
[2] Stravinsky and Craft: *Memories and Commentaries,* p. 135.
[3] *Stravinsky, a New Appraisal of His Work,* ed. Paul Henry Lang (New York: W. W. Norton and Co.; 1963), p. 12. The source is a letter from Debussy to his old friend Robert Godet.

Stravinsky: Le Sacre du printemps

Puccini: Turandot, Act III

1908 by the Paris publication *L'Éclair* to participate in a symposium commemorating the twenty-fifth anniversary of Wagner's death, Debussy at first refused and then consented to state his evaluation of that composer's influence in a sentence or two. Debussy wrote: "I consider Wagner's curve to have been accomplished. Wagner was and will remain a great artist."[4]

Debussy's characterization of Wagner's "curve" is an engrossing one. At his death in 1883, with *Parsifal* still to be absorbed into the world's musical experience, the tide of Wagnerism was still rising even in France. Twenty-five years later, it had begun to recede, as 1907–8 marked the flooding of Debussyism across the barriers separating France from the rest of musical Europe. Within a decade, in large part because of the pressures exerted by Stravinsky, Debussy's "curve" may also have been accomplished. It was not an awareness that would promote amiability toward one who had come rather too quickly onto the scene—and there is little doubt that Debussy had such an awareness.

[4] Seroff: *Debussy: Musician of France,* p. 269.

IX

Decision and Diffusion

I

WHEN A SUFFICIENTLY FINE ADJUSTMENT has been made of all the facts, dates, and occurrences brought together in this survey, it becomes unmistakably clear that the focal time of decision for the continuity traced herein is bracketed by the dates October 16, 1912, and May 29, 1913. With the hindsight of more than five decades, it can now be seen that the forces and counterforces that had been accumulating for a century and a half reached points of polarity in two conspicuous musical events of that artistically eventful era. They were, in order of occurrence, the first performance of Schoenberg's *Pierrot lunaire* in Berlin and the *première* of Stravinsky's *Le Sacre du printemps* in Paris. Had Diaghilev been more forehanded about producing the ballet (Stravinsky finished his score early in 1913 after it had been rescheduled from 1912 to 1913) the *premières* might have come in the same week rather than being separated by months.

Not merely the period but also the year (1912) was pivotal in other happenings related to the arts and intellectual activity in general. Writing of C. J. Jung's *Memories, Dreams, Reflections,* Cyril Connolly has observed: "It was not until 1912 that feelings of mutual ambivalence overwhelmed master [Freud] and disciple [Jung]. These [they had met in 1907] are also key years in the modern movement in literature and art, and the time will soon come when Freud's and Jung's findings are connected with Picasso, whose 'Demoiselles of Avignon' dates from their meeting, or Joyce, whose creative years in Zurich coincide with Jung's in the same city. All are stupendous products of the gigantic nineteenth-century crack-up. Nietzsche, in fact, is an obsessive father-figure to both Freud and Jung, with Schopenhauer running him second."[1]

Whether there is such a "connection" will depend on the findings of someone with the broadest kind of investigatory powers. The aftermath of the two musical happenings and their virtual coincidence have sufficiently broad implications on their own. At the time, the controversy, even sensation, they engendered was expressed in terms of equally radical departure from accepted norms. The temptation was to bracket Schoenberg and Stravinsky as like-minded revolutionists. In each, the reasoning went, a new impulse was manifest in an equal disregard for musical organization as it had been uncovered, expanded, amended, and expanded again over the course of this long chapter in musical history.

But from the present vantage point it can be seen that, for all its other innovations—displacement of metrical values, clarification of instrumental relationships, reconstruction of harmonic structure—*Le Sacre*, even at its most violent, is an affirmation of the tensile strength of tonality, its ability to rebound no matter how severely strained. It projects a line of procedure from which the composer deviated in many works of subsequent "periods" (including the "neoclassic," which is continuity reconstituted), without really turning his back on the compass course by which he had plotted his aesthetic. That was a tonal orientation as constant as the North Star (which, too, is sometimes obscured by clouds).

Equally apparent is the drift in *Pierrot lunaire* away from a fixed tonal point toward a Sargasso Sea of rudderless, anchorless craft without destiny or destination. Those who followed Schoenberg into it may be said to be, like the twelve tones of the method as he evolved it, related only to one another.

The perception being clear fifty years later, why was it not equally apparent then, or for two or three decades thereafter? To some adept at grasping fundamental distinctions, especially those who likened Stravinsky to T. S. Eliot as an artist trying to "refit old ships," whereas Schoenberg, in the manner of James Joyce, "sought new forms of travel,"[2] the difference was not long in emerging. But to most others, it was at least a possibility that the outcome of the game could still be affected by the cards in the deck which remained to be played. Or, in a figure more closely related to the history of the subject itself, that

---

[1] In the *Sunday Times* of London, July 3, 1963.
[2] Igor Stravinsky and Robert Craft: *Dialogues* (New York: Doubleday and Company; 1963), p. 30.

the forces set in motion decades before had to complete their projected curves, exhaust their potential powers of attraction before a decision could be reached, a judgment assessed.

In addition to the relatively youthful protagonists themselves—neither yet forty in 1912—the world was inhabited by a whole lexicon of composers from D'Albert to Zandonai, active and productive. Included were those of such major accomplishment as Debussy, Strauss, Puccini, Fauré, Scriabin, Ravel, Janáček, and Sibelius; plus such others of lesser but substantial talent as Charpentier, Rachmaninoff, Elgar, Vaughan Williams, Bloch, Delius, Busoni, and Dukas. The Bartók career was barely begun; those of Prokofiev, Hindemith, Shostakovich, Poulenc, Milhaud, Honegger, Kodály, and Copland were in various stages of formation. Others, such as Britten, Ginastera, and Henze were yet to be born (not to mention Boulez, Stockhausen, and Schuller). Charles Ives was settling in to make a fortune as an insurance underwriter and to labor at making an intelligible transcript of ideas deemed "bizarre" by the few to whom they were known.

As of 1912—the year of Ravel's *Daphnis et Chloé*, Strauss's *Le Bourgeois Gentilhomme*, Sibelius's Fourth Symphony, Montemezzi's *L'Amore dei tre re*, Roussel's *Le Festin de l'araignée*, the Second Piano Sonata of Prokofiev and Eighth of Scriabin—there was still a substantial period to come in which the norm of production would continue to be represented by the numerical majority of composers. It was conceivable that a new way, unrelated to either Stravinsky's or Schoenberg's, might be found to tunnel through the mountain, in the phrase of Mahler. He had, after all, died only the year before, in his early fifties.

As time passed and the men of the time passed with it, lines of communication began to shred, and the old soil showed signs of erosion or exhaustion, leaving contacts more tenuous and roots closer to the surface. As new composers grew to adolescence and then to maturity, the schism defined in the events of 1912–13 grew wider as the "rebels" were revered by separate sects as new gods and lawgivers. In an earlier, short-range view—say, as of 1937, which would split the half century more or less evenly—the emergence first of Alban Berg and then of Anton Webern as partners in harness with Schoenberg lent believability to the latter's ecstatic pronouncement of 1922. That is to say, to his messianic prediction that TMOCWTTROWOA would "guarantee the supremacy of German music for the next hundred years" (p. 270). The dedication of *Lulu*, which Berg sent to Schoenberg as a sixtieth-birthday present (September 13, 1934, in advance of the work's completion), makes a clear allusion to that concept in the words: "The whole world, and the German world too, shall recognize in the dedication of this German opera that it is indigenous in the sphere of the most German music, which will bear *your* name for time everlasting."[3]

But in the longer view, which becomes longer with each year, it becomes a more than casual possibility that, rather than being the first of a New Order, Berg and Webern may have been the last of the Old. It would be absurd to suggest that each achieved his life's work in spite of an affinity to Schoenberg and a commitment to embrace his theories deeper than reason could question or affirm. But there is a reasonable possibility that each could have achieved substantially the same ends, if perhaps with different means, without dependence on the formulations that Schoenberg arrived at in the early twenties. Contrary to a general conception of chronology, *Wozzeck* was by then complete,[4] and Webern had created nearly half of his thirty-one opus numbers, including the orchestral pieces of opus 6.

2

ALMOST EVERY COMPOSER'S CAREER starts with an "Opus 1," whether so labeled or not. Alban Berg was no exception, though his work bearing that opus number is more than ordinarily misleading. To understand the composer Berg became after his opus 1, it is imperative to go back to the composer he was before it, in the earlier, less familiar phases of his total production.

These earlier, less familiar phases are by no means incidental or fragmentary, unless a total of more than seventy *Lieder* can be called incidental to any composer's mental functioning or a fragmentary part of his total production. In Berg's case, these three score and seventeen settings of texts by poets from Walther von der Vogelweide to Rainer Maria Rilke have been retired to a limbo of nonperformance (less than ten are in print) because, for the most part, they pre-date the beginning of his studies with Schoenberg, which is to say, his official birth as a composer.

Included in the published fraction-of-the-whole is the collection titled Seven Early Songs. These date from 1905–8, and thus are chrono-

---

[3] Willi Reich: *Alban Berg* (New York: Harcourt, Brace and World, Inc.; 1965), p. 177. The italics are in the original.

[4] H. F. Redlich: *Berg* (New York: Abelard-Schuman, Ltd.; 1957), p. 109. "By April 1921, the orchestration of *Wozzeck* was completed." Schoenberg's celebrated walk with Rufer dates from 1922.

logically within the span (1903–10) of his apprenticeship to Schoenberg. (They were not published—without opus number—until 1928, when his fame was already substantial.) What they have to offer defines Berg not merely as a lineal descendant of Hugo Wolf, but also as in the same line of descent from Wagner. Berg's range of attachments includes not only *Tristan* and some of the harmonic sophistications of Richard Strauss, but also the use of the wholetone scale as pioneered by Debussy.

Even more, they affirm him as a German composer at one with such others as Schubert and Schumann, Brahms, Strauss, and Mahler in possessing the motive power of original melody, which gives music soaring flight. There is, in these Seven Early Songs, an easy flow of curves and dips, peaks and valleys, which exists not merely in response to the texts of Carl Hauptmann, Nikolaus Lenau, Theodor Storm, Johannes Schlaf, Otto Erich Hartleben, Paul Hohenberg, and Rainer Maria Rilke, but also as a thing in itself. That is to say that, rather than being confined to the vocal line alone, it moves the basses, weaves the intertwining inner voices, and arranges the "planes of sonority" (to which Mahler was partial) as though problems of mechanics and poverty of means were nonexistent.

In these songs, one can sense Berg responding to the models of which he was enamored, almost as Stravinsky was at the same time (p. 300). Thus in *"Traumgekrönt"* there are allusions to *Tristan* (in measure 5 Berg not only reproduces the contour of a phrase in the Shepherd's answer to Kurvenal in Act III, but also uses the same pitches —C, G, A flat, B flat—to which the words *"Wacht er noch nicht?"* are sung).

Debussy is recalled in *"Nacht"* (wholetone progressions, chains of thirds, empty octaves); Hugo Wolf in *"Schilflied,"* and Richard Strauss in *"Die Nachtigall"* (a narrative kind of melodic declamation, a rising inflection beyond the expected cadence point, a three-wave interweaving of bass, alto, and treble lines in the piano postlude). But at no point is there a sense of helpless imitation. The objective is almost always attained by an arching projection of line and sentiment distinctly Berg's own. The most characteristic element of it is a lyric ecstasy that bears out a predisposition recalled later by Berg: "Before I started to compose I wanted to become a poet."[5]

Whatever the outward form Berg's artistic urge took—and one can be grateful that it was in tones rather than words—this inward poetic impulse again and again asserts itself against all obstacles and despite any alteration of means. Without the evidence of these early songs,

[5] Redlich: *Berg*, p. 225.

Berg: Traumgekrönt

the contours and stylistic references of the Piano Sonata (his official opus 1) might strike one as willful and arbitrary. Published in 1910, it is a public testimonial to the private supervision of Schoenberg. In the context of what had preceded, it conveys Berg's effort to achieve a discipline in which his attachment to others would be minimized or eliminated. The result is neither Berg nor Schoenberg, but an amalgam of elements as varied as Scriabin and Massenet (a bass line in measures 9, 8, and 7 before the end).

In the String Quartet, opus 3, other pulls and counterpulls assert themselves. Redlich notes a parallel of its beginning and Strauss's *Tod und Verklärung*[6] while remarking a more inclusive likeness of its larger design to Schoenberg's quartets opus 7 and opus 10, then but recently finished. What had been noted in them (p. 260) as an infusion of Brahms had now become so diffused that, in Berg's reaction to Schoenberg's reaction, it measures scarcely a trace. Also present is a

Berg: String Quartet (op. 3)

[6] Ibid., p. 51.

Strauss: Tod und Verklärung *(op. 24)*

repeated reference to the principal motive of Mahler's Second Symphony which must be considered volitional:

Mahler   Berg (measures 5–6, movement
                          2, measures 181–2, movement 3)

There are also references to Wagner which may be part of an unexplained skein of allusion, or else are nonvolitional:

Götterdämmerung	Berg (measures 151–2, movement 1)
Tristan ("*Barg im Busen*," etc., p. 166, Schirmer piano score)	Berg (measures 119–29, movement 3)

Clearly, where so much can be affiliated with a line of continuity, a tonal orientation should be implicit. Redlich defines it as "the polarized conflict between the tonal centers of F and D" in which their natural affinities are "neglected or deliberately ignored."[7] As I read the words, this is not a denial of tonal gravity but, rather, a striving to employ or deploy its attraction in a new way. Redlich's expressive phrase for the outcome is "tonal ambiguity," a fair counterpart to my earlier description of certain procedures of Mahler and Schoenberg as neither "tonal" nor "atonal," but "untonal [p. 244]."

Between the two instrumental efforts of Berg's early publications came a sequence of songs bearing the opus number 2. These are rather more characteristic of the composer to come. As in almost every instance in which Berg utilizes a text—which includes, of course, *Wozzeck* and *Lulu*—he is keenly responsive to the implications of the poet's words. In these Four Songs of opus 2, his selections include an except from Friedrich Hebbel's "*Dem Schmerz sein Recht*" and the freer, less conventionally conceived "mystical visions" of Alfred Mombert's "*Der Glühende.*" Musically, the span is from a Tristanish harmonic change under a repeated pattern in the vocal line (Hebbel) to a more epigrammatic, appropriately disjointed outline for Mombert. A clingingly close-knit chord of fourths that Berg evolved—out of the *Tristan* derivatives —for the Hebbel text recurs in the Mombert settings.

In these few opus numbers, then, are contained the contemporary evidence of the work Berg did under Schoenberg's direct guidance. Soon after 1910 he passed into a new relationship of amanuensis and co-worker, undertaking so massive a task as the reduction for the piano of the enormous expanse of the *Gurrelieder*. He also produced a verbal exposition of it which was published in 1913, the year after the publication of the piano score. Largely speaking, whatever the alteration of status or the eventual permanent physical separation, Berg was a part of the Schoenberg environment—perhaps in response to the fa-

[7] Ibid., p. 52.

mous "intellectual pre-eminence" of which Alma Mahler has written (p. 254)—as long as he lived.

However, the extent to which Schoenberg remained *the* dominant force of Berg's expanding creative being demands some scrutiny. Bestriding the point of separation is the year 1910, when Berg published his opus 1, formalizing the end of his student period. He married Helene Nahowski, thus establishing a new center of emotional gravity for himself. Late in the year, he became acquainted with Mahler, who was about to leave for his last journey to America. From the meeting emerged an opportunity for Berg to study the score of Mahler's unpublished Ninth Symphony. Both happenings kindled further the glow of kinship which had been aroused by Mahler's work in general. Berg was particularly attracted to the Second and Sixth symphonies. The attraction became a deep, abiding absorption after Mahler's death.

For a time the close physical presence of Schoenberg continued to magnetize Berg's activities more than the remoter, more abstract appeal of Mahler. He was exposed to *Pierrot lunaire* as early, in all probability, as anyone, and participated in the excitement incidental to its first performance in 1912. That year, the history books confirm, was also the year of the first performance of Schoenberg's Five Orchestral Pieces (opus 16) in London, and of their Holland *première* later that year. But they do not say that Berg accompanied Schoenberg to attend the rehearsals as well as the performance in Holland and thus became intimately acquainted (much earlier than most others) with the trend of thought they embodied.

These momentous happenings in the musical world of which Berg was a part were deeply influential on both the substance and the shape of the projects to which he was attracted. His selection of poems by Peter Altenberg as the subject of a work for soprano voice was quite in accord with his choice of texts for previous settings. But the affiliation of them with a large orchestra was almost certainly a reflection of his Mahler enthusiasm. The result, from the very first, was a new sense of direction, a freshness of purpose in Berg's writing. For all the presence of a sizeable wind group (brass and reeds) of more than thirty and of a large percussion section, there is rarely a feeling of obstruction or curtain between the voice and the listener. There is, rather, a Mahlerish tendency to the use of the instruments individually or, as Redlich expresses it, to "cushioning the sound impact by frequent glissandi, trills, flutter-tonguing, harmonics and mutes,"[8] even to having the string

[8] Redlich: *Berg*, p. 62.

players bow over the f-holes to produce an eerie, breezelike flutter of sound in the final measure. Among the performing instructions are injunctions for the soprano to sing with "tightly closed lips" and with "half-open mouth" and "to start and finish with a mere breath."

A further striving for subtly defined sound-values may be found in the Four Pieces for Clarinet and Piano written in the following year (1913). These miniatures, like others of the time by Schoenberg and Webern (and such others outside their immediate circle as Bartók and Busoni), expressed a reaction against giantism as contained in the swollen sonorities of Strauss and of Schoenberg himself (in the *Gurrelieder*). Berg's undertaking followed this trend, but was not really of it. Rather, he was impelled by the impulse to work out certain structural ideas embodied in the Altenberg songs (such as the use, in the last of them, of a passacaglia).

Berg's next inclination was toward another work for large orchestra, perhaps with a solo vocal finale (in itself a Mahlerish conception). Much thought and no little emotional agitation were expended on plans for evolving the same kind of separated, stranded tonal texture he had conceived for the Altenberg settings. In the end, Berg abandoned the idea. In its stead, he turned to the composition of a series of separate orchestral movements which, in their grouping, occupied the same kind of formal middle ground as Schoenberg's pioneering Five Pieces for Orchestra and Webern's later opus 6. By coincidence, Berg's score also bears the designation opus 6. He never used such a sequential numbering again.

The focal point of Berg's compositional thinking at this time was the approaching fortieth birthday of Schoenberg (September 13, 1914). As a proper expression of regard and affection, Berg set himself to the creation of a work worthy of the person as well as of the time. When the date arrived, however, Berg had to confess that the middle movement—titled "*Reigen*"—was still unfinished. In his letter of apology for his "boldness in dedicating to you something incomplete," Berg described the missing movement as "a piece of dance-character, about 100 bars long." When it was finished, it turned out to be something rather more consequential: a parody-waltz ("*Ländler*") which is almost a sketch for the beer garden scene of *Wozzeck*. The other pieces begun in late 1913 gave him much less trouble.

It was only with the decision of May 1914, when he encountered Büchner's play *Woyzeck* on the stage of the Wiener Kammerspiele[9] and decided that his destiny and its destiny were inextricably inter-

9 Ibid., p. 234.

twined, that the direction of the dance piece was truly defined. In the Altenberg songs, in the clarinet-piano pieces, and the opus 6 orchestral movements—all along Berg had been working, in one form or another, with materials from which the tonal texture of *Wozzeck* was eventually evolved.

What went into that tonal texture has been analyzed and isolated by Redlich with skill and perception in his extended comments on *Wozzeck*.[1] Its derivations range from Beethoven's *Fidelio* and Weber's *Der Freischütz* to Strauss's *Der Rosenkavalier* and back to Mozart's *Don Giovanni*[2] (among operas), to Mahler's Ninth Symphony (see p. 249) and various works of Schoenberg (among instrumental compositions). For purposes of this inquiry, it is sufficient to note that the relationships with his predecessors do exist and can be identified in their germinal form. The outline that had been soft and supple in Berg's Seven Early Songs had been firmed and hardened under Schoenberg's attentive eye, as new ways of extending their melodic implications and expanding their harmonic explorations were provided by the prompting of Schoenberg's evaluating ear. It appeared (in the Quartet) that, for the refinement of technique thus acquired, Berg might be sacrificing something precious of his own for something merely novel of his mentor's. It was, fortunately, just then that the attraction to Mahler made itself felt, providing a counterforce that might be likened to a rudder against a strong current. At a moment when the strong impulse from Schoenberg might have pushed him off course into a backwater where he could have been becalmed, the corrective effect of Mahler asserted a contrary, enormously important influence to steady him on a way of his own.

It was, indeed, as a consequence of the subtle—and sometimes not so subtle—interplay of pressures that Berg arrived at an identity previously unknown and scarcely achieved by anyone since: a Mahler-composer-for-the-stage. Added to a lexicon of compositional techniques acquired from his studies with Schoenberg and to a formidable range of orchestral resources that he had evolved from his studies of Mahler was his own strong sense of meaningful vocal line. Together, they enabled him to articulate the mundane but mortal woes of the most bedraggled of theatrical *Untermenschen*, the half-dumb, wholly human Franz Wozzeck.

As the songs, Piano Sonata, Quartet, etc., are still far from being a part of the general listening experience, it is understandable that the listener who comes upon Berg's great first achievement should be in-

[1] Ibid., pp. 55–111.   [2] Ibid., p. 92.

clined to regard it as a typical expression, no matter how isolated or self-generating as a phenomenon. As the foregoing suggests, and a close attention to the work itself makes unmistakably clear, *Wozzeck* is as much a product of the continuity of which Berg was a part as *Tristan* had been under the stimulus of Liszt or Stravinsky's *Le Sacre* became under the compulsions provided by Mussorgsky, Debussy, et al.

To an even greater degree, the commitment to *Wozzeck* engaged the totality of Berg, including literary tastes that had been formed in youth and were responsive, as they flourished, to Balzac, Strindberg, and Dostoevsky as well as to Altenberg. They served him not only in educating his taste to a discriminating choice, but also in the way he proceeded to make the outcome a success. To fulfill the impulses the subject had generated within him, *Wozzeck* would have to be something more than a monodrama like Schoenberg's *Erwartung*, something less than an opera as customarily conceived. The scope of Berg's achievement is the greater for the extent to which it avoids the doctrinaire and the narrowly "stylistic" to which some others nurtured in the Schoenberg discipline have been prone. It embodies whatever technical elements suit the expressive purpose—from invention, passacaglia, and sonata movement to the folklike *"Soldaten"* (a close kin to the middle part of Mahler's *"Revelge,"* in the *Wunderhorn* songs, whose words are *"Ach, Bruder, Ach Bruder"*) or the final *"Hopp, hopp,"* which conveys with chilling simplicity the innocence of Marie's orphaned child. From the depths of his own poetic nature Berg speaks with eloquence of the beer garden and the Bible, the barracks and the tavern, the doctor and the fool (the latter a derivation, in Stravinsky's opinion,[3] from the idiot in Mussorgsky's *Boris*).

To be sure, this arsenal of assets did not come ready-made to Berg's hand. Even the parts within reach had to be matched, assembled, fitted, made workable. Included were the *Erwartung-Pierrot lunaire-Glückliche Hand* patterns of song-speech for some aspects of Marie and the vocal thrust of Strauss's *Salome* for others, the separate strands of Mahler's orchestral texture to keep the sound properly transparent, and the framework of Schoenberg's contrapuntal practices to sustain the musical structure. A full seven years lay between the impulse of May 1914 and the final fulfillment of April 1921. During that time Berg had, first of all, to make his own performable text from Büchner's twenty-seven scenes. Part of the time was committed to military service in World War I. Berg was trained for active duty but assigned to the War Ministry in Vienna when his asthma interfered with field service. However, his

[3] Stravinsky and Craft: *Dialogues*, p. 232.

experience with barracks life and general military atmosphere was sufficient to serve as basic training for the relevant scenes of *Wozzeck*. The verbal text was completed in mid-1917, the greater part of the score between the autumn of 1918 and the autumn of 1920.[4]

If my reasons for describing Berg as a "Mahler-composer-for-the-stage" have not yet become clear, the reader may be reminded of the prevalence of fanfares and drum rolls in Mahler's symphonies, the recurrence of marches among their movements (the long opening movement of the Sixth Symphony, of which Berg was particularly fond, is derived from *"Revelge,"* though not the part of it which contains *"Ach, Bruder"*), and his partiality, in the *Wunderhorn* songs, to such themes as *"Der Tamboursg'sell"* ("The Drummer Boy") and *"Der Schildwache Nachtlied"* ("Sentinel's Night Song"). It is a fundamental fact of Mahler's physical existence that he spent much of his early life near a barracks in Litomerice.[5] The amply apparent results in his music became, in turn, a part of Berg's spiritual life when he became absorbed in the problems of *Wozzeck*.

It is to the interaction of these many strains and cross-currents that *Wozzeck* owes its special appeal. It is an appeal that has, over four decades, transcended considerations of idiom and subject matter, language, locale, or custom to insinuate its way into the affections of operagoers world-wide. Much of this, in my belief, relates to the tonal orientation of Berg's melodic impulse. Whether or not the requirements of tonality are served at any given time, there is almost always the implication of a tonal center to provide for the participation of many to whom *Wozzeck's* frame of reference might, otherwise, be elusive.

The axes of this frame comprise not only the elements previously mentioned (and sundry others instanced by Redlich[6]), but also other, more remote ones. These include the orchestral interludes, functionally similar to those of *Pelléas* (its 1911 performance at the Vienna Opera under the direction of Bruno Walter was attended by Berg[7]) but vastly different in emotional impact from the impassioned *"Blut!"* (Wozzeck's last word, with its overtones of Tristan's third-act ravings) and the outspoken emotionalism of the succeeding episode in which

[4] Redlich: *Berg,* p. 109.

[5] J. F. Redlich: *Bruckner and Mahler* (London: J. M. Dent and Sons; 1955), p. 113.

[6] Redlich: *Berg,* pp. 80–94. Among the operas he mentions as being recalled, in one detail or another, by *Wozzeck* are *Don Giovanni, Fidelio, Der Freischütz,* and *Der Rosenkavalier.* (See p. 333.)

[7] Edward Lockspeiser: *Debussy: His Life and Mind* (New York: The Macmillan Company; 1962), II, 130 n.

Berg expresses his compassion for the characters of the drama in terms that affiliate him with such composers for the stage as Verdi and Mussorgsky.

Of the thousands who have learned to love *Wozzeck* and to look forward with enthusiasm to every new opportunity to expand their acquaintance with it, only one known to me has construed its breadth of appeal as, somehow, discreditable. That is Igor Stravinsky, who has written (in *Dialogues and a Diary*, p. 24): "What disturbs me about *Wozzeck*, a work I love, is the level of its appeal to 'ignorant' audiences." Among the elements cited by Stravinsky are the Bible, sex, brevity, dynamics, muted brass, *col legno*—which comprise a lexicon of means, rather than ends in themselves. Perhaps Stravinsky should be similarly "disturbed" about the broad appeal of *Orfeo*, *Figaro*, *Fidelio*, *Boris*, and *Otello* (among many others) to those who might, in Stravinskyan terms, be labeled "ignorant." It is the glorious distinction of these works that they, too, can be heard on several levels, listened to on others, according to the understanding of the individual participant. Masterpieces—including *Le Sacre du printemps*—are generally thus distinguished.

3

BERG'S TOTAL INVOLVEMENT with the realization of *Wozzeck*, which had occupied him mentally, spiritually, and physically for seven years, is embedded in the urgency and meaningfulness of the work itself. The consequence, unremarkably, was a period of deflation which left him without the impulse to compose for nearly two years. Such incapacity after a long period of concentration is normal enough. But there was another aspect to Berg's depletion. He had, in a large sense, used up the means he had previously amassed out of his own thought and the thinking of others, those elements of vocabulary and development rooted deep in his background.

For purposes of replenishment and regeneration, Berg turned once more to the example of Schoenberg, this time to the *Kammersymphonie* (opus 9), which Mahler had declared unintelligible to him. The result was the *Kammerkonzert* (Chamber Concerto), the dedication of which became Berg's gift to Schoenberg on his fiftieth birthday (as the composer noted in his letter of transmission, it was not completed until February 9, 1925, more than six months after the Schoenberg anniversary but in time for his own fortieth birthday four days later). What appealed to him in the Schoenberg work was the example it provided of maximum sonorous contrast with a minimum of performing elements. However, Berg's choice of a title defines the difference of direction in his work as well as the individuality of its purpose. He elected to use a wind ensemble of thirteen as a continuing basic ensemble, with a solo piano in the first movement and a solo violin in the second. The finale utilizes both.

The *Kammerkonzert* is by any standard a brilliant tapestry of sound, which, from the composer of *Wozzeck*, is the least one could expect. Somewhat in the manner of the early Quartet (opus 3), it reveals a struggle for domination of a formal problem rather than complete control of its manifold details. Needless to say, Berg's resources at thirty-eight were vastly more sophisticated than they had been at twenty-three. The uses to which they are put suggest a work cleverly constructed rather than spontaneously generated.

The musical matter itself is neither thematic in the conventional sense nor derived from a "row" according to the procedures arrived at by Schoenberg. It was begun in the summer of 1923, when Schoenberg's doctrines were just beginning to find expression in such works as the Five Piano Pieces, the Serenade, the Suite for Piano, and the Wind Quintet. It was not finished until the summer of 1925, and thus progressed without the benefit of Schoenberg's precepts (though the letter previously mentioned attests to Berg's knowledge of their existence in his reference to "passages that correspond to the laws set up by you for 'composition with twelve notes related only to one another' "[8]).

In place of a row it offers a verbal motto: *"Aller guten Dinge,"* which can be approximated by the English expression: "All good things come in threes." From this Berg evolved not only a physical but also a metaphysical scheme, in which the names of the three companions—Schoenberg, Webern, and himself—were rendered into their musical equivalents as generating tones. As each of their first names—Arnold, Anton, and Alban—begins with A, so does each generative sequence, providing a recurring point of reference for each phrase. These, in turn, are made up of pitches paralleling the letters from A to G, plus H and S, which have musical equivalents in German (exploited, for similarly derived mottos, by Bach from his own name, and by Schumann, in *Carnaval*, from the town of Asch).

From each group of letters Berg made up a five-measure phrase somewhat akin to the four measures that precede the *sehr rasch* (first) movement of Schoenberg's *Kammersymphonie*. Thereafter the procedure is quite different. Berg's first movement consists of five variations that can also be construed as the component parts of a sonata movement.

[8] Reich: *Alban Berg*, p. 147.

The second movement is a contrapuntal structure in which the last 120 measures are the retrograde form of the first 120 measures. The finale is a rondo whose recurrent motif is a rhythmic pattern rather than an intervalic one.

The reference to the second movement's being made up of two sections of the same length which together total 240 measures should not be construed as a mere coincidence. This total of 240 measures is precisely the same as the sum of the five variations in the first movement. Thus warned, the reader can readily anticipate the count for the final rondo. It not only adds the solo instrument from one movement to the solo instrument of the other, but also combines the mathematical disposition of measures to a total of 480 (uninformed players who omit the repeat of 175 measures in the finale are clearly falsifying Berg's intent). Pressing on to ultimate figures, it should not be overlooked that 120 and 480 are both divisible by three—the "Open, Sesame" of this particular combination—and also by thirty, the typical number of measures in each variation of movement one.

The reason this much space has been devoted to Berg's *Kammerkonzert* is not to provide a dissertation on its numerology, but rather to convey the striving it represents on the part of singularly gifted, intelligent, and honest craftsmen to evolve a substitute for the functional struts and trusses of harmonic relationships and the formal possibilities they provide.

As most music-minded persons are aware, tonality is not merely a contrivance for the avoidance of unpleasant or harsh combinations. It is an elaborate, almost infinitely variable resource whose modulatory values, enharmonic changes, opportunities for back-reference, and reminiscence around the circle of keys give rise to those sensations of departure and return, leave-taking and homecoming, serenity and agitation which make up but a small number of the emotional conflicts, humors, good and bad, moods, high and low, which color the expressions of composers over nearly two centuries.

Deprived of such relationships, and lacking a text to perform a supporting function, Berg was forced to evolve another unifying element. In his quest, it seems to me, he was distracted from anything like an expressive motivation to the mere fulfillment of a functional pattern. We are no longer absorbed, as in the Early Songs or *Wozzeck*, with the view from the corner of a poet's world; we are, rather, sharing the artisan's bench.

In the *Lyric Suite*, which Berg began almost immediately after the completion of the *Kammerkonzert* in 1925, he had the problem

of a structural plan well in hand from the outset. This time the Schoenberg impulse did not come from an example of the past, but from the
dogma of the present. In the suite's six movements, Berg utilizes a
twelve-tone row and its serial elaboration for the first time. It is, by
the measure of those versed in such matters, both respectful and
successful in its employment of Schoenberg's specifications.

According to Redlich,[9] the *Lyric Suite* embodies many poetic
references to works of Zemlinsky and Mahler, but they are even less
apparent to the ear—my ear, that is—than to the eye. Aside from the
agreeable curve of line which Berg is able to evolve from his innately
superior melodic sense, even within the confines of TMOCWTTROWOA, I
find little to absorb the attention in the *Lyric Suite*. The clearly audible
quotation from *Tristan* in the finale is there, I take it, to show that it
can be done (the line conforms to a retrograde inversion of his own
row)[1] rather than in fulfillment of an inner compulsion (as existed
in the parallel instance of the quartet, p. 330). This is, perhaps, the
sum of the difference between creation and construction. In any case,
the outcome is a world away from the bitter kind of communication
Berg achieved in *Wozzeck*.

Had the fatal bee sting that caused Berg's death in 1935 afflicted
him in 1927, it would have been reasonable to conclude that he would
not, could not, or at least did not, succeed in attaining that lofty plane
again. Meaningless and tragic as his death at fifty was, he did live long
enough to combine what he knew and what he felt into a new affirmation of purpose. What he achieved in the last span of time left to him
—1927-35—demonstrated two things: it was possible for a poet of
Berg's impulses to weave a new texture from the old ball of yarn and,
in such utilization of the new techniques, to prove that there was something more than aesthetic madness in Schoenberg's method.

Even more compelling was Berg's success in projecting the proof
in two divergent ways. Had the demonstration been confined to the
text he evolved from Frank Wedekind's *Erdgeist* and *Büchse der Pan-
dora* for the purposes of *Lulu*, it might have been concluded that
without the stage and supporting action, Berg's soaring song was muted,
his strain of eloquence only partially engaged. But the Concerto for
Violin and Orchestra which he wrote in the last year of his life not
only contradicts such a theory of exclusivity, but also validates everything in his prior artistic searchings.

Lulu exists as a sizeable portion of an incompletely disclosed whole.

[9] Redlich: *Berg*, pp. 141–2.
[1] Ibid., p. 143.

In the opinion of some, it could be presented as a totality, given the will to convert the nearly complete sketches of the third act into a likeness of the form Berg imagined. The two acts customarily heard are full of strongly sculptured theatrical outlines; some excruciating, but by no means insoluble, vocal difficulties; and a trenchant kind of character projection. Given the subject matter, the rows serve their assigned purpose of intensifying or enhancing the gruesome, mordant, decadent episodes in Lulu's progress from willful amoralist to prostitute victim of Jack the Ripper. If it can be said with conviction that the technique serves the special purpose well, then it may be said with equal conviction that the same special purpose could have been served just as well with some other technique.

The Violin Concerto is complete not merely in the sense that it was finished in every detail before the composer's death: it is also a perfect, complete whole in fulfilling every phase of the creative process from conception to realization. Ingrained with the warm sympathy for human misery which carries *Wozzeck* to the heart, it strikes deeper, flows even more strongly because the tragedy from which it stemmed was personal to Berg. This was the death, at the senseless age of eighteen, of the beautiful, gifted Manon Gropius (daughter of Mahler's widow by her marriage to Walter Gropius in 1915). Berg was mulling over a commission from Louis Krasner when the girl's year-long illness ended in death in April 1934. The impact of the event, with its effect on the composer's widow, to whom Berg felt a strong attachment, stimulated his emotional adrenalin so powerfully that he was drawn from the completion of *Lulu* to the new, more urgent task. Fresh as the emotion was, the expression of it was nevertheless guided, controlled, and directed by the calm hand and cool head of the superior artist.

In the Violin Concerto's swing from tender reminiscence to resentment and back again to grief-laden resignation is embodied a respect for the discipline that is the best of Schoenberg's Method, and a rejection of the rigor that is the worst in it. In achieving the most expressive exemplification of its possibilities to that time—or to now, for that matter—Berg was impelled to use not one row, but two (a flagrant disregard for BSD, or Basic Schoenberg Doctrine). He also felt free to employ a sequence of tones, based on the fifths to which the open strings of the violin are tuned, in contradiction to Schoenberg's contention that such a sequence should be avoided because of its "diatonic implications."[2] At certain strategic moments, he was impelled not merely to flirt with, but even to embrace, the seductive

[2] Ibid., p. 207.

charms of tonality. In a final flight of insubordination, he utilizes a chorale from the Bach Cantata No. 60 (in its original harmonization) as the wings on which his eloquence becomes airborne.

Whereas the *Kammerkonzert* was a mere tapestry of sound, the Violin Concerto transcends method as well as the Method to involve the listener with the poet's eulogy for promise unfulfilled and purpose insanely thwarted. One cannot exclude from it the recollection of Mahler's *Kindertotenlieder*, which subsequent sad events converted into a premature requiem for an offspring of his own by the same woman. Berg's sorrowing echo of that injustice is as much related to the woman on whom it was twice visited as to the innocent victim of circumstance. Berg's work finds consolation in reference to a Deity to whom Mahler also acknowledged devotion, making it the most Mahlerish achievement of all by the Mahler-composer-for-the-stage.

In its profoundly purposeful way, the Violin Concerto is also an acute criticism of the prohibitions and proscriptions of the Law (to revert to Berg's own characterization of it [p. 337]) as promulgated. It repeats notes before proper serial procedure permits; it calls upon a number of *wienerisch* devices (including the citation of a Carinthian folk song) to convey capriciousness as well as contrast; it takes advantage of the eloquence inherent in the violin to seek out phrases as sensuous as those of Chausson's *Poème*; and otherwise constrains itself to be unconstrained.

The final, summarizing variations on the Bach chorale (the text embodies the sentiment "It is enough! Lord, if it is Thy pleasure, relieve me of my yoke") pursue an unwinding pattern of motivic development along serial lines which give a new context of sequence, variety, and locale to the place of the solo violin amid the intermingled orchestral voices. It is the authentic masterpiece of this whole Viennese development, no more for what it realizes in present values than for what it implies of future possibilities.

Alas for music, these were not possibilities that Berg was privileged to explore. Like Mahler before him, he was permitted only to point a way, not to follow it to fulfillment. The reconciliations that Berg might have effected in his fifties and sixties were voided by death. His curve, in Debussy's use of the term, was never fully projected, and thus could never be fully accomplished.

But on its rising line one can discern a profound and meaningful truth. In rejecting the restrictions of the Method, Berg nevertheless affiliated himself strongly with the serial principle of "developing variations." In so doing, and very likely with no real awareness of the significance of his choice, he rejected that part of it which was one individual's arbitrary formulation and accepted the portion of it which is demonstrably an evolution from the continuity of the past.

4

IF THERE IS ANY SUGGESTION, in the preceding pages, of a desire to decry the place of Arnold Schoenberg in the history of music, it is a failure of expression rather than an expression of intent. The question is, rather, in which of his several capacities and at what period of his long career did Schoenberg influence the course of music most decisively? One can argue this aspect or that with heat, and perhaps with conviction. But there is likely to be uniform agreement that whoever supervised the development of a composer with the range and power of Alban Berg was a pedagogue of outstanding ability. For the same man to have sensed the vastly different capacities of Anton Webern and responded to them equally well qualifies him as unique. Each acquired from Schoenberg what was required for self-realization without being deprived of the elements that determine individuality.

By the evidence of the Webern works known to us from the period prior to his orchestral Passacaglia (his official opus 1), he no less than Berg was mentally and spiritually disposed to the continuity of Brahms and Wagner. Unlike Berg, he was disposed from the first to the instrumental rather than the vocal means of musical expression, and so remained. Though deeply affected by a visit to Bayreuth early in life (1902), Webern showed little indication of any such instinct for the theater as Berg possessed and was possessed by.

The earliest work of Webern known today is *Im Sommerwind*, an orchestral essay of 1904 which predated the beginning of his studies with Schoenberg in the fall of the same year.[3] At one moment it might be judged an early example of Delius, who had by then written some of his better-known works, at another a derivative of the kind of Richard Strauss contained in the A-flat chorale of *Zarathustra*. Before, between, and after these moments, the attraction is consistently to the man whose works were a source for both: Richard Wagner. Of the later Webern, there is little forewarning, save, perhaps, in the use of variation as a formal principle.

By 1907, when Webern had been working with Schoenberg for three years, his fundamental bent was slightly redirected. Rather than

---

[3] All dates for Webern's career are from the chronology published in *Die Reihe*, 2, ed. Herbert Einert and Karlheinz Stockhausen (Bryn Mawr: Theodore Presser Co.; 1959).

being Wagner-Brahms, it had become Brahms-Wagner. Its expression found an outlet in a Quintet for Piano and Strings (of which the first movement, as edited by Jacques Monod, is included in the "complete" edition of Webern supervised by Robert Craft for Columbia Records). It projects a counterpoise of conventionally characteristic first and second subjects, developed along Brahmsian lines and enriched with Wagnerian chromaticism. Now and again it is laced with a dash of French dressing, of the wholetone variety.

Contemporary with it, though published later, are half a dozen songs of indeterminate character, now known as opus 2 and opus 3. They are, however, both earlier and less revealing of the true Webern than the Passacaglia for orchestra published as opus 1. At first inspection, it would appear that Webern's inclinations, when writing this contrapuntal manipulation of an eight-measure theme, had made a sharp turn away from earlier expressions. Closer scrutiny discloses that it is less a change of direction than a "correction of course" for navigational reasons. The orchestra has much of the sound, if not the components of *Im Sommerwind*, and a variation of the variation principle prevails. The link to Brahms is maintained, by intent or otherwise, by Webern's use of the passacaglia form that his predecessor had utilized in the last movement of his last symphony. To be sure, Brahms avoided the use of passacaglia as a description of the finale of his Fourth Symphony, but the associations are clear enough. Webern's work utilizes the eight-measure theme as the "ground" for thirty or so variations (some are of double length and hence may be counted either as one or two), as Brahms did before him. Both themes consist of eight notes, or one per measure. In both, there is a reminiscence of the opening theme following the "turn," or beginning of the homeward sequence, after variation 15. As Schoenberg made clear in written form, the finale of the Fourth Symphony was a movement by Brahms which he held in high esteem.[4]

With or without regard to such an antecedent, the Passacaglia is prophetic in several respects of the Webern to come. It shows a gravitation to contrapuntal discipline which runs like a *cantus firmus* through much of what he wrote, between the opus 1 of 1908 and the opus 31 of 1940. Though its 240 (8 × 30) measures[5] are assigned a performance time of but eleven minutes (in the Universal Edition score), they make up the longest work of his entire catalogue.

To a degree, such brevity might be construed as a by-product of

---

[4] Arnold Schoenberg: *Style and Idea* (New York: Philosophical Library; 1950), pp. 62–3.
[5] See Berg's *Kammerkonzert* (p. 338).

the procedures the Passacaglia embodies: an eight-measure theme varied thirty times in a sequence of 240 measures has a finite limit of minutes and seconds. Such was hardly the case with the five movements for the String Quartet (opus 5) of 1909 (if Beethoven's opus 131 is chosen as the basis for comparison, a five-movement quartet could extend for rather more than half an hour). But Webern's opus 5 is an even briefer work than his opus 1. Some of the means—explosive pizzicati, wide skips across the strings, intricate patterns of time values—relate to procedures pioneered by Mahler in the Sixth and Seventh symphonies, and also utilized by Schoenberg in his early quartets. But the concentration of thought, the frugality of means, the economy of statement are decidedly Webern's own.

Thus, while still in his mid-twenties, Webern had discovered a second guiding principle to which he would retain a lifelong fidelity. In obedience to the discipline itself, it can be best conveyed in a single word: brevity. This is sometimes ascribed[6] to the specific example of Schoenberg's opus 19 Piano Pieces, which are, in truth, Webern-brief. But this does not explain Webern's trend *before* Schoenberg's composition of them in 1911. Whether or not prior examples of such brevity were known to Schoenberg's pupils, the impulse to brevity might have come from another quarter altogether. Erik Satie's vignettes suggest one provocative possibility, or it could have been a direct reaction to the compulsion to length embodied in the symphonies of Bruckner and Mahler and in Schoenberg's own *Gurrelieder*. The swing from the epic to the epigrammatic might have occurred to any clever musician of the same time and place.

What raised Webern's work from the category of the clever to the plane of an artistic credo was its control by and responsiveness to his other guiding principles: contrapuntal formulation, variational exposition. In a search for basic truths of his own, Webern divested himself of first one and then another of the compositional resources in which he had garbed his earlier efforts. First to go was melody per se; then harmonic structure; soon thereafter, in response to Schoenberg's development of free dissonance, tonal orientation. Sequences, repetitions, thematic recurrences were further inevitable encumbrances to be discarded as he attained a clearer conception of the objective for which he was striving and clarified his perception of the minimum resources required to achieve it.

Unlike some others of the time, to whom guiding principles served

[6] H. H. Stuckenschmidt: *Arnold Schoenberg* (New York: Grove Press; 1959), p. 59. "The style of this work [opus 19] has found its strongest (or rather its most tender) echo in the music of Anton von Webern."

as ends in themselves (Scriabin and his chordal constructions, Reger and his love of complication), Webern remained strongly aware of the listener as the final link in the chain of creator and re-creator. He was, during much of his compositional career, also a professional conductor who earned a living on the podium. He was, thus, constantly concerned with music as communication, aware of its existence both as subject and object.[7] As one who was aware also of the magnitude of interest conveyed by what he discarded, he realized that something would have to take its place. Some other means of attracting and retaining the interest of the ear, as well as of ministering to the spirit, would have to be evolved.

This was by no means a unique awareness among those who were making the same voyage of discovery as Schoenberg, if in the wake of their captain, rather than in his lead ship. He, too, was aware of the danger that arose from the jettisoning of all such ballast as key relations, modulations, enharmonic change, and the referential values that make thematic back-reference possible. In his "free dissonant" period of *Herzgewächse, Pierrot lunaire,* and *Die glückliche Hand,* it was the Word that provided a structural skeleton to support his vibrational fantasies. Indeed, as of 1940[8] he was much concerned that the "light, ironical, satirical tone" in which *Pierrot lunaire* was conceived should be conveyed in its performance, for "times and ideas have changed a lot, so that what might have sounded Wagnerian or at worst Tchaikovskian to us then [1912] would remind us of Puccini, Lehár or worse today." Here the emphasis is on the manner in which the text, rather than the setting of it, is deployed. Eventually, in the promulgation of TMOCWTTROWOA it was the serial skein that was intended to catch and retain the interest of the ear.

Webern's solution was both more personal and less encompassing. He was not by disposition a vocal composer: the Word served him only incidentally and occasionally. Thus it could not present itself as a way out of his dilemma. Nor was he a theoretician of Schoenberg's grand illusion, thirsting after definitive doctrines designed to last for a hundred years. He was concerned, primarily, with accomplishing his own artistic destiny. That he succeeded in evolving procedures valid for others was a by-product rather than a guiding principle of his intent. Proceeding cautiously, step by step, from the Passacaglia of 1908 to the

[7] In his introduction to the recorded works of Webern (Columbia K4L-232), Robert Craft cites Ernst Krenek's recollection of Webern as a superb interpreter of Haydn.

[8] Josef Rufer: *The Works of Arnold Schoenberg* (New York: The Free Press of Glencoe; 1963), p. 40.

Six Orchestral Pieces of 1910, Webern retained such typical factors of his aesthetic as brevity, contrapuntal discipline, and the variation principle. But the means by which they were expressed gave Webern access to a world of sound not even hinted at in the Passacaglia.

This is the equivalent of saying that, in 1910, at the age of twenty-seven, Webern already had put together the complex of elements which, when refined and intensified, would constitute the musical identity recognized only decades later. As in numerous parallel instances previously cited, this acceleration from anonymity to identity was not to be found wholly within Webern himself. It was, rather, another instance of one man's atypical becoming the typical of another. For Webern, the impulse was the pioneering Five Orchestral Pieces of Schoenberg. Though they were not performed until 1912 (see p. 331), the date of the last section to be completed (No. 5) is August 11, 1909. Therein are to be found the "schematics" (see p. 267) on which Webern built his highly personalized, carefully colored "new sounding" structures. In the words of Robert Craft "Schoenberg's 'changing colours' in the orchestra pieces of opus 16 are Webern's undeniable source."[9]

The association of a literary or descriptive phrase with each of the studies may suggest that Schoenberg was motivated by some form of illustrative intent. The titles were, rather, produced by Schoenberg at the urging of his publisher. As cited in his diary for January 27, 1912, they were (together with his justification to himself for each): "Premonitions (everybody has those): The Past (everybody has that, too): Chord-Colours (technical): Peripetie (general enough, I think): The Obbligato (perhaps better the 'fully developed' or the 'endless') Recitative."[1] In its early performances, perhaps to facilitate acceptance, No. 3 was titled "Summer Morning by a Lake." In the published edition of 1922 No. 3 bears the title *"Farben"* ("Colors"), which conforms to Schoenberg's original designation of 1912. This is altogether more appropriate to a work in which interest derives almost wholly from shifting glints of aural color radiating from the constantly changing sound-sources. Substantively, *"Farben"* is hardly more than a single chord: procedurally, the sound evoked by the combinations of instruments and the alterations of register in which they are added and subtracted, blended and amended provides imagery, variety, and interest vastly beyond the raw materials utilized. It was to this demonstration of

[9] Introduction to Webern's *Complete Works* (Columbia K4L-232).
[1] Rufer: *Works of Arnold Schoenberg*, p. 34.

the interest latent in such instrumental blending that Schoenberg gave the title *Klangfarbenmelodie*—"the melody of tone colors"—in his *Harmonielehre*, completed in 1911.[2]

My reference to it as a "demonstration" rather than a "discovery" relates to the earlier discussion of the whole phenomenon of tone colors and instrumental combinations *vis-à-vis Tristan* (p. 78). There I made reference to the well-known acoustical principle that the weight and value that the ear attaches to clashes of intervals and interactions of melodic lines can be intensified or alleviated not only by the volume of the instrument utilized but also by the octave, or octaves, by which they are separated on the frequency scale. A pioneering instance of "changing colors" may be found in Act III of *Tristan* (Schirmer piano score, p. 259). Behind Kurvenal's anxious question *"Bist du nun todt? Lebst du noch?"* the clarinet, French horn, and bass clarinet are joined in their pulsations first by the oboe, then by the cello. A few measures farther on, the clarinet is replaced by the oboe. In a later chordal combination, the clarinet is subtracted and the oboe added (miniature score, pp. 860–1).

Mahler made a practice of Wagner's pioneering preachment, and Schoenberg gave it an identity as well as a name. But it remained for Webern to make of tone color a guiding principle co-equal with contra-

(*continued*)

2 Ibid., p. 133.

(*continued*)

Wagner: Tristan und Isolde, *Act III*

puntal manipulation, alteration by variation, and time expanse (either length or its opposite, brevity). It thus takes rank with many other vital elements of music which, in the contemporary terminology, were "spun off" from the incidental expressions of one composer to become the generative factor of another.

In Webern's opus 6, the act of propagation distinguishing creative thought from sterile imitation comes in his application of *Klang-farbenmelodie* to a fast-moving pattern as well as to the slower ones in which it was utilized by Schoenberg. The melodic line, or what passes for it, is broken up and distributed among the many instruments of the orchestra. Little new has been added to *how* the instruments play; but everything new has been added to *when* they play, and in what part of their frequency ranges. No longer is color conceived in terms of a weave or pattern of interrelated lines: range and contrast, blend and proportion may vary from chord to chord, determining the harshness or blandness of the sounds separated by silence.

Of the many elements involved in Webern's fully formed works, the one exploited for the first time as an equal component of the total result is—silence. When Webern is at his most characteristic, silence takes on the function of more than a period of nonsound. It is the continuing condition, like the carrier wave of a radio transmission, into which sound is injected, the tissue of thought embodying the deep emotional state that is interrupted or disturbed by a tone, a figure, a pattern of percussion, the flick of a finger on a cello string pizzicato, or the rasp of a bow *sul ponticello* (on the bridge). One is conscious not only of the musical context in which the instruments vibrate together or separately, but also of the silences that set them apart. It might be likened to a painter who has found a striking new use for canvas. Rather than being merely the surface on which a design is imposed, the canvas has become, in itself, a part of the total experience.

Taken together, the bits and pieces of sound used by Webern make up a mosaic that might be likened to the fragments fitted together to form a stained-glass window. To the viewer within the cathedral, it is the light beamed from the outside that activates and completes the image. To the listener within Webern's sound world, silence is the intermediate element that fulfills and rounds out the aural image, defines the lightness or density of tonal mass. It is thus not sound alone, but also the absence of it that coerces the senses and creates a *new factor of attention* for the ear.

As Schubert had created one new factor of attention from the enharmonic modulation (hinted at but not developed by Mozart), or Chopin had projected another in his concept of bitonality, to be acted

upon eventually by Stravinsky, or as Debussy had added to the resources of the keyboard composer by formalizing and codifying the
kind of pedaling improvised by Liszt, so Webern made of the barely
audible pulsations in the third act of *Tristan*, as formalized and codified
by Mahler and Schoenberg, the substance of another aesthetic innovation. One listens to Webern not to be beguiled by the rise and fall of
a melodic line or to derive aural satisfaction from the give and take
of thematic discussion, or to react to a play of expectation, evasion, and
fulfillment in harmonic ingenuities, but with a concentration height-
ened by the slightest interruption of the prevailing silence.

Even as one is most acutely conscious of small disturbances (a
bird call, a dog's bark, a cricket's chirp) on a perfectly still night in
a noiseless countryside, so there is a similar physiological command to
the attention in the minutiae of Webern's tonal incidents. The strain
of listening for such sound as there is induces a hypnotic concentration
in which absolute time is suspended and any customary conception of
musical time must be reconstituted.

Taken together, Webern's guiding principles remain a valid, responsive *centrum* for the musical faculties, provided that: (a) they are
not required to sustain a burden longer than, in his acute judgment,
Webern postulated (nine minutes, thirty seconds for the Six Pieces
of opus 9; eight minutes, fifty seconds for the Symphony, opus 21; five
minutes, fifty-six seconds for the Concerto, opus 24; five minutes, forty
seconds for the Variations, opus 30, are some typical timings of the
performances directed by Craft in Columbia album K4L-232); (b)
they are treated with respect for the hypnotic power they exert and
not exploited as just one more compositional tool.

The first tentative but arresting application by Webern of this
"new factor of attention" in the opus 6 pieces resulted in a sometimes
coarse-grained, but always absorbing, panorama of change. In the opus
10 pieces for an ensemble of seventeen players we move closer to the
quintessential Webern. The sound has depth, gloss, opacity, or brilliance, according to his preference: but the context is more abstracted,
less palpable, laconic, like telegraphic statements of fact lacking a
connecting tissue of syntax: "dead" . . . "four a.m." . . . "stroke . . ."
A message is conveyed, but very little else. In the succeeding, more
highly refined application of his guiding principles—brevity, contrapuntal interweavings, alteration by variation, sound-interrupting silence
—Webern learned ever more productively the art of omission, approached ever more closely the finest fulfillment of his exceptional
sensitivities.

In one of several verbal tributes that Stravinsky lavished on the questing mind of Webern, he summarized Webern's innovation by saying that he had discovered "a new distance between the musical object and ourselves, and therefore . . . a new measure of musical time . . ."[3] This is the equivalent, in another formulation, of my contention that Webern discovered "a new factor of attention." The combination of sound-interrupting silences and the elimination of repetitions, sequences, developments, recapitulations, and all the other factors that extend the typical work of the preceding continuity commands as much concentrated attention for a five-minute work of Webern as to, say, a forty-minute work of Grieg.

As with anything that is all essence—whether food, perfume, or a thought-provoking epigram—the dosage need only be small. Indeed, quantity might negate the effect of what has been compressed, condensed, and compacted into the aural equivalent of a food from which all but nutrition has been removed. However, the discovery of an effective formula for one kind of communication did not guarantee its universal application. Indeed, the infrequency of Webern's production between 1913, the year of the opus 10 pieces, and 1927, when he attained his opus 20, suggests the difficulty that confronted Webern in the employment of the resources he had evolved. After much of the kind of futile military service in which Berg and Schoenberg had spent time on Austria's behalf during World War I, Webern returned to his conducting career. This was a modest means to the necessary end of survival: first at the Deutsches Landestheater in Prague, then as a collaborator with Schoenberg in performances of the works that the Viennese group had been incubating in the early twenties, and finally as director of the Vienna Workers' Symphony Concerts and the Vienna Workers' Choral Union, both of which he continued until 1934.

This was the period, also, of Webern's greatest concentration on vocal writing—one might almost say the period of his refuge in vocal music—as if he had been unable to function without verbal symbols to give shape and meaning to the tonal. For that matter, it is something of a misnomer to describe the six songs of opus 14 (1917–21) as "vocal writing," for their wide skips and angular outlines are the negation of what is commonly considered "vocal." Possibly if Webern had been able to find a clarinet that would intone such lines as *"Täglich kommt die gelbe Sonne über den Hügel"* (opus 14, No. 1) or a bassoon that could pronounce *"die purpurnen Male der Schwermut"* (opus 14, No.

[3] Igor Stravinsky and Robert Craft: *Memories and Commentaries* (New York: Doubleday and Company, Inc.; 1960), p. 97.

3), he would have been just as content. Certainly the musical thought would have been as well served.

Significantly, Webern's return to instrumental music can be dated to 1927, when he completed the String Trio which now bears the opus number 20. It had been preceded by three sets of songs (nine in all) with a combined performance time of seven minutes, thirty-two seconds. In these products of three years' application (1924–6), Webern had applied the imperatives of Schoenberg's Method, and found them absorbing. If it is too much to say that TMOCWTTROWOA provided Webern with a way out, it did afford him a way into a new world of fragmentation, elimination, and omission. For Webern, the discipline inherent in the "row" and its manipulation as decreed by Schoenberg doubtless seemed divinely derived to promote further his rarefied command of sonority and silence.

The audible results, however, did not duplicate, let alone excel, the achievements of opus 6 and opus 10. The difference, as I hear it, is clear. In the early works, the association of Webern's means with tonal materials that shared the background from which they were derived established a frame of reference enabling him to include the listener in the circle of his thought. In the later works, the disassociation of manner and matter does not promote such inclusiveness. It does not strike me as a failure in execution, for Webern was adept as early as the Passacaglia (1908) in the contrapuntal modes of thought inherent in serial elaboration. But the restrictions of TMOCWTTROWOA did not allow the principles of *Klangfarbenmelodie* to be applied at anything like maximum advantage in the symphony (eight minutes) for chamber orchestra or the concerto (less than six minutes) for nine instruments. In effect, the "distance between the listener" and "the musical object" (in Stravinsky's phrase) became more difficult to bridge, the "new factor of attention" (in my phrase) less hypnotic than it had been.

Of his later works, only the Variations (1940) convey to me something like the attention-absorbing values of opus 6 and opus 10. The message is conveyed with even greater terseness, with the appeals to the ear restricted to fewer occurrences of tone colors in the combination; instead, each sound source is utilized more as an entity in itself. Oddly, this tends to diminish rather than enhance the intrusion of silence, which is no longer a carrier wave as previously described but, rather, like the interior of a completely soundproofed chamber, dead air with an inert quality all its own. Indeed, the artificial injection of silence into either opus 6 or opus 10—by suddenly turning down the volume control of a unit on which it is being reproduced and as suddenly turning it up again—leaves some sense of interruption, of discontinuity. In opus 30, the same procedure leaves little sense of anything omitted or absent: the next burst of sound has as much identity, or lack of it, as it does when heard in the original context.

In dealing with these later, and last, works, it is customary for Webern's partisans to dwell on the marvels of construction embodied in the score, on the miracles of the canonic relationships they contain, the occurrence in reverse, at a later point, of what originally had been written forward, etc. (though George Perle properly notes: "The appearance of strict canonic forms in a twelve-tone work is in itself no indication of any remarkable ingenuity . . . since the relationships that define these forms are automatically provided by the precompositional operations of the twelve-tone system").[4] In the Variations, the technical feat that prompts the enthusiasts to enthusiasm is the derivation of the work's total content from the first two measures.

Rarely is there reference to connotations of *meaning* in the music. In describing these Variations to the critic Willi Reich, Webern insisted: "This new system does not overlook the laws that are inherent in the nature of tone. This would indeed be impossible if what is expressed in tones is still to make sense. And no one will seriously maintain that we do not want to make sense."[5]

It would be comforting, indeed reassuring, if the implication of "making sense" carried the inevitable corollary of "making music." It has never necessarily been so, nor is it likely ever to be. To achieve the end and then be able to explain it is admirable; but to proclaim an explanation without providing the persuasion that an end demands is to falsify the nature of the experience and deny the nature of the problem.

What could be more demonstrably the *reductio ad absurdum* of an art on which so much time, thought, and genius have been expended to evolve ever more meaningful combinations of sound than that terminal consideration be given to a composer who was at his most distinctive in the utilization of silence? But it is no more a contradiction than a discussion, at length and on a high level of learning, of structural details that can be seen but not heard; or of derivations

[4] George Perle: *Serial Composition and Atonality* (Berkeley and Los Angeles: University of California Press; 1963), p. 131.

[5] *Composers on Music*, ed. Sam Morgenstern (New York: Pantheon Books, Inc.; 1956), p. 457. The letter is dated May 3, 1941.

and analogies that can be charted but not articulated; or definitions of values in an art long considered peerless for what it expresses, arouses or assuages in terms of "events," "happenings," "incidents," and "regions of influence."

If Webern's projection of what "makes sense" does not "make music," it is nevertheless logical that those who deny not merely development of a theme but also the old need for one, and who proclaim the new need to "do away with the last two mainstays of tonal music: theme and the continuity of musical discourse"[6] should not merely welcome but rejoice that continuity itself, in this sector of the musical experience, has come to an end and that the rest, in the words of the most memorable of poets, may be silence.

[6] André Hodeir: *Since Debussy* (New York: Grove Press; 1961), p. 52.

X

Isolation or Synthesis?

WHAT EMERGES FROM the accumulated evidence of the preceding pages is inevitable, indeed inescapable. It is the clear evidence of an interruption in the long sequence of continuity which prevailed over centuries, a division of direction in which some of the ablest and most greatly talented men of this century have turned away from the common path and set out upon one of their own.

Fundamentally, the Pan-European musical language that served the needs of composers for a long series of decades (in the New World as well as the Old) has been challenged by another procedure, the proponents of which make the apparently persuasive claim that it is a no less satisfactory means of expression, with the attractive advantages of a ready-made, built-in discipline.

No music lover with a serious interest in his avocation is unaware of this challenge. Nor would he deny the conclusion reached by those for whom it is a vocation that the Pan-European musical language has, for some time, been in crisis. For whatever cause, and despite the appearance of much work of high quality, there has not been, for more than fifty years, a forward thrust to its development such as was imparted by Stravinsky, and before him by Debussy, when, in the words of the latter, "Wagner's curve" had been accomplished.

Both the serious interest and the crisis demand consideration of and, if at all possible, an answer to the questions:

Do the results possible with the alternatives devised by Schoenberg satisfy the criteria that were applied to the works of the former period, from which emerged a musical literature recognized as great?

Do these alternatives provide a valid way around the "mountain" whose existence Mahler and Strauss recognized as a block on the highway of musical travel, or do they amount, actually, to a detour into a cul-de-sac?

To resolve this dilemma and substitute clarity for confusion, at least in the minds of listeners, it might be well to review the range of possibilities presented by what I call the "Pan-European" language and compare them with those available in Schoenberg's alternative.

There is, in the older system, an infinity of concepts and values that have enabled generations of composers from a wide variety of backgrounds to find an idiom of their own within it, or to shape an existing idiom into a dialect suitable for their purposes. It works, it endures, it communicates. For an alternative to be acceptable it must bear scrutiny in terms of the same requirements: Does it work? Will it endure? Can it communicate?

From the mass of material previously cited emerges the inescapable conclusion that there exists, within the music created during the eighteenth and nineteenth centuries, a network of interrelated elements from which a fabric of musical meaning has evolved. It is made up of enormously variegated, flexible, and responsive tonal values. They have an extraordinary affinity for aural recognition, mental recollection, and emotional response. According to the ingenuity and resourcefulness of the user, these tonal values can be used separately or in combination; they can be drawn out, abbreviated, and subjected to an infinity of interweavings, tensions, and counterpulls.

The implications of this conclusion are far-reaching and pervasive. They go to the heart of musical comprehension, meaning, and emotional response. It is the durable relationship of these values, however much stress is put upon them, however much color is added to them, which makes a language out of a scientific phenomenon. It is much more than the *lingua franca* of a time or place. It affiliates those who spoke it with one vocabulary in the eighteenth century with those who speak it in a vastly expanded form in the twentieth. Indeed the elaboration of the vocabulary has vastly broadened the appeal of what is being said. Even today, it is those with the strongest links to the past in their writing who have the clearest channel of communication to the audience of the present.

Whether or not the composers of today who sustain such a link are conscious of their continuity, they unquestionably reacted to it. That, in a short sentence, is the way in which music evolved in this whole long period, and continues to evolve.

Whether or not the composers of the past were conscious of continuity, it is present in the music they wrote. That is the way it has been heard, understood, evaluated: in a frame of reference to other music, in response to the typical and the atypical, with an awareness of imitation or propagation, whether or not the listener has analyzed it as such.

It may be stated as an axiom (additional to all the other axioms previously set forth in this text) that music possessed of lasting appeal is rarely *all* new, *totally* different from what has been heard and enjoyed previously. Often enough, the listening experience is on two levels, in which sustaining threads of the old carry the seemingly strange threads of the new. There is, for example, more than enough in *Le Sacre du printemps* which is profoundly, essentially Russian to give Stravinsky an honored place in the continuity of Mussorgsky and Rimsky-Korsakov. *Le Sacre* makes the ground shudder under its revolutionary rhythmic impact, but the ground itself is adjacent to that occupied by Stravinsky's predecessors. The schism that has put those firmly attached to the Pan-European musical language on one side of an aesthetic chasm and those committed to Schoenberg's alternative on the other is the result of more than a theoretical disagreement.

On the one side are grouped all those (and their number includes much the larger segment of the musical community) who are neither enslaved to tonality as it existed, expanded, and altered through the decades, nor committed to its negation. Whether by reason or by instinct, they recognize the need for a tonal border. Its existence, like that of the physical border of a state or the metaphysical border of the universe, is a *necessary frame of reference within which, or even outside of which, related happenings occur.* In the absence of such a perimeter, border, or point of reference, space is a vacuum, time is without meaning, and the elements of order dissolve into chaos.

No law that is anarchical can establish sense by the vigor of its pronouncement, if the basis for sense is lacking in it. No stern pronouncement that sea water should be drunk instead of fresh water will sustain life if sea water is not a life-sustaining substance. If Schoenberg's alternative is lacking an element vital to comprehension, no jubilant pronouncement of its logic, mathematical justice, or, even, divine ordination will make it what it is not or enable those on its side of the chasm to communicate with those on the other.

Without a point of tonal reference—stated or implied, established or understood—aural relationships are deprived of an element as vital to musical comprehension as syntax is to verbal comprehension. The lack of such a link does more than isolate one section of a musical statement from another: it isolates the successive sections of a work from each other and, of course, isolates any single work of a composer from all his others. It inevitably follows that an aural continuity from one composer to another, such as herein described, becomes an impossibility.

In dispensing with all the infinity of resources that have accrued to the Pan-European language over the decades and are lacking in Schoenberg's alternative—the psychological effect of the interchange of major and minor, modulation, enharmony, the cadential play and its delay, extension, or evasion (to name but a few)—the most serious deprivation of all is isolation from the aural interchange of thought or influence with others. What is created with the Method remains an impersonal experience for the listener because its available resources permit little play of personality on the part of the composer. In the recently increasing instances in which volitional exception has been taken to the Law, it is obvious that the basic premise has been flouted, that something other than Schoenberg's alternative is at work.

If this conclusion seems arbitrary and the precepts derived from such a hypothetical concept as "continuity" insufficient for so sweeping a judgment, the case is by no means closed. It is subject to sustaining evidence from other sources, based on other points of view. Indeed, the variety of such points of view serves to supplement rather than merely to duplicate the weight of influence they convey. Tangential as the direction may be from which each point of view emerges, they tend to converge on the same focal finding.

In his study titled *Tonality Atonality Pantonality* the late Rudolph Reti addressed himself to the embracing concept known to Schoenberg and his disciples as "the emancipation of the dissonance." Says Reti: "Schoenberg believed that whether an interval, or for that matter a combination of intervals, a chord, constitutes a consonance or a dissonance is only a question of habit, of convention, almost of fashion. . . . Alluring as it may have seemed around the turn of the century when the musical avant-garde searched for a way out of the old restrictive tenets, it can hardly from any sober historical or musical point of view be maintained as serious thesis.[1]

"As a justification for the general introduction of more and more dissonance," Reti continues, Schoenberg "suggested that the disso-

[1] Rudolph Reti: *Tonality Atonality Pantonality* (New York: The Macmillan Company; 1958), p. 38.

nances represent the 'remote overtones' (in contrast to the close overtones called consonances in traditional theory). Now it is all too well-known that in a physical-acoustical sense the overtone series can be expanded beyond the third, seventh, or even ninth. But it is very doubtful whether in a musical sense we hear these further intervals as overtones . . ."

In sum, Reti says (p. 39): "Schoenberg confused two different problems. He was entirely right and only expressed the trend of the time in his *aesthetic* claim that further intervals and chord combinations, apart from the customary ones, should be permitted in the harmonic palette. But he was somewhat naïvely wrong in assuming that therefore the musical difference between all these intervals would be . . . done away with."

So much for the legitimacy of dissonance as the guiding factor in composition. Suppose that Reti is in error, what is the possibility of the listener's relating, mentally, to what he hears in a typical example of a work produced with Schoenberg's alternative? In his volume titled *40,000 Years of Music*, Jacques Chailley dwells on just that consideration. He cites a series of experiments reported by R. Frances in *La Perception de la musique*.[2] They showed, says Chailley, "that professionals, experts in the serial technique, were unable, even in quite simple examples conforming to the principles laid down by the theoreticians in this field, to determine which of the pre-arranged series was the one on which the piece in question was based."[3]

Recognizing the possibility that a composer may nevertheless derive mental stimulation from the manipulation of his materials, Chailley asks if it is possible for this "speculative satisfaction" to be conveyed to the listener. In answer to his own question, he declares: "If we take as a criterion the ability on the part of the hearer to identify and reconstruct mentally the composer's often elaborate treament of his series, we shall be obliged in the light of the experiment described above to answer frankly no."

Should both "the emancipation of the dissonance" and the recognizability of the row be accepted as valid principles in spite of the arguments cited herein, what of the scheme of using the twelve evenly separated steps of the chromatic scale as the nucleus of an alternative? After years of investigation prompted by his twin interests, music and mathematics, the noted Swiss conductor Ernest Ansermet reached the

[2] R. Frances: *La Perception de la musique* (Paris: Vrin; 1958), p. 140.
[3] Jacques Chailley: *40,000 Years of Music* (New York: Farrar, Straus and Giroux; 1960), p. 133.

conclusion that the premise of a method built on the division of the octave into twelve equidistant tones was, of itself, unsound. Aside from the practical consequences of robbing one scale step of the influence it may possess *vis-à-vis* another (the leading tone's inclination to a resolution or the super-tonic's gravitational pull to the tonic), "the principle," Ansermet says, "of twelve-tone technique is to found tonal structures on a series of twelve tones—our twelve chromatic notes taken in any order —which, says Schoenberg, are *not related to each other . . .*

1   2   3   4   5   6   7   8   9   10   11   12

"Now, our auditory preception being logarithmic, the law of auditory perception, like that of a logarithmic series, is to relate the tonal positions which come into play in music to the first position to appear.

1

2

3

5

4   .

"Twelve-tone music may have an external form: it cannot have an internal form, it is without foundation and this is enough to condemn it."[4]

The whole of Ansermet's presentation, I have no hesitation in saying, invokes mathematical principles beyond my comprehension. But I can understand, support, and endorse his contention—based on his investigations as well as the intuitions that motivated them—that it is the natural impulse of man to express himself tonally: "If the musician does not write 'tonally' it is because he compels himself not to write tonally, and in this case his music is as incomprehensible as the speech of a man who does not comply with the syntax of his language."[5]

In a series of papers devoted to the phenomenon of "Mind and Matter in Music,"[6] Gerhard Albersheim of the Department of Music

[4] *Recorded Sound: The Journal of the British Institute of Recorded Sound,* No. 13 (January 1964), p. 175.

[5] Ibid., p. 171.

[6] *The Journal of Aesthetics and Art Criticism* (U.S.), XXII, 3 (Spring 1964).

of the Los Angeles State College of Applied Arts and Sciences goes a step beyond Reti, Frances, Chailley, and Ansermet to take a piercing view of the Schoenberg alternative as a totality. Rather than challenging the legitimacy of the dissonance (which may find ears better attuned to it fifty years hence than those of this generation), the memorability of the row (perhaps in a hundred years it may be more memorable), or the logarithmics of Schoenberg's principle (figures, too, may lie), Albersheim applies his analysis to the basic, underlying consideration: Is the creation of a method without tonal feeling a positive achievement from which productive results can flow? Says Albersheim, "Atonality is not the positive achievement of a new order in music, but . . . the conscious abrogation of the hitherto prevailing order."[7] To paraphrase his contention in lay language: the Schoenberg alternative is based less on a breakthrough than on a breakdown.

What remains, then, of Schoenberg's prognosis of the future of his method? The answer is: Nothing.

If dissonance is not the same, physically, as consonance, and objection to a method based upon it is conditioned by more than custom, as Reti contends, then the resistance to it will not be overcome "in time."

If the fundamental premise is faulty, as Ansermet suggests, then the twelve notes are not "related only to each other," as Schoenberg's alternative proclaims, but are in unhappy contention with each other.

If the constructions made of them have no connection with a memory of the elements that entered into them, they are no longer contingencies of meaning, symbols of thought conveyed from a creative source to a conscious respondent, but mere counters of vibrational values in what Albersheim appropriately terms "noise music." Or, as Ansermet phrases the phenomenon of a "reaction" to such an expression: "However bizarre the structures, the listener receives affective *impressions* from them, but these are momentary impressions which do not add up, which do not link up in an event of unitary meaning. . . . In short, one can no longer comprehend, because to comprehend is to grasp the whole, the unity of meaning in a thing."[8]

As counters of what I call "vibrational values," the individual tones may take on the role of "parameters." That is to say, they have length, degrees of force, impact, timbre—all of which are indices to memorability. But they are like the index to a nonexistent book. They relate to no ordered structure possessed of memorability as it is musically under-

[7] Ibid., p. 27.　　　　　　　　　　[8] *Recorded Sound*, p. 175.

stood. Without memorability, all other attributes are meaningless and the claims made on their behalf are fatuous.

As stated previously (p. 357), a quintessential trait of the Pan-European musical language is that it possesses "an extraordinary affinity for aural recognition, mental recollection, and emotional response." An acceptable alternative to it, though failing on one count, could command consideration if it possessed the two others; or it could claim attention by sustaining one requirement now, and giving promise of satisfying others in the future. But when it fails, after nearly fifty years of prominence and promotion, to fulfill even *one* of these criteria, the chances of its eventually being accepted as a useful alternative to a tonal language that has, for centuries, satisfied all three may be described as negligible.

It would, however, be unrealistic to ignore the efforts of some composers to make Schoenberg's alternative less rigorous and more usable. Indeed, the clear evidence is that doctrinaire adherence to Schoenberg's alternative as he conceived it is dwindling (save in circles where it is taught as a kind of Academic Modern). A variety of modified but still codified alternatives to his alternative has come into currency. In one scheme, the twelve tones may be divided into two series of six tones each (which provide an illusion of contrast) or grouped vertically in a sonority that has a chordlike formation. Or they may serve the purpose that Milton Babbitt has defined as "combinatoriality." If they maintain allegiance to the concept of twelve tones separated by half steps, in a discipline that forbids use of the octave or any repetition with the mere implication of tonality, they remain, in my view, hostile to what Ansermet calls "the natural impulse of man to express himself tonally." Such modifications may offer greater latitude for manipulation —they do not provide increased opportunity for understanding.

Nor is the dissatisfaction with such weaknesses—acoustical, aesthetic, and psychological—of the Schoenberg alternative restricted to those with, perhaps, a built-in opposition to it, as Berlioz had a built-in opposition to enharmony. A conductor of my acquaintance who had but recently performed the Schoenberg Piano Concerto answered, in response to my question: "No, I cannot bring any portions of it to mind, as I can recollect literally thousands of older works . . . except a spot here and there where it becomes almost tonal." In a lecture delivered at the University of Cincinnati a few years ago, pianist-composer Glenn Gould, who has recorded sizeable quantities of Schoenberg, raised the query: "What, then, has really been the effect of this new world of sound introduced by Schoenberg?" The answer to his own question was: "I think there can be no doubt that its fundamental effect has been to separate audience and composer. One doesn't like to admit this, but it is true nevertheless."[9]

In separating himself, as a performer, from those who comprised his presumptive listeners, Gould was, in a sense, affiliating himself with others, like the late Dimitri Mitropoulos, who were absorbed by what was happening "in the kitchen,"[1] and thus were participants in the "speculative satisfaction" recognized by Chailley (p. 360). But, as Chailley makes clear, this cannot be passed on to the listener.

It is, however, essential to recognize that Schoenberg's alternative embodies not one principle, but two principles. By far the better known, because it can be verbalized readily, is the fundamental *dictat*, the arrangement of tones from which TMOCWTTROWOA takes its name. But there is also the mode of elaboration Schoenberg devised to provide a structural element that would, in the absence of cadences, key relationships, or the vaguest suggestion of them, otherwise be lacking.

The part of it invented by Schoenberg, and promulgated as his Law, has been examined and rejected for several divergent but complementary reasons: the twelve-tone idiom is without relevance to a prior aural continuity and shows no possibility of becoming part of a future one; what is expressed within it is not recognizable as an intelligible entity even by practiced listeners; it is in contempt of fundamental acoustical principles; it conveys only random impressions that result in "noise music."

But the concept of "developing variations"—Perle provides the alternate phrasing of "perpetually varied restatements"[2]—has a relationship to prior practice; it confers some advantages of manipulation and procedure; it is an acceptable alternative to other means of coordinating the interplay of sound and sustaining lines of thought; it has an application to broader aesthetic, emotional, and acoustical needs than the limited ones set forth by Schoenberg.

Lest it be supposed that the reference is simply to the classical kind of variation in which a theme was stated, then reharmonized, fragmented, or otherwise disguised before being given a triumphal restate-

[9] Glenn Gould: *Arnold Schoenberg, A Perspective* (Cincinnati: University of Cincinnati; 1964), Occasional Papers No. 3, p. 17.
[1] Mitropoulos used the expression to me when I encountered him in the aftermath of a performance of the Schoenberg Piano Concerto in which the soloist, by a curious coincidence, was Gould.
[2] George Perle: *Serial Composition and Atonality* (Berkeley and Los Angeles: University of California Press; 1963), p. 4.

Brahms: String Quartet, A minor (op. 51, No. 2), andante

ment in its original form, citation may be made of a movement of
Brahms that Schoenberg admired as generative of "developing variations"[3]: the andante of the A-minor Quartet (opus 51, No. 2). It was
also a procedure to which Mahler was partial, whether by derivation
from Brahms or not, and which he extolled in a letter to Bauer-Lechner
(p. 263) in the words: "According to my belief there should be no
plain repetition, but everything should go forward developing." Such
an unfolding, unwinding, constantly altering line provides the adagio
of Mahler's incomplete Tenth Symphony with a fascinating prevision
of things to come—preferably in his way rather than Schoenberg's, or
in Berg's way of the Violin Cóncerto.

Some composers of considerable stature—among them Stravinsky,
Ginastera, Britten, and Copland—have explored the possibilties of
adapting the principle of "developing variations" to musical shapes or

[3] Arnold Schoenberg: *Style and Idea* (New York: Philosophical Library; 1950),
p. 88.

germinal phrases that are not dodecaphonic. Some of the results, as encountered in Britten's *War Requiem,* Ginastera's Violin Concerto and *Bomarzo,* and Copland's *Inscape,* are not merely hopeful but also promising.

The laws of logic as well as the lessons of history suggest that the dilemma confronting contemporary composition must and will be resolved by a synthesis of the values presently available on both sides of the chasm (which, providentially, the dictionary defines as "the interruption of continuity . . ."). As synthesis itself has the meaning (in surgery) of "reuniting divided or separated structures," the outcome would be to bring together the strengths latent in the Pan-European language with the one element of the Schoenberg alternative derived from the past: the principle of "developing variations."

Thus would isolation be resolved, community of impulse restored, and continuity confirmed.

POSTSCRIPT

I N THE TONS OF PAPER turned over to produce the foregoing text, perhaps the weightiest ounce was the one on which W. A. Mozart was denounced as a "sectary (*settore*) of the false system that divides the octave into twelve equal semi-tones."[1] To be sure, in his scathing condemnation of Mozart, Giuseppe Sarti (1729–1802) was referring to quite another kind of "twelve-tone" writing than that proposed in the Schoenberg alternative and its alternatives. Sarti was baring his fangs at a "clavier player who could not distinguish between D-sharp and E-flat" in writing the introduction, with its crossing voices and clashing dissonances, to Mozart's C-major Quartet (K. 465).

Whether Sarti was irked more by what he saw than by what he heard is undocumented. But his comment is indicative of an aesthetic division of that time which had to be resolved, exactly as there is an aesthetic division of this time which has to be resolved. To say that its resolution would guarantee the emergence of a new Mozart would be to invoke a rare order of clairvoyance. It is, however, a certainty that without such a resolution there will not again be anything remotely comparable to Mozart.

[1] Ernest Newman: *A Musical Critic's Holiday* (New York: Alfred A. Knopf; 1925), p. 158.

Index

Abbiati, Franco: on Berlioz's views of Verdi, 124

Abraham, Gerald: on origins of Chopin's musical style, 41–3; on Chopin's pianistic orientation, 48; on Chopin's influence on Liszt and Wagner, 80, 84; on comparison of Berlioz and Wagner, 112–13

"Affaire Ravel, L'," 294

Albéniz, Isaac: Ernest Newman on, 61

Albersheim, Gerhard: on atonality, 361–362

D'Albert, Eugène, and Strauss's *Burleske*, 186

Alfvén, Hugo, 59–60

Altenberg, Peter, 331–2; *see also* Berg, Alban

D'Annunzio, Gabriele: on Debussy, 274; *Martyre de Saint Sébastien, Le*, 290

Ansermet, Ernest: on twelve-tone composition, 360

Antheil, George: in re *Le Sacre du printemps*, 318

Artaria (publishers), 13, 15

Auer, Max: on Wagner's influence on Bruckner, 169

Axioms: I, 32; II, 32; III, 32; IV, 43; V, 44; VI, 88; VII, 89

Babbitt, Milton, 363

Bach, Carl Philip Emanuel, 9, 12; Beethoven's admiration for, 14

Bach, Johann Sebastian, 3–5, 9–10, 14, 41, 52; and the enharmonic, 104

Well-Tempered Clavier, The, 104

Bach Gesellschaft, Die Neue, 239

Baillot Quartet, 96

Balakirev, Mili, 134–8, 140–3; and

Glinka, 135, 137; and Mussorgsky, 136

Fantasy on Czech Themes, 137

Ballet Russe, 303, 316, 318, 322

Barricelli, Jean-Pierre and Weinstein, Leo: on Chausson and Debussy, 292–293

Bartók, Béla, 38, 200, 220, 249, 296–9; and Beethoven, 38; and Strauss, 200; and Mahler, 249; and Debussy, 296–9; and Stravinsky, 318

Concerto for Orchestra, 219–20, 249

Music for Strings, Percussion, and Celesta, 38, 249

Barzun, Jacques: on Berlioz's early years, 90, 95; on Berlioz and Beethoven, 95–6; on Berlioz's criticism of abuse of appoggiaturas, 107; similarities of Verdi's Requiem and Berlioz's, 125; on Berlioz in the continuity of music, 156

Bauer-Lechner, Natalie: Mahler correspondence, 214, 217, 226–7, 230, 263

Bayreuth Festival (1876), 153

Beethoven, Ludwig van, 5, 11, 12–30, 33, 38–9, 41, 46–7, 51, 58, 64, 96, 98–9, 101, 162, 168, 173–5, 177, 202–3, 231; and Bach, 5, 14; and Cimarosa, 13; and Dittersdorf, 13; and Gluck, 13; and Haydn, 13–14, 22, 24; and Mozart, 13, 16–20, 24–5, 202–3; and Paisiello, 13; and Carl Philip Emanuel Bach, 14; and Clementi, 14; and Handel, 14; and Rossini, 14; and Spohr, 14; his use of dissonance, 51

Choral Fantasy, C minor (op. 80), 22–3

Beethoven (*continued*)
  Fidelio, 22, 26
  Piano Concerto No. 3 (op. 37), 19
  Piano Concerto No. 4 (op. 58), 23
  Piano Concerto No. 5 (op. 73), 23
  Piano Sonata (op. 13) ("*Pathétique*"), 25
  Piano Sonata (op. 90), 26
  Piano Sonata (op. 106) ("*Hammerklavier*"), 33, 41
  Quartets (op. 59) ("*Rasumovsky*"), 58
  Quartet (op. 131): Wagner on, 69–70; Berlioz on, 96
  Quartet (op. 135), 231
  symphonies, 16, 17, 20, 22, 24, 27–8, 30, 39, 98–9, 162, 168, 173–5, 176–7, 201–2; No. 3 ("*Eroica*"), 20, 22, 27–8, 39, 201–2; No. 9, 22, 98–9, 162, 168, 174, 176–7
  Violin Concerto in D major (op. 61), 18–19, 23
Bekker, Paul: on Wagner as a composer for the stage, 65
Bellini, Vincenzo, 4, 44–5
  Pirata, Il, 45
  Sonnambula, La, 45
Berg, Alban, 210, 267, 324–40; and Mahler, 210, 325, 329, 331, 333, 341; and Schoenberg, 267, 324–6, 328, 330, 332, 336–7, 339–42; and Wagner, 326–7, 330; and Hugo Wolf, 326; and Strauss, 328–9
  Altenberg songs, 331–2
  Concerto for Violin and Orchestra, 339–40
  Kammerkonzert, 336–8
  Lulu, 267, 324, 339–40
  Lyric Suite, 338–9
  Piano Sonata (op. 1), 328
  Seven Early Songs, 325–7
  String Quartet (op. 3), 328
  Wozzeck, 267, 325, 332–6
Berg, Helene (Nahowski), 331
Berger, Arthur: on *Petrouchka*, 308, 311
Berio, Luciano, 4
Berlioz, Hector, 24, 30, 53, 66, 71, 85–122, 124–34, 136, 138–9, 141, 213; and Beethoven, 24, 30, 95–101; and Chopin, 53, 57, 101–2, 106, 113; and Wagner, 85–8, 109–10, 112, 114–15, 122; on *Tristan* prelude, 85; his early years, 90–2; and Gluck, 90–2; and Weber, 92–3; and the piano, 103–4; and harmony, 106–8; his *Treatise on Instrumentation*, 111; and Gounod, 117; and Verdi, 124–9; and Russian composers, 129–34, 136, 138–9, 141
  Béatrice et Bénédict, 129
  Carnaval romain, 87

  Damnation de Faust, La, 87, 97, 117–19, 129–30, 141
  Enfance du Christ, L', 124
  Francs-Juges, Les, 91–2, 95, 102
  Grande Symphonie funèbre et triomphale, 66
  Harold en Italie, 66, 90, 98, 100–1, 106, 120
  Nuits d'été, 114, 116,
  Roméo et Juliette, 66, 71, 87, 98, 108, 112, 117
  Requiem, 87, 126
  Symphonie fantastique, 66, 87, 97–98, 102, 213
  Troyens, Les, 90, 122
  Waverley Overture, 89, 91
Bizet, Georges, 55, 152–3; and Wagner, 152–3
  Carmen, 153
  Djamileh, 153
  Pêcheurs de perles, Les, 153
Borodin, Alexander, 34, 136, 143
Boulanger, Nadia: on origins of Debussy's pianistic style, 50–1; on Debussy and Mussorgsky, 278, 281; on origins of Debussy's harmonic style, 50–1, 281; on Debussy and impressionist painting style, 287; on Debussy and Stravinsky, 299; on *Le Sacre du printemps*, 311
Boulez, Pierre: and Olivier Messiaen, 311
Brahms, Johannes, 17, 19, 27, 29–33, 35, 38, 160–3, 166, 168, 185, 194, 245, 365; and Beethoven, 27, 31, 33, 38, 162; and Wagner, 160–3
  Academic Festival Overture, 163, 166
  Alto Rhapsody (op. 53), 245
  Gesang der Parzen, 185
  Piano Concerto No. 1, D minor, 187
  Piano Concerto No. 2, B flat (op. 83), 35
  Piano Sonata No. 1 (op. 1), 33
  Piano Sonata No. 3 (op. 5), 168
  Serenade in D (op. 11), 17
  Symphony No. 1, C minor (op. 68), 27, 29–31
  Violin Concerto in D (op. 77), 19
Braunstein, Joseph, 74
Brayer, Julien de, 274
Breitkopf und Härtel (publishers), 12
Bruch, Max, 106, 148–9, 184; and Wagner, 148
  Kol Nidrei, 148
  Violin Concerto, G minor, 148–9, 184
Bruckner, Anton, 7, 31, 149, 163, 168–178; visits to Vienna for studies with Sechter, 170, 182–3; and Beethoven, 31, 168, 172–7; and Wagner, 149,

Bruckner (*continued*)
 163, 168–9, 171, 176–7, 182–3; and
 Mahler, 211–13, 252
 masses, 169
 symphonies, 163, 170–2, 174–8,
 183
 Te Deum, 171
Büchner, Georg, 332, 334
Bülow, Hans von: and Wagner, 79,
 146; and Strauss, 185–6, 198; and
 Mahler, 209
Busoni, Ferruccio, 4
Buxtehude, Dietrich, 9

Cage, John, 7
Cardus, Neville: on Mahler and Wagner,
 226
Chabrier, Emmanuel, 56, 133, 153–7,
 282; and Wagner, 153–7
 España, 133
 *Quadrille sur les principaux motifs
 de Tristan*, 157
 Roi malgré lui, Le, 154
Chailley, Jacques: on serialism, 360
Charpentier, Gustave, 110–11
 Impressions of Italy, 111
 Louise, 111
Chausson, Ernest, 5, 56, 154–5, 292–3;
 and Wagner, 5, 56, 155, 292; and
 Debussy, 292–3
 Hélène, 155
 Poème, 155, 293
 Roi Arthus, Le, 155
Cherubini, Luigi, 14
Chopin, Frédéric, 41–62, 81–4, 101–2,
 106; and Field, 43; and Hummel, 43–
 44; and Schubert, 43; and Bellini, 44–
 45; and Berlioz, 53, 101–2; and Liszt,
 54; and Rimsky-Korsakov, 62; and
 Wagner, 81, 83–4
 Ballade No. 1, G minor (op. 23),
 48–50
 Ballade No. 2, F major (op. 38),
 41
 Études, 48
 Mazurkas, 58–62, 84
 Nocturnes (op. 37), 41
 Prelude No. 23, F (op. 28), 50
Cimarosa, Domenico, 4, 13
Clementi, Muzio, 12, 14
Cooke, Deryck, 251
Cooper, Martin: on French music, 144;
 on French music and Wagner, 154–7
Copland, Aaron, 61, 291, 318
Couperin, François, 56
Cowell, Henry, 7
Craft, Robert: on Schoenberg and We-
 bern, 346
Cui, César, 136, 143

Dallapiccola, Luigi, 4

Dannreuther, Edward: on Wagner and
 Goethe's *Faust*, 70,
Dargomijsky, Alexander, 136, 143
Debussy, Claude Achille, 3, 50, 55–6,
 110–11, 144–5, 157, 159, 258, 261,
 274–83, 286–91, 299, 313, 319, 321;
 and Chopin, 50, 55–6, 286–7; and
 Berlioz, 110–11, 144–5, 289; and
 Mussorgsky, 274, 276, 278, 283; and
 Naḍejda von Meck, 275–6; and
 Tchaikovsky, 275–7; and Wagner,
 276–7, 288, 291, 321; and Fauré, 277,
 281, 283; and D'Indy, 278–9; and
 Chabrier, 281; and Liszt, 281–7; and
 Ravel, 287, 293–4; and Stravinsky,
 300, 316–17, 319, 321
 Après-midi d'un faune, L', 111, 276–
 277, 283, 286, 293
 "Beau Soir," 275–7
 Damoiselle élue, La, 276, 279–83
 Douze Études, 288
 Enfant prodigue, L', 275
 "Fêtes," 111, 278, 289
 Golliwog's Cakewalk, 159
 Hommage à Rameau, 3
 Île Joyeuse, L', 286
 Jardins sous la pluie (prelude), 55
 Jeux, 290
 Martyre de Saint Sébastien, Le, 290–
 291
 Mer, La, 289–90
 "Nuages," 289, 313
 Nuit d'étoiles, 275
 Pelléas et Mélisande, 111, 258, 293
 Suite bergamasque, 286
 Vent dans la plaine, Le ("Winter
 Wind" Étude), 55
Debussysme, 293–4
Delibes, Léo, 122
 Sylvia, 122
Del Mar, Norman: on Bruch and Strauss,
 184–5; on Strauss, 186, 189
Deutsch, Otto E.: on Schubert, 44
Diaghilev, Serge, 290, 303, 306, 316,
 318–19, 322
Dittersdorf, Karl Ditters von, 13
Donizetti, Gaetano, 4
Downes, Olin, 74
Dukas, Paul, 122
Duparc, Henri, 153–4
Dvořák, Antonin, 4, 34–7; and Brahms,
 34–5; and Wagner, 34–6
 Carnival Overture, 36
 Slavonic Dances, 34
 Slavonic Rhapsodies, 34
 Suite (op. 39), 34
 Symphony No. 7, D minor (op. 70),
 35–6
 Symphony No. 9 (op. 95) ("New
 World"), 34
École Boulanger, 61

Eisler, Hanns, 268
Engel, Gabriel: on Mahler and Wagner, 226
Enharmony, 104–8, 154; and the piano, 104–5
Exposition universelle (1899): Russian music at the, 143–4, 157, 181

Falla, Manuel de, 30, 61, 295–7; and Beethoven, 30; and Debussy, 295–6; and Stravinsky, 296
    Noches en los jardines de España, 295
    Sombrero de tres picos, El, 30, 296–7
    Vida breve, La, 295
Fauré, Gabriel, 56, 122, 153; and Wagner, 153; and Debussy, 277
    "Après un rêve," 277
    Ballade (op. 19), 153
    Bonne Chanson, La, 153
    Shylock, 153
Felber, Rudolf: on Hummel, 44
Fétis, François-Joseph, 42–3, 46; on Chopin, 42–3, 46; *Revue musicale*, 42
Field, John, 41, 43, 54
Franck, César, 154
    Éolides, Les, 154
    Quartet in D minor, 154
    Sonata for piano and violin, 154

Gade, Niels, 5
Gál, Hans: on Brahms and Beethoven, 162; on Bruckner and Wagner, 183 *n.*
Gesangsperiode, 174
Gilman, Lawrence: on Liszt and Wagner, 73–4, 74 *n.*
Gershwin, George: and Chopin, 55
Giordano, Umberto, 4
Glazunov, Alexander, 143, 181
Glinka, Mikhail, 61, 130–5, 143; and Berlioz, 130–3; and Liszt, 132
    Jota aragonesa, 133
    Kamarinskaya, 133, 135
    Life for the Tsar, A, 130
    Russlan and Ludmilla, 130–1
    Summer Night in Madrid, 133
Gluck, Christoph Willibald, 4, 13, 93
    Alceste, 92–3
Gounod, Charles, 116–17, 119, 121; and Berlioz, 87, 116–17
    Faust, 87, 116–17, 119, 121
Granados, Enrique: and Chopin, 61 and *n.*
Gretchaninoff, Alexander, 181
Grétry, André, 13
Grieg, Edvard: 4–5, 222; his "Law," 5
    Piano Concerto, A minor (op. 16), 5
    Peer Gynt Suite No. 1, 222
Grundgestalt, 271

Habeneck, François-Antoine, 67, 95
Hale, Philip: on Strauss's *Ein Heldenleben*, 201
Halski, Czeslaw R.: on Chopin's mazurkas, 59
Handel, George Frideric, 3, 9–11, 14; Westminster Abbey Festival (1791), 10–11
    Israel in Egypt, 11
    Messiah, 11
    Solomon, 9
    Zadok the Priest, 11
Haraucourt, Edmund, 153
Härtel, Gottfried Christoph, 12; *see also* Breitkopf und Härtel
Haydn, Franz Joseph, 10–14; trip to England, 10–11; and Handel, 11, 17, 22–4, 57–8; and Mozart, 11; and Beethoven, 14, 22; and other composers, 24
    Creation, The, 11, 17
    quartets (op. 33 and 76), 11
    Seasons, The, 11
    "Salomon" symphonies, 14
Hebbel, Friedrich, 330
Hedley, Arthur: on Chopin and the Italian school, 45
Hell, Henry: on Poulenc and Debussy, 294
Henschel, Georg, 161–2
Heuberger, Richard: on Brahms and Wagner, 162
Hérold, Louis Joseph, 107
    Zampa, 107
Hindemith, Paul, 3, 249; on Beethoven, 39
    Mathis der Mahler, 249
Hodeir, André, *vis-à-vis* continuity, 355
Hofmannsthal, Hugo von, 206–7
Holst, Gustav, 318
Honegger, Arthur, 122, 291; on absolute originality, 284
    Jeanne d'Arc au bûcher, 122, 291
    Roi David, Le, 122
Hummel, Johann Nepomuk, 41, 43–4
    Septet (op. 74), 44
Humperdinck, Engelbert, 182, 200
    Hänsel und Gretel, 182, 200
Huneker, James G.: on Chopin's G-minor Ballade, 48
Hungerford, Bruce: recordings of Wagner's piano music, 64 *n.*

Idée fixe, 98–101
Indy, Vincent d', 153, 156–7, 279; and *Aïda*, 125; and Wagner, 157
    Chant de la cloche, Le, 157
    Étranger, L', 157
    Fervaal, 157
    Symphony on a French Mountain Air, 57

"Innsbruck, ich muss dich lassen," 57
Ippolitov-Ivanov, Mikhail, 181
Ives, Charles, 205, 324

Jacobsen, Jens Peter, 257
Janáček, Leoš, 6, 33
Joachim, Joseph: and Liszt, 77; and
  Wagner, 147
Johnson, C. Ashton: on Chopin's G-
  minor Ballade, 49
Journal des débats, 85
Jones, Ernest: on Mahler's interview with
  Freud, 264
Jullien, Adolph: on Chabrier and Wag-
  ner, 154

Kalbeck, Max: on Brahms and *Tristan,*
  161–2
Kalkbrenner, Friedrich Wilhelm, 41
Kapellmeistermusik, 209
Klangfarbenmelodie, 78, 347, 350, 353
Klindworth, Karl, 72, 146
Knaben Wunderhorn, Des, 216
Kolisch, Rudolf, 268
Korngold, Erich Wolfgang, 34, 201
Koussevitzky, Serge, 318
Kukolnik, Nestor, 132

La Grange, Henry-Louis de: on Mahler
  and conducting, 209; on Mahler and
  Wagner, 226; on Mahler and chamber music, 232 n.; on Mahler and melodic invention, 234
Laloy, Louis: on Debussy and Stravinsky's *Le Sacre du printemps,* 316
Landon, H. C. Robbins: on Haydn, 11
Lawrence, Robert A.: on Berlioz's or-
  chestration, 91
Lekeu, Guillaume, 157
Lesueur, Jean-François, 91
Liadov, Anatol, 143, 181, 303, 306
Liszt, Franz, 4, 24, 54–5, 63, 68–9, 72,
  74–5, 83, 146–7, 284; and Chopin, 55,
  59; and Wagner, 68–9, 72, 74–5, 146–
  147; and Berlioz, 111 n.
    Dante Symphony, 76
    Faust Symphony, 68, 72–3, 83
    Jeux d'eaux à la Villa d'Este, 54
    Mazeppa, 68
    Orpheus, 68
    Piano Concerto No. 1, E flat, 24
    Préludes, Les, 68
    Tasso, 68
Lockspeiser, Edward: on Debussy and
  Mussorgsky, 274, 276; on Debussy and
  Tchaikovsky, 276–7; on *L'Enfant
  prodigue,* 275; on *Pelléas,* 335 n.
Long, Marguerite: on Debussy and Cho-
  pin, 287
Ludwig II (King of Bavaria), 146

Lully, Jean Baptiste, 204
Lvov, Alexis, 134

Mahler, Alma, 223, 263, 340; on Schoenberg, 254
Mahler, Gustav, 6, 31, 149, 208–19, 221,
  223–6, 228, 230–4, 236–53, 263–4,
  266, 335; and Beethoven, 31–2, 230–
  231, 234; and Wagner, 149, 214, 226,
  232, 248, 252; and Berg, 210; and
  Schoenberg, 210, 254–5, 262; and
  Webern, 210, 237; and Strauss, 210,
  223–4; and Bruckner, 211–13, 252; as
  lyricist, 214–16; his concept of the
  symphony, 217–18; and Schubert, 234;
  at Metropolitan Opera, 241; meeting
  with Freud, 263–4
    Aus der Jugendzeit, 214
    Kindertotenlieder, 215
    Klagende Lied, Das, 212–15
    Lied von der Erde, Das, 208, 215,
      217, 238, 241–7
    Lieder eines fahrenden Gesellen,
      214–15, 218–19
    symphonies, 215, 217–42, 248–53
    Wunderhorn songs, 215–17
Malipiero, Gian Francesco: evaluation of
  Debussy, 284
Margret, Arthur W.: on Liszt and Wag-
  ner, 78
Marschner, Heinrich, 66
    Templar und die Jüdin, Der, 66
Massenet, Jules, 156, 159
    Manon, 156
Meck, Nadejda von, 37, 133, 144, 275–6
Medtner, Nicholas, 5
Méhul, Étienne Nicolas, 92
Mendelssohn, Felix, 5, 23, 30–1, 41, 55;
  and Beethoven, 23, 30–1
    Midsummer Night's Dream, A, 30–1
    Songs Without Words, 55
    Symphony ("Italian"), A major
      (op. 90), 30
    Violin Concerto, E minor, 23
Mengelberg, (Josef) Willem, 210
Messiaen, Olivier, 311
"Mighty Heap" ("Mighty Five"), 138,
  140, 143, 300
Milhaud, Darius, 122, 291, 294; and
  Debussy, 291, 294; and Stravinsky, 318
    Christophe Colomb, 122
Mitchell, Donald: on Mahler's *Das Kla-
  gende Lied,* 212–13
"Moguchaya Kuchka": see "Mighty
  Heap"
Mombert, Alfred, 330
Mompou, Federico, 296
Montagu-Nathan, M.: on Glinka, 131
Montemezzi, Italo, 324
Monteux, Pierre: and Stravinsky's *Le
  Sacre du printemps,* 316–17
Montsalvatge, Xavier, 296

Moreux, Serge: on Bartók and French music, 296
Morin-Chevillard Quartet Society, 70–1
Mossolov, Alexander: and Stravinsky, 318
Mottl, Felix, 179, 191, 199, 209
Mozart, Leopold, 10, 12
Mozart, Wolfgang Amadeus, 4, 10–13, 18, 20, 25, 33–4, 51–7, 64, 99; travels, 10; and Haydn quartets, 11; and Beethoven, 16–22; and dissonance, 51
   Così fan tutte, 22
   Don Giovanni, 13
   Entführung aus dem Serail, Die, 13
   Fantasia, C minor (K. 475), 25
   Musikalischer Spass, Ein, 51
   Nozze di Figaro, Le, 13, 99
   Piano Concerto No. 24, C minor (K. 491), 17–18, 20
   Quartet (K. 465) ("Dissonant"), 51
   Quintet (Viola), G minor (K. 516), 51
   Symphony No. 23 (K. 425) ("Linz"), 16–17
   Zauberflöte, Die, 19–22, 57
Muck, Karl, 179
Munch, Charles: on Berlioz, 89
Music publishing, 12–13; *see also* Artaria, Breitkopf und Härtel, Ricordi, Schlesinger
Mussorgsky, Modest, 9, 55, 120, 136, 138–9, 143–5; and Berlioz, 120, 139
   Boris Godunov, 9, 131
   Night on the Bald Mountain, 138, 143
Myers, Rollo H.: on Debussy's *Douze Études*, 288; on Ravel and Stravinsky's *Le Sacre du printemps*, 317

Neue Zeitschrift für Musik, 79
Neumann, Angelo, 178–9
Newlin, Dika: on Mahler's Symphony No. 8, 240; on Schoenberg and Wagner, 256; on Schoenberg and Strauss, 258; on Schoenberg and Beethoven, 260; on Schoenberg and Mahler, 263; on logic of *Verklärte Nacht*, 269
Newman, Ernest: on Chopin and Granados, 61 *n.*; on Wagner, 63–4, 70 *n.*, 72, 110
Niecks, Frederick: on Chopin and Schubert, 43; on Chopin's G-minor Ballade, 49, 51
Nielsen, Carl, 6, 33
Nikisch, Artur, 179
Nono, Luigi, 4

Ornstein, Leo, 7

Paganini, Niccolò, 4
Paisiello, Giovanni, 4, 13
Pasdeloup concerts, 157 *n.*, 158; *see also* Wagner, Richard

Perle, George: on twelve-tone composition, 354
Pittaluga, Gustavo, 296
Pohl, C. Ferdinand, 12
Pohl, Richard, 79
Ponchielli, Amilcare, 4
Poulenc, Francis, 3, 39, 55, 294; and Debussy, 294
Pourtalès, Guy de: on Chopin's "Polonism," 56
Prokofiev, Serge, 39, 55, 317–18, 324; and Chopin, 55; and Stravinsky, 317–318
   Scythian Suite, 318
Puccini, Giacomo, 4, 6, 318–19, 321; and Stravinsky, 318–19
   Bohème, La, 120
   Fanciulla del West, La, 6
   Turandot, 321

Rameau, Jean Philippe, 56, 111 *n.*
Ravel, Maurice, 3, 9, 23, 54, 56, 122, 144, 287, 293–4, 317; and Beethoven, 23; and Debussy, 293–4; and Stravinsky, 317
   Boléro, 23
   Daphnis et Chloé, 9, 122, 324
   Jeux d'eau, 54, 287
   Ma Mère L'Oye, 290
   Tombeau de Couperin, Le, 3
Redlich, J. F.: on Mahler and Bruckner, 168, 170, 183 *n.*, 252; on Mahler's *Das Klagende Lied*, 212; on Mahler's Symphony No. 7, 237; on Mahler's Symphony No. 8, 240; on Mahler's Symphony No. 10, 252; on Mahler's early life, 335; on Alban Berg and "tonal ambiguity," 330; on Berg's Altenberg songs, 331; on Berg's *Wozzeck*, 333, 335, 335 *n.*; on Berg's *Lyric Suite*, 339
Respighi, Ottorino, 4
Reti, Rudolph: on Schoenberg and atonality, 359–60
Revue musicale, La, 42, 295
Revue wagnérienne, La, 157
Reynaud, Louis: on Paris success of *Lohengrin*, 158
Ricordi (publishers), 13
Rimsky-Korsakov, Nikolai, 4, 62, 91, 131, 136, 140, 143, 157, 180–2, 299; and Chopin, 62; and Berlioz, 136 (*Treatise on Instrumentation*), 140; his *Principles of Instrumentation*, 181; and Wagner, 180, 182; and Debussy, 299; and Tchaikovsky, 301
   Capriccio espagnol, 91, 133
   Mlada, 62
   Snegurochka, 62
Ritter, Alexander: and Strauss, 189–90
Rodrigo, Joaquín, 296
Rosé, Arnold, 254

Rossini, Gioacchino, 4, 14
Roussel, Albert, 324
Rubinstein, Arthur: on Chopin, 58 *n.*
Rückert, Friedrich, 235
Rufer, Josef, 268, 270; on Schoenberg's twelve-tone composition, 270; on *Pierrot lunaire*, 345

Saint-Saëns, Camille, 49, 51, 56, 105, 107–8, 122, 144, 150–3; on Chopin, 49; and enharmony, 105, 108; and Berlioz, 107–8, 122; and Wagner, 150–3
 Danse macabre, 152
 Rouet d'Omphale, Le, 152
 Samson et Dalila, 152
Satie, Erik, 56, 157
Scarlatti, Domenico, 3, 10
Schiller, Friedrich, 26
Schillings, Max von, 209
Schlesinger (publishers), 13, 15
Schmitz, E. Robert: on elements in Debussy's keyboard music, 282, 287
Schoenberg, Arnold, 6, 7, 24, 33, 38, 149, 210, 254–73, 291–2, 322–5, 328, 330, 336–7, 339–40, 342–3, 345–7, 359–63; and Beethoven, 38, 260, 264; and Wagner, 149, 255–9, 262, 291; and Mahler, 210, 254–5, 258, 262–266; and Brahms, 255–8, 262, 272, 343; and Strauss, 258–9; "developing variations," 262, 272; *Harmonielehre*, 265, 347; drift from tonality, 265, 269; and Berg, 267, 324–5, 328, 330–332, 336–7, 339–40, 342; and Webern, 267, 342, *Sprechstimme*, 267; twelve-tone composition, 269–73; *Grundgestalt*, 271; *Klangfarbenmelodie*, 347
 Five Orchestral Pieces (op. 16), 331, 346
 Gurrelieder, 257–8, 330
 Kammersymphonie (Chamber Symphony), 24, 255, 261–2
 Moses und Aaron, 272
 Pelleas und Melisande, 258–9
 Piano Concerto (op. 42), 38
 Pierrot lunaire, 6, 265–7, 272, 322–323, 331, 345
 quartets, 259-64; No. 1, 259–60; No. 2, 263–4
 Satires, 272
 Verklärte Nacht, 254, 256, 269
Schubert, Franz, 17, 31, 41, 43–4, 55, 57, 64, 105, 215, 227; and Beethoven, 31; and Chopin, 43; and Hummel, 44
 "*Erlkönig, Der*," 64
 Impromptus, 55
 Moments Musicaux, 55
 Quintet for Piano and Strings ("*Forelle, Die*"), 43–4
 Sonata for Piano (Grand Duo) (op. 140), 17

Symphony No. 8, B minor ("Unfinished"), 215
Symphony No. 9, C major, 31, 227
Trio, B flat (op. 99), 105
Schuh, Willi: ed., Strauss correspondence, 190 *n.*
Schumann, Clara: on *Tristan*, 87 *n.*
Schumann, Robert, 4–5, 17, 26, 41, 55, 89, 102, 162; and Chopin, 41, 55; and Berlioz, 89, 102
 Album für die Jugend, 55
 Fantasiestücke, 55
 Kinderball, 55
 Kinderscenen, 55
 Symphony No. 4, D minor (op. 120), 17
Scriabin, Alexander, 55, 261, 324
Sechter, Simon, 170
Seidl, Anton, 179
Senefelder, Alois, 12
Serialism, 271, 340–1, 345, 353–4, 358–363; *see also* Schoenberg, Arnold; Stuckenschmidt, H. H.; Twelve-tone composition
Serkin, Rudolf, 268
Seroff, Victor: on the "Mighty Five," 136 *n.*; on Debussy, 144; on Ravel, 144
Serov, Alexander N., 150–2
"Shenandoah" (arr. Cecil Dougherty), 57
Shostakovich, Dmitri, 9, 39, 249
Sibelius, Jean, 24, 324
Slonimsky, Nicolas: on Schoenberg's aim in twelve-tone composition, 270; on Ravel's "massed sonorities," 288
Smetana, Bedřich, 34, 137–8; and Glinka, 137–8
 Prodaná Nevěstá (*Bartered Bride, The*), 137
Société des Concerts du Conservatoire, 95
Spencer, Emile: and *Petrouchka*, 307
Spohr, Ludwig, 14
Sprechstimme, 267
Stassov, Vladimir, 134, 138
Steuermann, Eduard, 268
Strauss, Franz, 184
Strauss, Johann, Jr., 186
Strauss, Richard, 20, 39, 59, 149, 183–208, 324, 329; and Beethoven, 20, 201–3, 206; and Mozart, 20, 184; and Wagner, 149, 193, 195–8, 206–7; and Mendelssohn, 184; and Bruch, 184–5; and Brahms, 185–6; and Johann Strauss, Jr., 186–7; and Alexander Ritter, 189–91; and Liszt, 192; and Berlioz, 199
 Also sprach Zarathustra, 200
 Arabella, 184
 Ariadne auf Naxos, 184, 204, 207
 Aus Italien, 190

Strauss (*continued*)
  Bourgeois Gentilhomme, Le, 204,
    324
  Burleske for piano and orchestra,
    185–6, 188
  Capriccio, 207
  Don Juan, 192–5
  Don Quixote, 193, 200
  Elektra, 205–6
  Four Last Songs, 208
  Frau ohne Schatten, Die, 207
  Guntram, 198
  Heldenleben, Ein, 20, 193, 200–1,
    203
  Macbeth, 191
  Metamorphosen, 39, 203, 208
  Rosenkavalier, Der, 184, 186–7,
    205
  Salome, 205
  songs, 191, 208
  Serenade for Thirteen Winds, 184
  Symphonia domestica, 201
  Till Eulenspiegel, 193, 199–200
  Tod und Verklärung, 189, 195–8,
    329
Stravinsky, Feodor, 301
Stravinsky, Igor, 3, 6, 39, 61–2, 131,
  181, 266, 296, 299–320, 322–3, 336,
  352; and Rimsky-Korsakov, 181, 301,
  303–4, 308; and Debussy, 290–1, 299–
  300, 312–13, 316–19; on Rimsky-
  Korsakov's evaluation of Debussy, 299;
  and Mussorgsky, 300, 305–6, 312; and
  Strauss, 302; and Tchaikovsky, 302–3;
  his youthful works, 302; and Ballet
  Russe, 303, 306, 316, 322; and Wag-
  ner, 305; and Ravel, 317; and Puccini,
  318–19; his opinion of *Wozzeck*, 336;
  his attitude toward Webern, 352
  Firebird, The, 131, 303–7
  Feux d'artifice, 302
  Petrouchka, 62, 302, 306–10
  Pulcinella, 296
  Sacre du printemps, Le, 6, 266, 299,
    307, 310–18, 320, 322–3
  Symphony in E flat (op. 1), 302–3
Stuckenschmidt, H. H.: on Schoenberg's
  Gurrelieder, 257–8; on twelve-tone
  composition, 271; on Schoenberg's op.
  19 Piano Pieces and Webern, 344 *n.*

Tausig, Carl, 146
Tchaikovsky, Peter Ilitch, 30, 37, 129–
  130, 141–3, 236; and Beethoven, 30,
  141; and Berlioz, 129–30, 141; and
  Wagner, 141–2
  Lac des cygnes (op. 20), 142
  Mozartiana, 3
  Piano Concerto No. 1, B flat minor
    (op. 23), 37, 186
  Symphony No. 6 ("*Pathétique*")
    (op. 74), 37, 236

Thayer, Alexander W.: his biography of
  Beethoven, 12–14, 17
Thomas, Ambroise, 150, 152
  Mignon, 150, 152
Thompson, Oscar: on Debussy's *Fan-
  taisie*, 278
Thomson, Virgil: his evaluation of De-
  bussy, 284
Tiersot, Julien: on Berlioz's *Les Francs-
  Juges Overture*, 92
Tommasini, Vincenzo, 4
Tovey, Sir Donald: on Beethoven's Sym-
  phony No. 1, 16; on Beethoven's
  Symphony No. 2, 17; on Beethoven's
  Symphony No. 9, 98–9; on Berlioz's
  Harold en Italie, 106; on Strauss's *Don
  Juan*, 193
Trend, J. B.: on Falla and Debussy, 295
Turina, Joaquín, 296
Turner, W. J.: on Berlioz, 53, 102
Twelve-tone composition, 98–9, 269–73,
  339–41, 353–4, 360–3; *see also* An-
  sermet, Ernest; Schoenberg, Arnold;
  Serialism

Unger, George, 178

Vallas, Léon: evaluation of Berlioz, 89
Varèse, Edgard: and Stravinsky, 318
Vaughan Williams, Ralph: on Debussy,
  291
Verdi, Giuseppe, 4, 34, 87, 107, 123–9,
  147, 160; and Berlioz, 87, 123–9; and
  Wagner, 147
  Aida, 124–5, 147
  Ballo in maschera, Un, 125
  Don Carlo, 125, 147
  Ernani, 123
  Falstaff, 124
  Forza del destino, La, 125
  Lombardi, I, 123
  Luisa Miller, 123
  Macbeth, 123, 125
  Masnadieri, I, 123
  Nabucco, 123
  Otello, 107, 124, 129
  Requiem, 87, 125, 128
  Rigoletto, 123–4
  Simon Boccanegra, 125, 147
  Stiffelio (Aroldo), 123
  Traviata, La, 123–4
  Trovatore, Il, 123–4
  Vêpres siciliennes, Les (*Vespri si-
    ciliani, I*), 124
Vieuxtemps, Henri, 106
Villa-Lobos, Heitor, 61
Vivaldi, Antonio, 4, 6
Vlad, Roman: on Puccini and Stravin-
  sky, 319
Vuillermoz Émile: on *debussysme*, 294

Wagner, Richard, 3–4, 25–7, 34, 38, 59,

Wagner (*continued*)
63–81, 84–9, 100, 106–15, 122–3,
140–2, 146–64, 168, 171, 176, 178–
181, 197, 225, 232, 253, 256, 304,
321, 327, 347; and Beethoven, 25–6,
38, 66–7, 70–8; and Chopin, 59, 63;
his piano music, 64; his *Mein Leben*,
65; and Berlioz, 66, 71, 78, 85, 88,
107, 109–15, 123; and Weber, 66, 78;
and Liszt, 67–8, 72–5, 78–9; visit to
Paris, 69; visit to London and Zürich,
71–2; visit to Russia, 140; and Bülow,
79; and Ludwig II, 146; and Bruckner,
149, 163, 171; and French composers,
150–60, 321; performances in Paris,
158; and Brahms, 160–6; and Angelo
Neumann Opera Company, 178–9;
performances in Russia, 179–80; and
Russian composers, 180–1
    Faust Overture, 26, 67, 73, 79–81
    Fliegende Holländer, Der, 66, 85
    Götterdämmerung, 158, 161, 179
    Lohengrin, 26–7, 66, 68, 72, 76, 85,
      112, 141–2, 158
    Meistersinger, Die, 64, 158, 163–4,
      168
    Parsifal, 64, 66, 158
    Piano Fantasy in F sharp minor, 25
    Piano Sonata in B flat, 25
    Rheingold, Das, 72, 78, 150, 160,
      179
    Rienzi, 66, 75, 158
    Siegfried, 72, 158, 161, 179
    Tannhäuser, 35–6, 66, 68, 75, 85,
      111, 158

    Tristan und Isolde, 64–5, 67, 71–5,
      78–9, 84–6, 100, 107, 109–10,
      112–15, 122, 152, 154, 157–60,
      197, 256, 327, 347
    Walküre, Die, 72, 77–8, 179
Walter, Bruno: on Mahler, 234; and
  Pelléas et Mélisande, 335
Weber, Carl Maria von, 41, 60
  Invitation to the Dance, 60, 93
  Oberon, 92
Webern, Anton, 210, 237, 267, 324–5,
  342–6, 350–5; and Mahler, 237; and
  Schoenberg, 267, 342, 345–6, 353;
  and Wagner, 342; and Brahms, 343
  Im Sommerwind, 342
  Passacaglia for orchestra, 343–4
  Variations, 353–4
Wedekind, Frank, 339
Weingartner, Felix von, 209–10
Weinstock, Herbert: on Berlioz and
  Tristan und Isolde, 86 and *n*.
Wesendonck, Mathilde, 77
Wheeler, Joseph, 251
White, Eric Walter: on Stravinsky's *The
  Firebird*, 304; on *Petrouchka*, 307; on
  Le Sacre du printemps, 310–11
Willeby, Charles: on Chopin's G-minor
  Ballade, 49 —

Yastrebtsev, V. V.: on Chopin, 62, 180;
  and Wagner, 180; on Rimsky-Korsakov's views on Stravinsky, 302–3

Zemlinsky, Alexander von, 254–5

A Note About the Author

IRVING KOLODIN was born in New York in 1908. He served on the music staff of the New York *Sun* from 1932 to 1949, as music editor and music critic from 1945 to 1949. Beginning in 1947, he was editor of the Recordings section of the *Saturday Review*, of which he became music editor and critic in 1949; he is now one of its associate editors. In addition to his well-known books on the Metropolitan Opera, Mr. Kolodin has published *Guide to Recorded Music* and *The Musical Life*, and was co-author of the *Saturday Review Home Book of Recorded Music and Sound Reproduction*. In recent years he has made trips across the United States and to Europe, reporting on the course of current musical events. Mr. Kolodin is married and lives in New York.

A Note on the Type

THE TEXT OF THIS BOOK is set in Electra, a typeface designed by W(illiam) A(ddison) Dwiggins for the Mergenthaler Linotype Company and first made available in 1935. Electra cannot be classified as either "modern" or "old style." It is not based on any historical model, and hence does not echo any particular period or style of type design. It avoids the extreme contrast between "thick" and "thin" elements that marks most modern faces, and is without eccentricities which catch the eye and interfere with reading. In general, Electra is a simple, readable typeface which attempts to give a feeling of fluidity, power, and speed.

Composed, printed, and bound by
The Haddon Craftsmen, Inc., Scranton, Pa.
Music scores by Maxwell Weaner
Typography and binding design
by Anita Karl